The masks of Menander

This book provides a detailed analysis of the conventions and techniques of performance characteristic of the Greek theatre of Menander and the subsequent Roman theatre of Plautus and Terence.

Drawing on literary and archaeological sources, and on scientific treatises, David Wiles identifies the mask as crucial to the actor's art, and shows how sophisticated the art of the mask-maker became. He also examines the other main elements which the audience learned to decode: costume, voice, movement, etc. In order to identify features that were unique to Hellenistic theatre he contrasts Greek New Comedy with other traditions of masked performance. A substantial part of the book is devoted to Roman comedy, and shows how different Roman conventions of performance rest upon different underlying assumptions about religion, marriage and class.

THE MASKS OF
MENANDER

*Sign and meaning in
Greek and Roman
Performance*

DAVID WILES

Reader in Drama
Royal Holloway and Bedford New College
University of London

CAMBRIDGE
UNIVERSITY PRESS

PUBLISHED BY THE PRESS SYNDICATE OF THE UNIVERSITY OF CAMBRIDGE
The Pitt Building, Trumpington Street, Cambridge, United Kingdom

CAMBRIDGE UNIVERSITY PRESS
The Edinburgh Building, Cambridge CB2 2RU, UK
40 West 20th Street, New York NY 10011–4211, USA
477 Williamstown Road, Port Melbourne, VIC 3207, Australia
Ruiz de Alarcón 13, 28014 Madrid, Spain
Dock House, The Waterfront, Cape Town 8001, South Africa

http://www.cambridge.org

First published 1991
Reprinted 1993
First paperback edition 2004

A catalogue record for this book is available from the British Library

Library of Congress cataloguing in publication data

Wiles, David
The masks of Menander: sign and meaning in Greek and Roman
performance/David Wiles.
p.   cm.
Includes bibliographical references and index.
ISBN 0 521 40135 6 hardback
1. Classical drama (Comedy) – History and criticism. 2. Menander, of Athens – Stage
history. 3. Plautus, Titus Maccius – Stage history. 4. Terence – Stage history. 5.
Theater – Greece – History. 6. Theater – Rome – History. 7. Masks – Greece –
History. 8. Masks – Rome – History. I. Title.
PA3161.W55 1991
882′. 0109 – dc20
90–2570
CIP

ISBN 0 521 40135 6 hardback
ISBN 0 521 54352 5 paperback

Contents

Plates

Abbreviations used in the notes

BICS   *Bulletin of the Institute of Classical Studies*

DFA   A. Pickard-Cambridge, *The Dramatic Festivals of Athens*, revised by John Gould and D. M. Lewis (Oxford, 1968)

HGRT   M. Bieber, *The History of the Greek and Roman Theater*, revised edition (Princeton, 1961)

MC   A. W. Gomme and F. H. Sandbach, *Menander – a Commentary* (Oxford, 1973)

MINC   T. B. L. Webster, *Monuments Illustrating New Comedy*, second edition, *Bulletin of the Institute of Classical Studies*, Supplement no. 24 (1969)

MTGTL   L. Bernabò-Brea, *Menandro e il teatro greco nelle terracotte liparesi* (Genoa, 1981)

RAGA   P. Ghiron-Bistagne, *Recherches sur les acteurs dans la Grèce antique* (Paris, 1976)

Note on conventions used in the text

Translations of ancient and modern material are my own unless otherwise stated. For the convenience of readers who do not read classical languages, I have used translated titles where there seems to be no risk of confusion. For Menander's plays I have used the titles in Norma Miller's Penguin edition, *Menander: Plays and Fragments* (Harmondsworth, 1987); for fragments which do not appear in this edition, I have used the translated titles in F. G. Allinson's Loeb edition, *Menander: the Principal Fragments* (London, 1921). For Terence's plays, I have used the titles in Betty Radice's Penguin edition, *The Brothers and Other Plays* (London, 1965) and *Phormio and Other Plays* (London, 1967). For Plautus, I have used the translated titles in Paul Nixon's Loeb edition, *Plautus*, 5 vols (London, New York & Cambridge, Mass., 1916–1938). For the text of Menander, I have used the Oxford Classical text edited by F. H. Sandbach (Oxford, 1972). For fragments not in the OCT, I have used the Teubner edition by A. Koerte and revised by A. Thierfelder (Leipzig, 1953/5).

Classical references are conveniently standardized, and I have not attempted to direct readers to the page numbers of particular translations. Note that for Aristotle two forms of reference are used: first, the book/chapter/section numbers of the specific work cited, and second, the page reference to Aristotle's *Complete Works*.

Preface

Within the study of ancient drama, obvious intellectual advances, it seems, have been made in recent years in two distinct directions. First there has been the structuralist approach. Scholars like J.-P. Vernant, Froma Zeitlin, Charles Segal, and Simon Goldhill, having absorbed the ideas of Saussure, Lévi-Strauss, Barthes, Derrida, Lacan, and other (mainly French) thinkers, have come back to ancient drama with new premises and new questions. Second, there has been the 'stagecraft' approach. Critics favouring this approach, usually inspired by Oliver Taplin's seminal study of Aeschylus, have refused to read classical plays as self-contained verbal constructs, and have insisted that a dramatic text is the score for an event located in space and time. These have until the last few years tended to constitute quite separate attacks on orthodox literary criticism.[1]

The present study of New Comedy attempts to place itself within the liminal area located between stagecraft and structuralism. Although in many respects my research is of an applied, pragmatic nature, the basic orientation is indebted to structural modes of thinking. Institutional structures tend to set up a sharp divide between people working in 'classics' and people working in 'drama and theatre studies', and I have attempted to draw insights from both these disciplines. I hope that this study will be found useful by a variety of people who may be seeking, like myself, to make connexions: social historians wanting to understand how drama functioned as part of the nexus of relationships that constitutes a 'society'; literary critics and archaeologists interested in seeing how their two spheres of exploration relate to a single artistic practice; and theatre historians interested in performance theory, wanting to see how a semiological approach can have practical application.

New Comedy tends to be overshadowed by Greek tragedy. While everyone with an interest in theatre knows something about Greek tragedy, New Comedy tends to be a historical byway. This is due in part to the accident that Menander's texts were not available to serve as an inspiration to the Renaissance. Now that texts are available, they tend to be read through Roman spectacles, to be read in the way that people have learned to read Terence. There is also a widespread feeling that New Comedy belongs to a period of decadence and decline. One keeps meeting the assumption that, in the twilight of Athenian democracy, playwrights ceased to handle major themes, and resorted to writing about domestic trivia. This 'decline' is of questionable value as a historical concept. The age of Menander was a period of great creativity, most obviously within the spheres of philosophy, science and the visual arts. In the theatre, it was a time of increasing interest in the art of the actor, an art less accessible to us than the art of the writer. As a period, Athens at the end of the third century seems to me, living in Europe at the end of the twentieth century, to be a period of very great interest, for it was a time when people were struggling to reconcile local democratic ideals with the awareness that they lived perforce in a cosmopolitan world in which national boundaries were disintegrating. By comparison with the classical period, the Hellenistic period proves rewarding to study because we are so much better informed about the intellectual context. We can form a good picture of how educated Athenians understood themselves in terms of morality, biology, psychology, politics, and the like. Such information allows us to piece together techniques used by the actor in order to communicate with an audience.

The Hellenistic period offers the theatre historian more data than the classical period in every respect save one – a supply of complete play texts. Terracotta masks, mosaics representing scenes, and treatises on rhetoric full of observations about acting reflect an increased interest in visual modes of communication. Although we lack integral texts from the period, we have an abundant supply of fragments of Menander's work. The lack of integral texts is demoralizing if one's object is to focus on the author as the unique and coherent source of meaning; the deficiency is far less demoralizing if one's object is to understand a theatrical language, a set of conventions used to produce meaning. The fact that we have a large and more-or-less random corpus of fragments allows us to reconstruct a dramatic technique, as distinct from a set of individual art works.

It seems to be time for a synthesis, now that papyrologists have finished the bulk of their valuable and necessary work on the texts of Menander, and now that archaeologists have compiled usable catalogues of masks and monuments.[2] We need to form an understanding of how the Greeks used texts and masks as their tools for producing meaning. Although I lack the same specialist expertise, my research in a sense takes up where T. B. L. Webster left off. Webster was a theatre historian: he catalogued masks, he examined papyri, and he wrote literary criticism. Because of this diversity of interest, he was able to make many useful suggestions about how monuments or portions of text related to the practicalities of performance. He seems in this catholicity of interest to have had no successors in the 1980s. In his last book, *Studies in Menander*, written in the early 1970s, Webster recognized the importance of Lévi-Strauss for the analysis of Menander. His willingness to accept structuralist ideas possibly derives from the fact that he was then working not in Britain but in the United States. Although, unfortunately, the structuralist methodology is skin-deep, and provides few fresh insights, it is significant that Webster saw the need for this kind of approach if he was to write about Menander with a view to integrating social, moral, and theatrical concerns. I have attempted to use in this book an intellectual apparatus that was not available to scholars of Webster's generation.

It is not by chance that I have turned to France to find a methodology. The semiotics of performance was first developed as a discipline in Prague in the 1930s. A second generation of theatre semioticians followed the lead offered by Barthes in the 1960s. Although better known for his studies of the novel, Barthes is a seminal figure for the semiotics of performance. Anne Ubersfeld and Patrice Pavis at the Sorbonne have subsequently done much patient work, making mechanistic theories more flexible, demonstrating how in practice an audience reads the minutiae of a performance, and teasing apart the different sign systems which a performance comprises. The same kind of work has not been developed in Britain, for complex cultural reasons. Until recent years, there has been within literary circles a hostility towards theory, and a Leavisite privileging of feeling over thought, of common sense over abstraction. Within theatre studies in Britain, there tends to have been more interest in the production of performances than in their reception. I have attempted to release myself from this British tradition. The attraction of structuralism is the way it establishes coherent patterns where previously there seemed to be only incoherence – within, for example, the jargon of advertising, the world of fashion, Indian myths, or the tenses of a narrative. I have attempted to find this kind of coherence, both within the performance in all its multiple aspects, and within the society which can be regarded, no less than the writer, as the 'author' of the play.

It may seem perverse, in the circumstances, to have entitled this book

The Masks of Menander, giving such prominence to the writer. The masks of New Comedy, I shall argue, were the focus of the audience's attentions. My purpose is to reconcile the evidence of artefacts (principally masks) with the evidence of texts (principally by Menander). It is the texts of this particular playwright that have survived because his plays were selected by subsequent generations as the core of the New Comedy tradition. The culture that will concern me is not specifically the culture of Athens, but rather that of the Hellenistic world. The fact that Menander's plays rapidly became canonical gives them a unique importance in relation to Hellenistic culture at large. Enough fragments survive from other dramatists of Menander's generation to reassure us that they observed broadly the same set of theatrical conventions. That having been said, the lack of any surviving plays by Philemon can only be lamented.

I have devoted considerable space in this book to Roman comedy. Plautus and Terence wrote at a time when Rome was establishing itself as an imperial power. The hierarchical, militaristic culture of Rome could scarcely be more different from that of Athens and the democratic Greek world. It is of great interest, therefore, to see how the genre of New Comedy changed its nature within the Roman world. Although the texts of Plautus and Terence survive in far better condition than the texts of Menander, we have very little information about the intellectual context, and a complete lack of any iconography related to the plays of those dramatists in the Republican period. Evidence has, almost exclusively, to be extrapolated from the texts. What is interesting about Plautus and Terence for my purposes is the way they differ from Menander. I have aimed to isolate and explore those differences.

Several people have been kind enough to read short sections of this book in draft form: Christopher Gill, Adam Mills, Karina Mitens, Masahiro Takenaka, Oliver Taplin. I am grateful to them for their comments and suggestions. I have also incorporated helpful suggestions from three readers at Cambridge University Press. Peter Brown supplied me with useful bibliographical information. Students at Oxford acting in my production of *Old Cantankerous* and at Royal Holloway and Bedford New College acting in my production of *Stichus* taught me much about Menander and Plautus. Colleagues in the Department of Drama at the University College of Wales, Aberystwyth, released me from teaching for a term, during which time I completed the initial reasearch for this book. UCW Aberystwyth gave me a grant in order to visit the Kelvingrove Museum in Glasgow. The British Academy gave me a grant in order to visit Lipari and Naples. Andrew Foxon at the Kelvingrove Museum and Madeleine Cavalier at the Museo Eoliano gave me all help and assistance and provided me with photographs. Andrew Foxon also arranged for an analysis of pigments to be made. Staff at the computer centres at RHBNC and the University of London transferred two chapters of typescript onto disquette. Gayna Wiles provided the line drawings, and back-up services over the years. My mother lent me her word processor. My thanks are due to all.

INTRODUCTION

Two traditions of writing

It is no accident of modern archaeology that Menander is the only writer of Greek New Comedy whose works have survived in anything more than tiny fragments. After his death, Menander was recognized as the outstanding exponent of the genre. Texts of his plays were widely circulated, and illustrations of scenes served to decorate the floors and walls of rich men's houses around the Mediterranean world. In his lifetime Menander won the prize for comedy only eight times in Athens, and there is no evidence that he was considered pre-eminent from the beginning. Whether modern readers would share the considered verdict of the Graeco-Roman world, if given the means of comparison, cannot be known.

Menander was an upper-class Athenian citizen and an intellectual, and this social placing distinguished him from his rivals. He was educated by Theophrastos, Aristotle's successor as head of the Lyceum, and he was an exact contemporary of Epicurus.[1] Because of his background, he was necessarily involved in the intense philosophical and political arguments of the time. He was also caught up in an aesthetic argument triggered by Plato's renunciation of a theatrical career and subsequent denunciation of drama. A man with such a background, in this turbulent political period, did not commit himself to theatre as a quick route to profit or glory, and can have done so only because he had clearly defined moral and aesthetic objectives. I would suggest that he was a great playwright (by which I mean that his plays seemed to repay rereading and reperforming over the centuries) because his historical position placed him at the centre of political and philosophical change. He was at the centre of the emotions and arguments which surrounded the demise of the autonomous *polis*. From this historical vantage point he developed perceptions that continued to seem relevant.

The apolitical format of New Comedy can be seen as a negative phenomenon, a product of caution. Today it is easy to see the genre as a

symptom of decadence and intellectual retreat. Yet at least one contemporary, Philippides, continued to make overt references to the
political scene when democratic freedom was offered.[2] The apparent
apoliticism of Menander and most other dramatists of the time can be
seen, paradoxically, as a political decision. A striking feature of
Menander's plays is their adherence to the aesthetic tenets of Aristotle.
Although the *Poetics* has in many respects had a distorting effect upon the
subsequent study of Greek tragedy, it proves an illuminating guide to the
methods and principles of Menander. Less obvious, from a modern
perspective, is the extent to which Aristotle's aesthetics and his politics
are enmeshed. Once one gains a sense of the coherence of Aristotelian
thinking, one can see how the apolitical aesthetic of Menander is, in fact, a
political strategy. While Aristophanes cast his democratic audience in the
role of political decision-makers, Menander, through offering his plays as
a mimesis of reality, cast his audience in the role of detached observers.
The audience are offered a mirror-image of themselves, not as a political
mass, but as private individuals. The *dêmos* can no longer be represented
theatrically by a single stage character.

Although the section of the *Poetics* which deals with comedy is lost,
there can be no doubt that Aristotle found the tragedies of Sophocles and
Euripides more to his taste than the comedies of Aristophanes. According
to Aristotle's definitions, while tragedy naturally represents the actions of
men better than we are, comedy represents the actions of men worse than
we are. The masks of Old Comedy provoke laughter because they are base
and distorted.[3] It follows from this analysis that tragedy must be a form
superior to comedy. A generation after Aristotle, Menander and his
contemporaries evidently accepted the logic of Aristotle's thinking, and
evolved a new concept of generic difference. The new dichotomy between
comedy and tragedy was to be that which differentiated Euripides from
Sophocles, Euripides portraying men as they are, Sophocles men as they
ought to be.[4] The new symbol of tragedy became the *onkos*: the elevated
hair-style which made the tragic mask larger than life. The same word,
onkos, was used at the same time of the elevated poetic style which raised
heroic verse above everyday speech.[5] Comedy, meanwhile, abandoned
phallic costumes, participant deities, and all other signs that the play was
a Dionysiac ritual acting upon reality, and the 'New Comedy' proclaimed
itself an accurate imitation of life. We do not know how precisely Aristotle
countered Plato's charge that, because *mimêsis* is a natural learning
procedure, comic *mimêsis* corrupts its spectators and actors who necessarily acquire the behaviour patterns of the persons imitated,[6] but clearly

the new concept of comic *mimêsis* drained Plato's charge of its force. New Comedy could claim some kind of moral parity with tragedy on account of its roots in the respected work of Euripides.

As in many Greek tragedies – *Oedipus Tyrannus* being the most obvious example – so in Menander, prior events may be extraordinary, but given the initial situation, everything that happens within the play is plausible. In accordance with Aristotle's prescription for good tragedy, Menander's comedies have single plots, and the *peripeteia* turns upon an *anagnôrisis*, a 'recognition' which is simultaneously factual and moral. *Old Cantankerous*, for example, turns upon the misanthropist's recognition that human beings cannot survive in isolation from society, hence his daughter must marry. *The Arbitration* turns upon the young man's recognition that he has raped his own future bride, and that he is guilty of sexual double standards. When the old man falls down a well by chance, or a ring identifies the rape victim, these trivial plot devices become the framework for the correction of a *hamartia* (error) that is strictly ethical. Sophocles' tragic heroes may, arguably, have no 'moral flaw', but Menander's characters certainly do.

The Aristotelian working method, to start with the whole and then complete the parts, yields a strong sense of form, and the formal perfection of Menander's plots is perhaps to a modern eye the most remarkable feature of his writing. The primacy which Menander gives to plot, however, often causes the modern reader to sense that something is lacking in his plays. Characters like Knemon and Smikrines seem pale and unmemorable when placed alongside some of the great comic characters of the European repertoire – Dikaiopolis, or Harpagon, or Malvolio, for example. In order to make sense of Menander's method, we need to replace our modern concept of dramatic 'character' with an Aristotelian concept. For Aristotle, people are born with certain capacities, they develop through their habits certain *êthê* (character traits), they experience habitually certain emotions – but virtue in the last analysis is separable from all of these and involves choice, *prohairesis*. In tragedy, Aristotle states, choice reveals *êthos* (character).[7] Within the limits imposed by capacity, one can *choose* to indulge or reject emotions, one can *choose* to adopt or abandon habits which, if adopted, will eventually shape one's *êthos*.[8] The study of character is necessarily the study of ethics in Aristotelian thinking. Modern thought finds this equation between character and morality hard to accept. The modern actor who constructs a character is not expected to think in the first instance about questions of morality.

The carefully constructed action of Menander's plays allows the choices of the *dramatis personae* to crystallize and become visible in a way that is impossible outside the framework of art. The playwright has learned from the tragedies of Sophocles and Euripides, which likewise focussed upon choice. The new and remarkable feature of New Comedy is its system of masks. The distinctive mask worn for each role depicted a 'character', that is, a pre-formed ethical disposition. The stage figure offered to the audience at the start of the play was no longer, as in tragedy, an ethical *tabula rasa*. Moral choices could only be made in the context of a person's pre-formed ethical disposition.

Menander's everyday scenes of bourgeois life take their apparently natural course within a rigorously organized artistic structure. The plays broadly observe the three unities of action, place and time. That is to say, the plays have single plots, they take place in a single location outside two adjacent houses, and the action is completed within a single day. Stage time is identical with the real time of the audience. The plays are written in five acts, and choral interludes mark time lapses when off-stage business is deemed to be accomplished. Finally, the action is organized so that the speaking roles are taken by only three actors. Menander profits from these limitations, creating plays of formal elegance and emotional concentration. The spectacle which Menander presents to his audience is a *mimêsis* of bourgeois life, but cannot be confused with life. The controlling hand of the author is far too obvious.

The number of the acts plainly meets the Aristotelian requirement of furnishing a beginning, a middle, and an end. The action is a closed structure containing a *desis* (entanglement) and a *lysis* (dénouement). One might contrast the Hellenistic five-act structure with the dialectical structure of Aeschylus' Oresteian trilogy, where the form suggests the possibility of an infinite progression of thesis, antithesis, and synthesis, and the end of the trilogy interpenetrates the contemporary world of the audience. The Aristotelian theory of *mimêsis* assumed a hermetic divide between the world of the audience and the mimetic world of the play.

Aristotelian theory, however influential upon Menander, cannot give us a complete picture of Menander's dramatic technique in the Theatre of Dionysus. For Aristotle, the Dionysiac context of performance was merely of antiquarian interest, but for Menander this context was an inescapable condition of his work. While the structure of Aristophanic comedy makes sense only within the context of an Athenian festival, Menander's comedy, on the model of Euripidean tragedy, makes no formal reference to the fact that its performance is part of a festival of

Dionysus. Yet the context is not forgotten, for the element of festival is, as it were, enclosed within the realistic frame of the plot. A repeated device of Menander is to build the action around the interruption of a festival. Through this device, Menander replicates the experience of his spectators, who interrupt their active participation in processions, dances, sacrifices, and extemporal ribaldry in order to sit passively watching a play.

The device of the interrupted festival is more noticeable in performance than in reading. *The Farmer, The Phantom, The Shield, The Girl from Samos*, and *The Girl from Perinthos* incorporate wedding feasts which go awry. Feasts evolve into wedding feasts in *Old Cantankerous* and *The Man She Hated*. The heroes of *The Arbitration* and *The Rape of the Locks* turn to revelry in an attempt to escape their troubles. More feasts appear in *The Girl from Andros, The Peplos-Bearer, The Confectioner, The Head-Dress, The Toady, The Girl from Messene, Drunkenness, Trophonios*, and *The False Heracles*. A literary analysis of the plays can easily miss the impact created by the procession of live animals across the stage, the arrival of cooks, and musicians and their equipment, the sight and smell of sacrificial fires, the wearing of ceremonial costume. It is frequently in the course of a festival that a young man is said to have raped a free girl, and the performance can thus in a double sense be seen as the restoration of order within the disorderly progress of the feast.[9] The action of the play is in some measure reintegrated with that of the festival when the *dramatis personae* appear with torches and garlands at the end of the play, anticipating the climax of the theatrical festival when the victorious poet and actor appear on the stage with garlands.[10]

When Plutarch asserted that a symposium was better conducted without wine than without the accompaniment of a recitation from Menander,[11] he took it for granted that Menander's plays made sense within a Dionysiac context. The chorus who enter the *orchêstra* during the four act breaks are not an irrelevance: rather, they help maintain a tension between the real and represented worlds of the performance. The inclusion within the play of recitative and direct address to the audience represents a compromise with the strict requirements of *mimêsis* theory. It has been plausibly argued that Menander became more purist, and abandoned the use of musical accompaniment in his later plays.[12]

Menander's surface realism conceals not only ritual but also mythic elements, for the plays can also be read, could also be watched, as metatheatrical reworkings of Euripides.[13] The theatre of Aristophanes had a symbiotic relationship with tragedy, reversing all the conventions of tragic performance, not least the relationship between actor and audience. Aristophanes parodied scenes from tragic performances, and in so doing helped audiences to see those tragedies as controversial and relevant. In a similar way, Menander wrote for an audience familiar with a now classic canon of fifth-century tragedies. Even more markedly than Aristophanes, Menander drew upon Euripides for his material. An apparently ephemeral theatrical situation – a youth hiding, watching a peasant girl come to draw water, a man reporting a democratic assembly, the anger of an Athenian who believes his son to have slept with his foreign consort – could be perceived as mythic, could be pondered and remembered by an audience which had seen parallel situations played out in Euripides' *Electra*, *Orestes*, or *Hippolytus*. Many scenes which appear slight to us would become semiologically dense for an audience familiar with tragedies now unknown to us.

This metatheatrical technique is not one that Menander tries to conceal. In the final act of *The Arbitration* a slave quotes a line from Euripides' *Auge* and cites the source in order to point up a parallel plot structure. In both *Auge* and *The Arbitration*, the hero rapes the heroine during a nocturnal festival, and leaves her a ring which later enables him to identify his child. The *Auge* is not the only metatext in *The Arbitration*, for the arbitration scene which occupies Act II is based on Euripides' *Alope*, where a grandfather likewise arbitrates over the fate of his changeling grandchild.[14] The tragic metatext helped the Greek audience read the ravisher, the heroine, the grandfather, not as mere social types, but as archetypes. The comedy is rooted simultaneously in the world of contemporary Athens and the world of myth. Here again we see the limitations of the theory that art is simply a *mimêsis* of life.

Menander and Terence belong to a single aesthetic tradition governing the role of the writer. Their assumptions differ almost totally from those of Plautus, and it is to Plautus that we must turn for comparison. Plautus was not a member of the intellectual elite, but was a common actor for whom writing was a natural extension of his craft. He did not see himself as a detached observer of life, nor did he see himself as a hidden *animateur* whose task was to efface his own activity as the creator of illusion. He ignores or overturns Aristotle's two basic premises about drama, that plot has primacy over character, and that the play imitates an exterior, separable reality. Plautus' *dramatis personae* owe much to an extemporal performance tradition, and scarcely need the excuse of a story-line in order to justify their presence on stage as entertainers of the audience. The plots are loosely organized and open in structure. The performance is not the *mimêsis* of an action, but is, rather, in itself an action, an integral part of the Roman *ludi* (the games or festival). In these assumptions, Plautus is closer to Aristophanes than to Menander.

The *Curculio* may serve as an example of how Plautus subordinates plot to character. The plot is designed to allow a sequence of comic grotesques to hold the stage: a lover grasping a phallic candle, an old bawd who walks with her nose to the ground, an owl-eyed nymphomaniac, a corpulent pimp with indigestion, the one-eyed 'maggot' who gives the play its title, a homosexual banker, a blustering *miles gloriosus* in a borrowed cloak. The slave alone provides some kind of initial touchstone of normality. The rhythm of the action is created by the musician, whose role becomes ever more dominant as the action accelerates. When the actors banter with each other or with the audience, they speak, but in burlesque narratives and scenes of rapid action or high emotion they adopt a quasi-operatic style of delivery. The audience are not offered any internally consistent replica of reality, and they can make no psychological deductions or predictions. The soldier is risible at one moment, ferocious at the next. The pleasures which the play offers have nothing to do with the hermeneutics of *êthos*.

It is now a commonplace of Plautine criticism to note the congruence between Plautus' plays and the Roman *ludi* of which they form part.[15] The action on Plautus' stage is a symbolic inversion of everyday life. Plautus disengages his *Curculio* from the Hellenistic unities of time, place, and action in order to locate the play within an other-world of festival where normality must seem to be suspended. Time is collapsible, for there are no act breaks to cover off-stage action, and real time is accelerated by the pace of events. Unity of place disintegrates when the costumier of the production appears and takes the audience on an imaginary tour of Rome. Just as words lose their expected meanings in Plautus and acquire double meanings, so there is a severance between cause and effect, between an action and its predictable consequences. Instead of unity of action, we find, effectively, a variety show.

While Menander relies upon Euripides, Plautus relies upon Greek New Comedy to provide his metatext.[16] Plautus uses the Greek stage world of Menander to create a utopia, a world which casts a strange illumination upon Roman moral stances. The sense of a festive transgression against morality is enhanced by the fact that a Roman writer is transgressing the rules of Greek comedy. A Greek story-line, with a ring for a recognition token, holds the action together – but the supposed prostitute acts like a prostitute, not like the bride she becomes, and her

soldier brother acts like a buffoon, not like a citizen. The parasite, like
many a Menandrean slave, may quote from what 'an ancient poet wrote in
a tragedy', but his quotation is bogus.[17] The pleasure of the audience lies
in its sense that it is an accomplice in transgression.

The linear structure of *Curculio* is acceptable because the play is short.
Recent Plautine criticism has tried to define a more complex narrative
strategy adopted in many plays, of which *Pseudolus* is the most striking
example. After the initial complexities of the plot have been clarified, the
slave Pseudolus declares: '*nunc ego poeta fiam*' ('now I shall be the poet')[18]
and he presents what follows as a sustained improvisation. The slave
develops what has been described as a play-within-a-play, with disguises
for himself and for his accomplice. The model of the play-within-a-play,
as a basis for the critical exegesis of Plautus, is misleading in its suggestion
of enclosure. Plautus' supposed 'framing' technique does not correlate
with the operatic structure of the writing, which keeps moving from
speech via optional arias to recitative and back to speech again. The
structure is not closed, but open and dialectical. There is a sustained
ambiguity as to whether the actor or the poet is controlling the
performance. This ambiguity, which reflects Plautus' own double
identity as actor and poet, is homologous with another, more important
ambiguity: who controls the *ludi*, the senatorial sponsor of the games, or
the massed populace who must at all costs be satisfied?

CHAPTER I

Text and performance

THE EMERGENCE OF THE PROBLEM

Tragedy produces its effect even without movement, just as epic does; for a reading makes its nature quite clear.[1]

Thus does Aristotle justify a division which has come to seem a common-sense intellectual practice, a division between the study of text and the study of performance. In Greek terminology, the writer is after all the *poiêtês*, the maker of the play, while the actor is the *hypokritês*, the interpreter of the oracular poet.[2] Sophocles and Euripides died some twenty years before Aristotle was born, so the philosopher saw not original performances but revivals. In Aristotle's day the performance existed independently of the text and might also involve corruption of the text when actors chose to rewrite their lines. A belief that the play has a true 'nature' not contingent upon the physical presence of the actor lies behind Aristotle's lament that in his generation 'actors now count for more than poets' – '*meidzon dynantai nyn tôn poiêtôn hoi hypokritai*'.[3] Students of the Lyceum who read or listened to the text of a play by Sophocles could approach the poet more closely, it must have seemed, than any actor or spectator in the theatre. Aristotle, with a new concept of scientific truth, had no truck with Plato's claim that 'a writing cannot distinguish between suitable and unsuitable readers', and that oral communication is therefore necessarily superior to written communication.[4] For Plato, truth inhered in the parent of the written word, and this parent needed therefore to be present to defend his progeny from misconstruction. For Aristotle every idea had an objective rendering in language. The written word could be regarded as a signifier with a fixed referent. It was assumed that the careful reader of Aristotle's books would know exactly what Aristotle meant.

This changed understanding of language has its parallel in the theatrical sphere. The statesman Lycurgus, who oversaw the building of a permanent stone theatre in Aristotle's day, was also the man who compelled actors to perform the authentic, authorial texts of classic plays.[5] Paradoxically, while Lycurgus preserved the texts of fifth-century writers, the design of his theatre confirmed or precipitated fundamental changes in the way those texts were delivered. The author's meaning was assumed to be inherent in the words of his play, whether or not the words were delivered in the way the author intended. In this manner, with the emergence of a classical repertory, text and performance were ruptured in Aristotle's day, and went their separate ways.

Some theatres are dominated by the writer, others by the actor. The history of theatre in post-war Britain could be charted in terms of a transition from actors' theatre through writers' and directors' theatre to the designers' theatre of the eighties. Aristotle's lament that 'actors now count for more than poets' reflects a historical situation in which the actor was becoming dominant. Actors like Polos and Theodoros were cosmopolitan individuals, famed across the Greek world, while the ideal of the *polis*, which inspired both the great themes of fifth-century tragedy and the dedication of amateur choral dancers, had a waning hold upon the Greek imagination. Theatre as an institution was not in decline in the fourth century.

When Menander began writing for the Athenian theatre in approximately the year of Aristotle's death, his experience was conditioned by the new theatrical environment – the new Lycurgan building, a new Aristotelian aesthetic code, and a profession dominated not by writers but by virtuoso actors. We can discern in Menander's texts ethical and aesthetic assumptions which give evidence of a profound debt to Aristotle.[6] I shall argue in the course of this chapter that Menander parted company with Aristotle's aesthetics at the point where Aristotle proposes that the visual element is superimposed upon the play and is not intrinsically part of it.

It is easy when we read Menander's texts today to ignore the conventions of the theatre for which he wrote. His social realism seems comfortingly familiar. It costs us no effort to envisage a style of performance similar to our own – the style used by modern actors when they play dramas of everyday life written by a Rattigan or an Ayckbourn. One might all too quickly conclude that, when all is said and done, theatre changes very little over the years. The blatant un-realism of Menander's plots, with their changelings, recognition tokens, and love affairs, no less than the cast lists, with their philosophical servants, introspective lovers, and ambitious fathers, seem instantly familiar to readers and theatre-goers acquainted with Shakespeare and Molière. *Plus ça change, plus c'est la même chose,* one might conclude, for human nature changes little over the years. This ahistorical analysis which I have caricatured carries two riders. First, Menander's plays would seem to be shallow or slight. A play of Menander's requires, apparently, barely an hour's playing time, and would seem to be conceived more on the scale of modern television comedy than of modern theatrical comedy. The rapid flow of the action seems to leave the audience no breathing-space in which to ponder weighty issues. The dialogue is not without subtlety, but the actor has no time in which to build a substantial character. The plotting is clever, but not sustained at length. The plays, it seems, are instantly digestible. The second and related rider is that the plays need to be dubbed 'escapist'. The idea that the poet is an educator, blending pleasure with instruction, cannot be argued with conviction. Reflections on matters like wealth, fate, and marriage seem to be swamped beneath the force of fantastic plots full of piracy, exposure, rape, and impossible coincidences which bring everything to a happy end. The plays purport to imitate reality, yet, plainly, this is not how life is.

So, for example, Eric Handley writes of Greek New Comedy that

> its characters and stories offer many people an escape into a world of wish-fulfilment, a world with which they can easily identify, but neater and more entertaining than the real one often is; and secondly, there is, to a greater or less degree, an enlightening or educating influence.[7]

Identification is seen as part of the mechanism of escape. Yet if the audience have escaped, how can they be educated? Handley's uncertainty about the degree of education provided is symptomatic of underlying theoretical problems. The wish-fulfilment theory was cogently argued by Claire Préaux in a seminal essay written in 1957:

> The spectator, thanks to delaying techniques, feels that he is master of a destiny as it unwinds. It is escape that he seeks, ultimate compensation for the setbacks of life ... Menander's comedy is not a portrait of the Athenian bourgeois – but it is a door that opens upon his dreams.[8]

This theory leaves a fundamental question unanswered. Spectators may seek escape, but are they content with a surrogate existence at the end of the performance, or have they gained, rather, an enhanced understanding of life's setbacks? Are the spectators dreaming, or awake? The answer of course must be both. The spectator can be entranced by the plot while simultaneously aware that he or she is watching a play in the theatre.

An example of Greek spectator behaviour illustrates this point clearly.

When a Greek tyrant was watching the actor Theodoros give an emotional rendering of a Euripidean heroine, he was moved to tears and left the theatre. He explained privately to Theodoros that he left in shame because the emotions (*pathê*) of an actor could move him to tears but not the emotions of his subjects. The tyrant is deeply moved, yet is at the same time aware of his own present and future actions. He is aware during the performance that his response to enacted suffering differs from his response to real suffering.[9] This anecdote illustrates a general feature of theatrical experience, namely that spectators enjoy a double awareness. They are at once entranced, and observant of the process whereby they are entranced.

Aristotle understood this double awareness when he yoked together the fear that one feels for oneself (imagining that oneself is the other) and the pity that one feels for the other (knowing that oneself is not the other).[10] In accordance with this self/other dynamic, Aristotle argues that a well-constructed dramatic character should neither be too much like ourselves, nor too different from ourselves.[11] Concerning the related double awareness of the performer, we find a better understanding in Plato. When Ion the rhapsode recites Homer – too much in the manner of an actor for Plato's taste – his eyes fill with tears and his hair stands on end (the physical correlatives of pity and fear), but at the same time Ion keeps a weather-eye on his audience to ensure that his performance is succeeding.[12] The actor may be in a Dionysiac trance, but he can also observe himself entranced. The condition of the spectator, Plato argued, is not different from that of the performer, for both are held as within the same magnetic field.[13]

Plato disliked the way theatre could manipulate an audience's emotions. Aristotle in his *Rhetoric* countered Plato by laying bare the cognitive basis of pity, fear, and other emotions. An emotion is seen as a form of knowledge – knowledge of what is to come, knowledge of cause and effect. Human beings must learn when they ought and ought not to experience pity and fear. These reflections should make us wary of viewing Menander's theatre as pure escape, pure emotional indulgence. The spectator's response is complex. If, as Claire Préaux suggests, Menander's theatre is a door which opens upon an Athenian's dreams, then we must enquire whether Menander's audience entered that door, or merely looked through it from without. We must consider whether the plays purveyed dreams to individuals, or exposed private dreams to the public gaze.

Aristotle's theory of catharsis was an attempt to define that which turns the pity and fear of an audience or reader into a species of pleasure. His theories of reception were sophisticated. With reference to mass juries, he formulated a proposition which has implications for all audiences:

> The mind works irrationally [and assumes] that a speaker tells the truth, that such and such are the circumstances, so that one believes a speaker's assertions to be facts, when they are not; the listener, likewise, always shares the emotions (*synhomoiopathei*) of the person who speaks with emotion even if what is said is nothing.

One can respond to emotion, in other words, while knowing intellectually that an argument has no substance. Aristotle goes on to state that the speaker in the lawcourt expresses not only *pathos* (emotion) but also *êthos* (character).

> Character (*êthikê*) may likewise be demonstrated through signs (*sêmeia*), because there is [a demonstration] appropriate to each genus and disposition.[14]

Aristotle glosses the term 'genus' by stating that it refers to age, sex, and race. This art of using signs to demonstrate character is one that I shall analyse at length.

Theatre differs from the lawcourt inasmuch as the facts of the case in a play are given from the outset. Though the theatrical spectator knows the enacted events to be fictitious, he nevertheless necessarily 'shares the emotions' of an emotional speaker. While the speaker in court learns to express character covertly through the deployment of appropriate signs, in the theatre signs are deployed overtly by a masked actor. In the theatre, the panel of judges prepares to reward, not the man deemed to have spoken the truth, but the man deemed to have expressed *pathos* and demonstrated *êthos* most successfully. In theatre and lawcourt alike, a Hellenistic audience enjoyed unravelling the rights and wrongs of domestic dramas normally concealed from the public gaze;[15] but signs concealed in the lawcourt were made manifest and clearly codified in the theatre. Theatre audiences learned not what judgement to make but how judgements are made.

The French semiologist Anne Ubersfeld argues that 'truly theatrical pleasure is pleasure in the sign'[16] – and as a way of defining theatrical pleasure this seems to me a more useful starting-point than Aristotle's metaphor of catharsis. A famous theatrical anecdote illustrates how an audience thrives on the process of signification. The actor Polos, according to the story, made a great impact in the role of Sophocles' Electra when he carried the ashes of his own son into the theatre in the urn supposed by Electra to carry the ashes of Orestes.[17] In an orthodox

performance of Sophocles' play, although the grief of Electra generates
fellow-feeling in an audience, that audience cannot be immersed empa-
thetically in the grief of a fictitious Electra, for it knows intellectually
that she is mistaken, and that Orestes is still alive. The audience enjoys
the double awareness (a) that Electra grieves, and (b) that Electra has no
cause for grief. Her grief, like the emotions of any theatre audience, is
provoked not by reality but by a visible sign – in this case, an urn. The
anecdote told of Polos (and its possibility is important, not its veracity)
calls the status of the sign into an uncertainty that is in the end
impenetrable. Electra, it seems, was right after all: the urn is filled with
ashes. The anecdote plays upon the delight which any audience takes in
its double level of awareness of actor and role. It is not the actor's power to
disappear, but the actor's power to be simultaneously himself – a flesh-
and-blood human being – and Electra – a fictional sufferer – which
generates theatrical pleasure.

My project in this book will be to analyse how Menander's theatre, and
that of his Roman successors, worked as a system of signs. The starting-
point for such a project must be to erect a distinction between the two key
terms of semiological analysis, *langue* and *parole* – language and speech-
act. The conventions of the genre, the system of theatrical signs which
Menander had at his disposal, may be described as the *langue* of
Hellenistic comedy. A plot is formed when masks and roles taken from a
lexicalized repertory are juxtaposed according to certain syntactical rules
of combination. A specific play text can be described as an instance of
parole, an individual speech-act. At a subsidiary level of analysis, we
should add the rider that a play text can in its turn be viewed as a *langue*,
and that any one specific performance of that text constitutes *parole*.
While the *langue* is the creation of Hellenistic society, the *parole* is the
utterance of an individual member of that society. Menander's Greek
audience understood the *langue* of New Comedy, and through knowing
the rules of the *langue* were able to decipher specific speech-acts in the
theatre. This speech-act or *parole* might be a new and unique play by
Menander, or, a generation later, it might be a new and unique rendering
of a now classic and often performed play. We today are familiar with
different theatrical *langues*. Even if we can translate Menander's Greek
iambics fluently, this particular linguistic skill does not save us from the
danger of decoding Menander's theatrical speech-acts in a historically
inappropriate way.

Any spectator or reader of a play is familiar with an enormous variety of
inter-related *langues* or codes – both theatrical codes relating to conven-

tions of performance, and broader cultural codes. Menander's audience, because all members belonged to a common culture, would have shared such cultural codes as – for example – a diagnostic code which required them to read certain physiological signs as symptoms of certain diseases, a gestural code used to signify certain emotions or a certain level of sexual availability, and a complex of linguistic codes governing spoken and written Attic Greek. The modern scholar tends to be competent in decoding written (not spoken) Attic Greek, and in respect of other codes must necessarily be ignorant, relative to the original audience. The problem which I shall address in this book must be defined in the light of these limitations. I shall not try to ask, what did Menander mean?, but what theatrical language did Menander and his audience share? I shall regard the object of my investigation as a foreign set of codes, an inter-related system of socially produced theatrical signs. Since it is impossible to discard or obliterate the present, I shall pay attention to differences, differences which distinguish contemporary theatrical languages from those of the Hellenistic theatre.

If theatrical signs are socially produced, we need at the outset to delimit and identify the society which produced and used these signs. If we are to regard Menander's audience as a homogeneous body of users, what constituted that body? Women, for certain, did not form a significant part of the audience. Where the audience of fifth-century tragedy consisted in the main of Athenian males, the audience of Menander's plays must be seen as an audience of Greek males. Menander cannot have presented all his 105 plays at the major Athenian festivals,[18] and the Corinthian setting of *The Rape of the Locks* suggests that that play was written for Corinth. When plays were written for Athens, Menander knew that actors would carry them later to other parts of the Greek-speaking world. Moreover, Attica contained one non-citizen resident to every two citizens in Menander's day,[19] and since these metics would have been city-dwellers in the main, one might guess that up to half the audience in the Lycurgan Theatre of Dionysus was non-Athenian. While Menander worked for the most part in Athens, the archaeological data upon which I shall rely in reconstructing the performance of New Comedy derive from many other parts of the Greek world. The theatrical *langue* which I shall analyse in this book, therefore, must be seen as a pan-Hellenic rather than an Athenian phenomenon.

Theatre played an important part in maintaining the cohesion of Greek-speaking society in despite of city-state boundaries. I shall contrast the drama shared by the Greek world with the drama of the city of Rome. Rome differed not only in its language but also in its basic political and religious structures, and in its ethical and psychological premises. The social spectrum of the Roman audience was different too: while Greek plays were, to all intents and purposes, performed for the benefit of free-born males, in Rome citizen wives and men of slave extraction clearly formed important elements in the audience. I shall concentrate upon Plautus rather than Terence, because it is easier to discern through Plautus' large corpus of plays a specifically Roman theatrical *langue*. Plautus adapted Greek plots and conventions to the needs of a Roman audience which he understood through acting and writing for it over many years. The philhellenism of Terence seems to tell us more about the ideology of a political fraction than about the assumptions of a mass audience.

TOWARDS A HISTORICAL SEMIOLOGY

In order to analyse the sign systems which the Greek or Roman audience was competent to decode, I shall have to classify and describe a sequence of codes. The linguistic metaphor seems for this purpose inescapable. The metaphor is an ancient one. Cicero observes that 'acting is effectively the speech of the body' – '*actio quasi sermo corporis*'. He states that a foreigner ignorant of a speaker's language may grasp his meaning through his 'acting'.[20] A careful process of dissection will be required if we are to analyse the independent languages which the spectator 'reads' in order to construct the overall meaning of a theatrical experience.

Barthes's essay on 'Theatre and Signification' provides a methodological starting-point:

What is theatre? A sort of cybernetic machine. When out of use, this machine is hidden behind a curtain. But once revealed, it begins to send out in one's direction a certain number of messages. A feature of these messages is that they are simultaneous, yet have different rhythms. At a given point in a performance, you receive, *at the same moment*, six or seven pieces of information (from the set, costume, lighting, the position of the actors, their gestures, their posture, their speech); but some of this information is *fixed* (as with the set), some is *in motion* (speech, gesture). So we are dealing with genuine informational polyphony, and this is what theatricality is: *a density of signs*.

Barthes does not underrate the complexities which arise when theatre is analysed in this mechanistic fashion:

Any performance is an extremely dense semantic act. The relationship between the code and the enactment (i.e. between *langue* and *parole*), the nature of the theatrical sign (analogue, symbol, convention), which of the variables signify, invariability where signs are interlocked, messages which may connote or denote – all these basic problems of semiology are present in the theatre.[21]

The tale of Polos' urn illustrates the difficulties of defining the nature of the theatrical sign. The problem stems from the fact that (although in rehearsal the actor might well have used a flower pot) in performance a funeral urn signified a funeral urn. This precise identity of signifier and signified is hard to imagine in any other art form. At a secondary level, this urn which signifies an urn can be decoded in different ways: the audience understands how Electra decodes the urn (as the remains of her beloved brother), and how Orestes decodes the urn (as an extension of his disguise), and it must also recognize the real urn as a symbol of death (the real death that awaits each spectator). It also imagines how the actor playing Electra decodes the urn in relation to his personal bereavement. It is the polyvalence of the sign that makes it theatrically powerful.

Barthes's principal concern is not with the polyvalence of a single sign but with separating out the six or seven discrete sign systems which carry messages simultaneously. In relation to these discrete sign systems, we need to consider the problem of hierarchy. In any given performance some sign systems are dominant, and serve as points of articulation for others. Thus a drag act is articulated upon costume, Marceau's mime upon gesture, soap opera upon facial poses, and so forth. In the case of New Comedy, I shall argue that the dominant sign system is the mask, the ancient emblem of Dionysus. It would be a mistake to assume, in the manner of early semiologists, that a fixed list of sign systems can serve for the analysis of any piece of theatre.[22] In the work of Edward Gordon Craig, it might be said that lighting and set design constitute a single sign system. In melodrama or Kabuki, eye movements might be considered to constitute a sign system independent of the face. In certain types of performance, where codified hand movements substitute for speech (Kathakali, for instance, or Renaissance oratory, or the mime of Marceau) it may seem reasonable to distinguish gesture from movement. In other types of performance (soap opera, or the mime of Decroux), such a distinction may seem entirely inapproriate. When we look at the classical world, we have to ask afresh which are the discrete sign systems recognized by actors and audiences as the means by which messages are encoded and decoded. Lighting, plainly, was not a major sign system in the ancient world – though even here it could be argued that Aeschylus in the *Oresteia* exploited the qualities of morning and evening light. Mask and costume plainly were discrete sign systems – Aristophanes mocked

Euripides for dressing a king in rags, using mask and costume to send contradictory messages. In the work of actors, as distinct from choral dancers and from orators, it does not seem helpful to distinguish between gesture and movement. The Latin term *gestus*, for example, cannot be translated adequately by our 'gesture', and it implies a bearing of the whole body.

Barthes's image of the 'cybernetic machine' does not make a clear enough distinction between the two human processes of production and reception. The sign systems which constitute the tools of the actor's trade do not necessarily coincide with those offered to the audience. Encoding and decoding can be very different processes. The actor, for example, relies upon his script and upon his vocal technique. The spectator may register and respond to the rhythm of the actor's speech, but be entirely unable to distinguish whether he is responding to the rhythm of the author's words, or to a rhythm supplied by the actor.

These are some of the theoretical problems which arise when one tries to work with Barthes's cybernetic understanding of theatre. We also need to confront at the outset the question of historical method which arises when one tries to reconstruct the long-vanished art of an actor. Ancient actors have left no first-hand account of their methods or aspirations. Little work has been done on Greek acting in recent years, and the only substantial study is an Italian monograph of 1935.[23] P. Ghiron-Bistagne has contributed a useful study of the actor's profession, as distinct from his art.[24] In Britain, Peter Walcot in 1976 devoted two chapters to Greek acting, and his conclusions may be taken to represent contemporary orthodoxy, so far as an orthodoxy exists.

Walcot is heavily influenced by the naturalist/formalist debate in Shakespearian studies, and an example may illustrate why this approach is unproductive. Walcot contrasts the classical Periclean style of oratory, which required speakers to keep their arms beneath their cloaks, with the new style which involved much gesticulation. When Walcot remarks: 'The departure from behaviour we may call natural appears to have begun with Cleon . . .',[25] his use of 'natural' is wholly subjective. There is nothing natural – one has only to think how most modern Greeks converse – in addressing a crowd while standing stock still. In the same way, there is nothing natural in Pericles' reported attempt to speak without emotion (*pathos*).[26] Pericles' concealment of his arms, and Cleon's decision to tie up his cloak in order to have two arms free, were both semiotically laden, were both in effect political statements. We must always bear in mind that melodramatic gestures which appeared 'natural' to a Victorian audience appear unnatural to a modern audience familiar with different conventions. A 'natural' gesture is one which harmonizes with our expectations, not one which harmonizes with an objective natural state of things.

Walcot's conclusion that broadly speaking 'the audience came wishing to hear rather than to see'[27] is equally vulnerable. Menander addresses his '*theatai*', Plautus his '*spectatores*' (watchers) alike.[28] It is we who speak of 'audiences' – *audientes*, listeners. It is no historical accident that Cleon, the first physically expressive Athenian orator, received a bad press from Athenian intellectuals. Aristotle's disdain for the visual element in theatre belongs to the same elite or anti-populist tradition that condemned Cleon. Aristotle perceived a dichotomous theatre audience, and argued that competition and spectacle needed to be included to please the second, lower-class element of artisans and thetes.[29] We must beware of sharing these ancient prejudices embedded in our sources.

Treatises on rhetoric contain much material upon *hypokrisis* (acting, or performance), the term used to describe the manner of the orator's delivery, and the authors of rhetorical treatises are free in their comparisons between the art of the public speaker and that of the actor. Aristotle's *Rhetoric* seems the obvious text with which to begin an enquiry into Hellenistic theories of performance.

The ambivalence about performance which characterizes the *Poetics* is found again in the *Rhetoric*. We find the same presupposition that the written text ought to be self-sufficient. According to his usual practice, Aristotle relies upon an evolutionary perspective in order to justify that which is claimed to be 'natural'. In the theatre, he states, poets at first acted in their own plays, and only later was *hypokrisis* added as a separate element. In rhetoric, first of all there were the facts and the thought-content (*dianoia*), then came *lexis* or 'verbal style', a kind of adornment decorating but also clarifying the content, and last in time and importance came *hypokrisis* – which, Aristotle alleges, contemporary speakers rely upon. It would be preferable, he argues, if one could manage without verbal style, for no one needs style to demonstrate truth in respect of such subjects as geometry; it would be greatly preferable if one could manage without *hypokrisis* – but alas the orator has to persuade, and because of the corruption of the listener, facts alone never suffice.

Torn as usual between an urge to describe and to prescribe, Aristotle compromises by describing only the vocal aspects of *hypokrisis*. The discussion is quickly diverted back to verbal style on the grounds that 'acting is a natural ability and not a *technê* (art, skill), except in respect of *lexis*'.[30] Aristotle erects this murky distinction in despite of his knowledge that actors deem themselves to be *technitai*,[31] and prejudice comes to the fore when he describes acting as vulgar (*phortikon*) from a proper (*kalôs*) standpoint.[32] Aristotle goes on to distinguish two types of *lexis*, a style for writings and an agonistic style. The former – his own scientific style – has the advantage of precision, but the latter is performable (*hypokritikô-tatê*).[33] Arguing along these lines, Aristotle circumvents the need to analyse *hypokrisis* as an element separable from the words of the text.

The democratic orator Demosthenes articulated the opposite view, insisting in a much-quoted dictum that *hypokrisis* was the first, second, and third element in successful oratory.[34] Professional actors coached him in performance technique, and differing accounts name four different actors as his trainers.[35] Demosthenes' position is summarized by one of his biographers: 'the *lexis* instructs those with a responsive *psychê* as to what kind of *hypokrisis* is needed for its expression'. The speeches of Demosthenes cannot be delivered successfully by someone whose 'stony nature is sluggish, insensitive, immovable, and unfeeling', the biographer states.[36] There was a broad difference of views between radical democrats who argued for the importance of feeling, and their opponents who argued for intellectual substance. Aeschines accused Demosthenes of displaying too much *pathos*, while Demosthenes accused Aeschines of acting with his voice but not with his soul (*psychê*).[37] Aristotle's *Rhetoric* gives no quarter to this intuitive approach of the democrats whereby the performer in some way surrenders to the prompting of his soul, and his treatise systematically analyses the intellectual substance underpinning common human emotions.

A generation later, these arguments about the nature and purpose of performance continued to have a political context. In 317 BC – during the earlier part of Menander's writing career – Athens became a Macedonian protectorate, and was ruled for ten years by Demetrios of Phaleron. Demetrios was both a philosopher and a politician. He was educated in the Lyceum, and tried to implement many of Aristotle's political ideas. The Macedonian court supported his regime, influenced by the personal links between Macedon and Aristotle, former tutor of Alexander, and by the fact that Aristotle's ideals involved the attenuation of radical democracy. In the previous cycle of political change, Aristotle a year before his death had had to leave Athens in the wake of a democratic counter-revolution. When Demetrios' regime fell in its turn, Demetrios was forced to leave the city, and so also was Theophrastos, Aristotle's successor as head of the Lyceum. Demetrios' aspiration had been to recreate the traditional values of pre-Periclean Athens, an Athens in which the populace had not yet gained hegemony. He restored old institutions like the Areopagus. Within the artistic sphere, he was concerned to revitalize rhapsodic performances of Homer, verbal performances uncontaminated by spectacle.[38] Plato's *Ion* satirizes the decadence into which this institution had lapsed under fourth-century 'theatrocracy', and implies that it had become indistinguishable from dramatic performance.[39] The need for spectacle was reduced when the rich were no longer required by Demetrios to make a display of status by funding choruses, and the poor were no longer given money to buy theatre tickets.[40] The element of display in Athenian culture was generally discouraged – at funeral feasts and on funeral monuments, for example. Demetrios wrote a biography of Demosthenes in which he attacked the performative element in the democrat's political style. He criticized Demosthenes' *hypokrisis* because it was not of the old school, but was 'inconsistent' and 'excessive', inclining to 'softness' and 'baseness'.[41]

Despite these efforts to turn back the clock, an irrevocable change had taken place. Aristotle's attempt to dissolve performance away, his denial that it had an integral place either within the business of conducting politics or within the business of creating theatre, came to seem untenable. The view that *hypokrisis* was not a *technê* but a natural endowment was abandoned by Theophrastos, who wrote a seminal treatise on the subject. Theophrastos accepted that performance should be a major contributor to a speaker's success, and he analysed the sources of *hypokrisis* in the *pathê* (emotions) of the soul. For Theophrastos, mastery of *hypokrisis* involved harmonizing the movement of the body with the 'tone' of the *psychê*.[42] The meaning of this last phrase is made clear by Cicero, who writes of emotional impulses activating the voice just as touch activates the strings of the lyre.[43] Theophrastos accepted what Aristotle could not accept, namely the importance of the visual, physical elements in performance. We know, apparently via Demetrios' biography, that Demosthenes worked alike at the *pathê* of the voice and at the gestures of the body.[44] Theophrastos evidently came to accept the Demosthenic emphasis on sensibility, and his principle that speakers and actors must rely on movement as well as voice if they are to express that which the soul feels.

Later definitions of *hypokrisis* seem to be based upon Theophrastos' seminal treatise, and provide us with the bones of a Hellenistic vocabulary for describing acting. I have translated three key terms as follows:

> gesture – *schêma*: external form, configuration, hence how one holds oneself, bearing, posture, a step (in dancing);
> Mask – *prosôpon*: face, mask, a character (in a play), a character type;
> situation – *pragmata*: actions, things done.

The extant definitions are these:

Hypokrisis is a *mimêsis* made by speech and gesture to fit given Masks. For one must not only give a verbal imitation of Masks, one must also imitate the movements of the body.

Hypokrisis [can be defined as] (a) the *mimèsis* of given Masks and situations, or (b) the convincing disposition of voice and gesture suited to the given character trait and situation.

Hypokrisis is (a) the *mimêsis* of *êthê* and *pathê* which in each case approximates to truth, and (b) the disposition of body and tone of voice suited to the given situation.

Hypokrisis is like [the acting of] an excellent actor who by his gesture, gaze, and voice properly conforms his acting to what is said.

A *hypokrisis* which suits the *êthos* of given Masks comprises the mould of the voice, gesture, and the disposition [of these] to follow what is said.[45]

It may be, as Philodemos observed, that actors were commonly reluctant to turn to rhetoricians for instruction.[46] This does not alter the obvious fact that rhetoricians learned practical skills from actors, and that both groups used a common language in order to describe their art. These five definitions found in Greek rhetorical theory allow us to construct a coherent body of thinking about performance. This thinking assumes:

(i)   Performance (or *hypokrisis*) is a mimetic art, like dramatic writing or painting. Since a *mimêsis* may be a more or less accurate imitation of reality, it follows that performance is a *technê* and not merely a natural response to a text.

(ii) Any performance works with three givens (*hypokeimena*): situation (*pragmata*, what is done), character types (*prosôpa*), and dialogue (*legomena*, what is said: not so much the actual words as the thought behind the words).

(iii) Within the art of performance, control of the voice and control of bodily movement are always separable.

(iv) In respect of character types, the standard term is *prosôpon*, or mask. The character type represented and the mask worn are indisseverable.

(v) In respect of gesture, the standard term is *schêma*. This is a configuration of the whole body. The term emphasizes form rather than movement. Aristotle's theory of perception distinguished the perception of a *schêma* from the perception of *kinêsis* (movement).[47]

If we regard the script as a constant, we can say that a Hellenistic performance involved the deployment of three independent variables: mask, gesture (*schêma*), and voice. In our contemporary theatre, these three cannot be isolated so easily as independent semiological systems. The face is as mobile as the body in our maskless theatre, and the expressions of the face echo the expressivity of the voice. The importance of the classical distinction between voice and body may become clearer if we consider the alternative ideal of a Grotowskian theorist:

The voice as a physiological process engages the whole organism projecting it into space . . . The body is the visible part of the voice and one can see how and where the impulse which will become sound and speech is born. The voice is body – invisible body – operating in space. There is no separation, no duality: voice and body. There are only actions and reactions which engage our body in its entirety.[48]

The actor in Grotowskian theatre of this kind renders his body visible, reversing the norms of a society where the body is hidden and words are all. In the Greek world, where nakedness was common, theatre reversed normality by concealing the actor's body beneath robes, sleeves, and head masks. The body of the Hellenistic actor must seem to slip effortlessly from one mask and costume into the next. The actor subordinates his own physical presence to the transindividual presence of the mask and costume. While the corporality of the semi-nude Grotowskian actor fuses body and voice, the conventions of Hellenistic theatre separate the voice, which appears from within the mask, from the external signs which tell the audience who is speaking and what is happening.

In Stanislavskian theatre, the actor's primary task is seen as 'building a character'. Character work remains the basis of a modern actor's training. In Theophrastos' treatise on *hypokrisis*, the emphasis is very different.

The actor's basic task is to analyse and represent the emotions required by the play. The distinction between character and emotion, *êthos* and *pathos*, is fundamental to the performance of Greek New Comedy. Both *êthos* and *pathos* are implicit in the situation which the dramatist constructs: situations may be pitiful or fearful; they also involve choices which reveal the *êthos* of the doer. *Êthos* is a constant, a fixed moral disposition to undertake action *x* rather than action *y* in a given situation. *Pathos* is transient, it can only exist so long as it is felt. Thus *êthos* is signified by the unchanging element in theatrical communication, the mask, the *prosôpon*, the character type. *Pathos* is expressed by that which is of the moment, the voice. The body expresses both *êthos* and *pathos*, for it is both ever-present and always moving. In Stanislavskian theatre, the face expresses both character and emotion, and no distinction of the Greek kind is possible.

The mask is the *prosôpon* – in Latin the *persona* – the type of person that one is. The masks of New Comedy differed profoundly from those of classical tragedy. In New Comedy the mask was designed to be read frontally, and was – as I shall demonstrate at length – a synthesis of physiognomic signs identified by Hellenistic theorists. In classical tragedy, the mask was a neutral better-than-average face. The eyes of the audience could fix upon the shifting physical relationship of actor and chorus within the *orchêstra*, and a continuous view of the face was not essential. The *êthos* of the protagonists emerged exclusively through the action of the play, and was not revealed by the mask. Hellenistic theatre found new possibilities in the mask in accordance with new theories of perception. Aristotle argued that the visual image necessarily carries a higher information content than the voice. Colour, form, size, number, and movement offer human perception more possibilities of discrimination within a finite range of perceptible nuances than the voice can ever offer.[49] Hellenistic mask-makers used this kind of scientific insight in order to maximize the informational content of the mask. While the mask was fixed for the duration of the play, the voice could never be frozen in time. It was, as we have seen, regarded as a musical instrument activated by the *psychê*. The breath gave direct access to the roots of feeling. In Hellenistic theatre, where all the roles were shared amongst three actors, one voice, albeit slightly differentiated, served for many characters. The purpose of vocal technique was not to individuate and clarify character, but to individuate and clarify specific emotions.

The body in New Comedy has to conform to the mask. The two sign systems are in Barthes's terms 'interlocked'. But although the wearer of a given mask displays a fixed disposition to move in a certain way, any given movement expresses the emotion of a specific moment. We must recall that, in Aristotelian thinking, the emotions have no spiritual essence, but only exist materially as movements of the body. When the soul is angry or feels pity, the body changes.[50] A feeling necessarily has its physiological correlative. The actor must not, therefore, express emotion without using his body. The body of the actor, for this reason, expressed both *êthos* and *pathos*. Hellenistic painters and sculptors tended to be torn, to emphasize either the fixed moral condition of their subjects, or the passions of a particular moment.[51] Theatre was at an advantage over the visual arts because it existed in time as well as space. The actor's body could be a point of intersection where the fixed moral state (mask, bodily form) was tied to transient emotions (the voice, bodily movement). The dialectic is of course a subtle one, for a given *êthos* presupposes a disposition to feel certain emotions, and certain emotions presuppose an *êthos* with that capacity. Schematically, the underlying dialectic can be expressed in a simple diagram:

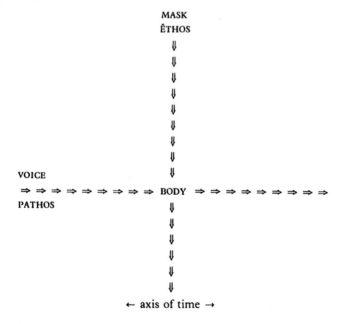

The task of the actor was to manipulate three sets of sign systems transmitted through sound and movement and located in the twin dimensions of time and space. This organization of performance signs differs profoundly from that of our naturalistic theatre, where the face is used to express emotion, where the voice is used to express character.

The great strength of the rule whereby all plays were performed by three actors[52] was that theatre became almost completely cybernetic. Everything that the audience saw and heard was part of a 'density of signs' – and in this density lay the audience's pleasure. In naturalistic performance based upon the merger of role and actor, the vagaries of casting introduce a chance element. The colour of the actor's hair, the grain of his or her voice, the shape of his or her body, may not be intended to signify anything. In Greek theatre, no information was redundant, everything signified: the conformation of the body, vocal intonation, the features of the face.

The actor's art of vanishing himself beneath his mask does not by any means imply that the double awareness of the spectator was lost. The spectator who weeps for Electra may weep simultaneously for Polos. The tyrant who wept for Euripides' heroine knew that Theodoros was playing on his emotions. Every Hellenistic spectator knew that he was watching actors participating in a competition designed to test skill in acting. Greek conventions never obscured the spectator's sense of double vision, his double awareness of signifier and signified. Analysing the phenomenon of mimesis in the theatre, Anne Ubersfeld argues that within mimesis

an articulation takes place between theatre-as-magic and theatre-as-scale-model. The spectator's pleasure oscillates between two tendencies: bewitchment by a magical recreation, and observation of an imitative practice. In the one case, as in the other, pleasure lies in the observation of a sign or system of signs.[53]

In the following chapters of this book I shall try to distinguish those aspects of performance where art conceals art, where actors and writers create theatre-as-magic through hiding their techniques beneath a guise of naturalness, and those aspects which, on the contrary, remind the audience that everything it sees is man-made, codified, and endlessly reproducible. This kind of balance can be discerned in Menander's plays first of all on the level of plot. We see an oscillation between extraordinary coincidences and an everyday bourgeois setting, an oscillation related to the Aristotelian polarities of the 'marvellous' and the 'convincing'.

THE NARRATIVE SUBSTRUCTURE

A well-known anecdote records that someone once said to Menander: 'It is nearly time for the Dionysia, Menander. Have you not finished your comedy?' The poet replied: 'Yes indeed, I have finished the comedy. The plot has been worked out. I have only to add the accompaniment of the verses.'[54] The anecdote illustrates Aristotle's advice that the poet should begin with what is most important, the arrangement of the incidents. Since a play is the imitation of an action, the poet's first task must be to construct the dramatic action, not the verses.[55] The *mythos* or plot is described by Aristotle as both the start and end of tragedy, being 'as it were its *psychê*'.[56] The *mythos* is thus the invisible soul of the play animating the language, just as the actor is the invisible soul animating the mask.

Although I shall be concerned in the remainder of this book with the material signifiers which constituted a performance, it is essential to begin with an analysis of the substructure. Without the *mythos*, the action on stage can have no shape. Menander, no less than Sophocles and Euripides, drew on myths which were a cultural property owned by all Greeks. Myths like those of Oedipus or the Atreids, transmitted and reworked in countless different versions, can be seen as a metalanguage used to define and resolve problems of patriarchy, kingship, divine intervention, and so forth. The myths used by Menander are, on the face of it, very different in kind, but they share nevertheless similar functions and properties. It is our language, and not that of the Greeks, which gives the word *mythos* two different renderings, myth (sacred, ancient, and mysterious) and story (any invented narrative). As in the case of *êthos*, it is helpful to return to the ancient vocabulary.

A myth like that of Clytemnestra tells a story: the mother kills her husband, and is in turn killed by her son. It was the job of the tragic dramatist in a specific play to invest each of these archetypal figures with an *êthos*, a character discernible through moral choices made. The play focusses upon moral choice, whether it is right or wrong to avenge a daughter, or to commit matricide. The 'character' of Orestes is a function of the decisions which he makes. Similarly, beneath Menander's plays we can perceive a mythic or narrational substructure, creating a framework for the organization of specific moral choices in specific plays. A convenient model for the analysis of this substructure is the actantial model of A. J. Greimas, a model inspired by the seminal researches of Propp into the Russian folktale.[57]

Greimas reduces all narratives to the syntatical form of a sentence. He deems all sentences to have a sender and a receiver, and to contain a subject and an object. The subject undertakes the action, the object undergoes the action; the subject desires to do, the object is desired. Two modalities act upon the verb, making it possible or impossible for the subject to realize its desire. All narratives can thus be reduced to a mythical model involving six actants or functions, thus:

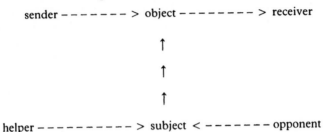

sender – – – – – – – > object – – – – – – – – > receiver

↑

↑

↑

helper – – – – – – – – – – > subject < – – – – – – – opponent

Greimas emphasizes that these actants are not actors but narrative functions. A cluster of individual actors can constitute one actantial function, one actor can fulfil two actantial functions, and so forth.

This model works very well for Menander, because of the underlying Aristotelian assumption that a play is an action. A play, like a sentence, should have as its core a single action. In each play of Menander we find a clear subject and object: a young citizen is subject, a free-born girl is object. The subject desires and seeks the object; when he has attained the object, the unitary action of the play is complete. In contrast to, for instance, Shakespearian comedy, the female is never the seeker, always the sought. In accordance with Greimas' model, one can map out the following schema for Menander's narratives:

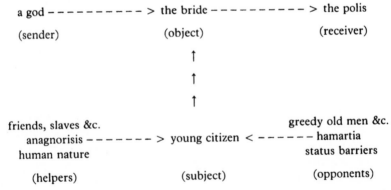

a god – – – – – – – – – > the bride – – – – – – – – – > the polis

(sender)   (object)   (receiver)

↑

↑

↑

friends, slaves &c.   greedy old men &c.
anagnorisis – – – – – – – > young citizen < – – – – – – hamartia
human nature   status barriers

(helpers)   (subject)   (opponents)

Effectively, four of the actantial functions in Menander are invariable: subject and object, sender and receiver. The subject always turns out to be an Athenian citizen (except in one play, perhaps written for Corinth, where he is a Corinthian citizen).[58] The object is always a citizen-born girl who, for reasons of status, seems to be unobtainable: she may be too poor, enslaved, mistakenly considered to be foreign, or considered not to be a virgin. The plot is set in motion by a semi-abstract divine force, embodied in prologues by such figures as *Tychê* (Chance or Fate) or *Agnoia* (Ignorance). It is left ambiguous whether this divine embodiment of universal law is purposive, or merely a personification of chance. There is never a division within the cosmic sphere such as we find in tragedy. The receiver is, in both literal and fictional terms, Athens, the political community which receives and judges a new play, which receives and accepts a new *oikos* (household). When the play ends, the marriage is cemented with the ritual formula: 'I plight my daughter for a harvest of legitimate [i.e. citizen] children.'[59] The central action of the play is that which permits the community to reproduce itself.

The modalities of helper and opponent are more complex, and provide the most obvious variables within the narrative formula. On the level of the *dramatis personae*, the subject encounters helpers who may be slaves, prostitutes, relatives or friends, and opponents who usually have some legal power over the bride. On the psychological level, '*anagnôrisis*' and '*hamartia*' seem to sum up the qualities which make resolution possible or impossible. The subject acquires both moral recognition (regarding himself) and intellectual recognition (regarding the facts of the plot); helpers and opponents may do the same. On another level, it is human nature – the spontaneous love of a man for a woman – which draws the couple together, and social barriers such as endogamy which keep them apart.

This schema helps to lay bare the sociological roots of Menander's comedy, and its ideological function. The plot solves a problem for the audience, namely, what is the relationship between humanity and citizenship. It offers a magical answer to a simple and stark problem: are Greek males first and foremost human beings, that is, capable of falling in love with a woman because of her nature, or are they citizens (or non-citizens), duty-bound (or forbidden) to marry endogamously in order to perpetuate the *polis*? The development of New Comedy as a form reflects this deep-rooted tension between the *polis* and the wider world. Though a performance was still part of a festival which affirmed the corporate identity of the *polis*, the actors were cosmopolitan individuals with a unique freedom to travel from city to city. The play was no longer anchored in the dancing of young citizens before their elders, and could be carried with the greatest ease to any city in the Greek world. The content and external form of the play are indisseverable, and expressive of the same tension: are the plays, like the characters within the plays, Athenian or merely Greek?

Aristotle was the last major philosopher to construe man as a political animal, arguing that 'the *polis* is both natural and prior to the individual'.[60] The new philosophy which emerged in Menander's generation put the individual first. Epicurus, Menander's exact contemporary, construed individuals as freely moving social atoms who bind themselves to others in order to secure individual happiness. The Stoics stressed the need for individuals to attune their souls to the law of nature, universal law not political law. These philosophical changes have an obvious political context in the hegemony of Macedon, and the declining autonomy of the Greek city-state. Menander's comedy marks the point of transition from Aristotelian to post-Aristotelian thinking, and could be said to dramatize the emergence of the autonomous individual. Autonomy is symbolized by the decision to marry for love. Fifth-century tragedy characteristically asked its audience to consider the question: 'who are you first – a member of your *oikos* or a member of your *polis*?' New Comedy posed a rather different question: 'who are you – a member of your *polis* or a member of humanity?' Sophocles expected his audience to understand and appreciate Creon's argument that the needs of the state must often override family responsibilities. By the time of Menander, the requirements of the state have become alien and almost incomprehensible. The legal requirement, for instance, that heiresses marry their nearest male relative in order to prevent the concentration of wealth was a theme for tragedy in Aeschylus' *Danaid* trilogy, but becomes an arbitrary and ludicrous piece of legislation in Menander's *The Shield*. Where classical tragedy dealt always with two equal and opposite moral forces, New Comedy dealt with the struggle of an individual moral agent against impersonal and arbitrary forces.

The presence of the citizen-born youth as narrative subject can be related to the prominent presence of ephebes in the Dionysiac festival. The ephebes – youths removed from their families and placed on military service – carried the statue of the god into the theatre, led the sacrificial bull to its altar in the precincts, and then sat together in a central block next to the Council.[61] The 'myth' of New Comedy represented the final reabsorption of the ephebe into the body politic as he married, formed a new *oikos*, and joined the assembly of mature males. A convention of direct address allowed the actor in a monologue formally to interpellate the audience as *andres* (sirs!) – implicitly the group of adult males who formed the political community.[62] The stage was, physically, a tangent upon the circle in which the community sat assembled, and the community necessarily contemplated itself in relation to the play on the stage. The spectator within this circle saw himself becoming that which, perforce or by nature, he had to be, a political animal, part of a group. The play explored the practical, philosophical, and emotional problems which made it difficult for men to identify themselves as members of the *polis* before all else; but also, through the fact of its performance, the play affirmed the corporate identity of the audience.

Women, confined to the margins of the auditorium, are excluded beings, not addressed by the actors, object but not subject of the play. Slaves have a place in the narrative only to help or hinder. This is not the world of Shakespeare, where a Rosalind or a Viola can be 'subject' of the narrative; nor is it the world of Beaumarchais where a servant is 'subject'. Slaves and women may be human beings but they are not political beings. That is how they must recognize their situation. The narrative structure of Menander's plays, like the organizational structure of the Greek *polis*, never yields in its privileging of the citizen male.

Terence's plays are interesting to examine as a control upon the model which I have proposed for Menander. Though Terence's plays are on the face of it adaptations of Greek New Comedy, the actantial model operates rather differently. Terence substitutes double plots for the single plots of Menander, and we are therefore confronted with two contrasted narratives:

BRIDE	PROSTITUTE
↑	↑
YOUNG CITIZEN B	YOUNG CITIZEN A

This model holds good for all six plays, with minor reservations: A and B are one and the same youth in *The Mother-in-Law*; in *The Girl from Andros* the supposed prostitute turns out to be an Athenian; and a second marriage is tacked onto the end of the *The Self-Tormentor*. The functions of sender and receiver change also. In accordance with Stoic thinking, there is no cosmic *primum mobile*, no divine prologue to inform the audience about the facts of the plot. All knowledge is empirical, hence the audience must deduce the facts of the plot from the dialogue alone. The audience are not formally receivers of the narrative. They are not directly addressed in monologues, but seem to be voyeurs unrelated to the action, eavesdropping upon dialogues which do not directly concern them. The fact that an action set in Athens is played to a Roman audience points rather to the universality of human experience. The spectator in this Roman theatre must see him- or herself as a member not of a closed community but of the human race, with an eternal moral choice to be made between duty (symbolized by the bride) and pleasure (the prostitute).[63]

We must take note also of a change of emphasis within the helper/opponent dimension. There seems to be an increased interest in the moral qualities of the narrative subjects, and a decreased interest in the barriers thrown up by status. Citizenship was far more open to newcomers in Rome than in Athens, although there was less mobility within the citizen body. The central problematic in Terence is no longer: 'Is natural human behaviour compatible with citizenship?' – as Aristotle strenuously maintained – but rather the great question of the Stoics: 'Is natural human behaviour congruent with virtue?'

An attempt to analyse the surviving plays of Plautus according to the model of A. J. Greimas has been made by Maurizio Bettini.[64] Bettini argues that the use of stock roles allowed the audience to perceive the paradigmatic nature of the plots. Permutations of actor/actant relationships proposed by the narrative allow the audience to test out the logic and flexibility of the Roman social structure. In Bettini's analysis, the plays all involve the transference of women and/or wealth from the opponent to the receiver. All Romans were concerned by such problems of transference in a culture where children remained under the economic and legal power of their fathers until the fathers' deaths. While Greek New Comedy is concerned fundamentally with problems of status, Plautine comedy, as Bettini perceives it, is concerned with ownership. I fully endorse Bettini's critical premise, that the Plautine corpus, qua *langue*, is a collective creation, and that laughter in the Roman theatre can be examined in terms of its anthropological function. Bettini encounters, unfortunately, insoluble problems when he tries to lay individual texts upon Greimas' template. These problems are inherent in the material, but are exacerbated by Bettini's failure to distinguish text from performance. The Roman actor was not a vanishing physical presence in quite the manner of the Greek actor. The actor playing Pseudolus, for instance, was required to present three façades to the audience: (i) as an Athenian domestic slave, (ii) as an actor participating in the Megalesian games, and (iii) as the mouthpiece of Plautus the Roman poet. Pseudolus (i) is the helper, Pseudolus (ii) presents himself as the sender, but Pseudolus (iii) is always known to be the receiver of an authorial text and musical score. While Calidorus the lover, the subject of the Greek metatext, remains the formal subject of Plautus' narrative, Pseudolus (ii/iii) is the subject of another drama whose declared object is to win the audience's applause and laughter.

Bettini is not unaware of the problems which the slave poses for his analysis. He maps out a paradigm in which the slave is permitted to be subject of the narrative but never sender or receiver in accordance with the sociological status of the slave as an outsider:

The fact is that the slave – this subaltern-hero – is simultaneously within the action (because he acts in it) but also outside it (because he does not benefit from the outcome). Qua mere subject, he can mediate between inner and outer, between the position of 'author' of the play and that of 'actor' inside it.[65]

It is difficult to know how a 'subject' is now to be defined, and Bettini relies upon some seemingly arbitrary choices when he nominates subjects for Plautus' individual plays. It seems that in Plautus, unlike Menander, it is impossible to pin down the subject of a given play. Plautus' technique consists precisely in disrupting the Greek narrative formula, and in creating a sense of dislocation between the narrative and the performance.

If we are to analyse Plautine theatre, we need to start with an understanding of the shifting relationship between stage and auditorium. The simple cybernetic model of performance analysis breaks down at this point, just as Greimas' model of narrative analysis breaks down. The audience are not merely passive recipients of messages, they are also part of the play. In order to illustrate this point let us consider Plautus' technique in the *Stichus*. The first part of the play is the sentimental Menandrean story of two faithful brides and their hypocritical father. Neither brides nor father formally address the audience. The women establish physical remoteness at the outset, sitting on seats inside a house. The father first addresses his unseen slaves, in a parody of Greek entrance conventions. When the parasite appears, he establishes an intimate relationship with the audience, which he maintains whenever he is on stage. He tries to auction his stories and other non-existent effects to the spectators, whom he castigates ironically as idlers with nothing better to do than gawp. A slave arrives to announce the husbands' return, and play-acts, implicitly for the audience's benefit, as a messenger drawn from a tragedy. The father expresses his desire for a prostitute, framing his request as a set piece apologue delivered to a stage audience – a device which again distances the real audience. The finale is played out by three slaves who celebrate an *eleutheria* or slaves' freedom festival to replicate the off-stage banquet of their masters. The slaves expend great efforts in persuading the stage musician to drink in order that he may play suitably orgiastic music for their erotic dancing. This finale ensures that the fictional Athenian *eleutheria* merges with the real Plebeian games in

Rome, as actors seem to disrupt the orthodox, planned order of performance.

Plautus has marked out the shifts in the actor–audience relationship. The figures on stage move freely between three levels of self-presentation: as actors, as stock Menandrean characters, and as characters engaged in role-play. The assumed identity of the audience is equally unstable. At the start, the audience are deemed to be a Hellenistic audience concerned with questions of virtue. En route, they are insulted as penniless loafers, with nothing better to do than come to the theatre. By the time the play ends, they have been recast as carefree fellow revellers. The audience must finally recognize themselves as Romans, people quite distinct from Athenians. Rome was not noted as a trading nation, and Roman spectators could not easily identify themselves with the two rather unattractive husbands who belong to an entrepreneurial bourgeoisie. By implication, the peers and interlocutors of the audience are the under-dogs, the hard-working slaves and the starving parasite. In the finale, it is established that the festival is the people's festival. The audience are shown that it is their power which ensures that the rules of an imported cultural form are going to be broken recklessly.

Menander's theatre and that of Plautus are both deeply ideological. We cannot understand either form of theatre unless we see each as a relationship set up between specific actors and a specific audience. We cannot analyse the audience unless we grasp its historical particularity. Menander's writing career embraced a unique period when a philosopher became absolute ruler of Athens and an attempt was made to implement Aristotelian theory in the form of a practical political programme. Aristotle's espousal of moderate oligarchy – a mean between the rule of the very rich and the rule of the people – rested on a massive framework of ethical, psychological, and historical, not to mention literary, research. The aesthetic ideal of Menander cannot be disengaged from the political aspirations of the elite group within which he moved. When the philosopher-ruler went into exile, Menander was almost brought to trial 'merely because he was his friend'.[66] In the event, Menander did not go into exile, but continued to write for an Athenian audience, many of whom must have been radical democrats, and passionately anti-Macedonian. One must presume that such spectators nevertheless found something they could recognize as truth in Menander's plays. Menander was a writer of plays not of tracts, and he gave expression to multiple and contradictory currents of thought.

No similar political experiment took place in Rome, but Plautus too wrote at a time of cultural change. Through its conquests, the Roman world was opening itself up to Greek influences. Roman traditionalists and Roman philhellenists were implacably opposed. A Greek life style and Greek art attracted many aristocrats for whom Greek democratic ideals were repellent. Plautus' treatment of the Greek world plays upon an uncertainty about how Greeks should be regarded. The Roman aristocracy was clearly not divided in its desire that the common citizens should understand two things – first, that they were destined to remain in the lower ranks of a tiered society, and second, that they belonged to a triumphant and uniquely successful state destined to rule. This double message, that the citizen is both ruler and ruled, seems connected to the lack of a clear narrative subject. One does not know whose story the play is telling, that of the slave, or that of the rich roué. The clearest message which emerges from the plays is the message that the different orders of society are interdependent. Without the help of the lower orders, the master can achieve nothing.

CHAPTER 2

Space

THE VITRUVIAN DISTINCTION

Thus the platform will be made wider than that of the Greeks because [in Rome] the artists all play their parts on stage, while the orchestra is used for the seating of senators. The height of the platform is not to be more than five feet so that those who are seated in the orchestra can see the movements of all actors ... The Greeks have a more spacious orchestra, and their stage wall is further back. The stage platform is narrower and called the *logeion* [lit. speaking-place], for the reason that in Greece tragic and comic actors perform on stage while other performers play their parts using the whole orchestra. For this reason *scenic* [i.e. on stage] and *thymelic* [i.e. around the orchestral altar] actors are given separate names in Greek. The height of the [Greek] stage should not be less than ten feet nor more than twelve.[1]

Vitruvius here describes some fundamental distinctions. Hellenistic actors played on a shallow stage positioned at a tangent to the orchestral circle. The *orchêstra* was used for the choral interludes of a play and was not invaded by the three 'actors'. Actors and audience were separated, therefore, by a vast empty space which served as an acoustical sounding board. In the Roman theatre, the stage reduces the shape of the *orchêstra* to a semicircle, and the orchestral floor is filled with seats. There is no intervening void to set actors and audience apart. While the Roman stage is deep enough to accommodate a substantial group of actors, and perhaps some spectators too,[2] the Greek stage only needed to hold three actors plus a few supernumeraries. While the Roman spectator looks at a three-dimensional stage image, the effect for the Greek spectator resembled that of looking at a carving in relief.

The Hellenistic tradition saw art as a reflection of reality. Alkidamas, a century before Menander, first saw the *Odyssey* as a 'mirror of human life',[3] and Plato's simile of the cave suggested that life itself was but a reflected image.[4] One portrait of a Hellenistic dramatist seems to depict, emblematically, a mirror propped against a column, signifying that the play which the dramatist is planning mirrors reality.[5] The stage action was like a mirror in the way it created a flat two-dimensional image. The stage world in the Greek-style theatre can be seen as completing the circle suggested by the shape of the auditorium. The world of the play is contiguous with the normal world of the audience, but at the same time inhabits a separate architectural structure. The openness of the Hellenistic stage makes it quite unlike the enclosed and private stage of modern naturalistic theatre, which spectators looks into from without. A troublesome problem concerns the structures known as 'paraskênia' (though the term may be incorrectly used[6]) which are found in some but not all Hellenistic theatres and seem designed to support projecting wings framing the stage. These wings may be slightly angled or tapered in the manner of a picture frame in order to prevent the stage from seeming to recede.[7] Archaeologists have in the past often gone too far in reconstructing pseudo-Victorian stages, ignoring problems of sight-lines in order to reproduce an equivalent to the nineteenth-century proscenium arch.[8] The world of the Hellenistic stage is a world opened to public gaze. It does not draw the audience into an interior world so much as reflect an image back to the audience.

The world of the stage is necessarily divided off from the real world, and the function of paraskênia must be to emphasize this division. The acting space, like the plot, has a clear beginning, middle, and end. Boundaries defined in time and space give the performance its artistic shape, and the audience are free to imagine the world of the play extending beyond these boundaries. In the Roman theatre of Plautus, no such rigid bounds enclose the play. Spectators are seated at the foot of the stage, and the actors do not tower high above them. The theatre is a single architectural structure. Actors and audience are bonded by their sharing of a common environment, and their two worlds interpenetrate. As we saw in the Stichus, the two worlds of actors and audience merge in the final dance of the slaves, who inhabit not an Athenian street so much as a Roman theatre. No future punishment awaits these slaves, for they have no off-stage reality. There is no dichotomy of imitation and reality, only the single shared world of the festival.

Vitruvius' distinction between Greek and Roman theatres correlates broadly with the archaeological evidence, but his writing is prescriptive, and contains no historical information about how this distinction arose. Since the deep, low Roman stage was not drawn from the Hellenistic tradition, we can only conclude that it derives from an earlier tradition of performance which could not be discarded because of its cultural importance. Livy tells us that stage performance was introduced in lieu of circus-style performance in 364 BC. The change was made to placate the gods, and the new stage was used for Etruscan dancing.[9] When Greek-style plays were introduced over a century later, these plays must have been made to accommodate themselves with the Etruscan spatial arrangements that had been used in the *ludi* for so long.

I have assumed, and will continue to assume in this book, that Menander's comedy was written for the 'high' Hellenistic stage described by Vitruvius. No one doubts that within Menander's lifetime his plays were performed on high stages in some parts of Greece, and that after his death these high stages became the norm, but there has been scholarly uncertainty as to whether there was such a stage in the theatre built by Lycurgus, where most of Menander's plays received their first perform-ance. Pickard-Cambridge argued that, compared with other parts of Greece, 'in Athens there was a more conservative spirit'.[10] The need to continue performing tragedy in the traditional manner, he claimed, meant that Menander's plays also had to be performed in the *orchêstra* long after the new mode of staging had been introduced in Epidaurus, Eretria, Priene, and elsewhere. Bieber accepted this notion of Athenian 'conservatism', and reconstructed two alternative stagings of Menander's *The Arbitration*: an Athenian style using the *orchêstra* and an 'eastern' style using the high stage.[11] This 'eastern' style, however, is not only found in Asia Minor, but also in Sicily and in mainland theatres like Corinth and Epidaurus early in the third century. The traditional theory envisages that, for a century or more, an Athenian guild of actors could have taken Athenian plays to new-style theatres throughout the Greek world, and yet remained content with a fundamentally unsuitable mode of performance in their home city. This view is no longer in fashion, and I endorse the contrary view of one recent scholar that it is 'absurd to question Athenian leadership, either in dramatic composition or in techniques of production, at a time when New Comedy was at its height'.[12] The myth of Athenian 'decline' needs to be resisted. Athens remained a centre of innovation in dramatic writing, philosophy, science, and the visual arts, and was not in any obvious sense conservative.

When the Athenian auditorium was reconstructed by Lycurgus in stone rather than wood, and extended half as high again up the slope of the Acropolis, it is inconceivable that minute and scientific attention was not paid to the acoustical properties of the new structure. Vitruvius assures us that the ancient architects studied music and mathematics for this purpose.[13] In the Greek theatre, the actor's voice was to a large extent reflected off the beaten earth floor of the *orchêstra*. From this floor, the voice rises in circular waves to the audience seated around it in the auditorium. This type of reflected sound is called by Vitruvius 'consonant' from the Greek *synechountes*: 'Consonant places are those in which the voice, with the assistance of the ground, increases as it rises, and is distinct when it reaches the ear, making the words clear.' Voices rising direct from the *orchêstra* create more 'resonant' sound – *antechountes* – which is an effect more appropriate to song than to speech.[14] While the Greek auditorium was made of stone, the Plautine actor played in a temporary theatre made of wood – a material which, Vitruvius tells us, naturally creates 'consonance' in a way that stone cannot.[15] The voice may therefore travel directly from stage to auditorium.

The logic of the high stage is that actors and chorus should occupy different spaces in order to carry out their respective functions: the chorus had to display their dances, and make their singing resonate; the actor had in the manner of an orator to display his *êthos* and *pathos* to an audience which needed to see everything in order to judge. A move towards differentiating the two functions of actor and chorus is already in evidence in the last play of Aristophanes, some half-century before the new theatre was built.

THE HELLENISTIC STAGE WALL

There is no communication between actors and chorus in New Comedy. When the chorus of Dionysiac dancers invades the *orchêstra* at the end of Act I of a Menandrean comedy, diverting the audience's attention from the stage, the actors by convention retire with the complaint that a crowd of drunks has arrived. Hellenistic comedy deals with the actions of individuals, not with the actions of communities, and it is no longer the property of Hellenistic choruses to be 'doers'.[16] The art of the individual actor is increasingly under scrutiny, and New Comedy is written to exploit the possibilities which the high stage opened up for the actor. The proximity of actors and doorways permits the virtuoso doubling that is so striking a feature of Hellenistic performance. Entries and exits are accomplished much faster than they were in Aristophanes, and this gives time a new importance. There is always the sense that something must be done before something else happens. Perhaps most important of all, from the point of view of the actor, the high stage gives new possibilities to the mask. All spectators now have an identical view of the mask, which the actor can display frontally or in profile as he chooses. When the actors performed in the *orchêstra*, different spectators had different views of the mask, and often only the wig would be visible. This was not considered a problem in fifth-century performance, where the focus was upon the physical relationship of actor and chorus. The Hellenistic mask had a completely new purpose and served to impart much psychological information to the audience. Raised, framed against a background, and facing the audience, the masks could be studied and deciphered. I shall examine in subsequent chapters the complex system of masks which the new stage made possible, and which Greek writers exploited.

Our best pictorial representations of Menander's theatre are the two mosaics by Dioskourides which illustrate scenes from Menander's *The Ladies at Luncheon* and *The Girl Possessed*. These mosaics are copies of a Hellenistic original of Menander's day or soon after.[17] Details of mask, costume, supernumeraries, and light are so precise that we may be confident that the Hellenistic artist was trying to capture the sense of the play in performance. The mosaic of *The Girl Possessed* (plate I) depicts clearly the shallowness of the stage, and includes the edge of a doorway, an edge faced with a simple purple stripe. We see no perspective scenography or elaborate architectural features. The movements and masks of the actors show up clearly against an off-white stage wall. Frescoes without exception represent actors playing against a neutral background which allowed the masks to be seen clearly from a distance. Nothing was permitted to distract the eye from reading details of mask, costume, and gesture. The question of sunlight is obviously important in relation to reading the mask, and we notice that painters are always at pains to represent the play of shadow on the mask.[18]

The stage building in fifth-century theatre was always made of wood, and the earliest stone auditoria seem likewise to have been used in conjunction with a wooden stage wall. The stone auditorium at Priene was built very soon after Lycurgus' theatre in Athens, but the stone stage wall was only built a generation later.[19] In the Lycurgan theatre, there is no trace of a stone stage wall in the position where Vitruvius and many later Hellenistic theatres place it, and we must presume that a wooden stage wall was used. The most likely reason for this must be acoustics, for a stone façade could have set up echoes, robbing the voice of its precision. Canac's acoustical research using models shows that a reflective surface immediately behind the actors and not extending far to the side can in fact serve as a useful reflector for the voice.[20] Later, stone *proskênia* must have exploited such a discovery. The auditorium in Athens did not have the perfect symmetrical form of Epidaurus or Priene, and the acoustical conditions may have been slightly different.

Canac's research confirms that, like the stage platform itself, the wall supporting the stage (the *hyposkênion* or sometimes *proskênion*)[21] always needed to absorb sound. For this reason, it was filled with columns and statues,[22] and painted wooden panels were inserted between the columns.[23] It was evidently in this space that, when the oligarchy of Demetrius of Phaleron ended, Demetrios Poliorketes, the 'liberator' of Athens, was painted in a godlike pose riding astride the Greek world.[24]

The edges of the stage wall between the side doorways and side *parodoi* were, according to Pollux and Vitruvius, given over to *periaktoi*, revolving units bearing painted panels.[25] We do not know when these units were introduced, though a revolving unit was constructed in Delos only thirteen years after Menander's death.[26] It is unlikely that these *periaktoi* appeared as from nowhere upon the sudden inspiration of some stage technologist, and I believe that they were the logical solution to a problem. If large panels of scenery (*skênai*) were regularly hung on pegs at the side of the acting area, changing them would have been laborious, and revolving units would have made it much quicker to change panels between plays.[27]

Pollux and Vitruvius associate these revolving units with a convention whereby entry via the *parodos* (side exit) on one side is an entry from the city, and entry from the other side is from the country. Vitruvius simply refers to 'one side' and 'the other'.[28] Pollux's evidence is compressed, but not as contradictory as it appears. He gives the right side as representing a scene outside the city, the left a scene 'from the city, and especially the harbour'. However, when the scene changes, the new 'locality' shows on the right, while the 'country' scene is exchanged between the two sides. This seems a logical way of effecting a move to, say, another part of the city. The triangular unit on the right, we are told, has three available faces signifying entries from the fields, the harbour and the city, so various permutations are possible. Pollux adds finally that people who come from elsewhere (i.e. not the specific locations shown) may enter via the *orchêstra* and climb up steps to the stage.[29] The assumption that consistently left = city, right = country is drawn from an anonymous commentator on Aristophanes, and 'left' is generally taken to mean stage left, the direction of the city in the Theatre of Dionysus.[30] Such a convention may be appropriate enough for Aristophanes, but Menander's theatre with its varied settings in different parts of Attica demands more flexible conventions. A small number of standard and reusable scenic devices are required: a view of the city to signify an entry from the *agora*, a prospect of the sea to signify an entry from the harbour, a view of mountains or of fields to signify different sorts of country, and so forth.

A typical juxtaposition is exemplified in *The Double Deceiver*, where one exit leads to the Athenian *agora* (line 89), and the other, as is clear from Plautus' adaptation, must lead to the Peiraeus where returning travellers dock.[31] If the harbour is on one side and the *agora* on the other, then the real topography of Athens becomes irrelevant. In *The Harpist*, we see another clear example of Menander's practice. One scene includes an exit to the *agora* (line 49); in the next, a man enters 'from the country'. The man says that he will go on 'to the *agora*' (lines 53–65), but in fact he goes into his house first, making it possible for the dramatist to bring on the man's son from the direction of the *agora* without a collision or hiatus. Menander's texts indicate the range of settings that New Comedy might require. A scene panel signifying a route to the country seems necessary also in *The Farmer* and *The Necklace*. The audience of *The Self-Tormentor* and *The Hero* must be shown that the setting is not the city but a village. Plautus' *The Rope*, based on an original by Diphilus, is set beside a beach, and Menander also apparently used beach scenes in *The Pilots* and *The Fishermen*.

The 'satyric' and comic wall paintings of Boscoreale give us an idea of how the contrast between rural and urban prospects was represented pictorially.[32] Vitruvius' description of comic, tragic, and satyric scenes follows immediately upon his description of *periaktoi*, placed in 'the spaces prepared for ornament', and it is clearly in these spaces that painted scenes, such as those from Boscoreale, were inserted. Pollux tells us that either curtains or wooden panels could be hung over the *periaktoi*, and that these contained designs appropriate to the need of the play, such as sea, mountain, or river.[33] Another source tells us that the curtains in Greek comedy were made of leather not of 'purple' (i.e. woven), and this was presumably because leather can be painted.[34] Our best representation of a *periaktos* is the well-known Naples relief (plate 3).[35] Like the Pompeian frescoes representing comic scenes, this relief seems to be based on an earlier Greek painting. Although the Greek original has been substantially Romanized, as is clear from the way an arch is used for the doorway, we cannot simply dismiss as Roman or as fantasy the curious curtain which conceals an urban setting with tower and arches. The broken line and dizzy angles suggest that we are actually looking at a sculptor's rendering of a *trompe l'œil* scene painting, set on a *periaktos* that is not quite flush. This city scene is covered by a curtain, probably because its grandeur belongs to tragedy. Faintly behind the curtains, we can trace the line of the pediment on which the *periaktos* rests. In front of the curtain, a drunken youth, slave, and piper enter from the *parodos* stage left, while two old men stand before the house, preparing to intervene. The uniqueness of this relief lies in the fact that it represents an entry from the side, whereas all our frescoes represent the main, focal acting area.

Representational scenery in Greek New Comedy, then, stands to the side of the main acting area. The actors are only backed by it temporarily when they walk in from a *parodos*. A simple verbal tag like '*pros agoran*' cues the audience to register the scenery as the actor walks past. Evocative descriptions of off-stage locations such as we find in Ibsen or Chekhov are absent in New Comedy, for such descriptions would call attention to the conventionalized nature of the scene panels, curtains, or *periaktoi*. The purpose of this scenery is, quite simply, to make it easy for the audience to follow the comings and goings of the plot. The Greek stage described by Pollux is admirably suited to the drama of Menander. With a minimum of conventional emblems in the form of painted landscapes, scenes could be changed quickly between plays, and any Greek New Comedy could be performed at short notice in any well-equipped Hellenistic theatre. There could be no question of the actor stepping forward on this shallow stage, and distancing himself from the two-dimensional world of the play, a world entirely separate from the world of the audience.

Once having entered, and having walked past the painted scenery which framed the action, the actors performed against a neutral wall, broken only by three doorways. These three doorways are the feature that we must now examine. I shall code Pollux's description in order to clarify his thinking. The central door, Pollux tells us, serves as (a) the palace, or (b) a cave, or (c) an important house, or (d) whatever is (appropriate to) the main actor of the drama; the right is occupied (d) by the second actor; the left is (d) for the most unimportant mask, or might be (b) an abandoned shrine or (c) an unused house. In tragedy, Pollux adds, when (a) the right door is for guests, the left is shut off.[36] Thus when the set represents a palace, the right door is used for guests and the left is sealed off; when the set represents a sanctuary, the left door is a grotto that does not house a god, and so forth. Vitruvius contradicts Pollux on a small point of detail when he states that, while the central swing-doors are 'royal', both right and left doors designate guest quarters.[37]

Pollux's description is only relevant to tragedy, for we should expect that the setting of a tragedy would often be the palace of the hero, or a sanctuary. The idea that the leading actor should use the central door is plainly not relevant to comedy. Pollux does go on to discuss comedy. On either side of the pair of doors in the middle, he says, are two more, one on each side, beside which the *periaktoi* are set up. His description of 'enclosures' which are 'by the house' (i.e. the central door) relates to the period of Middle Comedy, and need not concern us.[38]

The two side doors are domestic in scale, unlike the royal or divine central door, and are appropriate to the inhabitants of comedy. An important feature of Pollux's description of the theatre is the contrast which he sets up between left and right. Just as the painted panels offer contrasting scenes – the town versus the country, the sea versus the land – so the two doorways have contrasting meanings. When we turn to Menander's texts, we find that the conflict between the two families whose homes are represented by the two doors lies at the heart of the narrative and thematic tensions of the play. Usually this tension is reconciled when the girl who belongs to house A is married to the youth who belongs to house B. The tension between right and left is frequently one of social status. Plays like *The Girl from Samos* or *The Farmer* juxtapose a rich and a poor household. The marriage which joins the two houses is socially significant in its implications for how rich and poor should behave towards each other. In many plays we find not a sociological but a moral antithesis. A miserly elder brother lives next door to a generous younger brother in *The Shield*. A manipulative city youth lives next door to an impulsive soldier in *The Rape of the Locks*. In *The Self-Tormentor*, to judge from Terence's adaptation, the virtuous son of the 'self-tormentor' contrasts with the philandering son of the neighbour. The juxtaposition of left and right takes us to the heart of the moral debate proposed by Menander's play.

Pollux privileges right over left in accordance with the natural supremacy accorded to right over left in Aristotelian thought.[39] The right-hand door is used for the second actor, he tells us, the left may go unused. This suggests the possibility that the two doors on the stage wall were not symmetrical. None of Menander's moral oppositions between house A and house B are incompatible with the hypothesis that a relatively wealthy-looking house on the audience's right contrasts with a relatively neglected or austere house on the left. Webster cites *The Brothers 'B'*, *The Necklace*, and *Faithless* as plays where the doors may be visually differentiated according to wealth.[40] Two references in *Old Cantankerous* imply that the misanthropist whose estate is worth two talents lives on the right, while his penniless stepson lives on the left.[41] In the Naples relief (plate 3), one of the old men is marked out as richer than the other by the hem on his cloak,[42] and the doorway, which stands to the audience's right, is more ornate than we might expect from the mosaics. It is probably the son of this rich man whom we see returning home. The ornateness of the doorway is probably not just a Roman decorative feature, but also a stage sign signifying wealth.

The painted panels beside the doors were certainly different on each side. Here again, the contrast between the two sides points the audience towards the central narrative and dramatic tensions of the play. In *The Shield*, one side exit (*parodos*) leads to the *agora* (line 212), the other must lead to the Peiraeus. City is opposed to sea. The view of the city reminds the audience that Athenian law gives the miser power to marry his unwilling niece. The return of the slave Daos from overseas precipitates the entanglement, and the return of his supposedly dead master precipitates the dénouement. A view of the sea would remind the audience through the first three acts that the assumptions of all the characters will at some point be overturned. A view of the sea also highlights the decision of the Asiatic slave to return voluntarily to a land that is not his own. *The Girl from Samos* offers a similar juxtaposition: one exit again leads to the *agora* (lines 191, 281), the other to the port. The two old men describe the Black Sea region as they make their first entry, walking in front of the scenery as they speak. The young lover simultaneously exits towards the *agora*, seeking a 'deserted place' to practise his wedding ceremony. This youth has performed all the rituals proper to an Athenian, but has never travelled, and his search for a 'deserted place' in the direction of the *agora* creates an ironic moment. In the final act, the youth dreams of liberation from the marriage that he has hitherto sought, and threatens to leave Athens and go overseas. The tension between land and sea emphasizes the theme of escape, and serves as a reminder of this motif in the *Hippolytus*, so obviously parodied in Menander's play. Like Euripides' Phaedra, Menander's Samian concubine is also accused of sleeping with her partner's son. She, like Phaedra, has come from overseas to unite herself with an Athenian who prefers to travel the world.

While the central doorway is the focus of tragedy, the two side doors are the focus of comedy. While Hellenistic tragedy deals in unique heroes, Hellenistic comedy deals in binary oppositions – between rich and poor, town and country, male and female, helper and opponent, to

name the most obvious. The palatial central doorway nevertheless
remains present in comedy to dominate the stage, and we must examine
its function. An altar stood in front of the central doorway, for it is often
required in tragedy, and Pollux confirms its existence.[43] The altar allows
this doorway, which in tragedy represents the dwelling of kings, to
become in comedy the dwelling of gods. It is brought into active use when
it can serve as a shrine, as in *Old Cantankerous* where it represents the
shrine of Pan, or in Plautus' *The Pot of Gold*, based apparently on
Menander's *Faithless*,[44] where it represents the shrine of Faith. Elsewhere it is an unlocalized space from which divine prologues may make
their entry and exit. A pair of Pompeian frescoes from the house of
Sulpicius Rufus, now destroyed, evoke the Roman-style comic and tragic
stage, and these stages illustrate admirably the contrasting functions of
the central door in comedy and tragedy.[45] The tragic scene displays only a
central door, and a life-size statue stands to either side beneath a small
colonnade. The comic scene displays domestic doorways to left and right,
and a statue of a god stands directly in front of the grand central doorway.
Both scenes include the central altar, which stands midway between the
door and the front of the stage. Statues are a well-documented feature of
the ancient theatre, and movable statues offered a simple way of
transforming a tragic stage into a comic stage.[46]

On the shallow Greek stage, the altar in the centre is the obvious focus
for the finale, when the girl from one side and the boy from the other are
formally betrothed. It is used for libations or sacrifices when these form
part of the stage action. Libations are prepared in *The Toady*, and in a
Pompeian fresco a goose is laid on the altar ready for a priestess to sacrifice.[47] In the finale to *The Rape of the Locks*, when the impetuous hero
purloins a sacrificial garland from an altar (line 999), he probably tears a
garland from this central altar, indicating his intention to sacrifice the sow
upon it. In another fresco, a slave leans casually on the altar while his
master reprimands him.[48] The master's anger is more severe in
Menander's *The Girl from Perinthos* where firewood is stacked around the
altar upon which the errant slave has taken refuge. Props essential to a
recognition scene are laid upon the altar in a Delian fresco.[49] Given the
dimensions of the Greek stage, some 2.5 metres deep and 20 metres wide,
the central altar is both physically and symbolically a barrier which
divides left from right. It becomes a meeting point where, in association
with the god who is *primum mobile* of the plot, the spatial, narrative, and
thematic oppositions of the play are brought together.

Whether other altars stood beside the doorways is not certain. In fifth-century tragedy, a conical stone sacred to Apollo Agyieus apparently stood beside the central door. When characters in *The Girl from Samos* repeatedly invoke Apollo, they may be addressing such a stone. It is much more probable, however, that actors in New Comedy, in the interests of visual economy, used words and gestures to establish the central altar as the altar of Apollo as and when convenient. This would explain how the central altar acquired its conventional name, the '*agyieus* altar'.[50]

The moral parameters of left and right are complemented by another oposition between off stage and on – which is to say, between outdoors and indoors, revealed and hidden, public and private. The spatial opposition between private and public worlds helps to articulate the problem which I described in the last chapter: whether a human being is, in essence, an individual or a member of a *polis*; or, putting it another way, whether a man is a function of his domestic or of his corporate relationships. Since the play is set in a street, the Greek audience must always take account of the social convention whereby bourgeois citizen women did not venture into a public place unless force of circumstance or festive licence permitted them to cross the threshold. One husband in Menander puts the point directly:

In leaving the courtyard, you are overstepping the bounds of marriage. For a free woman, the courtyard door customarily marks the household boundary. To go charging into the street shouting abuse is to go acting like a dog.[51]

The plot is conventionally triggered by the rape of a virgin who has strayed beyond her threshold, and the action of the play thus takes place when private matters have intruded upon the public sphere. The status divide between citizen women who stay off the street and non-citizen courtesans who go freely on the street is commonly a point upon which the plot turns. The 'girl from Samos' in the play of that name can never become a wife; the 'girl from Andros' and many similar heroines are revealed to have citizen birth.

The Man She Hated examplifies how the tension between an invisible world behind the stage wall and a visible on-stage world is exploited. In the opening scene, as the 'hated' soldier stalks up and down the lane, enduring rain and the danger of thieves, a precise sense of place is created. The soldier has come out onto the street to describe the scene of intolerable personal emotion which faces him within. The 'hating' heroine comes onto the street when her long-lost father knocks on the door, and the plot gets under way when a slave misconstrues their public embrace. A mosaic and a clay cake mould portray the climax of the play in the final act, by which time the soldier has evidently resolved upon suicide, and the heroine has now to persuade him not to hang himself.[52] The female-dominated indoor space is associated with a hypertrophy of *pathos*; the male-dominated stage platform is the space where *êthos* is formed and demonstrated. The soldier's choice in the final act is either to go indoors, surrender to *pathos*, and kill himself, or remain on stage and regain control of his emotions. The betrothal which concludes the play takes place on the street, and the heroine is not present. Order is restored, and the woman is indoors where she belongs. This marriage, like all marriages in New Comedy, is a contract between the husband and the bride's father. The actors end the play by asking the audience to make the play victorious: the garlands which they put on celebrate simultaneously the fictional wedding and the real victory to which the actors aspire. The play starts with the hero's physical isolation, and ends with his incorporation in the world of the audience. The movement of the play as a whole can be seen as a progress from the hidden world of emotion and sexual desire to the public world of citizen responsibilities.[53]

The absolute divide between off stage and on stage can be broken down, if required, by the device of the *ekkyklêma* – the projecting platform used in tragedy to display interior scenes. The device is used to pseudo-tragic effect in the fourth act of *Old Cantankerous*, when the cantankerous old man, bedraggled, dirty, and recumbent after falling down a well, with his daughter and stepson at his side, makes an impressive entry.[54] The mock-heroic effect is completed when the musician accompanies his *apologia pro vita sua*. Although fifth-century tragedy never uses a side door for an *ekkyklêma*, we know from Pollux and from payments to a carpenter in Delos that the Hellenistic theatre had this facility.[55]

The *ekkyklêma* is illustrated in Dioskourides' mosaic which depicts the title scene from Act I of *The Ladies at Luncheon* (plate 2). A decorative three-stepped platform has been thrust forward of a doorway, and three bands of striping are used to suggest perspective into the recess behind. A boy actor stands on the platform to the rear of the stage wall, and half concealed. This domestic scene with three women at table could not be envisaged as taking place in the street, and Menander's staging of a domestic interior represents a bold theatrical experiment. The tragic code, whereby the *ekkylêma* is used at the end of a play for scenes of death, spectacle, and weighty sentiment has been systematically inverted by Menander. The grand effect comes not at the end but at the beginning. If the play was devised to initiate a day of performances, the artist may have intended, Webster suggests, to show that the stage was lit by morning light from the east.[56] Plautus commenced his adaptation of Menander's play when the repast was finished. An *ekkyklêma*, if one had been available to Plautus, could not have dominated the deep Roman stage to the same extent, or given the domestic scene a feeling of being close to the audience.

We see a further visual representation of the *ekkyklêma* in a mosaic depicting the title scene from *The Phantom*.[57] We learn from Menander's text that the heroine passes from one house to the next via a 'passageway' (*diexodos*) (line 21). This passageway, as a Latin summary tells us, is given the appearance of a sacred place, and is bound about with headbands and greenery. The text speaks of a passage rather than a simple hole in the wall because the passage is conceived as running behind the unlocalized central doorway. The mosaic depicts a scene from Act II where the heroine as 'phantom' makes her appearance to an old man, who is accompanied by a youth seemingly in the know. The phantom is framed by a doorway, the double doors having opened inwards, and stands on a three-tiered platform. Clearly the *ekkyklêma* has been pushed through the central doorway, which conventionally represents a shrine. Menander used this technique in order to stage a scene conceived as taking place indoors beside the fake shrine. He was not bound by a rigid 'unity of place', and used the stage in a surprisingly fluid manner.

NATURALISM AND ARTIFICE

For the dramatist, the advantage of using a neutral but framed background for his actors is that the stage platform can function as a localized or unlocalized space according to the needs of the moment. The actors can use a few words to create a very precise sense of place, but quickly that sense of place can become irrelevant. Once the *ekkyklêma* has been introduced in *Old Cantankerous*, actors can come on and off stage without worries about leaving through an appropriate front door. This is not nineteenth-century naturalistic theatre, where the audience looks through a proscenium arch at a scene which, theoretically, ignores its presence. It is not the three-dimensional theatre of the fifth century, where the spectators are gathered round as participants in a corporate rite. Nor is it the shallow forestage of Italian neo-classicism, where perspective scene-painting creates a sense of depth behind the actors. Like a relief carving, the stage image in Greek New Comedy is at once three-dimensional and two-dimensional. It is simultaneously an illusory, internally consistent world which the audience can look into, and a public platform upon which men stand in order to present words and emblems to a gathering. On the deeper Roman stage used by Terence, the audience learns about the facts of the plot through overhearing a dialogue which takes no formal account of its existence. This assumption of audience absence was not a convention that could develop on the Greek stage, where the action had to be presented frontally and projected across the orchestral void.

The presence of boy supernumeraries and of a stage musician enhances the sense that the Greek stage offers more than a *mimêsis* of visible reality. Unmasked boys function as slaves when mute slaves are required in the text to bring on props and furniture, and when not invoked by the text they become anonymous stagehands. Both of Dioskourides' mosaics and one other mosaic from Pompeii, together with some half a dozen Pompeian frescoes, all depict these boys, and testify to their ubiquity on the stage of Greek New Comedy.[58] In a Pompeian and a Delian fresco, an unmasked boy functions not as an attendant slave but as a child with a major place in the narrative.[59] In *The Ladies at Luncheon*, the boy in our mosaic is dressed in female clothes, and is described in the text as *hê barbaros*, 'the foreign girl'. In the course of the scene, her task is to carry off the wine and the table (frag. 385). A good example of how these boys were integrated in the action occurs in *The Shield*, where a cook addresses a tirade to his over-honest boy 'Spark', who has failed to steal anything from their employer. The great advantage of using these unmasked boys, who must in actuality have been sons or apprentices to the actors, was that they helped to fill the expanse of stage, but because of their scale did not divert attention from the three masked adults who 'acted' the play.

In the Roman theatre, the stage also had to find space for the piper with his double-reed pipes. Cicero tells us that the Roman piper moved across the stage following the actors.[60] On the shallow Greek stage there was no space for the piper to sit in front of the altar, and his place was in the *orchêstra*. The piper who appears in the mosaic of *The Girl Possessed* is a mute actor, miming while the real piper plays. This can be seen from the fact that the actor in the mosaic is masked, while the real musician had to secure the pipes to his mouth with a band.[61] Also, this actor does not wear Dionysiac but conventional female stage costume. Our fragment of text includes an instruction to the piper to play ecstatic music (lines 27–8), and this instruction must have been delivered to the mute. An actor representing a female piper is used in a similar way in *Old Cantankerous* (lines 432–4, 880–1). There is no equivalent in Greek New Comedy to the scene in Plautus' *Stichus* where the stage piper is forced by the actors to drink. This Roman use of the real stage musician is illustrated in a fresco from Herculaneum, which portrays a slave bantering with the piper seated on the altar.[62] The long ceremonial gown made it easy for the piper to be regarded as female. The piper in the Naples relief (plate 3) may or may not be masked. Since he again is not dressed as an actor, we seem to be looking at the piper of the Roman stage in the sculptor's interpretation.

The shallow stage imposed certain practical constraints, and provided certain opportunities. Two obvious ways of exploiting the space are chase sequences and processions. In *Old Cantankerous*, the procession takes the form of a string of worshippers visiting the shrine, including a cook with a fat sheep. The chase occurs in Act I, when a slave runs the length of the stage, wrongly assuming that the old man is still in pursuit. This 'running slave' routine was to become enormously popular in the Roman theatre.[63] In *The Girl from Samos*, the first chase occurs when the Samian concubine, carrying the baby, is driven from her house by her furious partner; the second chase follows when she and the baby are chased back home by the neighbour, this time to musical accompaniment. The procession is again centred on the cook, who brings all the paraphernalia for a wedding feast. The live sheep on this occasion is not fat, but the scrawniest that can be found. Pseudo-military processions, echoing visual motifs from tragedy, are another staple. As if from the Trojan War, a convoy of slaves and war spoils arrives in *The Shield*. A ragged mock army assaults a house in *The Rape of the Locks*. In *The Toady*, to judge from Terence's adaptation, there was a more impressive siege; wine was also borne processionally across the stage for a drinking ceremony. Large-scale movements and group scenes of this kind take advantage of the length of the stage, which might seem superfluous if it were occupied by a mere three actors.

The shallowness of the stage restricts the Greek dramatist's ability to use certain devices that we might consider stock devices of farce. Entries needed careful handling. An actor entering from the *parodos* must have lines written to cover his walk in front of the scenery. He must always be seen by characters on stage before he sees them, for he is not in a focal position, and the gaze of actors already on stage must cue the gaze of the audience. Entries through the doors impose different and more complex demands. An actor entering through internally opening doors will always be visible to the audience before he is visible to other actors on stage. The few seconds in which he walks through the door and onto the stage need to be covered. When he enters, his gaze must first take in the audience before he can turn to see an action taking place to one side of him. There is also a vocal problem in masked theatre: the audience needs to identify who is speaking, but the mask hides the actors' mouths; the possibility of confusion is increased by the fact that, in Greek New Comedy, the same mask may be worn by more than one actor in a given play. There is finally the aesthetic problem of suggesting depth on a shallow stage, so as to avoid the jack-in-the-box effect of an instant entry. In response to these requirements, Greek New Comedy evolved a set of strict conventions. When the doors open, the audience's attention is necessarily diverted from any other action in progress. Actors already on stage, therefore, either stop speaking, or remark on the noise made by the opening door. The actor made visible by the opening door usually addresses unseen people inside the house as he makes his entry – though this may be omitted if he enters in a hurry. Once on stage, his first remark is always addressed to the audience. Only then does he turn and observe what is happening on stage beside him.[64] Actors on the same side of the stage must notice the new entrant before he notices them. Only at the start of an act can two actors enter from a house in mid-conversation, since their entry does not then need to be covered.

The shallow stage sets up a relationship of distance between actor and audience. There is no such thing, therefore, as an 'aside' in Greek New Comedy. I mean by that, there is no scene in which an actor talking to another standing beside him abruptly changes direction and targets a remark at the audience.[65] An actor can stand in profile when listening, but he cannot afford to speak in full ninety degrees profile, since his voice would lose its clarity when it fails to encounter a reflective surface. All speech, whether to another character or to the audience, needs to be directed via the orchestral floor at the foot of the stage. The Greek stage thus differs completely from the Roman stage, as a simple pair of diagrams will illustrate (fig. 1). My Greek diagram represents the Athenian auditorium, together with a stage of the type described by Vitruvius and found in so many Hellenistic theatres – Priene, Epidaurus, Ephesus, Delos, Corinth, and elsewhere. For the Roman theatre, my proportions are derived from the ancient plan of the stone theatre built by Pompey, which we may assume followed the traditional Roman groundplan.[66]

On the Roman stage, actor B can easily turn from speaking to actor A, and throw a remark at a convenient spectator X nearby in the auditorium. Since the stage is enclosed at the side, there is less danger of the voice getting lost if the actor speaks at ninety degrees. The Greek actor speaks

ATHENS   ROME

fig. I

in a more public manner, addressing both audience and stage interlocutor simultaneously. He is too far from the nearest spectators to deliver an aside to any selected individual. Opportunities for eavesdropping are likewise more restricted on the Greek stage. Actor B can stand on the opposite side of the stage to A and pass comment on what he sees, but not on secrets he might hear, for he appears too distant to eavesdrop.[67] Alternatively, he can stand silently in the doorway behind A and listen, but he cannot pass comment to the audience without being heard by A. Eavesdropping is not used by Menander to nearly the extent that it is used by Plautus. In *The Girl from Samos*, where the plot turns upon an overheard conversation, Menander chooses to play this event as reported off-stage action. It is hard to imagine Plautus refraining from the chance of staging such an episode.

There are, of course, few constraints in the theatre which cannot be turned into assets. The frontal delivery required of the Greek actor means that there can be an unobtrusive elision between dialogue and monologue – from speech between characters to speech directly addressed to the audience. There is no question of characters being overheard thinking aloud. Everything that happens on the Greek stage is manifestly laid out for an audience's benefit. Characters tell the audience exactly what they are thinking and planning. Motivations are complex rather than concealed or withheld. While the naturalism of Ibsen, for example, is aetiological, and reveals the motives and past experiences which cause a present condition, Hellenistic comedy is teleological, and concerned with the future that a given *êthos* will bring into being. While Ibsen's stage is, visually speaking, recessive, the Hellenistic stage pushes forwards.

Before we turn to Plautine comedy, and see how it relies upon a quite different concept of theatre space, let us look at Menander's one text which has reached us intact, *Old Cantankerous*, in order to see how all the resources of the Hellenistic stage are exploited in a coherent manner.[68] Pan opens the play by asking the audience to assume that the setting is Phyle in Attica. He enters through the central door, which represents the entry to his shrine. In real life, as many in the audience would know, Pan's shrine was set half-way up a cliff face in a gorge, but the unlocalized background prevents the audience from being disturbed by the fact that, in this play, two farms stand on either side of it. The same freedom allows a journey to and from Athens to ignore the constraints of distance. The doorway on the right, Pan tells us, belongs to the cantankerous old man, and in the other direction live his wife and stepson. The two heads of household represent contrasting types of rural behaviour – the one open and philanthropic, the other closed and misanthropic. A major concern of the play is whether the country is the site of natural virtue, free from the corruption of the city, or whether peasants are degraded by the toil and poverty of country life. The pair of doorways help to fix these polarities for the audience. The two side exits are distinguished as exits in the direction of the mountains and the direction of the valley. The mountain, said to be visible from the stage (line 99), is where the misanthropist spends his days. The land in the valley is farmed by a rich city-dweller, the second old man of the play, and this side is established as the direction of Athens. The painted scenery must have suggested these two alternative settings, with rock and scrub on one side (lines 3, 170), and a distant village on the other (line 33). The scenery helps to fix important oppositions between rural and urban values, between the hostility and the beneficence of nature. The on/off-stage parameter is also important. The intrigue begins when the heroine strays across her threshold, for she encounters the hero when a domestic emergency forces her to come out and fetch water from the shrine. The reported action inside the shrine contrasts with the visible action on stage. At the start of the play, the shrine's occupants are said to be nymphs. The hero's mother invades this space in the course of the play, and at the end an erotic dance within the shrine is vividly evoked. Sexual innocence gives way to sexual experience. A concealed off-stage female-dominated world of sexual encounters contrasts with a public male world concerned with the disposition of wealth. Menander's careful deployment of stage space allows the complex strands of his play to become clear to his audience. There is no question of the visual element being subordinate to the verbal, for without Menander's organization of space, his play would be little more than ephemeral love story. When first performed, probably in little over an hour's playing time, *Old Cantankerous* offered its audience a density of signals not revealed by a simple reading of 'the text'.

THE ROMAN STAGE

While the operative parameters or polarities of the Hellenistic stage are left/right and shown/hidden, the most important parameter in Plautine theatre is close/distant in respect of the audience. The Hellenistic theatre is a democratic space, where no seats are obviously the best, either from the acoustical or from the visual aspect. The play cannot be heard better from the front, to any significant degree. The painted scenery must have profited from new impressionistic techniques of painting, and from the research of the Aristotelian school into the effects of distance.[69] The governing principle of painting with light and shade, Aristotle informs us, is that detail must be omitted since a large audience requires a distant viewing point.[70] No spectator in the Greek theatre has the sense of an intimate and privileged contact with the actors. The Roman theatre reversed Greek methods and did not counteract so much as exploit the effects of relative distance.

We do not know exactly what the stage wall used in Plautus and Terence looked like. We can see from their texts that no play requires more than two domestic doorways.[71] As a stimulus to thought, we might look at the two contrasting stage walls in Pompeii. In the small theatre, presumably frequented by the educated elite, we have a Greek-style simple flush plastered wall. In the large theatre we find embrasures and recesses in an Augustan stage wall similar to that of the first stone theatre in Rome. The austere wall of the small theatre would suit the presentation of plays by Menander, while the lavish wall of the large theatre would suit a play in which the visual detail of mask and costume was less significant. It is a reasonable guess that Plautus and Terence used a wooden stage wall which shared something of this ornateness. The actor was not normally seen by the spectator against this wall on the deep Roman stage, but against the stage floor. The recesses are helpful for eavesdropping, allowing the actor to merge into the background, just as he can merge also with the audience when he comes to the front of the stage.

The possibility exists, within this elaborate stage wall, for subsidiary points of entry. We should take seriously the evidence of the comedy fresco from the house of Sulpicius Rufus.[72] Unlike other para-theatrical

stages represented in Pompeii, this stage contains actors. It depicts two
narrow arched entries between the doors and the central shrine.
Whatever the exact positioning, entries such as these could serve as the
'alleyways' so often mentioned in Roman plays as giving back access to
the houses. Donatus, in his commentary on Terence, describes such an
alleyway as 'a narrow place, between the houses', and as a 'lane not giving
onto a public highway'.[73] Although Beare demonstrates that the plays
could be staged without separate entries for the alleys, he does not
demonstrate why the Roman dramatists so often introduce this feature
missing from Greek plays.[74]

There is no evidence for the use of scenic panels on the Roman stage.
They could not effectively frame the action, for many spectators are too
close to the stage to keep two downstage panels within their field of
vision, and in an upstage position painted scenery would be lost amidst
the ornamentation. In Menander's *The Brothers 'B'*, it is reasonable to
suppose that Menander used his pair of doorways to juxtapose wealth and
poverty, and used his pair of scenic panels to juxtapose town and country.
In Terence's adaptation, there is no sign that anyone makes an entry
'from the country', and characters come and go without stating to which
particular part of town they are going. Likewise in Terence's adaptation
of Menander's *The Girl from Andros*, town lies not in one direction but in
every direction. A slave can leave through one exit, and, having
supposedly doubled along a back-street, reappear elsewhere (lines
736–44). In Terence's *The Eunuch*, two of Menander's plays are
amalgamated, and the Roman text includes exits to the harbour, the
forum, and the country.[75] Clearly there was no exploitation of visual
oppositions in this theatre to trouble the audience. In *The Mother-in-
Law*, the courtesan's house is just off stage, and she is fetched in moments
(lines 720–7). Where Menander must have inserted an act break, Terence
substitutes continuous action. The liberties which Terence takes with
stage time correlate with liberties taken with stage space.

The scene panels in Greek New Comedy tie the action to the laws of
mimêsis. In the Roman theatre, these ties are lacking. I suggested in the
last chapter that each character in Plautus' *Stichus* negotiates a fresh
relationship with the audience. The fluid use of the stage in that play
seems closer to Elizabethan than to Hellenistic practice, if we examine the
staging carefully, and Plautus' subversion of Greek staging conventions
seems to be a deliberate ploy. The play opens with a dialogue between two
women played as an indoor scene on one side of the stage. Their father
then enters with what reads like an off-stage address to his slaves. This

speech is in fact far too long to play off stage, but would work theatrically if the audience were harangued and threatened as slaves. The father somehow goes out through his own doorway and passes through another door, with no time to go off stage, so as to find himself in his daughter's house. There is a further complication in that, through the rest of the play, the two regular doorways are needed to represent the two houses of the two brothers. One simple hypothesis disposes of all difficulties. I would suggest that the father entered at *orchêstra* level in order to interact with the audience and threaten them as his slaves. He could then mount the steps in order to find himself inside his daughter's house. Such an entry overcomes the problem of how to represent an indoor location, a problem which Menander overcame by using the *ekkyklêma*.[76] The text appears to indicate that the house of the second son is accessible via an alleyway as well as by the main door. However, when the slave Stichus refers to a rear entry to this dwelling, his speech turns into an excuse for obscene *double entendre*. The house becomes a metaphor for the slave-girl's body, and rear entry prevents the risk of pregnancy. We cannot therefore expect the speech to give us much help with the topography of the stage. The audience is expected to revel in the subversion of Greek spatial realism.

There is no unity of place in the *Stichus*. When the slave-girl sets off in one direction to find the parasite, the parasite immediately enters from the other side. The technique establishes a changed sense of place, and the scene becomes the forum. The parasite constructs the audience as loiterers in the forum with nothing to do but pry, and no doubt he tells the literal truth: the audience were idling in a place where normally they would be at work. The fictitious Athens dissolves into the here and now of the performance. The transition back to the house is accomplished in a surreal manner. A conventional 'running slave' figure appears and boasts that he is training for the Olympics. He fails to demonstrate his athletic prowess because the running track proves too short, and he reaches the door too soon. A few words suffice to expand or contract the space. The final scene, the slaves' banquet, is played out on stage, even though notionally it takes place indoors (lines 433, 439). The slave Stichus rolls a cask out through one exit, and establishes the new indoor location by reappearing with the cask through another (lines 670, 683). The central doorway is perhaps used as a shrine in the finale, when the slave-girl appears as an incarnation of Venus (line 745).[77] The setting within the slave's quarters is dissolved when the stage musician is plied with drinks, and the audience are invited to participate in the banquet (line 686).

Plautus' dramaturgy disintegrates the Greek distinction between
private and public worlds, off stage and on stage. This polarity had less
force in Rome, where the private off-stage world no longer correlates with
the female world. Roman women were not sequestered, and were an
important presence in the audience.[78] What we see instead in the finale of
Stichus is a contrast between the off-stage banquet of the two rich
brothers, from which the parasite, slaves, and audience are excluded, and
the on-stage banquet of the two slaves, brothers in love, from which the
audience are not excluded.

Plautus' *Curculio* also gives us much insight into the possibilities of the
Roman stage. As in the *Stichus* so in *Curculio* the arrangement of
doorways follows the Hellenistic scheme. The play requires a central
shrine to the god Aesculapius, and domestic doorways to left and right.
These domestic doorways are associated with the obvious narrative
opposition of subject and object: the youth and the girl he seeks. Since
these doors belong to a home and a brothel, they mark also a characteristically Roman polarization of duty and pleasure, in its many aspects:
negotium (non-leisure, business) versus *otium* (leisure, idleness), Roman
morality versus Greek libertinism, normality versus festival, order versus
anarchy, marriage versus prostitution. The central doorway representing
the shrine provides an entry for the principal 'opponent' of the narrative,
the pimp. In spatial terms, therefore, the pimp keeps the hero and heroine
apart. By contrast with the doors, no narrative or thematic significance is
attached to entries via the neutral side exits.

The action proceeds much faster than in any play of Menander's.
There are no act breaks, and there is more music to encourage physical
action. More actors are available, so there is no need to slow the pace for
changes of costume and mask. The play acquires a sense of momentum
when all major characters except the slave (who presumably doubles as
the soldier) gather on stage for the finale. On the shallow Greek stage,
where depth cannot be exploited, such ensemble scenes would have been
aesthetically unpleasing. The actors in Plautus' play also take less time
getting on and off stage. Although a Greek-style entrance – first an
address to someone indoors, then an address to the audience – is often
used, an actor is also free to enter and perform an immediate double-take
on the action (lines 231, 274, 599, 610). No significant time gap separates
the appearance of a new entrant and his perception of what is happening
on stage, for the action takes place in front of the new entrant and not to
his side. Conversely, the new entrant can also be addressed before he has
spoken (line 455).

The lowness of the Roman stage and proximity of the audience allow for an asiding technique. The slave conducts simultaneous banter with the audience and with the two embracing lovers, always making it clear to whom he is speaking. The technique relies upon the actor placing himself downstage of the lovers, becoming a kind of stage audience watching an erotic spectacle framed by the doorway of the brothel.[79] On the Roman stage, unlike the Greek, actor A can place himself physically closer to the audience than he is to actors B and C. He can thus function as an extension of the audience's consciousness, or as an *alter ego* of the poet, whilst B and C, under the eyes of the stage commentator, seem to inhabit a play world within a play world. In the Greek theatre, this framing technique was impossible. The high wall supporting the stage and the scenic panels together constituted a strong single frame around the action, and alternative frames could not easily be created. Stage reality was constructed within one internally consistent plane. In Plautus' theatre, unlike the Greek, actors and audience can encroach on each other's territory. We should bear in mind the strong likelihood that some members of the audience sat on the stage in Plautus' theatre – a practice well documented in seventeenth-century English and French theatre. The principal evidence is a Plautine prologue which refers to a prostitute sitting *in proscaenio*.[80]

The fluid barrier between actor and audience is decisively ruptured half-way through Plautus' play when Curculio the parasite makes his entry, apparently through the auditorium. Pollux tells us that travellers 'from other parts' could enter through the orchestra, and climb steps onto the stage, so an orchestral entry could be justified as a parody of a Hellenistic practice.[81] Steps from ground to stage were certainly used in the *phylax* farces of Southern Italy.[82] And there were wooden steps in the Greek theatre in Delos.[83] In the Roman theatre the steps would not have to be high as in the Greek theatre. The crucial difference between the Greek and Roman *orchêstra* is the fact that the Roman *orchêstra* was filled with spectators. In transposing the Greek entry convention to the Roman theatre, Plautus would have obliged his actor to make a passage through the audience. Even if my suggestion of an orchestral entry were shown to be incorrect, an entry at stage level could still have involved the Roman actor in pushing his way through spectators seated on stage. Curculio's entry speech is reminiscent of those which occur so frequently in English medieval theatre, where actors push through the crowd with scripted lines like: 'Aback, give me room! In my way do ye not stand!', or: 'Friends, of fellowship, let me go by ye!'.[84] Curculio asks the audience to stand clear because he has urgent business to perform: as Curculio, one understands, he must reach his master; as an actor, he must reach the stage. He threatens to collide with all manner of people – wealthy officials, scholars, drunks, undisciplined slaves, anyone who might inhabit a crowded Greek street. Actors already on stage help guide him to his target, and some thirty lines are allowed for him to make his epic journey to the acting area. As a mime routine, the speech is far too long to be playable, but as an exercise in audience involvement it is playable with ease.

This breaking of the barrier between stage and audience is in a sense symbolic of Plautine theatre as a whole. The status barriers which separate masters from slaves, fathers from sons, citizen women from prostitutes, are all subverted within the plays in accordance with the particular licence of the Roman festival. The Roman *ludi* were occasions of great political sensitivity. Plays were entertainments given to the people by members of the senatorial elite, who expected to gain prestige and thereby votes. The event was a recognition, symbolic but in material terms expensive, that the people had certain rights, certain obligations due to them. The *ludi* were, in a sense, a period when the elite no longer ruled, but gave the people what the people wanted. For a strictly limited span of time, the normal hierarchical divisions were obliterated. It is too easy to picture the 'saturnalian' or 'carnivalesque' reversal of order in Roman festivals as a timeless institution, continuing with the happy acquiescence of all social orders.[85] In the absence of any democratic assembly, the Roman theatre was – or became – the place where the public could best communicate their feelings to those who ruled them, as many passages in Cicero assure us.[86] In no sense was the theatre a place where people escaped from political reality: rather, it was a place where they found or created it. It was not without reason that the Senate refused, until almost the end of the Republic, to build a permanent stone theatre. The Hellenistic theatre doubled, from Menander's day onwards, as the normal place for democratic assemblies. There citizens no longer stood, as in the Pnyx, but sat at leisure to impose their will upon the state – a system which Cicero for one found abhorrent.[87] In Rome, temporary theatres were set up and pulled down at enormous expense to ensure that there could be no permanent site for the expression of mass opinion.

For both senators and populace, theatre was an expressive instrument. On the one hand, the logic of festival could be taken to imply that all signs of hierarchy should be suspended for the duration, and a more natural order observed; on the other, theatre could be seen as a public event, where the true order should be on display. The former, egalitarian view of festival became increasingly unacceptable to the senatorial class who, in the course of Plautus' writing career, decreed that they should be given separate seats in the *orchêstra*. Doubtless the wealthy had found ways and means to secure the best seats before legal measures formalized the situation. Many commoners saw this formal segregation as an arrogant move, threatening the harmony and ancient freedoms of the Republic.[88] There was similar antagonism when, later in the Republic, the lowest banked seats were reserved for knights.[89] Class divisions, therefore, were both visible and at issue in the Roman theatre.

Curculio's entry speech incorporates members of the audience in the play by turning them into a Greek crowd. He imagines he is passing a *stratêgos*, an inspector of the *agora*, a demarch, men in Greek clothes, men in Greek taverns. He locates his audience in an imaginary utopia where food and drink flow freely, and slaves play ball in the street – the same utopian Greece as that which reigns on the stage. As Curculio draws nearer to the stage, the social status of his fictitious Greeks becomes lower. The poorer Romans at the back or fringe of the auditorium, it seems, become the wealthy 'tyrants' and 'generals', while the richer people nearer the stage become porridge-eaters, drunks, and slaves. Beneath a pseudo-Greek mask, the Roman order can be safely inverted.

Later in the play, the audience are reconstituted as Romans. When the Costumier appears, actors and roles merge. The Costumier claims that 'Curculio' has stolen his costume, and he decides to 'observe' while waiting for the actor's return (lines 462ff). While he waits, he offers to help the audience distinguish good men from false, and proceeds to describe the inhabitants of a series of Roman locations. These are the locations which a man can see if he stands in the forum, faces south and looks from left to right through one hundred and eighty degrees. Plainly the forum is where Plautus' temporary theatre was erected. The auditorium, of course, blocks the normal view from the spot where the actor stands, and his remarks have to apply to the inhabitants of that part of the auditorium where his gaze falls. The perjurers of the Comitium, by analogy with speakers on a rostrum, are probably spectators seated on stage. The good men and rich are specified as those who 'walk' in 'the lower forum' – not the seated senators, therefore, but the ushers, who were doubtless bribable. 'In the centre by the canal' – that is, the real Cloaca, but also the lateral theatre gangway or *praecintio* – sit the ostentatious sort. Above them are the noisy sort who gratuitously insult others, and these must be the Roman poor who hurl raucous comments at actors and social superiors alike. Even more undesirable types lurk in the recesses of the theatre – prostitutes 'under the Basilica', crooks 'behind' a temple. The shameless morality of all characters on Plautus's stage is ascribed in equal measure to the Roman audience.

While Menander's audience is addressed as a homogeneous body of *andres* (sirs!), the Plautine audience is differentiated as a multitude of discrete groupings. This accords with the logic of the space: the Roman actor must select which part of the auditorium he wishes to address, while the Greek actor speaks for the benefit of the whole assembly. Plautus both displays the basic divisions in Roman society, and symbolically overturns them. The Greek narrative played out on his stage is no less paradoxical. Every role is type-cast: all social types – slave, pimp, youth, old man – are fixed in their preordained roles. And yet, all the relationships are inverted: pimps are bullied, old men consort with prostitutes, slaves give orders to masters, soldiers submit before adolescents, the impoverished parasite is fed, pampered, and becomes master of ceremonies. Through his simultaneous displaying and inverting of the norms of society, Plautus fulfils his double obligation to the aedile who buys his play and to the public who must give him applause.

Greek New Comedy, in its social detail if not in its plots, tells its audience how life is outside the theatre. Its referent is social reality. Plautine theatre contains no such referent. It is a temporary world which must end when the festival ends. There is no future in Plautus' world, and characters act only for present gratification. Behind the wooden walls of Plautus' theatre lie the real Forum, sewer, fish-market, and Comitium of Rome. While the spectator in the Theatre of Dionysus sees only wilderness above the stage wall, the spectator in the Roman Forum must see the Capitoline hill rise above the stage with its temples of Jupiter and Juno, symbols of state power and legitimate marriage. The Sulpicius Rufus fresco, like so many other Pompeian paintings, conveys this sense of a real world behind the flimsy stage façade, impinging upon the stage world.[90] In *Curculio*, the off-stage world at one moment contains praetors and the Capitol, at the next becomes Greek Epidaurus. The play is not a *mimêsis* of any 'elsewhere'. The audience are not invited to conjure up an imaginary scene behind the three doors of the stage wall, or beside the stage to left and right. Instead of making the audience visualize the scene inside the brothel, for instance, where his beloved may or may not be suffering, Plautus' hero delivers a serenade to the door itself. The actor sings his love for the double doors, and bids them become 'foreign players' (*ludii barbari*) like himself. The only available reality is the visible here and now of the signs which constitute the performance.

THE STAGE AS A SYSTEM OF SIGNS

I quoted in chapter 1 Anne Ubersfeld's observation that the spectator's pleasure oscillates between on the one hand bewitchment and on the other conscious observation. In Plautus' *Curculio*, the emphasis tends to be upon the latter, upon directing the spectator to observe the practice of creating theatre. Theatre is presented as an imported and thus an unnatural practice, unnatural in the sense that its conventions are man-made rather than inscribed in nature. Actors hire costumes, writers borrow story-lines from other writers, actors play stock roles – this is the 'reality' that is acknowledged and celebrated. In semiological terms, the emphasis is rather upon the signifiers than the signified: upon the phallic candle, for instance, which signifies the hero's love, or the auditorium which signifies another part of the city. The door in *Curculio* is a sign which does not simply denote the entry to a brothel but acquires other connotations. It becomes a player in the drama, is serenaded, and given water to drink to keep its pivots quiet; it is 'beautiful', 'taciturn' and 'unkind'. The heroine, when she displaces the door as object of the hero's erotic attention, is then to be seen as a theatrical sign no less than the door. Whether she is a prostitute or a free-born girl affects the hero's power to obtain her, but has no further importance in Plautus' stage world because she has no off-stage reality, no imaginable future. Her mask displays her nature instantaneously, and conceals no enigmas. The whole Hellenistic system of signs is at once celebrated and mocked by Plautus' actors in accordance with what Florence Dupont terms an 'aesthetics of re-dundance'[91] – the pure theatrical pleasure which Ubersfeld terms 'pleasure in the sign'.[92]

In modern naturalism, the emphasis is upon the signified, a specific other world represented by actors and objects on stage. Menander's theatre, though much closer than Plautus' to modern naturalism, differs in many essentials from the modern form with which we are familiar. A different balance was maintained between the magical recreation and the imitative practice, between signified and signifier. Our idea of what a 'realistic' play should be like has to yield in face of a theatre which has its actors play against a stage wall that is part representational and part neutral, which places masked actors alongside unmasked boys, which includes verbal references both to a precise topographical setting and to a watching audience. On the face of it, these are minor details. But if we lose sight of them and allow ourselves to assume that Menander's plays were performed in a way that we today consider to be 'natural', we shall fail to understand why the Hellenistic world found these plays important and powerful.

The similarities are obvious. Menander's *dramatis personae* have an off-stage reality, a past and a future. Their behaviour on stage is shaped by pre-existent character traits, and by events which take place off stage. The hero's aim is to secure his future after the play has ended. The painted scene panels frame the action so that the cut-off point between on stage and off stage seems an imposition of art, and one can imagine the stage world extending beyond this frame. The *orchêstra* has a similar function to the proscenium arch in isolating the audience from the stage, so that the stage action seems to progress without the audience being able to change it. The dissimilarities are less obvious.

The public mode of address is linked to the close relationship of actor and orator. Like public speakers on the platform of a lawcourt, the actors present their *mimêsis* to the audience in order that the audience may arrive at a corporate judgement. As in a lawcourt, the audience have to evaluate the moral stances of the various speakers. The spectator holds both the stage world and his fellow spectators in his field of vision, and necessarily relates the one to the other. He must judge whether the situation proposed by the play could be resolved so happily in the real world of the audience. He must judge whether he, or others around him, would make the same moral choices.

The design of the background is to us surprising. The scenographic tradition which stretches from Italian neo-classicism to modern naturalism places actors against a visual illusion of reality. This convention implies a relationship between human beings and the environment against which they are seen. If all human beings are latent Machiavells, this tradition implies, then it is Florence which allows that natural corruption to flourish; if Miss Julie differs from the servant, then the central explanation must be that she is unfamiliar with life in the kitchen, the kitchen which the audience sees displayed before it. In Menander's Athens, such assumptions about the effect of environment upon personality, though compatible with the ideals of a democracy, are incompatible with the preconceptions of a patriarchal slave-owning society. In response to endogamy, slavery, patriarchy, and related problems, Aristotelian ethical thinking evolved some complex theories about character. Character is not seen as a passive substance, subjected to the active operations of an environment, nor is it primarily genetic. *Êthos* is formed through a dialectic of choices made and habits acquired. 'Virtues are neither natural nor outside nature: we are naturally capable of acquiring them, and whether we succeed depends on *êthos*.'[93] Character and physiology are closely linked, and environment is only one of various factors which create a specific physiological condition. The physical environment in Menander's theatre is allowed the place due to it as but one influence on human conduct.

If the long, shallow stage has found few imitators in recent centuries, this is perhaps because of its essentially democratic quality. All actors are equidistant from the audience. Just as there is no hierarchy amongst the audience, so there is none amongst the *dramatis personae*. The deep-set illusionist stages which prevailed from the seventeenth to the nineteenth centuries, and on into the modern London West End, have tended to differentiate lead actors who occupy the foreground, from supporting actors who fill the background. In Menander's theatre, no one can retreat from the footlights and merge into the background. Supernumeraries are not further back but smaller-bodied. Within a given play, no single role stands out as significantly larger than several others. The same actor can play slave, woman and free man within a single play. The victorious lead actor must be versatile enough to play any sort of role. The speaking roles are thus in a sense of equal status. This is particularly significant in respect of the slave. Although three semiological systems – plot, mask, and costume – differentiate the slave from the free man, the two systems of language and space mark the slave as equal to the free man.

It is to be noted that Menander's theatre operates on a horizontal plane, and makes no use of height. Pollux, it is true, writes not only of entries through the *orchêstra* but also of an upper room. This was probably tucked under the roof, for it is at the level of the tiles. Here women are supposed to watch, pimps to spy.[94] Menander's texts offer no evidence that he tried to exploit the possibilities of an upper level offered by Aristophanes' *Wasps*, or by *phylax* farces.[95] His works contain no 'window scene' in the manner of *Romeo and Juliet*, expressing through a visual metaphor the association of carnal love with Heaven, the stars, and the spheres. In Menander, love is not a spiritual but an earthly affair. Medieval theatre, the ancestor of Shakespeare's, set God high up in Paradise, and Hell-mouth at ground level, in accordance with the assumption that man has both higher, spiritual, and lower, carnal, aspects to his nature. There is a similar assumption in Senecan theatre, which relies upon the high *scaenae frons* of the Imperial theatre to make sense of its constant invocation of gods in the heavens and the after-life down in Acheron. Here again we find an assumption that there is a higher principle, god or reason, and a lower principle, matter. In the purist

Aristotelian theatre of Menander, the parameters of higher and lower do not exist. All problems can be stated and resolved in human (i.e. horizontal) terms. The *psychê* or invisible soul which animates the body is conceived as being not above but within and inseparable from the body. Just as the actor is the unseen *psychê* animating the mask, so the off-stage action behind the stage wall animates the action on stage.

The Hellenistic theatre can be analysed as a model of what Ubersfeld terms 'psychic space'. 'The human psyche', she writes, 'can be regarded as a space, and the place of performance may be its image.'[96] The three doorways correspond not only with the three actors but also with the tripartite soul envisaged by Plato and Aristotle. Plato compared the *psychê* to a charioteer driving two winged horses towards heaven in pursuit of Zeus. This charioteer has to reconcile the obedient white horse of spirit with the unruly black horse of lust.[97] Aristotle rejected Plato's non-material, moralistic notion of an ignoble faculty, and the associated spatialization of the *psychê* in terms of high and low, winged and earthly. Without abandoning materialism, however, he retained the division between 'mind' and 'appetite', and between two types of appetite, reasoning and unreasoning, which is to say appetites for long-term and short-term gratification.[98] This concept of the *psychê* is reproduced on stage in the form of the three doorways: a central doorway associated with hidden and intangible forces, and a right and left which must somehow be held in equilibrium. The occupants of the two houses in Menander's plays display contrasting types of 'appetite', and the problem for the audience is to decide where reason lies. Aristotle's formulations are numerous, the plays tell many stories, but the patterning is a constant.

Aristotle's ethical and political thought displays the same tripartite structuring. His political ideal is a mid-point between the rule of the few and the rule of the many. Moral virtue can be defined likewise as a compromise or mid-point. 'It is in the nature of moral qualities', he asserts, 'that they are destroyed both by deficiency and by excess.[99] Virtue is not a matter of looking to an ideal form of the good, as Plato held, but a matter of striking a balance, finding the mean. The Hellenistic stage furthered this ethical endeavour. It does not lead the eye upwards to heaven (symbolic of truth and divine virtue), nor inwards to one of Ibsen's glimpsed inner rooms (symbolic of the unconscious), nor beyond the actor to a formative environment, but rather to the stage altar, a visible point on a long lateral line, equidistant from left and right.

In the Roman theatre, reality is not ultimately knowable. There are many competing angles from which the stage action can be viewed. Many different frames can be placed around the stage action to make it coherent. Actors can hide in recesses and disappear down alleyways, they may be more or less visible. Reality is not therefore a constant state, available for scientific analysis, for no common experience of that reality is shared by all. Truth resides not in but beyond the ephemeral casing in which man is housed. Roman *virtus* consists in imposing will upon matter, forcing the body to do what the mind compels. Observed material reality does not, therefore, yield the key to ultimate reality. On the Aristotelian stage of Menander, which completes the broken circle of the auditorium, pleasure and virtue become one. The theatre creates wholeness. On the Roman stage we see not unity but a binary divide. The stage bisects the orchestral circle, and Plautus plays tirelessly with the resultant line of demarcation. The god-given divide which separates mind and matter, *virtus* and pleasure, nobility and *plebs*, is more insistently present the more it is challenged.

CHAPTER 3

The system of masks

CRITICAL APPROACHES

As we saw in the last chapter, the adoption of the high stage, whatever the
historical relationship of cause and effect, correlates with a quite new use
of the theatrical mask. In Aristophanic comedy, the emphasis was not
upon the face but on the body. A leather phallus and padded stomach
signalled to the audience that an actor of Old Comedy represented man at
his most carnal and self-interested. In accordance with the principle that
Old Comedy represented men as worse than they really are, the masks of
Old Comedy, Aristotle tells us, are necessarily 'ugly and distorted, while
causing no pain to the spectator'.[1] New Comedy, as we have seen, owes
more to Euripides than it does to Old Comedy.[2] In Aristotelian terms,
New Comedy was to represent men as neither worse than they really are
(like Aristophanes), nor better than they really are (like Sophocles), but as
they are – like Euripides. The masks of New Comedy evolved in
accordance with this thinking. Their primary purpose was not to idealize
or caricature, but to express something of how people really are. With the
emergence of the high stage, it was not only the comic but also the tragic
masks which changed. The *onkos* or high head-dress added to the tragic
mask gave it a new larger-than-life grandeur. It thus portrayed people as
they 'ought to be' or as 'better than they are', in contrast to the comic
mask which portrayed people as they are.

The convention of the mask is never in question in Sophocles or
Aeschylus. It functions as a neutral face and obliterates all the idiosyncrasies which distinguish one individual, or one actor, from another. In
the classical tragic mask, as John Jones rightly states, 'the audience could
read a few simple, conventional signs determining rank and age and sex'
but it had 'no inside. Its being is exhausted in its features.'[3] This neutral
mask obliged the spectator to judge Agamemnon or Oedipus not by his
appearance but by his actions. It obliged the actor to externalize emotion

and develop the expressivity of his whole body. There could be no sense of the uniqueness of the individual once the actor donned his tragic mask, in accordance with the guiding principle that classical art should deal in universal truths. Observations on the neutral mask by Jacques Lecoq, the greatest living European teacher of masked acting, seem apposite in describing the effects of the classical mask:

With it, no means of trickery. The neutral mask, which might be thought a means of concealment, strips us naked. Our face mask of life falls off, the role that it played has no meaning ... The gestures become larger, become slower. At the beginning, you suffocated, but now your breath has expanded. The themes are simple in their meaning, difficult in their profundity ... You cannot imagine a neutral mask called Albert, waking up in bed. The neutral mask is a sort of common denominator ... It makes us discover the space, rhythm and weight of things. The dynamics of fear, of jealousy, of anger, of pride, belong to all.[4]

The convention of the mask does nevertheless come under some kind of pressure in the late plays of Euripides. John Jones perceives in Euripides 'a discrepancy of inner and outer' which 'threatens to destroy the masking convention'.[5] Froma Zeitlin has analysed the role-playing of Orestes in Euripides' *Orestes* and found that in this play the 'repertory of tragedy and epic provides, as it were, a closet of masks for the actors to raid at will, characters in search of an identity, a part to play'.[6] By the time of Menander, a century later, the human being seems to have been reconstituted as an integral psychosomatic entity. It can no longer be said that a person has 'no inside', but inside and outside are securely integrated. The scientific investigations of Hippocratic medicine and Aristotelian biology had helped to create a positivist climate in which it seemed theoretically possible to gauge a man's psychological state from his external appearance. New Comedy offered its audience the pleasure of engaging in this task. Up on a raised stage, the actor displayed his mask to the audience and controlled the angle at which it was to be viewed. The mask ceased to be a 'common denominator', directing the audience to sense the universality and grandeur of human feelings, and became a means of establishing fine distinctions between human beings.

Research into the masks of New Comedy has followed a well-trodden path since Carl Robert's seminal study of 1911. Webster, Gould and Lewis and Bernabò-Brea have concurred in their methods.[7] The starting-point for their analysis is the catalogue of forty-four masks preserved by Pollux. Correlatives for these masks are found in the archaeological remains, and all surviving monuments are subsequently, so far as is possible, allocated to one of the forty-four types. Once this operation has been performed, the complex psychology of characters in Menander's texts can be contrasted with the crude typology of the masks. Geoffrey Arnott, introducing the new Loeb edition of Menander, has digested the archaeological research when he writes:

Due weight of course needs to be given to the limitations put on Menander's character drawing by his genre and his time ... He apparently inherited a drama of conventional type-figures – braggart soldier, greedy parasite, garrulous cook, spineless lover, choleric father, selfish courtesan and the like – immediately identifiable by the audience from the masks these characters wore and the names they were given. These enabled an experienced member of the audience to predict the total personality of a character on his first entrance, provided the playwright had made it conform to type ... What Menander does is to take over the skeletal role, and then to add a series of characteristics which are either wholly unexpected, being outside the conventional gamut, or only half surprising, because they refine the grossness out of the conventional traits and so turn them inside out.[8]

Lurking in the background we notice the old assumption that text is qualitatively superior to performance, that what the audience hears is necessarily more complex and subtle than what it sees.

This established methodology is analytic rather than structural. It analyses Pollux's catalogue of masks not as an integrated system but as the sum of its independent parts. Much intellectual effort has been expended in marrying monument x with mask y in the catalogue, with little regard for the paucity of information which Pollux provides, and the lack of evidence that his list is comprehensive. The same piecemeal, analytic thinking then governs the critic's response to the text, as for example in Arnott's definition of 'character':

Playwrights like Menander saw 'character' as the sum of a person's idiosyncrasies in speech and behaviour, an externally viewed set of matching characteristics that slot into a conventional pattern like the tesserae of a mosaic.[9]

This must be Arnott's view rather than Menander's. It is the masks, with their multiple components of wig, complexion, brows, etcetera, which have prompted Arnott's definition. Aristotle's concept of êthos – the nearest equivalent to our word 'character' – is concerned with moral choice, and has nothing to do with external idiosyncrasies. Speech patterns are sometimes distinctive in Menander, but never quirky. The subordination of character to action prevents him from creating idiosyncratic monomaniacs in the manner of Molière. If we are to achieve a more satisfactory analysis of what Menander was trying to accomplish in the theatre, then we need to transcend the notion that character is a collection

of free-standing textual and visual bits. We must lay bare the organizational principles in New Comedy which integrated visual and verbal
components.

A well-known relief depicts Menander staring at a trio of masks while
his muse offers inspiration.[10] Menander did not write his plays around
specific actors whom he knew well, as Molière did, or Shakespeare, for
actors were allocated to poets through a lottery system.[11] Rather, he wrote
for the masks that were the characters of his plays. Mask and character are
now the subject of separate investigations by archaeologists and by
literary critics, yet they could not be analysed separately by the spectator
in the ancient theatre. The *prosôpon* or *persona* was the character which
the actor assumed. In modern naturalistic theatre, actor and role to some
degree merge as the actor finds within the role points of connexion with
his or her own experience. In Greek theatre, as Jones rightly states, 'at the
living heart of the tradition, the actor is the mask'.[12] In the Menander
relief, the poet stares at his trio of masks so intently because he is
interested in what they show, what they are, not in what lies behind them.
If the masks were really so predictable and gross as Arnott envisages,
Menander would have looked elsewhere for his creative inspiration. The
whole question of what the masks showed and meant to the Hellenistic
audience needs to be re-examined.

In order to undertake this task, we must lay down the initial
semiological principle that each mask is not an isolated unit, with a fixed
and definable meaning or personality, but that the corpus of masks
creates a system of distinctions. The example of colour will illustrate this
principle. The English system of colours – purple, red, pink, orange,
yellow, etc. – constitutes a system of distinctions within a spectrum
which, our science teaches us, ranges from infra-red to ultra-violet.
These terms have no exact equivalence in the Greek *porphyreos*, *kokkinos*,
erythros, *pyrrhos*, *xanthos*, *krokôtos*, etc. *Porphyreos* does not 'mean'
purple, *pyrrhos* does not 'mean' orange, because medieval dye processes
and modern fruit consumption give us new points of reference. Hellenistic science analysed colour in relation to a spectrum ranging from white
to black.[13] In order to understand what the Greeks meant by their various
colour terms, and to find English equivalents, we would have to analyse
an integral system of distinctions containing its own interior logic. This
then is the principle that we must apply in an analysis of masks.

Claude Lévi-Strauss's investigation of north-west Indian masks
provides a useful methodological guide. The features of the Swaihwé
mask had no comprehensible meaning for him, Lévi-Strauss records,

until he was able to relate this mask to a seemingly unconnected mask, the Dzonkwa. The latter systematically reversed the features of the former:

white → black
protruding eyes → concave eyes
lolling tongue → pursed mouth
feathers → fur

Pendulous breasts identify the Dzonkwa as female rather than male. Its ritual usage is different, and Lévi-Strauss observes the following reversals related to the usage of the two masks:

summer → winter
aristocratic wearer → rich wearer
energetic → passive
eyes attacked → eyes blind

The Dzonkwa is associated with a different body of myths which change its identity:

north/south locations → east/west locations
vertical origins → horizontal origins

Both masks are related by Lévi-Strauss to the transfer of wealth at marriage. The Swaihwé gives wealth voluntarily, the Dzonkwa has wealth taken from her. The former, by virtue of its shape, represents wealth, the latter owns wealth. Lévi-Strauss also records that the mythic and ritual features of the Swaihwé mask are inverted, while the form remains constant, when the mask is transferred to another group further south. This leads him to venture a conclusion which has broad application:

It would be misleading to imagine, therefore, as so many ethnologists and art historians still do today, that a mask and, more generally, a sculpture or a painting may be interpreted each for itself, according to what it represents or to the aesthetic or ritual use for which it is destined. We have seen that, on the contrary, a mask does not exist in isolation; it supposes other real or potential masks always by its side, masks that might have been chosen in its stead and substituted for it. In discussing a particular problem, I hope to have shown that a mask is not primarily what it represents but what it transforms, that is to say, what it chooses *not* to represent.[14]

Lévi-Strauss's methodology allows him to make sense of a body of data that seems at first disconnected. A similar method can be used to make sense of the apparently disconnected data that survive from the Hellenistic world.

It may seem a gargantuan step to move from ritual dances to theatre, from illiterate Indian tribes to the sophisticated culture of Greece. Lévi-Strauss's structural method is, however, particularly helpful in relation to Greek culture because the tendency to think in terms of binary oppositions is so apparent in Greece. As Aristotle observes in his survey of Greek philosophy, 'nearly everyone agrees that things and substance are composed of opposites'.[15] The Pythagoreans, for instance, based their philosophy upon the differentiation of odd and even, while the basis of number for Plato was the opposition of great and small. Empedocles based his philosophy upon the opposition of love and strife. Aristotle's polarizations in the *Poetics* of pity and fear, tragedy and comedy, drama and epic, better or worse than average, exemplify his own binary tendencies. I described in the last chapter the polarization of right and left which characterizes Hellenistic stagecraft. The structuralist approach, as we saw in relation to plot, proves particularly helpful in relation to a form so rigorously coded as New Comedy.

Aristotle's analytic procedure is similar to that of Lévi-Strauss in its insistence that we gain knowledge not through knowing what things are in themselves but through constructing differences. His method is always to work from the whole to the parts, from genus to species. While each genus has a different first cause or origin, each species is distinguished by an identifiable 'difference'.[16] Contraries susceptible of intermediates by definition belong to a single genus. Thus, for example, particular species of the genus colour – red, grey, etc. – were all seen as intermediate points between black and white, being more or less penetrative (diacritical) or compounding (syncritical).[17] This whole intellectual system becomes fraught with problems when Aristotle has to consider whether men and women, or black men and white men, belong to the same human genus. They do, Aristotle argues, because all humans contain the same formula (*logos*); the same semen can be the origin of male or female.[18]

These principles and methods were followed by Menander's teacher, Theophrastos, who considered problems of epistemology in much the same terms. 'Why', Theophrastos asked, 'does nature and all existence consist of contraries, so that the worse has virtually an equal share with the better, or is indeed much greater, so that a universal truth seems expressed in Euripides' words: "Good alone there cannot be!"?' Knowledge, Theophrastos continued, 'cannot exist without some differentiation'. He saw it as the task of science to find where things, in part or in whole, are not differentiated, and thus constitute a species or genus. Knowledge proceeds through distinguishing invariable first principles from naturally occurring variables.[19] Where Theophrastos' tone differs from that of Aristotle is in his doubt that nature always has a purpose. Art is tidier than life, and one of the pleasures of Menander's audience must have lain in sensing nature's hidden purpose.

In order to illustrate the importance of binary opposition as a fundamental principle in Hellenistic thinking, let us conclude by examining the Pompeian mosaic of the Seven Philosophers.[20] The seven philosophers are set within a decorative frame studded with theatrical masks. A perception of oppositions helps one to understand the relationship between theatre and philosophy which the mosaic proposes. A tree and a column in the centre of the mosaic establish a nature/culture opposition, related to the practice of philosophy in the groves or in the city. To the right is an Epicurean walled garden, on the left a portico signifying the Stoa. Tureens placed inaccessibly on top of the portico signify the denial of pleasure. Within the border of the mosaic, we find at the four corners fierce masks from satyr plays signifying the untamed wildness of nature. At the centre of the four sides we find four masks from New Comedy, the genre associated with urbanity and civilization. The pair on the vertical axis belong to a youth and a courtesan, the pair on the horizontal axis belong to slaves. The implicit philosophical question is whether those who surrender to desire become slaves of desire. The choice lies between following the dictates of nature or of civilization. The pairing of satyr masks − a satyr and Silenus against two omophagous maenads − must also relate to the unleashing of bestial passions. The mosaic is an object-lesson through the way it demonstrates how the ephemeral mode of comedy may become a vehicle for exploring major philosophical issues.

POLLUX'S CATALOGUE

Let us now examine Pollux's catalogue of New Comedy masks,[21] keeping in mind always the insistence of Lévi-Strauss that a mask is to be understood not through what it represents in itself but through the elements which it transforms, and the insistence of Aristotle and Theophrastos that nature consists of contraries, and that we understand through perceiving not things in themselves but similarities and differences. We must examine the catalogue not as a list of forty-four independent masks but as an exercise in taxonomy.

OLD MEN

first grandfather: oldest – hair cropped close to skin – gentle brows – full beard – thin cheeks – downcast gaze – pale complexion – forehead at ease

other grandfather: thinner – more taut around the eyes and gloomy – rather pale – well-bearded – russet hair – crushed ears

principal old man: has a wreath of hair round his head – hook-nosed – flat-faced – right brow raised

old man with long streamy beard: has a wreath of hair round his head – full beard – brows not raised – lethargic gaze

Hermon's*: bald forehead – well-bearded – raised brows – keen (or 'fierce') eyes

wedge-beard: bald forehead – brows raised – pointed beard – rather cussed

Lycomedes' (lit. 'wolf-cunning'): curly hair – long beard – other brow raised – represents a busybody

pimp: resembles 'Lycomedes' mask' except that he has a slight grin on his lips, his brows are clenched and he is bald on his forehead or pate

* *Hermon's No. 2*: shaven and has a wedge-shaped beard

YOUNG MEN

accomplished youth: ruddy – athletic – skin lightly tanned – a few wrinkles on his forehead, and a crown of hair – raised brows

dark youth: younger – lowered brows – appears cultured rather than athletic

curly youth: even younger – ruddy complexion – hair as his name implies – lowered brows – one wrinkle on his forehead

delicate youth: hair like the 'accomplished' youth – youngest of all – pallid – suggests the delicacy of one reared in the shade

in *the boor*, the complexion is darkened – lips broad – snub nose – wreath of hair

in the *wavy-haired*, who is a soldier and braggart, with a dark complexion and dark hair, the hair waves about – as also . . .

in *wavy-haired No. 2*, who is more delicate, and fair-haired the *toady* and *parasite**: dark – belong to the gymnasium – hook-nosed – comfort-loving – the 'parasite's' ears are more crushed and he looks more cheerful, while the 'toady' has his brows raised more maliciously

the *'portrait'* has a scattering of grey hairs, and his beard is shaven – he wears a purple hem, and is foreign

* the *Sicilian parasite* is a third version

SLAVES

grandfather: is the only grey-haired slave, and represents a freedman
*principal slave**: has a coil of red hair – raised brows with the tips drawn together – equivalent among slaves to the 'principal old man' among the free
low-hair: has a bald forehead and tawny hair – puffed brows
curly slave: obvious hair, tawny as also his complexion – bald forehead – twisted gaze

slave Maison: has a bald pate and is tawny
slave 'Cicada': a bald pate and dark – two or three dark curls lie on top – similar ones on the beard – twisted gaze

* the *wavy-haired principal* resembles the 'principal slave' except in the hair

WOMEN

(Old women)

she-wolf (or *withered old woman*): slightly elongated – small, close wrinkles – pale, close to ochre – eye squints
fat old woman: has fat wrinkles in ample flesh – headband going round her hair
little housekeeper (or *menial*, or *sharp old woman*): snub-nosed – in each jaw has two molars

(Young women)

talker: hair round about – hair discreetly smoothed down – straight brows – white complexion
curly: differs from the 'talker' in hair-style

virgin: has a parting and hair smoothed down – straight, dark brows –
pale, slightly ochre in complexion
pseudo-virgin: paler complexion – binds her hair round top of her head
– looks like a newly-wed
the *other pseudo-virgin*: is distinguished only by the lack of a parting

talker with grey strands: looks as the name implies – reveals herself as a
courtesan who has abandoned her trade
concubine: looks similar, except hair round about
mature courtesan: is redder than the 'pseudo-virgin' and has curls
round the ears
nubile courtesan: not made-up – hair bound tight with a little band
golden courtesan: has much gold about her hair
mitred courtesan: has head wrapped in a multicoloured turban
little torch: distinctive through her tresses of hair which culminate in a
point, whence her name

shorn poppet: is a slave-girl with hair cut short all round – wears only a
white chiton with a girdle
slave-girl with smoothed hair: has her hair parted – is slightly snub-
nosed and slave to a courtesan – scarlet chiton with a girdle

The original cataloguer, whose schema Pollux reproduces, has worked in
the manner of an Aristotelian biologist, and has tried to create order out of
the chaotic data which sensory experience presents to him. His first step
has been to divide the material into four or five genera – types with
different points of origin or first principles. He describes four major
genera, plus the small group of old women. When we examine the texts of
New Comedy, we find that no play can exist without representatives of
the four major genera, while old women are often absent and have only
minor roles when they appear. The division of humanity into four major
types is connected to the narrative structure which I explored in
chapter 1. The fourfold division is rooted in sociological and philosophical assumptions of the Hellenistic world, and I shall explore these
assumptions in chapter 6. The cataloguer does not concern himself with
the distinguishing features which differentiate one genus from another,
no doubt because these features seemed too obvious. He is only
concerned with distinctions of species.
    We must begin by seeing precisely how the cataloguer identifies the
existence of a species within a genus, and how he distinguishes a species
from a subspecies. In some instances, the cataloguer is classifying a mask

that has a recognized name, distinctive looks, and a specific dramatic function. The Cicada mask, we learn from Athenaeus, belongs to a cook.[22] Its curls create a distinctive identity, and the name must allude to the dark curls which lie across the bald scalp and look like grasshoppers flitting about. In other instances, the cataloguer seems to be inventing a title, like low-hair, for a mask which he has identified yet knows no traditional name for. It is clearly a moot point whether certain variables warrant the classification of a separate mask. Thus, for instance, the cataloguer has decided to note as an addendum that the principal slave may sometimes have curly hair. If he seems more confident in his decision to classify a separate talker mask on the basis of curly hair, this is probably because hair-style is the most prominent feature of female masks.

Although the cataloguer was not faced with an easy task, he has worked in a logical manner. First, we notice that the taxonomy observes a systematic hierarchical order. As far as possible, the genera and species are listed so that age precedes youth, free precedes slave, male precedes female. Secondly, we notice that in respect of the male masks the cataloguer has started by defining four normative types within each genus, and has followed these four with a number of particular masks, immediately recognizable by their name (Lycomedes', etc.), and/or by their social status (pimp, soldier, etc.), and generally also by their personality (braggart, busybody, etc.). When we examine these particular masks, we see that the cataloguer consistently thinks in terms of dyads, or contraries. The two bald cooks are distinguished by their hair and gaze, the two young men from the gymnasium are distinguished by their moods. The cataloguer takes two bald old men, and distinguishes them by their beard and mood, then takes the second and pairs it with another mask that has only one brow raised, then takes this third mask and distinguishes it from a fourth by mouth, brows and hair, and finally, having created a kind of spectrum, identifies an intermediate point between the first and second.

If we return now to the four normative types within each genus, we can see how the cataloguer, using binary oppositions as his constant analytic tool, has evolved his fourfold schema. Once the cataloguer has selected a standard or 'principal' type, the model generates new types like a self-reproducing amoeba. Tetrads are constructed in such a way that each normative mask embodies two polarities.

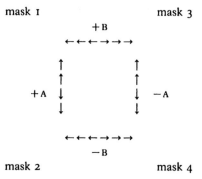

mask 1   mask 3

mask 2   mask 4

In respect of the slaves, $+A/-A$ = hirsute/bald, while $+B/-B$ = symmetrical brows/asymmetrical brows. In respect of the old men, $+A/-A$ = older/less old, while $+B/-B$ relates to a positive or negative mood about the eyes. And in respect of the young men, $+A/-A$ = reared in the sun/reared in the shade, while $+B/-B$ seems to relate to an upwards/downwards movement of the brows and hair.

When we turn to the female masks, we find that the cataloguer continues to form tetrads. Old women, citizen women, courtesans, and slave-girls are listed in four separate groupings. The schema works differently because the categories of slave and free are superimposed upon old and young. We see something more like a spectrum of ages, since grey-haired mature women are included in the 'younger' group. Assuming that crones are normally slaves or ex-slaves, we can set out the initial scheme as follows:

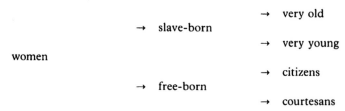

Within the major grouping of free-born women, the tetradic pattern re-emerges: $+A/-A$ = middle-aged/young, $+B/-B$ = citizen/non-citizen. This yields four terms: talker (or middle-aged citizen), middle-aged non-citizen, virgin, courtesan. Each of the four terms in this equation is then split again. Thus we find two talker masks differentiated by hair-style; a concubine and an ex-courtesan, again differentiated by hair; a virgin and a pseudo-virgin type; an adolescent courtesan and a mature courtesan. The pseudo-virgin type is again subdivided, another contrasted pair of mature courtesans are added, and the little torch is noted as a distinctive special mask.

Pollux's catalogue can now be seen for what it is: not a list of forty-four universally recognized types, nor the repertory of masks that happened to lie in the hands of one company, but a sophisticated attempt to codify a complex and subtle tradition of masking. This tradition would seem to have emerged without systematic planning, but in close accordance nevertheless with the intellectual structures of the Hellenistic world. In order to test out the usefulness of the cataloguer's work, and to see how well the observable data correspond with the theory, we need to turn to the evidence of archaeology, and to the evidence provided by dramatic texts.

THE EVIDENCE OF ARCHAEOLOGY

Our knowledge of Aristophanic and Middle Comedy owes much to the survival of terracotta figurines. The masks of Old and Middle Comedy have no meaning except in relation to the body of the human animal to which they belong. In the period of New Comedy, the face can be interpreted in isolation. Images of masks proliferate on frescoes, mosaics, archways, lamps, jewellery, theatre tickets, and – most valuable of all for our purposes – miniature terracotta replicas. While some larger terracotta masks were designed to be wall decorations, the miniatures were normally used, it would seem, as souvenirs of productions, or as dedicatory gifts to Dionysus. Terracotta masks helped to familiarize the Hellenistic world with the tradition of New Comic performance, so that the masks became a common currency within a far-flung culture. Local craftsmen who manufactured masks could either copy the real masks worn by travelling actors, or could reproduce – freehand or by taking moulds – models imported from Athens. The real masks worn in the theatre had to be light, easy to remove, and easy to transport. They were therefore perishable. Successful actors might dedicate their masks to the gods.[23] Models provided the simplest reference device for the manufacture of replacements, and for recording which masks belong to which play. There is an obvious parallel in the practice of Chinese actors, who use miniature models to record the complex make-up designs which they must reproduce for every performance.[24]

Our best source for terracotta miniatures is the island of Lipari. The sack of the city by the Romans in 252 BC ensures that all finds can be dated to within a generation of Menander's death. The double association of

Dionysus with the theatre and with the cult of the dead seems to explain why masks are so often found in cemeteries.[25] A few masks are found in tombs, but most seem to have been used as votive offerings before being collected up and laid in special trenches. Luigi Bernabò-Brea, curator of the museum in Lipari, has documented finds on the islands in a well-illustrated volume which makes it possible now to examine a set of masks as a synchronic system. Previous research has had to be content with assembling masks from different regions and different centuries, and the resultant diversity has frustrated any serious attempt to put Pollux to the test. The Lipari finds include masks from all the genera, together with masks of children, and of Menander himself. The principal lack is within the genus of old men, where few types are represented. The most plausible explanation is that emblems of old age were not thought appropriate companions for a person in the underworld, and emblems of youth, beauty, or mischief were preferred.

Brea allocates each of the Lipari masks to one of Pollux's forty-four types and alleges that:

The perfect correspondence of this new set of masks with the types in Pollux' catalogue demonstrates moreover that this catalogue is not the work of Alexandrian grammarians, or later redactors, but goes back to Menander himself, or almost to his period.[26]

Since the group of young men is the best represented in the Lipari finds, let us see how Brea proceeds in pursuit of his thesis.

Brea allocates four different mask 'groups' to the 'accomplished youth' defined by Pollux. Unfortunately, group 1 has striking *curly* hair, group 2 has *level* brows, group 3 has a twisted mouth and nose and a bulging brow, while group 4 has *level* brows and a *single* wrinkle. None therefore corresponds with the explicit or implicit description in Pollux. We pass on to the 'dark youth', and find that Brea has divided them into five 'types'. Dismissing the evidence of colour as inadequate, Brea takes almond eyes and a delineated, delicate nose as the characteristics which define this 'cultured' mask. Four of the 'types' have flowing tresses of hair, but one has a wreath of hair. Four have wrinkles in the forehead, one particular forehead being of a distinctive triangular shape, while the fifth has a smooth, calm forehead. When he seeks the 'curly youth', Brea bases his classification upon the single wrinkle cited by Pollux, and in order to do so has to argue in defiance of the Greek that 'curly' (*oulos*) does not actually mean 'curly' but 'wavy'. This time he classifies five 'sizes' of mask. Amongst the various individual masks said to belong to the 'curly youth', one has raised brows where Pollux stipulates lowered brows, and is distinguished by the elongated, oval shape of the face; one has a distinctive fleshy and protuberant nose, and a rectangular mouth; one has clenched brows. Various colours are used for the complexion in different examples – red, purple, red-brown, and brown. Only one example is offered for the 'delicate youth' – a boy with a small round face, wide nose, and smiling mouth, with no obvious suggestion of delicacy.

And so Brea's list continues. The clear descriptions and excellent photography in the book make it plain that the Lipari finds in fact exemplify a far wider range of variants than Pollux's taxonomy allows. We should not for this reason discard Pollux, however; we must simply read his catalogue in a different way. An obvious first step, followed by Robert,[27] is to extrapolate from it all the perceptible 'differences' or variables of which a mask was seen to be compounded. Hair-style, hair colour, forehead, brows, the eyes perhaps, mouth, beard, and skin colour seem to be isolable areas of the face, each with its own system of transformations. Pollux shows us how the mask functioned not as a naturalistic portrait but as a system of signs. In the words of one ancient critic, Platonios, 'we see in the masks of Menander's comedy what the eyebrows are like, and how the mouth is opened out, in a way that is not natural'.[28] We do not have to accept Platonios' account of why the masks diverge from 'nature' in order to accept the validity of the observation that the mask offers no 'natural' likeness.

We have only to look at the fineness of bone structure in the non-theatrical portrait masks found in Lipari to see how profoundly the art of the mask-maker differed from that of the portraitist. The subtle features which distinguish one individual human being from another cannot be rendered visible to a distant audience, and the mask-maker's job must be to highlight a set of features which can be discerned at a distance. Other criteria, such as the obvious need for an open mouth, also necessarily differentiate the art of the mask-maker from that of the portrait sculptor. Despite the height of the stage, the theatre mask is viewed from above by most spectators, and therefore certain slight adjustments are made to the normal proportions of the face. The eyes are rounder, the mouth is wider, the crown of hair is higher than in a portrait, in order that, when viewed from above, these features can flatten out and regain the proportions of a normal face viewed on the level. The masks also need to give the actor the opportunity of creating different moods by holding them at different angles. This is most apparent in the case of asymmetrical masks. Quintilian tells us that the old man with one brow raised can turn his normal brow to the audience to denote calm and his raised brow to denote excitement.[29] This is clearly a technique which can only work on the shallow Greek stage, for in Roman-style theatre the spectators have diverse angles of vision.

These are some of the refinements which condition the mask-maker's basic art of constructing a readable system of signs sufficient to differentiate one mask from another. If the Greek spectator, guided by the author and his mask-maker, perceived the masks of New Comedy in broadly the same way as the cataloguer in Pollux, then we may assume that his feelings and judgements during the performance were shaped not by a set of masks-in-themselves but by a set of transformations. We need to understand the spectator's perception as a process.

Since the Lipari masks are mostly found massed in trenches, we cannot use any given combination as evidence for the casting of a specific play. Let us turn instead to two further mosaics from Pompeii which, like that of the Seven Philosophers, now hang on the walls of the museum in Naples.[30] Both have, again, decorative borders studded with eight masks. The first depicts three pairs of doves drinking from a wine bowl, and the border offers a simple pairing of masks within each of the four genera. Two slaves are set at the bottom (sociologically inferior) corners, two old men at the top (superior) corners, two youths on the centre horizontal axis, two young women on the centre vertical axis. Like the wild satyrs, the four asymmetrical masks are relegated to the corners, while the symmetrical, good-looking masks occupy the median positions. To analyse these masks in relation to Pollux is a hopeless endeavour, but it is a simple exercise (hindered only by damage to the mosaic) to see how each pair is systematically differentiated according to hair-style, skin complexion, eye shape and eyebrows.

Both better preserved and more interesting is the mosaic portraying Eros astride a tiger, drinking wine (plate 4). Designed appropriately for a dining-room floor, the mosaic is again a meditation on the power of desire, and the possibility of taming it. The border contains the same complement of two old men, two slaves, two youths and two young women, but the arrangement is different and more informative. Let us attempt to read the story which the mosaic tells. The focal position, bottom centre at the base of the tiger, is given to the courtesan, the object of desire. She is eyed by the amorous youth on her left and the angry father on her right. The initial dramatic situation is apparent. Our eyes pick up the pairings. The angry father is contrasted with another old man top left:

	top left	*bottom right*
hair	brown	white
beard	straggly	neat corkscrew strands
complexion	brownish	yellowish
brows	symmetrical	asymmetrical
mouth	more rounded	more tensed

Our angry father is thus better groomed (i.e. richer), more bilious in colour, and less level in temperament than his friend. The courtesan is paired with another girl top centre:

	top centre	*bottom centre*
hair	curly, unadorned	wavy, with ribbon
brows	level (slight fall to temple)	shallow arch
complexion	slightly paler	slightly darker

We deduce that the girl at the top, with her plain hair, can be no courtesan. The eyebrows suggest a placid, less arch temperament, the complexion a more sheltered life. This must be the bride whom our amorous youth bottom left is supposed to marry. We note that she has the same soft, straggly brown hair as the old man top left, who is therefore her father. The youth bottom left has a neatly groomed crown of hair, the same shape as his father bottom right, but darker. We pass to the second young man, the rival, in the centre of the right-hand border:

	bottom left	*centre right*
hair	smooth	striated
brows	level, slight slope to temple	conjoined, snaky
forehead	level wrinkles	curved wrinkles
complexion	paler	darker
eyes	smaller pupil	larger pupil
nose	straight profile	less straight
jaw	squarer	smaller, rounder

The rival is darker, so more accustomed to the outdoor life than our amorous hero. Perhaps he has served in the army. His temperament is altogether more violent, as we see from the stiffer texture of the hair, and most obviously from the distorted eyebrows. He is also less good-looking, with a worse profile and weaker chin. The pair are obviously competing for the courtesan. Two slaves are available to help their respective masters: the slave top right gazes at the rival, while the other centre left gazes at the amorous hero, so we see who each serves:

	centre left	*top right*
hair	white	grey-brown
eyebrows	asymmetrical, rounded	symmetrical, angular
eyes	squinting	staring forwards
complexion	yellower	browner

We see from the complexion that the rival's slave has shared his master's outdoor life, and we see from the glowering stare that he also shares his master's aggressive temperament. The white-haired city slave has the wiliness of age. His squinting right eye is evasive, and his left eye winks knowingly. He is cleverer, just as his master is better looking, and the audience can look forward to a battle of brains against brawn. The only uncertainty in our story concerns the courtesan, and whether she turns out to be free born. Similarity of the eyebrows suggests that the placid maiden might yet be the proper match. The question refers us back to the central problematic of the mosaic: whether it is possible to tame the tiger of sexual passion.

Each of these Pompeian mosaics is constructed as a system of oppositions, just as Pollux's catalogue is constructed. By following a structural path, and seeking out differences rather than identities, we can rapidly establish a set of meanings. We must keep this principle in mind as we attempt to establish a semantics of the comic mask.

PHYSIOGNOMICS

The art of the mask-maker differs from that of the portraitist for reasons which go beyond the practical exigencies of performance. New Comedy, like Aristotelian tragedy, must demonstrate universal truth – which is to say, what a certain type of person would necessarily do in a given situation. The roots of the mask-maker's art plainly lie in the Aristotelian science of physiognomy – and here Brea is right to insist that the masks must be linked to a philosophical school of thought 'according to which the external features of an individual can reveal, besides his state of mind, the innermost aspects of his temperament'.[31] When Gould and Lewis dismiss 'the supposed relevance to the masks of the pseudo-Aristotelian

Physiognomica',[32] they close their eyes to a complex intellectual system which provides a semantic key to the system of masks in New Comedy.

The pseudo-Aristotelian *Physiognomics* conflates two separate treatises from the Aristotelian school. The first treatise identifies three established physiognomic methodologies. First is the zoological method which observes the different temperaments characteristic of different animals, and supposes that similar physical features in humans correlate likewise with temperaments. Aristotle's *History of Animals* is the seminal text for this method. Aristotle distinguished the noble and brave *êthos* of the lion from that of the boar, deer, hare, etc.[33] He analysed parts of the face in animals in order to show what dispositions they represent: a bulging forehead indicates quick temper, a broad forehead excitability, a small one fickleness, and a large one sluggishness.[34] Second is the ethnographic method which interprets the human physique as a response to climate. People from hot or cold, wet or dry climates display appropriate characteristics. This kind of thinking is rooted in Hippocratic medicine, exemplified in the treatise *Airs, Waters, Places* of about 400 BC. The third or 'ethical' method consists in analysing different types of *êthos* – a disposition towards anger, sexual desire, etc. – and finding empirically the physical traits which correspond. This is substantially the method followed in the first pseudo-Aristotelian treatise. Again, we see a method that is rooted in Aristotelian theory. The analysis of the emotions was undertaken systematically in the *Rhetoric*, the analysis of desirable and undesirable types of *êthos* was undertaken in the *Nicomachean Ethics*, and Theophrastos popularized the study of dispositions in his *Characters*. Where the first author of the *Physiognomics* diverges from the path mapped out by Aristotle is in his failure to work in an orderly way in terms of contrary states. The second author of the *Physiognomics* is particularly interested in correlations with animals, but is equally unsystematic in the way he orders his many sets of contrasting qualities. Other physiognomic methods were plainly also available in Menander's day. Loxus in the early fourth century argued that the soul was to be located in the blood and erected a body of physiognomic theory upon an analysis of the quantity and fluidity of the blood.[35]

Physiognomic theory deals not just with the face but with the whole body, and we shall see in later chapters how it relates to the voice and posture which the actor assumes in accordance with the mask. It is nevertheless a consistent assumption that the face is the most revealing area. As the second author of the *Physiognomics* concludes:

The most favourable area for examination is the area round the eyes, the brow, the head and the face; second is round the chest and shoulders; then the legs and feet.

Least favourable are the parts round the belly. In general, the parts which supply the clearest signs are those which are most used also to display a thought process.[36]

Within the facial area, it is the eyes which above all demand examination.[37]

The logical basis for a semiotics of the face receives close attention in the treatises. It is assumed that emotion is manifested according to processes which are not culturally conditioned, but are natural and biological. Body and soul are part of a single physiological whole, and no repressed, unconscious, or divine presence lurks behind a false facial façade. The second author of the *Physiognomics* sets out the general principle clearly:

When the disposition of the *psychê* changes, it changes also the form of the body; and conversely when the form of the body changes, it changes the character of the *psychê*.[38]

In the light of this theory, we must re-examine Arnott's assumption that the masks enabled the audience 'to predict the total personality of a character on his first entrance', and that the plays somehow 'refine the grossness of the conventional traits'. Brea, because of his rigid commitment to Pollux, echoes the idea that a character's temperament is revealed 'from his first appearance on stage'.[39] Yet, just as there is a dialectic between body and *psychê* in physiognomic theory, so there must be a dialectic between word and mask in Menander's theatre. The masks are capable of a bewildering complex of variants, and the isolable features of a given mask can only make sense to an audience in relation to other masks which they transform. The multiple features of the mask can only acquire coherence in the light of the action of the play, while the choices made in the play acquire coherence in the light of the character typology proposed by the mask.

Aristotle himself analysed the logical premise for physiognomy in his *Prior Analytics*:

Physiognomy is possible if one grants that body and *psychê* change together on the basis of natural emotions ... anger and desire being examples of 'natural' impulses. If this is granted, and that there is one sign for one affect, and that we can identify the particular affect of each species with the sign, then we can practise physiognomy.[40]

In practice, as Aristotle goes on to show, this is very difficult. If the lion is brave, one has to define which of the lion's many physical traits is reproduced in all other brave animals and therefore denotes bravery. In face of such problems, Aristotle in the *Rhetoric* develops a different concept of the sign as something which can connote rather than denote. The *tekmêrion* is described as a 'necessary' sign: if a woman, for example, has milk, this is a 'necessary' sign that she has a child. A *sêmion* is a 'probable' sign: if for example a man breathes hard, this is a 'probable' sign that he has a fever, but other explanations are possible.[41] When we analyse the semiotics of the mask, we are always analysing *sêmeia*, 'probable' or connotative signs susceptible of other explanations.

To decode the signs contained in the mask was not, then, a mechanical exercise. Menander in *The Sikyonian* presents to the audience two contrasting young men. Moschion ('bull-calf') is 'pale-skinned' (line 200), Stratophanes ('soldier-like') is 'manly' (line 215). Pale/dark corresponds with female/male in the colour code of the masks. Pallor is the result of coldness, lack of heat – but in Moschion's case this may be due to his youth and life reared in the shade, or it may be due to a physiological state of melancholia, yielding an unstable, sexually excitable personality.[42] Stratophanes may be darker because of a naturally sanguine temperament, or because as a mercenary he has long led an outdoor life. The spectator's hermeneutic reading of the mask can only be completed in the context of the stage action, which may supply answers to these uncertainties.

The masks of Moschion and Stratophanes would of course contain much more information besides complexion. Hair-styles no doubt provided another contrast. In Pollux, the identifying feature of a soldier's mask is its 'wavy hair', which is to say hair that moves about as the actor moves, suggesting a wild and unrestrained element in the soldier's temperament. There was probably, therefore, a contrast between the wilder hair of Stratophanes and the well-groomed hair of Moschion. Other differences would be more subtle. Let us pursue, for the sake of example, the question of how the spectator might read another trait, the eyebrows, moulded and painted a dark colour in order to be abundantly visible. Physiognomic theory appears to offer some easy correlations. One treatise from the Aristotelian school tells us that 'people with arched eyebrows are rascals, as in the masks of old men in comedy'.[43] Aristotle himself cites the following signs:[44]

straight eyebrow = soft *êthos*
curved to the nose = harshness
curved to the temple = mockery
drawn downwards = spitefulness

The second author of the *Physiognomics* adds:[45]

pulled down to nose, up to temple = piglike simplicity
conjoined = hard to please

We might add two more observations from Pollux:[46]

raised = supercilious
drawn together = thoughtful.

These signs, each denoting a single trait, sound as if they should be clear
to read, but in practice it is hard to isolate them in most masks, since the
shape of the eyebrow is related to the shape of the forehead, or the shape
of the eyes. In a given mask, it may be the eyes, or the forehead, or the
bridge between the eyes that is the most striking feature. It is not possible
for the spectator to decipher the mask in a strictly mechanical fashion, on
the lines of: eyebrows $= x$, forehead $= y$, complexion $= z$, therefore
personality $= (x + y + z) \div 3$. In practice spectators can only perceive
meaning through perceiving contrasts or opposites. They can contrast
striking features against a normative, intermediate or idealized face, and
they can register more subtle features when those features are inverted in
an otherwise similar mask. While the parasite Theron in *The Sikyonian*
probably displays strikingly deviant features, the features of Stratophanes and Moschion are probably subtle. One can imagine a contrast
emerging between two types of over-emotional disposition: Stratophanes, who is disposed to weep, and in need of rallying (brows pulled
towards the tear duct), and Moschion, who is excitable and impulsive
(brows drawn up). The eyebrows can help the spectator perceive two
different ways in which two young men cope with misfortune.

   The play probably effects similar pairings within the other role genera.
Of the two fathers, one has raised brows (line 160), which are taken by a
democrat to connote oligarchic arrogance; the other has a snub nose (line
352), which helps to establish him as man of no pretensions. The pseudo-
virgin mask of the play, with its 'fine eyes' and pure 'white face' (line 399),
must be contrasted with the mask of the courtesan whom the parasite
seeks to marry. The two slaves must likewise be contrasted: the military
slave has a mask that can seem to 'glower' (line 124), and he must
presumably look younger than the domestic slave who has protected the
heroine through years of captivity. This neat sequence of four pairs,
similar to that which we examined in the mosaic, is complemented by
another old man who delivers the paratragic messenger speech, and by
the anomalous figure of the parasite.

   We can approach pictorial representations of scenes in the same way, searching for distinctions. We can, for instance, look at the two old men in the Naples relief (plate 3),[47] and compare their reactions to the youth's drunkenness. One of the old men restrains the other. The one being restrained is marked as aggressive in temperament by the fall of his beard, the sharper corners to his mouth, larger eyes, and a thick asymmetrical eyebrow. The one who exercises restraint has a wider, more rounded mouth, and a well-tended beard. His raised eyebrow is turned away from the audience, suggesting that a less equable mood will apear at another time. We do not know from what play this scene is taken, but we can turn for comparison to Menander's *The Girl from Samos*, where two old men display contrasting reactions to youthful intemperance. Demeas, described by Nikeratos as 'sweet-tempered' (*hêdus* – line 412), is comic through the way he constantly represses his own anger, while Nikeratos, described by Demeas as 'rough-tempered' (*trachys* – line 550), is comic through the speed with which his anger develops. The temperaments of the two old men, represented through their masks, interact with situation in order that the audience may enjoy the spectacle of an equable man compelled to be angry, an irascible man compelled to be calm.[48]

MASK NAMES

The mask typology used by Menander and his contemporaries is implicit in the system of names which we find in the texts. The hypothesis that each role name in Menander correlates with a fixed mask type was proposed and argued by T. W. MacCary in a sequence of articles in 1969–72,[49] and the substance of MacCary's arguments has been rejected in a recent and careful re-examination of the evidence by P. G. McC. Brown. I shall re-examine the evidence myself in order to demonstrate that MacCary's hypothesis is in essence sound.

Brown is concerned to argue for the primacy of the literary text:

I shall argue that, as far as the evidence of Menander goes, masks and names normally conveyed very little. A character's external appearance (his costume and equipment as well as his mask) told the audience his age, sex, status and (sometimes) profession: and certain stock characters were thus instantly recognizable... As to names, the names of characters in New Comedy were subject to certain artificial conventions; but these too were of limited scope.

This negative conclusion has its positive side. For, if I am right, the texts which we have got provide us with the essential clues for understanding the plays. We do not need to know exactly what sort of mask was worn by each character: and we do not need to know much about what the audience would have expected when they saw a particular mask or heard a particular name.[50]

Brown's conclusion is clearly 'positive' for literary critics who wish to
view the written text as a self-contained system; it is a negative conclusion
for those like myself who prefer to understand a play as a synthesis of
inter-related verbal and visual messages. Theatrical conventions are by
definition 'artificial'. If we accept Barthes's axiom that theatricality is 'a
density of signs', then we should not accept a hypothesis which allows
an apparent signifier to carry no signified. The system of names found in
Menander's texts has a logic that we must seek to uncover.

Brown concedes that although a male name like Sostratos might in
Athenian life belong to a slave, a young citizen or an old citizen, in
comedy a given name normally belongs to only one of these categories.
On the face of it, there is an obvious correlation between the division of
masks into four or five genera, and the distribution of names. Brown cites,
however, two names attributable to old and to young men in different
comedies, and presents these as firm evidence against the correlation of
names and masks. In *The Girl from Samos* Nikeratos is an old man, but in
a papyrus fragment from the work of a dramatist later than Menander,
Nikeratos is presumed to be a young man. This presumption rests upon
the premise that a young man could not have an old man for his 'friend' –
which in Greek social life he plainly could.[51] Brown's second and more
compelling example is 'Chairestratos', a name which appears at least
three times in Menander. In *The Arbitration* he is a householder and
landowner, interested in a prostitute but not in marriage. In *The Shield* he
is the father of a daughter who, however, need not be more than a child. In
The Eunuch, he is the elder brother (renamed Phaedria in Terence's
adaptation) who consorts with a prostitute in preference to marriage.[52]
We meet the name again when Cicero remembers 'Chairestratos' as the
elder brother in a Roman adaptation of Menander's *The Changeling*[53] –
and it is Cicero's sense of plausibility that is significant here. I conclude
from these examples that the mask of Chairestratos belongs to a man who
is approaching his prime, and has passed the age at which a young man
normally takes a wife. Pollux assures us that the masks of young men
established differences of age. Chairestratos should be in his late thirties,
perhaps forty. Menander uses the mask of Chairestratos for clear artistic
purposes. In *The Arbitration*, he contrasts a man who has opted for
marriage and regrets his decision with Chairestratos, who has elected to
be single. In the other three examples, Chairestratos is one of a pair of
brothers, and the audience needs to know which brother is the older. In
The Eunuch it falls to the younger brother – not Chairestratos – to be the
one who marries and perpetuates the family line.[54] In *The Shield*,

Chairestratos is the younger brother of Smikrines the miser. Since
Menander's concern is to isolate the grotesque figure of an old man set
upon marrying a girl, he makes Smikrines the only wearer of an 'old man'
mask, and gives the oldest available 'young man' mask to his brother.[55]

There is no evidence, therefore, to refute the general rule that the
distribution of mask names correlates with the four or five genera of
masks. Since this rule holds good, let us proceed to examine the division
of genera into species. Brown accepts that two names do seem to correlate
with a specific mask type. The name 'Gorgias' is given to a young rustic or
'boor' in three of Menander's plays, while the name 'Smikrines' belongs
in three examples to a miser.[56] Amongst the female names, which Brown
and MacCary do not analyse, we find that Myrrhine (myrtle) at least four
times belongs to a free-born mother;[57] Chrysis (golden) is twice used for a
mature good-hearted courtesan – and the name suggests the 'golden
courtesan of Pollux;[58] Habrotonon (wormwood) is twice used for a slave
prostitute;[59] Sophrone is twice a nurse;[60] Doris (Dorian) is at least twice a
maidservant (though only one of our texts is definitely by Menander).[61]
In these instances, the correlation of mask and name is clear.

Secondary sources provide some further evidence. When Lucian
writes of the 'risible masks of Daoi, Tibeioi and cooks', we must infer that
he has in mind specific species of slave mask associated respectively with
Daos, Tibeios, and a cook.[62] When a schoolboy, having won a prize for a
recitation, dedicates a mask or image of 'Chares, old man in Comedy', or
when a victorious Rhodian actor dedicates his mask of 'Pamphilos the
lover',[63] we should assume that the features of the mask are linked in
recognizable ways to the specific name used.

MacCary places much emphasis upon a late text by Choricius, in which
an apologist for acting argues:

Is it really the case that, of the masks (*prosôpa*) created by Menander, 'Moschion'
has taught us to rape virgins? 'Chairestratos' to fall in love with harp-girls? that
'Knemon' has made us cantankerous? and 'Smikrines' has turned us into misers –
Smikrines who is afraid that smoke may have stolen something from inside his
house and made his getaway?[64]

Brown will not countenance this text as evidence, since on the one hand
Knemon appears – so far as we know – only in *Old Cantankerous*, while
Moschion appears in many plays, and neither consistently rapes virgins,
nor is unique in doing so sometimes. These cavils miss the point of the
quotation. Choricius refers to antisocial traits typical of a given mask. He
goes on to specify that Knemon represents misanthropy, Chairestratos
the love of harp-girls, Smikrines the love of money and Moschion

debauchery (*moicheia*). Although Smikrines is a miser in several plays, the quotation refers us to one in particular – probably *Faithless*[65] – where miserliness is the dominant trait. The mask of Smikrines does not create a money-hoarder so much as a man of the type who tends to hoard money. It seems to be given to the obnoxious oligarch in *The Sikyonian*,[66] whose greed is implicit rather than explicit. When Chairestratos falls in love with a harp-girl in *The Arbitration*, this can be seen as a typical failing for an older young man. Moschion does not always rape virgins, but debauchery of this kind is typical of his more impulsive and adolescent temperament. Thinking in fours, as so often in Greek thought, Choricius juxtaposes the sexual failings of two young men – one older than average, one younger – and then contrasts these vices with the antisocial tendencies of another duo, the old misanthropist and the old miser. It is to be noted that the same pair, Knemon and Smikrines, are taken also by the emperor Julian to represent archetypal old men, and in the case of Smikrines it is not the text but the character's ill-kempt visual appearance that is alluded to.[67]

The general principles regarding names in New Comedy are clearly set out by Donatus in his commentary on Terence:

The names of characters, in comedy, need to have a connection and an etymology. It is pointless for a comic writer, when he works out the details of his plot, to make either the name of the mask incongruous, or its status divergent from the name. Thus Parmeno is a faithful servant, Syrus and Geta unfaithful, Thraso and Polemon are soldiers, Pamphilus a youth, Myrrhina a matron, and Storax (from his smell) or Scirtus (from his acting and gesture) are slave-boys, and so forth. In these matters, when a name is distinguished from an opposite, the ultimate offence in a writer is to use that direct opposite – the exception being when a writer humorously employs such a name in 'antiphrasis': e.g. the banker in Plautus (*The Haunted House* line 568) who is called Misargyrides (money-hater).[68]

Etymology points to the nature of the mask. Names are suggestive rather than allegorical, and retain a veneer of social plausibility. The ethnic names of the unfaithful slaves, the Syrian and the Gete, distinguish them from Parmeno – 'Stand-by'. The military names of Thraso (reckless) and Polemon (warrior) distinguish them from Pamphilus (complete lover). Myrrhine's name relates to the fragrance of myrtle: not an aphrodisiac like wormwood, but a fragrant plant used for garlands in the wedding ceremony.[69] Storax is a resin used in incense, while Scirtus means 'frisky'. We can trace similar etymological links in the four mask names cited by Choricius. Smikrines (*smikros* = small) suggests small-mindedness; Knemon (*knêmê* = tibia) suggests the lower leg visible in a farmer; Chairestratos (*chairein* = to delight in) suggests a pleasure lover; and Moschion (*moschion* = young shoot, or little calf) suggests the age and sexuality of the mask, with an echo of *moicheia* (adultery, debauchery). Naming conventions, for Donatus, are significant and rule-bound, they help establish complex sets of oppositions used to construct meaning, and it is essential to decipher their logic.

An apparent peculiarity in Menander's system of names is the fact that some are common, some are rare. According to Brown's count, over half the names found in our remains of Greek New Comedy are found in one play only. Other names occur frequently. Amongst the old men, Demeas is found in four or five plays of Menander, and in two anonymous papyri.[70] Laches is found in at least five plays by Menander, and in three papyri.[71] Demeas also appears in a play by Alexis, Laches in a play by Krobylos.[72] In order to make sense of this apparent imbalance, we need to return to the labours of the cataloguer in Pollux. For the cataloguer, certain masks are easily identifiable, and can be given a familiar name – the Cicada, the 'little torch', and so on; some are identified as principal masks; others are classified with difficulty because of minor variations. Names tell the same story. Some names belong to principal types which crop up in play after play; some are unique, and belong to variants created for a single play; some belong to types with idiosyncratic traits recognizable at a glance. Demeas and Laches can be associated with normative types in Pollux's catalogue, while Smikrines and Knemon can be associated with masks that have idiosyncratic features, masks such as those which the cataloguer links to the names of Hermon and Lycomedes.

Brown rejects MacCary's theory that the mask allowed the dramatist to economize on explanation, for he does not himself feel deprived of information as he reads the text. He rejects also the theory of Webster and Arnott that Menander develops character by playing against the expect-ations set up by the mask, for then a character's mask would be 'a *misleading* guide to his personality' and the real personality is again to be discerned in the text.[73] These theories are indeed all unsatisfactory because they fail to take account of the dialectical relationship between mask and text, between verbal and visual signals. As I argued in chapter I, the dialectic of mask and text correlates with the dialectic of *êthos* and *pathos*. While the mask conveys a fixed disposition, the words convey a transient state of thought and feeling. Though a man's behaviour is shaped by his *êthos*, he has also the free will to change himself and his pattern of behaviour. This dialectic, so subtle in its ability to tease out problems of free will and moral choice, was a unique asset of the theatrical medium.

With the exception of Gorgias and Smikrines, Brown finds that he cannot relate any stock name to any distinct personality. He cannot find any traits to typify, for instance, the slave Daos, who appears in nine plays of Menander as well as in six papyri. He gives no weight to MacCary's pertinent observation that Daos is everywhere a schemer.[74] It is in an Oxyrrhyncus papyrus, not by Menander, that Daos' role as the archetypal schemer perhaps emerges most clearly, for here the dialectic of text and mask is apparently less subtle. Daos asserts that cheating a master in the matter of a music-girl is no job for a newly purchased slave, but demands intellect.[75] I would add to MacCary's formulation the rider that Daos is also a natural victim or fall guy. His mask, I believe, served to fix these two dominant traits. The typical slave traits of raised brows, furrowed forehead, and grinning mouth eloquently express mischief when the face is raised and a grimace of pain when the mask is lowered. Alternative slave traits which seem to be lacking in Daos' mask would include greed, stoicism in adversity, malice, and physical aggression. The two traits which I have isolated can be tabulated, as far as the surviving fragments allow.

Play	Daos as schemer	Daos as victim
Old Cantankerous	anticipates downfall of Sostratos	reprimanded by Gorgias, terrified of Knemon
The Arbitration	manoeuvres to retain birth tokens	vanquished by Syrus
The Rape of the Locks	attracts heroine to Moschion's house, guides Moschion's conduct	threatened and accused of lies by Moschion
The Shield	plans fake death of Chairestratos	grieves for Kleostratos, feigns grief for Chair., insulted by waiter
The Farmer	manages to be first with the news	?
The Hero	?	suffers for love of girl
The Girl from Perinthos	declares how easy it is to cheat master	threatened with burning on altar

The Eunuch	proposes hero's disguise as a eunuch	terrified of old master
Pap. Oxy. 11	plans a risky scheme to rescue young master	?
Pap. Hibeh 5	expounds plan to help Strobilos' master	?
Pap. Lund 4[76]	?	threatened with branding

Daos' two traits of mischievous scheming and anguish are not in fact completely disconnected for, whatever his plight, Daos never loses his sense of humour, his ability to present himself as a comic figure. A short extract from *The Girl from Perinthos* – which I quote in Norma Miller's translation – will illustrate how the two elements combine. Daos has taken refuge on the stage altar, and a pyre is being set up around him . . .

LACHES   Now, Daos, show us your low cunning. Think up some trick to get out of my clutches!
DAOS   Trick? *Me?*
LACHES   You, Daos. For 'deceiving an easy-going and empty-headed master is a piece of cake!'
DAOS   Oh, help!
LACHES   And if the '*crème de la crème* of intelligence . . .' (DAOS *winces*)
SOSIAS   That registered, did it?
DAOS   (*reproachfully*) This is not like you, sir.[77]

Lines spoken by Daos-the-schemer are quoted back to Daos-the-victim by his old master. Daos' terror is only momentary, and he attempts to turn the situation round by reproaching his master. The actor playing Daos lowers his mask to express dismay on '"*crème de la crème* of intelligence"' and raises his mask in mischief to try a new ploy with 'This is not like you, sir.' The audience knows from Laches' mask whether this behaviour is in fact characteristic of Laches.

We should be clear about what the mask does not establish. It tells us nothing of Daos' status, beyond the fact that he is a foreign slave. He may be a shepherd, farm labourer, urban domestic, or pedagogue, depending on the play. It tells us nothing about the plot, or about the importance of the role in a given play. It tells us little about the moral judgements that the audience should form. Daos in *The Shield* is a paragon of altruistic loyalty, in *The Arbitration* he is exclusively self-interested. Brown's failure to find a 'personality' for Daos is in large part the consequence of imposing a modern psychological discourse upon Greek material. If we are to understand the nature of 'personality' in Menander's theatre, then it is to a Greek, and specifically to an Aristotelian discourse that we must turn.

I have suggested that the dialectic of *êthos* and *pathos* is the key to understanding the relationship of mask and text. This is a useful generalization, but one that now needs qualification. In the *Poetics*, Aristotle defines dramatic character as that which is revealed through choice. Moral choice, in the *Ethics*, springs from the interaction of two human functions, reason and desire.[78] Exploring this dichotomy in different terms, Aristotle states that choice cannot exist without, on the one hand, 'thought' (*dianoia*), and on the other hand a moral disposition (*hexis êthikê*).[79] A person's moral disposition stems from habits formed, specifically upon what he or she has been brought up to find pleasurable or painful. Virtue, for Aristotle, is related to a person's acquired or chosen disposition, as distinct from his or her innate capacities, or from passing emotions.[80] In accordance with his binary methodology, Aristotle identifies two types of virtue: intellectual virtue (*dianoetikê*), located in a thought process, and virtues of character (*êthikê*), acquired through habit.[81] Supreme virtue is then conceived as a dialectical unity of these two. It is neither mere reason, as Socrates argued, nor is it mere desire, developed in conformity with reason (*kata logon*) as some sophists argued; it is desire united with reason (*meta logon*).[82]

This complex analysis of the *psychê* has implications for the constructing of character in the theatre. *Logos* means both 'reason' and 'language'. In the scene which I have quoted from *The Girl from Perinthos*, the language expresses a reasoning process. An intellectual duel is afoot between Laches and Daos. Although this reasoning process can be grasped from a reading of the written text, it is only through hearing how actors deliver the text that one can form a firm opinion about the emotions of the moment. Without the contribution of the actor, one cannot tell whether the apparent anger of Laches, glee of Sosias, or fear of Daos are deeply felt, or feigned to create an effect. We need to see the masks in order to form a moral judgement, in order to gauge whether Laches' anger and Daos' fear are triggered easily, or are the result of great provocation. The masks allow us to judge whether the characters' actions are the result of rational thought processes or of preformed desires, desires to experience certain types of pleasure, or to avoid certain types of pain. The central moral questions presented by the scene – whether Daos deserves to burn, whether Laches should relent, or Daos apologize – can only be resolved when, in the course of the action of the play, we see character, in relation to thought and emotion, emerging in an act of moral choice. Without the masks, Menander's text may be complete, but part of his play will be missing.

The mask of Daos was so popular because it was polyvalent, it could be interpreted in a variety of ways. It revealed what the slave found pleasurable and painful. It manifested a disposition towards mirth, affection, thought, anguish, and no disposition towards anger, malice, gloom. It did not permit the audience to form an instant moral evaluation. We have to keep reminding ourselves that the Greek concept of *êthos* does not correspond with our 'character' or 'total personality'. Our culture thinks in terms of 'individuals' who are by definition each unique, and we instinctively identify and admire that which is unique in a 'character' whom we see on stage. The Hellenistic spectator instinctively identified that which was typical. In Athens a boy learned from birth that he belonged first and foremost to a group – be that group family, deme, clan, tribe, fellow ephebes, fellow citizens, fellow dancers in a chorus, members of a mass jury, oarsmen in a trireme, or whatever. The individual was the point where a series of corporate identities intersected. Psychology has no independent existence in Aristotelian thinking, but is an aspect of ethics (the study of *êthos* or character), which is in turn an aspect of politics, for ethics and politics are both concerned with defining the good life. The good of the *polis*, in Aristotelian thinking, necessarily has precedence over the good of the individual citizen.[83] Virtue is not seen as an essence but as a means to an end, not a state but an activity of the mind.[84] We shall study the masks in vain if we seek to find in them an essential character, transcendental moral qualities, a unique personality. We must seek instead for a complex of typical traits.

Modern theatre is obsessed with motivation. A motivation for an action might be described as an act of will precipitating that action. There has been much debate as to whether there is a classical concept of the will. Vernant described the will as 'the person seen as an agent, the self seen as the source of actions for which it is held responsible before others'.[85] Greek thought lacks a vocabulary to define the self/individual/ person/subject whom we regard without question as the source of moral action. In Aristotelian thinking, an act of will cannot be separated from the dialectic between a reasoning process and a pre-existing disposition. An 'ethical' choice, as we have seen, relates not to a single existential act of will, but to an accumulated selection of habits.

Menander's theatre of masks makes sense within the context of Greek moral debate because the mask crystallizes a disposition, while language crystallizes thought. In modern theatre, in order to identify acts of free will, we have to look behind the text to a subtext, behind the actor's face to a motive. In consequence, when we read today a text of Menander, we tend to perceive, by virtue of cultural conditioning, that which makes a character unique. We reconstruct motives and acts of free will. A fixed disposition is something we are trained to dismiss, or consider less significant than 'individual' qualities. This different psychological orientation does much to explain why modern scholarship has found such difficulty in reconciling Menander's texts with a system of masks.

Aristotle had a clear grasp of the way comedy was developing in his time:

Poetry speaks in generalities, history in specifics. A 'generality' means that this kind of person says or does this kind of thing, probably or necessarily: which is what poetry aims at in the names that it bestows. Specifics are what Alcibiades did, or what happened to him. In comedy, the thing has now been made plain. They construct a plot out of probabilities, and then attach the names that happen to fit (*tychônta*) – unlike the comic satirists who write about specific people.[86]

Tychônta is difficult to render, implying the agency of both chance and destiny in hitting the mark. The logic of the passage makes it clear that the naming conventions of this emergent post-Aristophanic comedy both were and were not arbitrary. Names were part of a coherent system of signs, and although the initial selection of the corpus owed much to chance, their clear purpose was to signify 'generality', typical traits. Names and masks served to locate figures on the comic stage not as individuals but as representative members of society.

CHAPTER 4

Masks east and west: contrasts and comparisons

I have suggested that the mask is at the centre of the New Comedy tradition. All the other semiotic systems constituting the performance of New Comedy – gesture, voice, costume, and so on – are structured in a way that links them directly to the system of masks. We saw in the last chapter how the mask was perceived by audiences of New Comedy not as a thing in itself but as part of a system of differences. In this chapter I shall lay the Hellenistic system of comic masks alongside other theatrical masking traditions. This comparative exercise will demonstrate (a) that the theories which I have advanced regarding the primacy of the mask and the conventions governing its use are inherently *plausible*, given the evidence offered by more accessible cultures; and (b) that the use which the Hellenistic theatre made of the mask was in various ways unique and culturally specific. I shall therefore be looking both for similarities and for differences. We shall begin with the Noh tradition of Japan, which is of particular interest because it is a living form. We will then turn to two areas within the western performance tradition which owe a profound debt to the principles of Hellenistic theatre.

NOH THEATRE

TAXONOMY

The catalogue in Pollux should be seen as a serious but in no way definitive attempt to assemble into a logical shape raw data drawn from observed theatrical practice. We may assume that Pollux's catalogue differed in points of detail from other taxonomies, such as that of Aristophanes of Byzantium. Aristophanes in his book on masks seems to have regarded 'cook' and 'slave' as separate genera, where Pollux regards 'cook' as a species of the genus slave.[1] Modern attempts to construct taxonomies of Noh masks encounter similar problems. All scholars and practitioners agree that a system exists, with types and subtypes, but none agree on the precise details, and the point where a variant becomes a new type. There is no definitive body of data, since different masters have different collections of masks which can never be laid side by side. There is, nevertheless, a shared sense of structure, for a typology of masks governs the classic structure of a Noh performance. Plays written for different types of *shite* (masked protagonist) follow each other in the prescribed order of divine plays, warrior plays, women plays, present-life or miscellaneous plays, and demon plays. While this order of performance creates a need for contrast and balance, it does not in itself structure a system of masks, for a given mask may be used in plays of more than one genre.[2] In many plays the *shite* will change masks, and in some there may be a masked supporting actor (*shite-tsure*), in addition to the unmasked *waki* or regular supporting actor. The *shite*, moreover, will sometimes play unmasked, though with expressionless face, when playing an 'ordinary' person in some present-life plays.

The classic fifteenth-century writings of Zeami offer no clear guidance on the subject of mask types. Zeami in one treatise distinguishes nine role types, but includes Chinese roles and Buddhist priests, which later taxonomies see as minor subtypes.[3] In another treatise on dramatic construction, he isolates old men, women, and warriors as the three principal types, subsuming such groups as demons and lunatics.[4] Today, modern authorities on the Noh[5] agree on the existence of four principal types:

> *Jo* (old man)
> *Onna* (woman)
> *Otoko* (man)
> *Kijin* (demon, god)

but they have difficulty in accommodating a miscellany of masks which do not fit into these categories. The category of old women fits uneasily alongside the much larger group of young women. The *sho-jo* mask of a water-sprite may be placed within a 'boy' category distinguished from the *otoko* category, or it may be placed in the 'demon' category. *Tenjin*, as a god who was once human, may be placed within a 'spirit' category as distinct from a 'god' category. The *aku-jo* (angry old man) may be regarded as human or demonic in different plays. As in the Hellenistic theatre, the outlines of the system of masks are clear, but the details are not.

The Japanese system interestingly mirrors the Hellenistic tetrad of old man, young man, woman, and slave, substituting a divine figure for the Greek male slave. This prompts the reflection that the Greek slave mask has certain affinities with the demonic satyr mask. It represents the less than fully human, and is scarcely more anthropomorphic than a Japanese demon mask. This parallel should not obscure obvious differences. While the Hellenistic system works synchronically through the juxtaposition of one mask with another, the Japanese works diachronically through the replacement of one mask by another. Characteristically, the *shite* will exchange a human mask for a demonic mask in the second part of the play.

While the Noh theatre serves to articulate differences between the human and the spiritual, the Hellenistic theatre is concerned with social relations on an exclusively human plane. In both cases, masks constitute a system of distinctions. The boundaries between god and human on the one hand, servile and free on the other, are clarified by a system of masks. Specific plays explore the tension between these opposites.

The Noh tradition helps to illuminate the system of mask names in Menander. Some Noh masks are popular types that can be used in many plays, while others are specific to a single play. Young-girl masks, for instance, like the *Ko-omote* or the *Zo-onna*, can be used in many plays, while the warrior mask of the *Kageyiko* is worn only by the *shite* in the play of that name.[6] The names given to masks reflect this diversity of use. Some are descriptive. *Ko-omote*, for instance, meaning 'small-face', refers to the closeness of eyes, nose, and mouth in a mask of a young girl. *Zo-onna* (Zoami's woman) refers to the actor Zoami who first wore the mask. Another young woman's mask, the *Magojiro*, is named after the sixteenth-century mask-maker who created the style, allegedly as a portrait of his dead wife. Others, like *Kageyiko*, are named after characters in specific plays. Subtypes exist for more popular masks, such as two variants on the serene *Zo-onna* mask favoured by the Hosho school: *Naki-zo* (weeping *Zo-onna*) used for the classic *Zo-onna* roles, and *Fushiki-zo* (wood-knot *Zo-onna*) used for lower-status roles.[7] With this diversity in mind, we can look with fresh understanding at the struggles of the cataloguer in Pollux to incorporate masks like *Maison* (an actor's name[8]) and *Hermon* (an actor's or perhaps a mask-maker's name[9]) within a lexicon of predominantly descriptive names. We can sympathize with the cataloguer's uncertainty whether or not to record variants on Hermon's mask, or on the two parasite masks. Theatre in Greece, as in Japan, was never planned, it evolved. While its detail owes much to the chance contribution of individuals, the underlying system contains a logic which is also the logic of the culture to which the theatre belongs.

While Noh masks are made of wood, as were Greek cultic masks used in the worship of Artemis, Dionysiac masks were made of perishable linen and glue.[10] Victorious Greek actors had no hesitation in dedicating their masks to a god[11] because they knew that these masks would in due course need to be replaced. While Noh theatre is concerned with the past, and thus loves masks of great physical antiquity, Hellenistic theatre was concerned with the present, and its masks were ephemeral, like performance itself. Since Greek masks were perishable, we must consider how continuity was maintained. Modern Japanese mask-makers speak of the difficulty of reproducing accurately the features of a particular mask, and, though this is not an ancient technique, they use a series of cut-out templates to check the precision of their work.[12] In the Hellenistic theatre, I have suggested that clay miniatures, reproduced by means of moulds, offered a method of maintaining and transmitting a sophisticated artistic tradition as the actors travelled far afield.

We need to distinguish between the conditions in which Menander's plays were originally presented in the Theatre of Dionysus in Athens, and the conditions which governed subsequent performances when the plays were taken by itinerant troupes of actors to all parts of the Greek-speaking world. The poet had control over the first production. I commented in the last chapter on the relief which represents Menander, in the act of composition, gazing at the masks for which he is writing. He was in a position to stipulate whether new masks or familiar masks would be used. A touring troupe of actors, moving from one festival to another with a large repertory of scripts, would have to rely upon the stock of masks that they could carry, or that could be provided for them. In the third century it was necessarily the actors, not the poet, who decided which mask to allocate to a given role. With the passage of time, the exact correlation of mask and role conceived by the dramatist necessarily became obscured.

Zeami speaks of the need to select a mask 'with the particular artistry in mind of the actor who wears it', and of the way the choice of mask determines the emotional atmosphere of the play.[13] A modern Noh actor, Kongô Iwao, speaks of the way he chooses a mask five days before the performance. For the play *Sumidagawa* he must choose between two versions of the *Shakumi* (hollowed) mask: although his grandfather preferred the more mature-looking version, which emphasizes the harsh reality of a bereaved mother's madness, Iwao often prefers a lighter and younger-looking mask, created by a different carver, which seems more appropriate to the absurd madness which precedes the mother's certain knowledge that her child is dead. The particular qualities of the actor are all-important. Iwao states that he cannot wear a *Magojiro* mask worn by his father because his face is too thin, and as an actor he lacks the right sensual quality: 'the spirit of the mask and the actor must complement each other'. The choice of mask subsequently governs Iwao's decisions about costume, about posture and movement, and about music. The mask is in this sense the pivotal element upon which all else turns.[14] I would suggest that the experience of actors in Hellenistic Greece was not dissimilar. When Menander wrote his plays for the festival of Dionysus in Athens, he knew which actors would play which parts. He might know, for instance, that the mask of Daos would work well for the actor Diopeithes, while the mask of Demeas would suit Theophilos. When the scripts became the property of actors' guilds, the precise correlation of name and mask necessarily loosened. The actor would be tempted to choose a mask that suited his own particular artistry as an actor, his own interpretation of the play's meaning, and his sense of how to make the play work for a specific audience. We should expect the Hellenistic tradition to be more rigid than the Noh tradition in this respect. The names used in Menander's text would continue to provide a clue to the mask style to be chosen, but would not be seen as constituting a precise and binding instruction.

PERFORMANCE

I argued in the last chapter that the 'Daos' mask changes its emotional connotations depending on the angle at which it is set. This is a universal principle governing masked acting. Lecoq, in response to the question 'what is a good mask?', answers:

It is a mask which changes expression when it moves. If it stays the same when the actor changes posture and situation, it is a dead mask... It must not bear an expression that is distinctly transient. One cannot conceive of a mask that is always laughing, for it would not be able to stay on stage for long, it would only be a passing shadow. To understand the merits of a mask, it is not enough to read the meaning yielded by its formal and ideological propositions. One has to understand its behaviour through the actor's movements which it instigates.[15]

These principles apply to Greek and to Japanese actors as much as to the pupils of Lecoq.

The ability of the mask to change its meaning depending upon whether it is raised or lowered is a starting-point for the Japanese actor's and mask-maker's art. It is a general principle of Noh performance that 'lowered the mask seems sad; raised it seems happy'.[16] An analysis of the *Ko-omote* mask reveals a technique which ensures that:

the Nô mask, moved only the slightest degree, can delicately, almost imperceptibly, express the full range of human feeling: joy, anger, grief, anticipation . . . Thus if the mask is tilted up slightly it takes on a cheery, bright expression, while if it is tilted forward slightly a melancholy expression is produced.[17]

The same move in the *Sanko-jo* (old man of (the mask-maker) Sankobo) mask can be defined as a transition from good-naturedness to physical suffering.[18] From at least the seventeenth century, a sophisticated technical vocabulary has been used to relate the physical and the emotional aspects of mask control. To look up is to 'make the mask shine', to lower the mask is to 'shade' or 'cloud' the face, while to lower it further, as in weeping, is to make the face 'fade'.[19] A similar vocabulary extends to sidewards movements of the mask: to move it quickly from side to side in a moment of intense emotion is to 'cut' the mask; to move it more slowly is to 'use' the mask.[20] Kongô Iwao records how he gazes at length into a mirror in order to train himself to control the angle of his mask, since 'just the slightest shift can change the expression'.[21]

The best Noh masks are described as having an 'intermediate' expression. The Noh actor Kanze Hisao contrasts demon masks which 'have such a clear-cut emotional expression that they can be used for only a short time on the stage' with apparently expressionless female masks which, precisely because of their lack of specific expression, are 'capable of expressing a broad range of emotions and holding the interest of an audience over a long period of stage time'. He concludes that:

in the final analysis, the Nô mask has no intrinsic expressive powers of its own. Rather it is designed in such a way that it melds with all the other elements of presentation on the stage to draw out and excite the rich imaginative powers of the audience.[22]

These are important principles that we must bear in mind when analysing Hellenistic masks. While certain masks – Lycomedes, or the Cicada, for instance – have a clear-cut expression, and might be described in loose modern terminology as 'character masks', the best and most important masks have the potential to create a broad range of emotions once they are integrated with movement and costume. The masks of young men and courtesans in New Comedy have an 'intermediate' quality similar to *Otoko* and *Onna* masks. While old man and slave masks in New Comedy will display sharply contrasting moods as the mask is turned or tilted, the masks of young men and women allow for a more subtly graduated range of emotions. In photographs, terracotta models of these 'intermediate' Greek masks necessarily seem frozen and lifeless, with their gaping mouths, hollow eyes, and lack of bone structure. We have to reconstruct the life that the masks possessed when worn by an actor.

The technique of the Hellenistic mask-maker can be related to that of the sculptor. Sculptors in Menander's day achieved a new sense of movement in time and space. A particular moment was captured – Aphrodite, for instance, surprised in the act of bathing. A portrait caught not just a timeless *êthos* but the *pathos* of a particular moment. There was much interest in illusion. Lysippus no longer tried to capture ideal human proportions as calculated from a real body, but tried to show men 'as they appeared'. By reducing the size of the head and elongating the legs, he countered the massive, square solidity which seemed to result from reconstituting flesh in the medium of marble.[23] This new interest in illusion, movement, and materials had its influence upon mask-making. While a sculptor had to give an immobile mass the suggestion of past and future movements, the mask-maker had to make a fluid form suggest a series of present states. The form of the actor had to be moulded, not out of marble or bronze, but out of hair and fabric. The techniques of portrait sculpture had to be reversed in the theatre, and the Japanese experience can help us to understand the principles involved.

The carver of Noh masks understands that he must keep the eyes unfocussed so that, whilst in a photograph or on a museum wall the mask may seem to have two separate lines of vision and an impersonal expression, in motion in performance the mask will seem to be caught in the act of focussing, and thus to be alive. Likewise a square-cut iris seems round when the mask is moved, whereas a genuinely round iris would create the effect of an unblinking expressionless stare.[24] The Hellenistic theatre demonstrates a similar understanding. The eyes of a tragic mask, we are told, are turned towards the nose in order to create a gaze full of thought.[25] In comedy, asymmetrical and 'squinting' masks, viewed from in front, create an impression of movement and energy within the face when the mask itself is in movement. Such masks necessarily belong to energetic characters. The eyes of young men are often wide open, and stretch further round the side of the mask than they would on a real face, thereby creating the sense of a mobile gaze: when the head moves, the eyes seem to remain fixed on a point. If we look closely at the most impressive example of an apparently idealized young man in Lipari, we see that the left eyebrow and eye are pulled further back, creating a sense of movement, and preventing the face from looking like a deity on a pediment (cf. plate 1A).[26] A similar point can be made about the mouth. Although the mouths of young men seem to be wide open, the upper lip is unnaturally foreshortened to create the sense of a lip that is moving up and down.

As in 'intermediate' Noh masks, there is no defined bone structure around the eyes and jaw of such a youth. The mask-maker's art, as in the Noh, lies not in the creation of projections but in the creation of hollows that will catch the shadow.[27] The actor relies upon the play of light, together with some toning of colour, to create a sense of mobility in the face. The high crown of hair, characteristic of so many Hellenistic masks, creates more shadow, 'clouding' the brow when the mask is tilted forwards. The importance of light cannot be overestimated. While masks in museums tend to be displayed under an even fluorescent light, Greek painters representing actors are always scrupulous in the way they represent the angle of sunlight. Although Greek theatres faced in different directions according to the lie of the hillside, the Theatre of Dionysus at least faced south: the stage, that is to say, faced north, and the audience looked into the direction of the sun.[28] In a north-facing theatre, direct sunlight would have flattened the masks by eliminating all shadow, and glare from the stage would have made watching them more tiring. On the Athenian stage there was always shadow to give the masks depth, and create a play of light to bring the masks to life.

Greek techniques for simulating facial mobility can be illustrated from the mosaic depicting the opening scene of Menander's The Ladies at Luncheon (plate 2). I shall analyse the scene again in my chapter on costume in order to explore the dramatic situation.[29] For the present, we shall simply note the technique. The asymmetrical eyebrows of the old bawd seem to be moving upwards in indignation. As the actor lowers the goblet, the unfocussed squint of the mask directs our thoughts to what the bawd is seeing in her mind. The eye of the girl on the left is plainly visible despite the fact that the face is seen in ninety degrees profile. The alignment of the eye suggests the eye movement of someone trying to escape her situation. The shortened upper lip gives movement to the mouth. The strong profile of the nose, contrasting with the snub nose of the bawd, does not create movement, but reminds us of the girl's identity at birth. The actor in the centre turns his body towards the bawd, but his mask towards the audience. As the actor makes a reasoning gesture, the mask is tilted slightly downwards, expressing seriousness of intent. The face seems to be turning from the bawd's goblet to the hands of the left-hand figure, which are anxiously fingering the tassels of the cloak. While the two 'intermediate' masks are brought to life by the play of shadow upon them, the bawd's more strongly characterized mask seems to be an outgrowth of the hunched body because of the way it is swathed in fabric.

I argued in chapter 2 that the shallowness of the Hellenistic stage platform and its distance from the audience gave the actor a high degree of control over the angle at which he presented his mask to the audience. The fact remains that spectators viewed the actor from a variety of different angles. Keith Johnstone's experiments with masks at the Royal Court helped him to understand the illusion whereby 'we "read" the body, and especially the head–neck relationship, but we experience ourselves as reading the Mask'.[30] A Noh actor, Takabayashi Kôji, describes the same phenomenon in more detail:

After all, people watching from the side see the same play as people watching from the front. The whole body, not just the mask, expresses the emotions read as being in the mask. When one lowers the face (*kumorasu*, 'cloud mask'), one lowers not only the head but the whole upper torso. When such a pattern is meant to express sadness (as opposed to looking into the depths of a river) the chest also caves slightly. Looking up (*terasu*, 'brighten mask') likewise involves a lifting of the upper torso. Therefore one might say that the audience, influenced by the words, melody, rhythms, and body posture, sees the feelings it is experiencing as if they emanated from the mask.[31]

While the Japanese spectators are placed on two sides of the stage (or three in earlier times), the Greek audience viewed the action from a range of vertical levels. In both theatres, all spectators 'see the same play' because whatever their angle of vision they see the same relationship of body, neck, and head. A difference should nevertheless be noted. The Hellenistic actor on his shallow stage can more easily differentiate between frontal and profile presentation of the mask, and for this reason asymmetrical masks are common so that alternative moods can be established through moving the face sideways. In the Japanese theatre, where the spectators all sit at approximately the same height as the stage, a more subtle manipulation of the mask within the vertical plane is possible.

Takabayashi Kôji explains also the technical problem of proportion that arises because the mask projects forward of the actor's own face. This problem is partly overcome when the Noh actor learns to draw his head backward, adding to the effect of the padded costume, which serves to bring the chest forward. The actor learns also not to make over-large gestures, since these would accentuate the shoulders and make the mask appear to jump away from the body.[32] Similar problems had to be overcome in the Hellenistic theatre. An experiment was carried out in Lipari when Luigi Bernabò-Brea commissioned replicas of miniature masks found on the island in order that actors trained in *commedia dell'arte* techniques might mount a production of *The Girl from Samos*.[33] One can see from photographs that the masks envisaged by Brea are larger than those we see in frescoes and mosaics. The effect is to give the actors a comically grotesque appearance, since the regular proportions of the human body are lost. A reviewer commented that the director, 'through the use of these masks was led almost fatally to pull the play towards farce. To be sure, this is one aspect of Menandrean comedy, but here it overwhelmed and crushed all others.'[34] The proportions of Brea's actors are particularly disconcerting if we recall that in Hellenistic sculpture the convention was to make the head smaller than life in order to create an ideal of beauty.

The Hellenistic theatre evolved some solutions to this problem of proportion. First, the ample cloak worn by most characters gave the body extra bulk, and so prevented the head from looking so large. The slave in his scantier costume might be allowed to look ill-proportioned. It was important that the mask should seem contained by the body, rather than isolated from it, and the actors therefore ensured that the focus was always on the torso rather than the extremities. Secondly, where elegance was required, the masks themselves were often made higher by the addition of a high head-dress for women, a crown of hair for men. The optical effect of the crown of hair on a young man's mask is particularly interesting (fig. 2). From in front, the crown conceals the large dome which covers the actor's head. When the mask dips forward slightly, only the top of the dome appears over the crest of the crown, preventing the intrusion of a massive cranium from spoiling the illusion of perfect features. When the head dips forward slightly, the silhouette does not change as much as it would on a normal human head, and the spectator does not register a tilt of the head so much as a change of expression.

The Japanese theatre has a different kind of solution to the problem of perspective. The Noh mask is placed in front of the face, leaving the outline of the actor's natural face visible. The audience thus has a sense of the actual bodily proportion of the actor as well as the proportion of the character represented. Greek masks covered the head rather than simply the face, so the audience was not offered the same double image. The two traditions assume quite different relationships between actor and mask. A vital institution in the Japanese theatre is the mirror room where the actor, having donned his mask with due ritual solemnity, gazes at himself in the

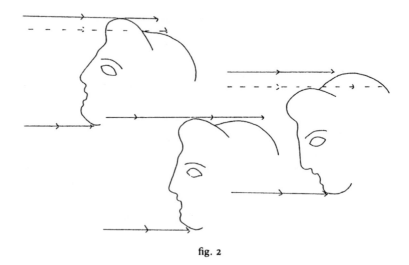

fig. 2

mirror so that mask and actor become as one.[35] In the Hellenistic theatre, we hear of the actor Aesopus staring at his mask *before* putting it on in order to suit his voice and gestures to its appearances.[36] The iconographic tradition seems to confirm that the actor, like the dramatist, regarded the mask as having a life of its own before the actor inhabits it. A mosaic from Pompeii shows a satyr chorus-man, apparently invited to graduate to the position of actor, recoiling in dismay from the tearful heroine's mask which he must wear.[37] A relief in Istanbul shows *Skênê*, the personification of the stage, gazing into the features of a mask held up by Euripides.[38] In such images, the actor's relationship to the mask is one of observation rather than immersion. This emphasis belongs to a theatre where the actor must prepare himself to take not one role but several in the course of a single play. While Japanese spectators see both face and mask and admire the miracle of merging which seems to take place before their eyes, Greek spectators saw only the mask, and admired the way the actor's personality was effaced.

Underlying these differences of convention are differences of philosophy. Kanze Hisao expands upon this Japanese convention whereby a real face frames the theatrical mask:

From the standpoint of realism, it would seem that it would look more natural to have the actor's face covered completely by the mask, and that this would bring the mask to more vivid life, but in fact, just the opposite is the case, for when the whole face is covered, the mask takes on the aspect of a lifeless doll.

Hisao conceives of actor and mask existing in a kind of mutual confrontation:

The Nô mask has the power not only to cover the face of the actor like an ordinary mask, but also to become one with his flesh. At the same time it also has the power to act and react in opposition to the performer. In other words, it must support the inner space of the actor.[39]

This emphasis upon the 'inner space' of the actor connects with the broad Buddhist tradition which gives the inner life of the spirit primacy over the external life of the body. The medieval Noh theorist Zenchiku identified six roots of sensory perception immanent in the mask. Four – eyes, ears, nose, and mouth – are readily visible; the fifth, body, is transmitted to the mask by the actor's body; the sixth, the organ of mind, can only exist once the actor has meditated upon the mask, perceived how it operates, and obtained the appropriate spiritual awakening.[40] The Aristotelian and Stoic traditions admit no such dichotomy between body and spirit. The emphasis is rather upon how mind and body are part of a single organism.

The Greek mask covers the entire face. It does not become one with the actor's face before the audience's eyes, but substitutes for it. The mask is thus a façade, offering no glimpses of a hidden 'inner space', and its meanings are all on the surface. The materialistic philosophy of the Hellenistic world insisted that all reality was available to sensory perception. Mind and body were seen as part of a single organism, and there was no distinct sixth 'organ of mind'. There was of course known to be a *psychê* animating the body just as there was known to be a person animating the mask, but the Hellenistic audience expected to deduce or infer from the evidence the nature of this hidden presence. There could be no question of any perceptible traffic between the material and the spiritual worlds, the kind of traffic that is the essence of Noh theatre. Aesopus was not concerned with attuning his spirit to the hidden 'mind' of the mask implanted by the chisel of the mask-maker: rather, he was concerned with externals – with the voice and movement which observation and convention taught him were characteristic of the mask type that he held in his hand. The features of the mask displayed not the inner essence of the character but the way the character interacted with the external world.

The concern of Noh theatre with 'mind' and 'inner space' does not make its masks any the less susceptible of semiotic analysis. In the Noh as in the Hellenistic theatre, the mask broadly defines a character type while the costume signifies a specific social status. The wig, physically separate from the mask in the Noh, can be seen as a separate semiotic system, helping to differentiate the human from the supernatural.[41] The eyes of the Japanese mask are obvious signifiers. In contrast to the staring eyes of demons, the half-closed eyes of *Ko-omote* suggest that her contemplation is directed inward as much as outward. The spine of the Japanese actor has been described as a second pair of eyes, working in opposition to the face, and capable of seeing what is behind the head.[42] The Noh actor learns to sense and respond with his body because his real vision is so restricted. Hellenistic masks for the most part have enlarged eyes, and the movement of the torso flows with the head rather than in opposition to it. Hellenistic comedy always turns upon the chaos caused by ignorance of ascertainable material facts. Lightweight masks allow the actor good vision, so that the mask seems to see with an outer eye, not an inner eye. We can analyse the forehead in a similar way. On Hellenistic masks of young men, the brows are usually contracted as if in thought; Noh masks do not have intellectual problems to solve, and the Noh brow is characteristically a blank translucent space suggestive of the mind that is ever invisible. The Hellenistic brow may be furrowed as if in physical pain, for physical and mental pain are indistinguishable, but in the Noh mask the pain lies within, leaving no tangible mark upon the flesh. The flesh can be contrasted too. The complexion painted onto the Hellenistic mask suggests a physiological condition, or an environment which the mask has inhabited, while beneath the varnish of the Noh mask can be seen the texture of the solid wood in which the eternal spirit of the mask is housed.

The Noh mask contains some more specific signifying elements. The three strands of hair which frame *Ko-omote*'s brow, for instance, signify purity and chastity. The gold eyes of *Deigan* signify that she is neither fully human nor fully spirit.[43] Signs like these may be described in semiotic terms as 'symbols' bearing an arbitrary relationship to an abstract signified. Signs on the Hellenistic mask tend to be 'indices', pointing to the physiological whole which is their referent. While there is no physical or measurable link between gold and the world of Japanese spirits, there is such a link between tanned skin and the life of a Greek mercenary. The signs embedded in the Noh mask assume that reality extends beyond the superficial reality accessible to sensory awareness.

The Hellenistic mask reflects a materialist philosophy, and yet it was also, paradoxically, like the Noh mask, a sacred object. It was an emblem of Dionysus and worn in his honour. In order to understand the religious dimension of the Greek mask, one might consider an epigram by

Callimachus which ironically commemorates the dedication of the mask of Pamphilos (=complete lover) by a victorious actor. The skin has shrivelled with the passing of the years, for the epigram states that Pamphilos has not been consumed by love but looks like a cross between a dried fig and a torch of Demeter.[44] The mask, Callimachus implies, is as ephemeral as love, and as ephemeral as performance, for the perfect lover of yesterday has disintegrated. Within Greek religion, transitions and liminal states are the particular sphere of Dionysus, who crosses the boundaries between life and death, land and sea, city and wilderness, civilization and savagery, reality and illusion.[45] Dionysus is associated with temporary states: spring, drunkenness, the return of dead souls, and theatrical performance. His vehicle is neither a ship nor a cart but a combination of both; his sanctuary in the marshes is neither on land nor water; his statue has no permanent place in the theatre but lives on the mountain roadside. In accordance with this understanding of the god, the mask of Dionysus functions as a symbol of transition. In performance, it is put on, removed, and exchanged by actors at great speed, and it is perhaps removed in view of the audience at the end of the play.[46] The actors represent passing emotions, the narratives represent a rite of passage, marriage. The Dionysiac mask is the reverse of the Noh mask, which embodies not transience but permanence. The Noh actor spends much time before the performance trying to become one with his mask. There is, paradoxically, no loss of illusion when the actor plays without a mask, for his face becomes immobile like the mask. The action of the play concerns permanence – memories that cannot be exorcized, souls of the dead that cannot rest. The mask has its own permanent identity, longer-lasting than the identity of the actor, and it carries with it its own past. In a phrase of Kanze Hisao, the mask always carries into performance 'its sad memories of being shut up inside a box'.[47]

According to a medieval theorist of the Noh, when the actor gazes through the seven orifices bored into the mask, he perceives the seven stars which point north.[48] The Noh mask, in other words, gives access to a truth beyond the material present. In the worship of Dionysus the meaning of life is rather to be found in the flux of the natural, physical world. It is the Greek spectator rather than the Greek actor whom we should conceive to be possessed by Dionysus, thanks to the operation of the mask. Under the influence of Dionysus the spectator gains not a perception of a different world in the deep north but an enhanced perception of the present. Plato in The Laws describes how the influence of Dionysus in the theatre renders people more child-like, more emotional, and more malleable.[49] Here, for Plato, lay both the power and the danger of theatre.

THE WESTERN MASK

THE PASSIONS OF THE SOUL

If the mask has never found a comfortable home in modern western theatre, this is perhaps because western culture cannot accept either the classical or the eastern concept of the mask. Broadly speaking, under the influence of romanticism, western culture has come to understand the mask as a concealment designed to prevent one from seeing the *real* thoughts and feelings of the wearer. It has become an emblem for the disguise which is seen as a condition of social survival. In Nietzsche's words, 'to avoid everlasting crucifixion, you need your mask'.[50] Theatre is seen as a place where truth is made visible, and the convention of masking is thus by definition alien to the spirit of most modern theatre.

The man renowned for driving the mask from the Italian stage is Carlo Goldoni, the great 'reformer' of the *commedia dell'arte*. Goldoni looked back in his memoirs to the early eighteenth century and argued:

Passions and feelings had not at that time been brought to the point of refinement that is nowadays required. People now want the actor to have a soul, and the soul beneath a mask is like a fire beneath ashes.[51]

It was no great step from Goldoni's sentimental theatre of the mid-eighteenth century to the naturalistic theatre of the late nineteenth and early twentieth centuries. In Stanislavski we see, as in Goldoni, a scientific interest in social processes blended with the mystic idea that the actor's 'soul' is all-important. For Stanislavski it is through 'masking himself in a created image' that the actor succeeds in displaying his own personal emotions to an audience. Thus 'a characterization is the mask which hides the actor-individual. Protected by it, he can lay bare his soul down to the last intimate detail.'[52] We must take care to distinguish this soul-orientated naturalism of the post-romantic era from the materialist naturalism of the Hellenistic period. If the modern audience searches to reconstruct a soul beneath the mask of characterization, then a physical mask must necessarily be an impediment to that search. The nature of such a soul cannot be deduced from external signs, it can only be inferred. With a different concept of self, the Hellenistic audience did not find the mask a hindrance but an essential guide.

In modern naturalism, depth is the dominant spatial metaphor which expresses the nature of the soul. Our imaginations are led past the three walls of the set to the hidden reality behind. A brief vista of a fjord, a roof-garden, or a cherry orchard stimulates our sense of the infinite that lies beyond. These half-glimpsed places are understood to have shaped the souls of the characters who walk the stage. In the Hellenistic world, character is understood to be the product of autonomous moral decision-making. Character is therefore detachable from background. Everything is laid out in two dimensions, and the stage has no depth. The mask belongs to this Hellenistic theatre because it too has no depth. While the modern actor's face is felt to have a soul hidden behind it, the face behind the classical mask has no significance. The classical mask does not hide but reveal the *psychê*. While the Christian or Buddhist soul lingers after the body has disintegrated, the Hellenistic *psychê* can have no existence except in relation to the body.

As in Japanese theatre, so in western theatre the concern of an audience to find a hidden 'soul' does not in the least inhibit it in practice from carrying out a semiotic reading of the face. A stage direction by George Bernard Shaw humorously establishes the point:

He must, one thinks, be the jeune premier; for it is not in reason to suppose that a second such attractive male figure should appear in one story. The slim, shapely frame, the elegant suit of new mourning, the small head and rectangular features, the pretty little moustache, the frank clear eyes, the wholesome bloom on the youthful complexion, the well brushed glossy hair, not curly, but of fine texture and good dark colour, the arch of good nature in the eyebrows, the erect forehead and neatly pointed chin, all announce the man who will love and suffer later on.[53]

As in the Hellenistic theatre, so in the theatre parodied by Shaw, the audience constructs the nature of the character out of the information offered by the eyes, complexion, texture and colour of hair, eyebrows, forehead, and so on. Its familiarity with the physiological codes and narrative structures of nineteenth-century theatre allows it to make a multitude of deductions. Shaw's tone is of course satirical, for this was a semiotic system which, by the start of the twentieth century, had become fossilized. It was a theatrical system which rested upon a body of ideas no longer espoused by intellectually minded dramatists.

Shaw evokes the tail-end of a tradition which, approximately speaking, begins with Descartes and ends with Freud. The serious theatre of western Europe during this period was in a very real sense a theatre of masks. Although, for reasons that I have indicated, the wearing of physical masks was not acceptable outside the realm of farce, masks of a different kind were nevertheless created by the features of the face. If we

turn back to the heyday of this system of 'masks' in the eighteenth
century, we find that it no more troubled an English audience to see
Garrick at the age of 24 play King Lear than it would have troubled a
Greek audience to see a 24-year-old play Oedipus at Colonus. Garrick's
concern was not to be Lear, but to present the masks of Lear's passions.
When playing Lear, a witness recalls,

> Garrick had displayed all the force of quick transitions from one passion to
> another: he had, from the most violent rage, descended to sedate calmness; he had
> seized, with unutterable sensibility, the various impressions of terror, and
> faithfully represented all the turbid passions of the soul; he had pursued the
> progress of agonized feelings to madness in its several stages.[54]

Garrick's method is not to analyse Lear's character, but to analyse the
different 'passions' of Lear's soul, and then to represent these by means of
a series of sharp transitions.

   The theoretical basis for this neo-classical system of representing the
passions can be found in Descartes's treatise on *The Passions of the Soul*
(1649). Descartes analysed the different human emotions, according to a
model which can be traced via Aquinas to the analysis of the *pathê* in
Aristotle's *Rhetoric*. Descartes's ideas were adopted by Charles LeBrun,
court painter to Louis XIV and director of the Academy, and became the
basis of an illustrated treatise on drawing the passions. LeBrun's treatise
influenced actors as much as painters, and in 1827 LeBrun was still the
basis of Jelgerhuis's course of instruction given to actors in Amsterdam.
LeBrun follows the guiding Cartesian principle that the body is a
machine, and thus 'whatever causes Passions in the Soul, creates also
some Action in the Body'.[55] The brain is understood to transmit fluids,
released from the blood and called 'animal spirits', via the nerves to
the muscles. The muscle that receives most spirits becomes the most
active and swollen. When Descartes dispensed with the bipartite
(noble/appetitive) soul of Plato and Aquinas, and replaced this with a
unitary soul located within the pituitary gland at the base of the brain, he
built upon Aristotle and Aristotle's theory of *pneuma* (breath/spirit).
Descartes makes no distinction between the moral qualities of different
emotions, but merely distinguishes those which are simple from those
which are complex. Reason or will remains separable from the passions,
and a strong or well-trained will can conquer the passions. LeBrun's
treatise includes sketches illustrating the six simple passions isolated by
Descartes – Admiration, Love and Hatred, Desire, Joy and Sadness – and
many of the compound passions – Fear, Hope, and so forth.

   Descartes's analysis of the mechanics of the body translates itself into

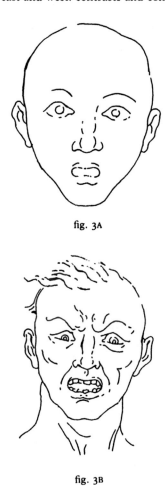

fig. 3A

fig. 3B

some basic rules for the artist and actor. LeBrun lays special emphasis on
the eyebrows, which are closest to the brain – for 'as the gland in the
middle of the brain, is the place where the Soul receives the images of the
Passions; so the Eye-brow is the only part of the whole face, where the
Passions best make themselves known'.[56] Simple passions generate
simple movements of the brow. The nose and mouth, by contrast, follow
the emotions received by the heart, and have a less direct relationship to
the will. Admiration is a simple passion, according to this scheme (fig.
3A), while fright is an example of a compound passion (fig. 3B).

The implications of this Cartesian system for the work of the actor are set out in an essay by the dramatist Aaron Hill, a contemporary of Garrick. Hill was concerned to stress the place of the actor's imagination, and to restrain him from merely reproducing learned gestures and faces. He maps out four steps which lead from the actor's imagination to a realized performance:

1st   The imagination must conceive a *strong idea* of the passion.

2dly,   But that idea cannot *strongly* be conceived, without expressing its own form upon the muscles of the *face*.

3dly,   Nor *can* the look be muscularly stamp'd, without communicating, instantly, the same impression, to the muscles of the *body*.

4thly   The muscles of the body (brac'd or slack, as the idea was an active or a passive one) must, in their natural and not to be avoided consequence, by impelling or retarding the flow of the animal spirits, transmit their own conceiv'd sensation, to the sound of the *voice*, and to the disposition of the *gesture*.[57]

He goes on to define the 'ten Dramatic Passions', and describes how the eyes and muscles are used to create them. The imagination, in Hill's analysis, first stimulates physiological change. Since the face is closest to the brain, the face expresses the passion first; the animal spirits subsequently move on to the other parts of the body, to voice and to gesture. This analysis of the relationship between mind and body results in certain conventions of performance. The actor learns to express an emotion first through the face, then through the body; only thereafter comes delivery of the authorial text from which the emotion was first extrapolated. When the spectators hear the tone of the actor's voice, and see the actor's gestures, they see – if emotion is involved – the resolution of the primal Cartesian conflict between the body and the will. In the case of fear, for instance, the object of fear directs certain spirits in the gland towards the muscles, while the will also acts upon the gland and sets off a contrary movement of the spirits. The result, in the case of fear, is 'sharpness in the eye', while the muscles, unable to obey the will, are unbraced and reduced to a 'debility'.[58] This physical tension within the actor becomes the focus of the audience's interest. The product of this conflict is action.

I have examined this neo-classical Cartesian system of performance because of obvious parallels with the way an Aristotelian system of ideas governed Hellenistic performance. In both cases we see a widely disseminated materialist philosophy shaping theatrical conventions. Both New Comedy and this theatre of the passions were notable for their ubiquity and longevity. Both forms required an audience that was familiar with a specific physiognomic code, and we can turn to physiognomic treatises for assistance.[59] LeBrun's descriptions of the faces required for each emotion sound very much like the descriptions of a cataloguer of Hellenistic masks. Each element is isolated – eyebrows, eyes, pupils, nostrils, lips upper and lower, mouth, corners of mouth, complexion. We have to remember, if this all sounds too mechanistic and uncreative for late twentieth-century taste, that the kind of analysis provided by LeBrun was found to be of great value by generations of actors.

Although the Cartesian system was rooted in Aristotelian thinking, we must take stock of major differences between the two theatrical forms. The bourgeois neo-classical world was concerned to stress individual sense experience, escaping thereby from an aristocratic code of values which celebrated the suppression of visible emotion. This bourgeois world was obsessed with identifying the 'natural' behaviour of human individuals. In Hill's essay we find a dialectic between the natural flow of the animal spirits and the muscular responses prompted by the mind. In Aristotle's thinking, the emotions are not simply natural but have a cognitive aspect, since they are related to a concept of 'the good'. Feeling and reasoning are not ultimately separable. Virtue is not a matter of being strong enough to overcome the (natural) passions, but of being wise enough to admit the right (learned) passions in the right situation. A different dialectic therefore obtains.

In eighteenth-century neo-classical theatre, the face is used for the expression of *pathos* in its analytically purest form. Character, as, for instance, the character of a tyrant, is a function of the emotions of fear and hate characteristic of a tyrant. In the Hellenistic theatre, by contrast, the mask expresses an *êthos* in its purest form, and emotion is rather a function of character. The character of a certain old man will imply a disposition to feel anger. The neo-classical face in a sense performs the function of the Hellenistic voice as the direct physiological route to the *pathê* of the soul. The neo-classical spectator passed from the actor's face to his body and voice in order to watch an emotion progressively taking hold. The Hellenistic spectator necessarily passed from the voice and body back to the mask in order to 'read' an emotion into the inert form of the mask. While the neo-classical spectator learns in the theatre how emotion governs behaviour, the Hellenistic spectator learns how emotion, and subsequently action, is the product of character. In each case, theatre reinforces the basic assumptions of the culture.

The 'face-playing' of the neo-classical theatre can give us some practical insights into the working of a theatre of masks. The most comprehensive manual to which we can turn is probably Jelgerhuis's *Lessons* of 1827. Jelgerhuis warned his Dutch students of the danger of expressing their personal emotions, for 'there are many people who ordinarily laugh as if they were crying and when they cry give the impression that they are laughing'.[60] Imagination is, therefore, as for Aaron Hill, not sufficient, and the actor needs knowledge. Natural feelings are indeed a snare, for 'too many natural feelings can constrain our genius, which we must instead set free'.[61] With this paradox, Jelgerhuis underscores the point that the actor's creativity lies not in becoming something but in signifying something. The first practical step which Jelgerhuis requires is for the actor to study his own face. By the accident of nature the actor's own eyebrows, for example, may happen to be 'drawn down at the outer corners of the eyes, thus constantly giving an impression of sadness. Or perhaps they are arched high over the eyes and so constantly give the impression of rage'.[62] The judicious application of make-up serves to eliminate such idiosyncracies. For Jelgerhuis, the eyebrows are again the most important of all the facial elements. The difference between astonishment and fright, for example, is marked solely by the way the eyebrows of fright are drawn towards the nose. Eyes, nostrils, and mouth are constant for these two emotions. Conversely, the transition from horror to fear is marked by a movement of the mouth.[63] This method of analysis is sustained at length through a gamut of subtly differentiated emotions.

Both New Comedy and eighteenth-century theatre of the passions share an emphasis upon the neutral mean as a starting-point. Jelgerhuis's actors have to create a neutral face before they can superimpose specific facial signs. The Cartesian tradition construes the distinct 'simple' emotions of joy and sadness, love and hate, and compound emotions such as fear and hope, despair and certainty, as opposites on either side of a mean. Desire and Admiration, for Descartes, exist only in relation to an opposite of calm, an absence of passion. Starting from a neutral state, the actor must learn to twist the features one way to create love, the other way to create hate. Aristotle's analysis of the emotions in the *Rhetoric* is structured in the same way around the discernment of opposites. The components of Hellenistic masks, as we have seen, are constructed as variations either side of a norm. The masks of free-born young men and women come more-or-less close to a norm of physical beauty, from which slaves and crones are far removed. Beauty is understood to comprise perfect proportion, and an absence of blemishes. This idealization of the norm or mean is antipathetic to twentieth-century individualism, and in the theatre or cinema we prefer to admire an idiosyncratic, 'characterful' face, regarding such a face as a sign of authenticity. While mimes like Jacques Lecoq continue to regard the neutral face as a starting-point for an actor's work upon the body, mainstream theatre relies upon type-casting, employing actors on the basis of their unique voice and physique.

The Cartesian system of performance adapted itself easily to romanti-cism, which was concerned like neo-classicism with a tension between reason and emotion. It could not be adapted to the post-Freudian era, with its theory of the unconscious. Since Freud, the relationship between the dynamics of the mind and the mechanics of the body has become subject to new and unfathomable laws. Twentieth-century theatre has experimented with a bewildering variety of forms in a search for points of anchorage. For many theatre practitioners, Shavian intellectualism and Stanislavskian psychologism have seemed to place too many constraints upon the theatrical medium. Many dramatic theorists – such as Vakhtangov, Meyerhold, and Copeau – have called for a return to masked performance, and specifically to the traditions of the *commedia dell'arte*.

COMMEDIA DELL'ARTE

The *commedia dell'arte* is the only major tradition of masked acting to have flourished within the post-classical western theatre. It is not an easy tradition to analyse. What we tend to think of today as '*commedia dell arte*' should perhaps be considered a creation of the eighteenth century. Only then did the term '*commedia dell'arte*' come into use: until then, people spoke of 'comedy of Zanies', of 'Italian comedy' or of 'comedy to a scenario' in an effort to describe the phenomenon.[64] Eighteenth-century theorists like Riccoboni, Gozzi and Goldoni were able to describe a more-or-less rigidly codified form of theatre within which names could be attached at a glance to a given costume, and specialist companies had a standard format. In the late sixteenth and early seventeenth centuries, it is much less easy to describe the system of performance involved in presenting masked, extemporal comedies. The Italian companies who presented plays based on scenarios using charac-ters like Arlecchino and Pantalone offered this mode as one of several available genres. It was a genre that came to be seen as the quintessenti-ally Italian genre only when Italian actors travelled abroad, and found that such plays were particularly well able to transcend linguistic boundaries.

At this formative stage of the *commedia dell'arte*, each actor tended to create an original stage name and stage identity, and these would serve the actor whenever he or she presented a play within this genre. This stage identity had to be located within a loosely defined set of role types: old man, *zanni* (i.e. servant), lover, and so on. Pantalone is probably the only character who, from the beginning, had a fixed name, costume, and mask. Plays in the *commedia dell'arte* style were 'improvised' principally in the sense that the dialogue was composed not by a single author but by the actors responsible for speaking specific lines. The plot outlines used for these 'improvised' plays followed exactly the same formula as the outlines used for scripted plays of the '*commedia erudita*', which the same actors would present, playing similar kinds of roles.[65] For this reason, we find a very close correlation between the role structures of the *commedia dell'arte* and the role structures of the Graeco-Roman comedy that served as a model for classically trained writers of *commedia erudita*.

In order to analyse the role structures of the early *commedia dell'arte*, let us consider the earliest surviving collection of scenarios, the volume published by Flaminio Scala in 1611.[66] Scala was actor-manager in one of the most successful troupes of the time. His scenarios, though clearly based upon plays actually performed, were reworked for publication. The purpose of publication was to enhance the cultural and intellectual standing of actors. The plays are written for an idealized company. The names of the characters can all be identified with the stage names of the most famous actors of the day, a set of individuals who were never in fact united within a single troupe. Within this ideal troupe, we find that the role structure of a play breaks down into two tetradic groupings. We have on the one hand two pairs of unmasked lovers, and on the other two pairs of masked actors, namely a pair of old men and a pair of Bergomask servants. The troupe is completed by a few marginal characters who may or may not be masked – the Spanish Captain, the servant-girl, a third male servant. A system of oppositions thus governs the role typology:

Arlecchino (i.e. the actor T. Martinelli) is Scala's example of the stupid *zanni*, Pedrolino (i.e. G. Pellesini) of the clever *zanni*. One pair of lovers is normally more emotional, the other more rational. In actuality, it was not normally possible for companies to construct themselves in such a tidy manner at the start of the seventeenth century. Scala's model represents the ideal towards which aspirant companies were moving. We see a similar emphasis on binary oppositions in the theoretical writings of another ambitious actor-manager of the period, P. M. Cecchini.[67]

The central articulation within this system is of masked and unmasked. While each masked character has a distinctive regional dialect, the unmasked lovers use the Tuscan dialect that was, in effect, the lingua franca of educated Italians. In some measure, this divide relates to the Hellenistic principle that the masks of young men and women should be variations upon a normative ideal, while the masks of old men and slaves are distorted. Taviani calls attention to the fact that a Latin translation of Pollux was available to early exponents of the *commedia dell'arte*, and this text may have helped them to systematize their masking practices.[68] In the early *commedia dell'arte*, however, the absolute division between masked and unmasked has implications that go far beyond Pollux, and these can only be understood when we place the *commedia dell'arte* in context in relation to the Italian carnival.

The theatrical mask flourished in Italy because the mask was the central emblem of carnival. There was no equivalent tradition of masquerading in England, a country where masked acting never took root. The importance of the social context emerges in Nahum Tate's apologia for an English theatrical experiment of 1684 in the use of *commedia* techniques. Tate felt it incumbent on him, while defending the mask as a theatrical device, to castigate the abuse of masking in the Italian carnival. 'Can all their mortifications of the ensuing Lent', he writes, 'make any tolerable amends for the lewdness then committed?', and he praises the medieval English legislation which prescribed capital punishment for masquerading.[69] Such an attempt to sever theatrical practice from its cultural context was destined to fail in the long term. In Italy there was a symbiotic relationship between *commedia dell'arte* and the world of carnival. While those who penned scenarios looked to the plays of Plautus and Terence, the actors who had to find masks and costumes in order to play those scenarios looked to the world of carnival. Subsequently, we often find that characters modified and refined on stage reappear in the streets at carnival time.[70] It was taken for granted that carnival constituted the theatrical season, the period when plays could be presented. Masks were worn not only by theatrical performers in seventeenth-century Italy but also by spectators. Even when masking was banned for reasons of state, an exception was made for theatre-goers.[71] This masking convention characterized court audiences as much as public audiences.[72] The anarchic inversion of normal moral behaviour within the world of the play was indisseverable from the inversion of everyday conduct permitted under the rules of carnival. The sense that a *commedia dell'arte* performance was improvised both encouraged and was encouraged by participatory behaviour from the audience. A vivid account of the Venetian theatre by a French visitor, Limojon de St-Didier, describes how 'young nobles go to the theatre not so much to laugh at the buffoonery of the actors as to play parts themselves ... The licence taken by those in the pit, in imitation of the nobility, completes the disorder.[73] The stage was, for St-Didier, a microcosm of 'the great theatre' of St Mark's Square, where deceptions, loves, and intrigues took place on a grander scale.[74] The conventions of masking and improvisation served to dissolve boundaries between stage and auditorium.

In order to understand the working of the *commedia* mask, we have therefore to understand the nature of the carnival mask. This mask was a symbolic rather than a real disguise. In Goldoni's studies of Venetian life, maskers are often recognized by their eyes or gait.[75] Castiglione makes the symbolic element explicit. A gentleman, he allows, may perform indecorous dances in private, 'but not in public, unless he is at a masked ball, when it does no harm even if he is recognized'. Castiglione adds that a prince, even though his mask does not conceal his identity, becomes free to mix with social inferiors.[76] Masked plebeians, conversely, became free to mingle with patricians in the coffee-house or in the gambling-house.[77] The mask created a symbolic levelling. St-Didier believed that the subjection of the Venetian commoners was rendered less harsh by the freedom which masks gave them to mix with the nobility.[78] The nobility, for their part, obviously relished the liberation from decorum which masks provided. They often unmasked in the theatre and gambling-house in order to distinguish themselves from commoners dressed as nobles, but they always assumed their masks when decorum was in jeopardy – when consorting with courtesans, for example.[79]

The conventions of the *commedia dell'arte* at once reproduce and invert the contiguous world of carnival inhabited by the audience. The unmasked lovers are expected to be young and beautiful, their manners to be refined. Young gentlemen and courtesans who go masked to the theatre see themselves unmasked on stage. Conversely, those too old, too dignified, or too poor to take a prominent part in the carnival appear masked and ridiculous on the stage. Within the theatrical performance, the actor's mask dissolves completely the boundaries which govern everyday life outside the carnival – as, for instance, sexual boundaries (the virility of Pantalone), linguistic boundaries (the pseudo-reasoning of the Doctor), spatial boundaries (the acrobatics of Arlecchino), or hierarchical boundaries (Pedrolino's practical jokes). While the unmasked actors have educated voices, the masks use travesties of regional dialects. Through voice, face, and movement, the masked characters are a negative imprint of the unmasked characters. Old is opposed to young, low status to high status. The oppositions embodied by the *commedia* correspond to those which set carnival apart from everyday life: sin and virtue, body and soul, satisfaction and denial, equality and hierarchy, anarchy and order.

It was a very different form of *commedia dell'arte* which established itself in Paris in the second half of the seventeenth and first half of the eighteenth centuries. The link between *commedia* and carnival was broken, as was the link between mask and dialect. The dramaturgy was no longer based on classical principles. Characters like Scaramouche no longer took their dynamic from the master–servant relationship. There was a new focus on the world of court. Arlecchino became a pivotal figure, and tended to represent the noble savage, a creature comprising only emotion, with no admixture of reason. The character of Arlecchino could, for this reason, be related to central areas of philosophical enquiry. We must not, therefore, confuse the French *commedia dell'arte*, performed by foreigners for the benefit of Parisians, with the indigenous Italian version of the genre.

A semiotics of the *commedia* mask is not easily undertaken because of the diversity of masks used for the same character type at different periods, or by different actors. If, however, we consider the masks worn by Arlecchino and Pantalone in the formative period of the *commedia dell'arte*, we can say that the dominant feature in Arlecchino is his circular eyes, in Pantalone his hooked nose. The nose of Pantalone suggests the Jew of the Venetian Rialto. The line of the nose is continued by the line of the beard, and echoes the phallus worn by early wearers of the mask. The round eyes of Arlecchino are framed by curved brows, and echoed by a rounded beard. These shapes transform themselves into the movements of the actors. When Arlecchino doffs his hat, his arm describes a curve. His body is never held erect, and his limbs always seem to move towards the circumference of an imaginary circle.[80] The movements of Pantalone, on the other hand, always start from his extremities – his red slippers, his nose, his phallus – and the rest of the body is drawn after.

The sense is of linear rather than circular movement. While Arlecchino has no rational purpose, his mind aiming nowhere and everywhere, Pantalone is subject to single and inflexible drives that may be either sexual or financial.

Carlo Boso, the director of 'TAG teatro', the leading contemporary company working in the *commedia dell'arte* tradition, elaborates in his teaching upon the semiotics of the mask. The wen on Arlecchino's mask represents a devil's horn, like the little points above the eye on Pantalone's mask. While Pantalone's nose is like the beak of a crow, Arlecchino resembles an ape, with physiognomic elements also of a dog and a cat. The blackness of Arlecchino's mask suggests the slavery of a Negro. The height of Pantalone's brow and the slant of his eyes signify intelligence, while the low forehead of the *zanni* mask signifies lack of intelligence. Boso also speaks of the actor's choice, whether to present the mask frontally or in profile. The beak-nosed *zanni* looks stupid when the mask is presented frontally, but aggressive when the mask is seen in profile. The mask of Pantalone works in the same way whether the mask is seen frontally or in profile, but the flat mask of Arlecchino works best when the mask is presented frontally: the actor needs always to bounce a response off the audience.[81]

Commedia dell'arte masks are constructed of leather. They do not suggest man's power to create substance out of nothing, nor are they, like Noh masks, imbued with the spirit of antiquity; rather, they are animal skins superimposed upon human skin, and they liberate non-civilized animal behaviour. In common with all *commedia* masks, Pantalone and Arlecchino are half-masks. They therefore change rather than conceal the actor's identity. They are overtly symbols, and do not attempt a mimetic reproduction of psychologically significant traits. While the white domino masks of the carnival outside the theatre proclaim the wearer empty of status and empty of malice, these dark theatrical masks signal a more active presence of evil.

Ferdinando Taviani develops an interesting contrast between the iconography of the Hellenistic theatre and that of the *commedia dell'arte*. In the Hellenistic period, actors, muses, and poets are, as we have seen, consistently represented as gazing into the eyes of the mask as if engaged in silent dialogue. Portraits of *commedia dell'arte* actors, by contrast, represent the actor holding his mask casually, and gazing at the audience. When the Hellenistic actor expresses his questions or gratitude to the mask, that mask, according to Taviani, 'transmits to him the continuity of a tradition, dictates to him a way of performing, and suggests to him the character of a person whom the poet has created, and who reaches the actor from without'. Portraits of *commedia* actors reverse these principles. While the actor's face suggests his interior life, the mask becomes a mere symbol of his profession, with no personality of its own separable from that of the actor.[82] The *commedia* mask, in Taviani's view, is a shell rather than a face, and exists to depersonalize rather than to impersonate.[83] The power of the *commedia dell'arte*, therefore, relates to a perceived dualism of the actor and his disguise.

Andrea Perrucci, a theorist of the *commedia dell'arte* writing at the end of the seventeenth century, accepts the theory derived from Platonios that the Athenians invented theatrical masks in order to speak of the Macedonians without fear.[84] Perrucci's acceptance of this spurious tradition tells us something of his own carnivalesque understanding of the mask as a vehicle for the expression of taboo behaviour. The Greek mask, as we have seen, empowered the actor to cast off his own individual identity; it did not allow him to express a natural self concealed in everyday living. The real historical origins of the Greek theatrical mask seem to be bound up with the cult of Dionysus. Vase paintings depict a life-like mask of Dionysus laid in a basket or set on a column.[85] Masks were required wear for komasts in the Dionysiac procession when the statue was carried to the theatre.[86] In democratic Greek society, the mask did not have the job of obliterating social hierarchy, for hierarchy was deemed not to exist; rather, it marked the equal ability of all men to be changed by the god. So, for example, in the Delian Dionysia satyr-type masks were worn by the komasts who announced the arrival of the statue in the theatre and called for space, but no masks were worn by the phallus-bearers whose duty was to hurl insults at individual members of the audience.[87] The free citizen in a democracy is one who can speak unmasked.

The *commedia dell'arte* offers parallels to Menander's theatre when it shows us how a mask can impose certain patterns of movement upon the actor, and how a particular mask needs to be presented in a particular way to the audience. In other respects, we must beware of allowing the *commedia* tradition, based upon the principle of inversion, to influence our understanding of a Helenistic tradition based upon *mimêsis*. The recent Italian production of Menander's *The Girl from Samos* clearly did not make this distinction (see p. 109). The Plautine tradition, as we shall see, is more closely related to *commedia dell'arte*. The *commedia* tradition was far more fluid in its initial development than Greek New Comedy because artistic control lay in the hands of a large number of actors, not a small number of authors, and there was no city like Athens to serve as a geographical focus. Loose generalizations about 'masked acting' conceal the different meanings and uses which a mask has in different cultures, and a failure to grasp the complexity of the mask perhaps explains why so many twentieth-century attempts to revive masked performance have seemed to lead up a cul-de-sac. Both the eighteenth-century theatre of passions and the *commedia dell'arte* belong to a western tradition that is linked through literary and artistic channels to the Hellenistic world. What is important is to notice the differences: to notice how similar external forms acquire quite different meanings within different historical circumstances. The *commedia dell'arte*, as we shall see in the next chapter, had far more in common with the theatre of Rome than with the theatre of Greece.

CHAPTER 5

The Roman mask

THE CONTEXT

Before we examine the use of the mask in Roman comedy, we need to look at the place of the mask in Roman culture, within a political and religious context very different to Greece. Lucian's description of how Greeks in Asia Minor perform as satyrs, corybants, and so forth points up the essential difference: for the Ionians, Lucian observes, these performances are a greater source of pride than family trees, public service, and ancestral distinctions.[1] For a Roman of good family, it was inconceivable that dancing in a mask should be a source of pride and public celebration. This was not part of a citizen's upbringing. The Latin word *persona* serves as a fairly exact translation of the Greek *prosôpon*, but there is no precise Greek equivalent to the Latin synonym *larva* which means both a 'mask' and a 'ghost', and derives etymologically from *lar*, a household god. Roman culture was far more concerned than Greek culture with the after-life. It encouraged constant thoughts of death through institutions such as the gladiator fight, the 'decimation' of a disgraced regiment, and the power of a *paterfamilias* to kill his sons. Its religion was bound up with death. The Greek observer Polybius wrote, perhaps cynically, that Roman religion was theatricalized in order that the masses could be controlled by unseen terrors and suchlike *tragôidia*.[2] While the Greek who put on a mask created a new form of life, I would suggest that the Roman who put on a mask resurrected a dead being. This is a sweeping generalization, but sums up, I think, a fundamental difference between the life cults of Dionysus and the death cults of Rome. Replica masks of Greek New Comedy are found in graveyards because they represent the life that a dead person might wish to retain. They are not objects which induce fear, unlike the gaping Roman *persona* which, as Juvenal, Martial, and Seneca all tell us, was used to terrorize children.[3] It is symptomatic of the difference between the two cultures that the mask of Greek Dionysus was

129

made of linen rags and glue, while the mask worn in the worship of
Roman Bacchus was made of wood.[4] The mask of Bacchus, like a Noh
mask, was an object that might be inhabited by a spirit.

The most important use of the mask in Roman culture was in the cult of
the *imago*. When a man of noble family died, a death mask was made using
a wax mould. A person who had the same physique as the dead man, and
had been trained in life to imitate him, sometimes a professional actor,
would participate in the funeral as the living incarnation of the dead man.
Others would wear the robes of office and masks of the deceased man's
ancestors, and would take their places on ivory chairs mounted on rostra,
so that the entire family line was, as it were, brought back to life on stage.
The masks, which became blackened with age, were normally kept on
display in the atrium of the ancestral home, and were put on public
display at state sacrifices. The purpose of this gruesome cult, Polybius
tells us, was to inspire the young, so that young men would be willing to
suffer for the public good, knowing the immortalization that would
follow.[5] To be a noble in Roman society was to have the right of receiving
a death mask; a commoner elected to curule office acquired this right, and
transmitted it to his descendants. This cult of the death mask has a
bearing upon the theatre. The theatrical mask needed a quite different
identity in order to avoid any risk that it might be mistaken for an *imago*,
and thus offend a noble family. There could be no question of Roman
mask-makers following in the tradition of the fifth-century Athenians
who made theatrical masks resembling Cleon or Pericles.[6] Caricature
portraiture and the whole principle of *mimêsis* had to be avoided. The
mask of Roman comedy became something like a negative imprint of the
imago, a face imbued with such ignobility that a young man would shun
the idea of imitating such a person.

A second notable use of the mask was in the Atellan comedy. Although
the exact chronology supplied by our sources is suspect, the way the
tradition developed is clear enough. It was a more or less improvised form
of comedy associated with the town of Atella near Naples, and performed
in Oscan dialect. By Plautus' time Atellan comedy had become an integral
part of the Roman festival. Stock characters such as Old Pappus,
Manducus with his large jaw, or Lamia the child-eating ogress appeared
in play after play. In the Imperial period, we know that Atellan actors
were able to voice forbidden political views.[7] The freedom of political
expression permitted by the Atellan mask seems to explain the information in Livy that the early Atellan actors were amateurs of good family
who would have been derogated had they become professional actors in

regular plays.[8] Symbolic or real anonymity was preserved because, unlike Greek actors, an Atellan actor 'did not take off his mask on stage'.[9] This would seem to refer to a practice whereby the Greek actor would remove his mask at the end of a play when presenting himself to the judges.[10] Plautus' comedy was evidently influenced by the Atellan form. Horace regarded the parasites of Plautus as versions of Dossenus, an Atellan mask.[11] Plautus refers to Atellan characters in his plays, and in two prologues refers to himself as 'Maccus', prompting the speculation that he might himself have performed this Atellan role.[12] I shall argue in the course of this chapter that Plautus, like the Atellan actors, and like the actors of the *commedia dell'arte*, was content with a very limited repertory of stock masks. The masks of Plautus, like those of Atellan comedy and of the *commedia dell'arte*, had as their principal function to legitimate taboo behaviour.

A third masking tradition that we must keep in mind is that of the flute-players. On the Ides of June, during the festival of Minerva, masked flute-players would take to the streets, drink, and wear long, floral, feminine gowns. The festival commemorated the return of the musicians from banishment, a return which saved the city from divine displeasure.[13] Ovid derives the masks from a ruse used to conceal identities from the Senate, while Valerius explains them as a concealment for embarrassment. Though neither explanation carries any weight, what is clear is that the festive mask allowed abnormal liberty to the wearer. A commemorative coin shows an ugly Gorgon's mask of the kind worn by flute-players at this festival.[14] The grotesqueness of this mask must have had an apotropaic function. From the various accounts it is clear that the whole masked ritual was seen as conferring protection from evil. Since Minerva was the patroness not only of musicians but also of actors and dramatists, we may infer that actors received from their masks similar protection against both men and gods.

Finally we should recall that scenic games in Rome were introduced in imitation of Etruscan games as a means of placating the gods.[15] The Latin term for an actor – *histrio* – derives from the Etruscan, and the Latin term *persona* (mask) derives likewise from the Etruscan *phersu*. The *phersu* was a masked dancer and is represented on a sixth-century tomb conducting some sort of human sacrifice. The Etruscans also used masks in connexion with death when they covered the faces of valorous warriors fallen in battle with masks.[16] We can glimpse from such details how an Etruscan masking tradition shaped the way the Romans adapted a Greek tradition of masks.

Unfortunately the Plautine mask is a vexed topic. While French and Italian scholars often still assume that Plautus' actors performed unmasked,[17] English-language scholars now tend to accept William Beare's careful sifting of the evidence and his conclusion that Greek-style masks were used.[18] A. S. Gratwick voices the prevailing British view when he dismisses as incredible the old idea that Plautus' theatre 'could have borrowed the plots, verse-form, and costume of the Greek tradition, but not its masks'.[19] Continental scholars cling to the 'unmasked' theory partly because they do not share the philhellenism of British classicists and wish to stress the independent Italian origins of Plautine theatre, and partly because they lack a pragmatic approach to the practicalities of performance.

The argument against masks rests heavily upon a text of Diomedes, of unknown but late date, which asserts that Plautus' actors wore wigs rather than masks. This text alleges that the mask was invented by Roscius to conceal his squint, for he was only handsome enough to play the parasite.[20] As a historical explanation, this is unacceptable, and it is plainly a speculation based on two passages in Cicero. One might perhaps give more credit to a reversal of this theory, whereby Roscius could have developed a squint from constantly peering through a mask. Diomedes alleges that the colour of the wig – white, black, or red – signified the age of the character, and he makes no mention of status despite the fact that a tawny wig in Greek practice signifies a slave. We have no evidence, written or iconographic, for this theatre of wigs and faces, and Diomedes' chronology is contradicted by the statement of Donatus, the meticulous editor of Terence, that Terence's actors 'even then' – a century before Roscius' death – wore masks.[21]

It is safer to return to Gratwick's common-sense observation that if the Romans decided to incorporate 'Greek games' within their festivals, as they had previously incorporated Etruscan and Oscan games, they would not have excluded the central feature of Greek theatre, the Dionysiac mask. The institution of new rituals and the assimilation of foreign deities was commonly seen as a means of warding off divine displeasure.[22] Livius Andronicus, for example, the first writer of Greek-style comedy in Rome, is said to have brought success to the city through composing a traditional song for performance by a chorus of maidens.[23] It is reasonable to assume that the external ritual forms of the Greek Dionysia – its masks, costumes, and music – were seen as more important than the aesthetic principles of poets. From a practical point of view, moreover, it is hard to see what could be gained by an abandonment of the mask, since the actor needed to be seen at a distance. Pliny states that a temporary wooden theatre in

58 BC held 80,000 spectators, an impressionistic figure which does at least confirm that Roman drama, like Greek, was presented to a vast gathering of the community.[24] Singers and dancers could perhaps have dispensed with masks, since they did not need to differentiate characters, but actors could not have done so. The mask was a ubiquitous convention. Masked acting flourished in Italy in its Oscan form, in its Etruscan form,[25] and in the *phlyax* farces of the south. Statuettes in the British Museum suggest that the *togata* – comedy in Roman dress – was played with masks.[26] Itinerant Greek actors were playing in Rome by the end of Plautus' lifetime.[27] Greek theatrical masks were a familiar sight to most Roman men both from their visits to foreign parts on military service, and from Greek monuments and souvenirs carried home for public and private display, either purchased by philhellenist aesthetes or plundered by victorious soldiers.[28] The only grounds for arguing that Plautus' actors played unmasked is the modern assumption that playing with a bare face is somehow more natural.

The question should not be whether but how Plautus' actors used masks. Since Plautus' texts conflate Roman and Greek elements, it is reasonable to assume that the masks of his theatre were likewise more or less syncretic. We have no definite iconographic evidence for Plautine performance, despite the fact that Plautus' plays remained in repertory for over a century – a lack which suggests that the Roman version of New Comedy had no completely independent visual style. Two versions of a Hellenistic painting of a scene from New Comedy, one from Pompeii and one from Herculaneum,[29] give us an idea of the kind of variation that was possible. While the Pompeian version captures the precision and elegance of the Greek original, the version from Herculaneum portrays masks that are crude and lumpish, but have nevertheless far more energy than those in the Pompeian version. The contrast, I believe, is not between the work of a skilled and an unskilled artist, but between one artist who attempted to copy his Hellenistic original and another who preferred to interpret his original, inspired by the actual masks that he had seen on the Roman stage. For lack of further archaeological evidence, we must turn to Plautus' texts in order to see what visual information they assume the audience to be receiving.

THE EVIDENCE OF PLAUTUS' TEXTS

An analysis of terminology in Plautus' prologues by Cesare Questa suggests that the Roman audience was expected to recognize by sight a simplified version of the Greek taxonomy. Questa extracts from the texts a lexicon of role types, which I have adapted in the list below. I have reorganized Questa's list in order to align it with the taxonomy of Pollux. I have also rejected some of his more tentative suggestions, and have added the two slave types of *lorarius* and *puer* which appear in several plays, but have insufficient narrative importance to feature in prologues.[30]

old men	young men	slaves	women	
senex (old man) leno (pimp)	adulescens (youth) miles (soldier) parasitus (parasite) danista/trapezita (money-lender)	servus (slave) cocus (cook) lorarius (flogger) puer (slave-boy)	lena (bawd) nutrix (nurse)	anus (old woman)
			matrona (mother) virgo (maiden)	
			mulier (young woman) meretrix (courtesan) ancilla (maid-servant)	mulier

Questa argues that where Menander's prologues lay the emphasis upon relationships between characters, Plautus' prologues offer a gratuitous or unmotivated pointer to a fixed role type. The list which I have adapted from his study gives us the basis of a Roman system – a system which follows the outlines of the Greek, and borrows all its masks from identifiable Greek types, yet obliterates the sense of a spectrum and sets up sharp demarcations between each type. The Greek system has been adapted, in other words, to create a restricted and fixed repertory of masks on the model of Atellan farce.[31] The strength of the Greek system lay in its ability to juxtapose two people of contrasting character: two old men, one quick to anger, the other slow to anger; two young men, one a decadent city youth, the other a soldier or countryman; two slaves, one in love, one concerned with his stomach; and so forth. This possibility no longer exists in Plautine theatre. Instead, Plautus uses his fixed repertory of masks to subvert the narrative and aesthetic codes of Hellenistic theatre. In chapter 1 I examined and broadly endorsed Bettini's argument that, through using stock roles, Plautus was enabled to work ever-new variations upon the relationship of actor and actant. The Greek spectator could read the complex signs of the mask because the narrative structure was fixed and given. The Roman spectator, because the mask was fixed and given, was able to enjoy unfamiliar narrative structures.

I shall look now at some representative Plautine texts in order to demonstrate how the Roman system of masks operated in practice. I shall begin with the *Curculio*, since I have used the play as my example in earlier chapters. The major mask types are represented, and there is no duplication.

The *leno* is announced by his mask name before he arrives, and is addressed by that name. The name *leno* is in fact used at least eighteen times. The audience are assumed to be as familiar as the actor with the nature of a *leno*. The typicality of this *leno* is celebrated in a speech by the parasite about the genus of *leno*s (lines 499–504). The terms of praise used of a nobleman are all reversed. The wearer of this *imago* belongs to the same genus as a flea, and the man who associates with him in the forum is doomed to lose his *res* (estate) and his *fides* (credit, good name). Once the audience have been prepared for the arrival of a typical *leno* mask based on the Greek type, what they are actually shown turns out to be a novel variant designed to suggest ill health. The slave is taken aback by green eyes, and comments: 'the form I recognize, the colour I cannot recognize' (lines 232–3).

The play contains several young men. The *adulescens* is in love, and love represents the totality of his existence. His words celebrate his role as the typical lover when he wagers that temperate lovers do not exist. On his first appearance, however, the *adulescens* acts the part of the slave by walking ahead with the light. The *miles* like the *leno* is established before his entry as a typical specimen, and at first he conforms to type by playing the swaggerer. In the course of the play he undergoes a sudden change of character when he turns out to be the brother of the *adulescens*. As with all the masks, the audience sees a metamorphosis. The *leno* is sick, the lover acts the slave, the *miles* acts the *adulescens*. We see a similar metamorphosis in the money-lender, who acts the part of an *adulescens*. The so-called '*trapezita*' (= banker) in this play can be identified with the '*danista*' (= usurer) in other plays. Athenian bankers were metics, so this role would seem to be based on the 'portrait' mask of Pollux. Pollux states that this mask was shaven, a feature which fits with the middle-aged pederasty of Plautus' *trapezita*. His name, Lyco, means 'wolfish', implying his predatory nature. The *trapezita* conceals his age by covering his head (line 389), following the normal Roman practice when worshipping a god,[32] and he is therefore addressed as '*adulescens*' by the parasite (line 399).

It is the parasite who gives the play its title. The parasite takes over the conventional narrative functions of the slave, and is the resourceful schemer who allows the *adulescens* to obtain the heroine. The term *parasitus* is used six times before the actor's entry in order to build expectations. When he makes his entry, the parasite marks his new function by playing the well-known Greek routine of the 'running slave'. Although the mask may be recognizably a parasite's, the costume is not, for the character wears a *chlamys* (short pinned cloak) stolen from the soldier. This novel costume justifies the arrogance with which he pushes his way through the audience. When he meets the disguised *trapezita* – whom he already knows (line 342) – the parasite promptly disguises his own identity in order to pose as the freedman of the soldier whose cloak he wears. The *trapezita* refers to the parasite as a one-eyed Cyclops (lines 393–4), and asks whether the eye has been shot out or burnt out. The parasite replies that the hole was acquired as a sign of public service. The service of a parasite is of course to eat. Evidently the eyes of the mask have been covered by a hat, the head is tilted back so the parasite can see, and the central Cyclopian eye-socket is in fact the parasite's mouth – a mouth previously described as 'bleary' with hunger (line 318). The parasite's name – meaning 'weevil' – evokes the appearance and movement of the actor when eyeless and noseless. Later in the play the parasite uncovers his face in order that the *miles* can see that he is no slave but a free man (line 623). This extended visual joke tells us something about the Roman mask. A gaping mouth is not the most striking feature of the Greek parasite mask, and reflects the Roman reconception of the role.

The name of the slave Palinurus means 'ever-pissing', and it sums up his role as coward and fall-guy. The slave starts the play in a dominant position as commentator on his master's follies, then is humiliated successively by the *mulier* (who prompts his master to beat him), the cook, and the parasite. The cook, in his brief scene, adopts the role of seer and interprets the *leno*'s dream, without ever concluding what the dream foretells.

We pass finally to the women of the play. The bawd is called Leaina (= lioness) in a name which punningly conflates *lena* with *lykaina* (= she-wolf – Pollux's term for the mask, equivalent also to the Latin term for a whore). The feline agility with which the bawd scents and drinks her wine

correlates with her change of animal identity. The name of the *mulier* –
the pseudo-virgin of the plot – proclaims her a 'little vagabond'. The
parasite evokes her role-label when he looks to tragedy in search of an
example of a more evil *mulier*. The *mulier* undergoes the usual metamorphosis. First, before her arrival, she is introduced as an *ancilla* (line 43),
and she embraces her lover erotically in the manner of a professional
meretrix; before her second appearance, she is reclassified as a *virgo*, and is
then consistently referred to by this term as she plays the part of an
innocent virgin, untouched by her years of slavery. The appearance of her
mask is evoked when the slave insults her for her 'owl eyes' (line 191) –
which must therefore be round and staring. He then describes her as a
'masked performance' (*persollae nugae*), which her lover counters by
dubbing her 'Venus'. Clearly this striking mask did not display the
idealized beauty of a narrow-eyed Hellenistic 'wronged maiden' type,
but is rendered grotesque by its owlish features. This theatrical mask is a
deliberate distortion or inversion of the perfect Venus created by
sculptors, and by Greek mask-makers.

The pattern is clear. In each case an expectation is set up in order to be
overturned. Each mask undergoes a metamorphosis when its wearer in
some way acts contrary to type. Conventional Hellenistic masks are
variants or distortions constructed upon a normative base, an ideal of
male or female beauty. There is no such norm or ideal implicit in Plautine
theatre, where a theatrical mask is the inversion of a noble *imago*, and is
necessarily an emblem of ignobility. The animal references in *Curculio*
are more than coincidental. Names assimilate characters to a lioness, a
wolf, a weevil. While the *mulier* looks like an owl, the *leno* with his
stomach and green eyes must look like a frog. The name of the *miles*,
Therapontigonus, suggests a 'beast born from the sea'. Plautus' characters do not act with the noble qualities of men but with the instincts of
beasts. The masks of Plautus preserve the outline structure of the Greek
system, but their meaning is wholly changed.

The basic differentiating signs of the Greek masking system are
preserved in Plautus' theatre. The evidence is necessarily sparse because
theatrical signs are rarely redundant, and a good dramatist does not use
language to duplicate information available to the eye. We observe that in
Plautus, as in Greek comedy, old men have beards, young men do not.
This is a theatrical convention, for it is reasonable to guess that in Roman
life some young men grew beards, and some old men shaved.[33] We have to
glean our information from jokes. We know, for instance, that Nicobulus
in *The Two Bacchises* had white hair and a white beard because of a

sustained joke about sheep-shearing (lines 241–2, 1100ff). His slave has twice shorn him of his gold. When he plays the *adulescens* and propositions the courtesans he is mocked for his lack of wool, presumably because he is bald, and is offered a third shearing. This time he wants to be shorn, so his hair starts to itch. The conventional white beard of the Greek mask has not been discarded, but it becomes a self-conscious convention. Nicobulus compares himself to the Atellan mask Bucco (line 1084), encouraging the audience to think of his mask as a theatrical property. We see again how a Greek visual convention has been subverted, so that the mask is drained of all psychological content, and becomes the emblem of an animal identity.

Slaves in Pollux have tawny hair, and we know that the principal slave in *Pseudolus* has red hair (line 1218). A passage in *The Comedy of Asses* gives us good information about a slave's appearance. The slave is said to have 'thin cheek-bones, reddish complexion, a paunch, wild eyes, moderate height, and a dejected brow' (lines 400–1). The hair is not mentioned in this instance because the slave is at the barber's, and his presumably red hair is about to undergo an exotic transformation. The other features receive an accurate description in order to enhance the surprise value of the apparition, and they seem entirely consistent with Greek convention. Equally consistent is the description of the *leno* in *The Rope*. This *leno* is bald and has 'twisted' eyebrows. His hair is curly and his brow clenched (lines 125, 317–18). Although these details replicate precisely the description of the pimp given in Pollux, no mention is made of the mouth, which in Pollux displays 'a slight grin'. Plautus' *leno* offers to hire himself out as the Atellan mask Manducus because of his chattering teeth (line 535). One suspects that the most ambivalent area of the Greek mask has been subverted. In both *The Comedy of Asses* and *The Rope*, the Greek image provides the base for a transformation. The grotesque qualities of the mask are drawn to the audience's attention.

Now that we have grasped the basic elements with which Plautus works, I shall turn to two plays, which literary criticism tends to place at opposite ends of a spectrum, in order to clarify the structural principles underlying Plautus' plot construction, and thus the use he makes of his system of masks. *The Captives* is generally seen as Plautus' most serious or moral play, *The Persian* as his most farcical and trivial. In the first, the playwright eliminates the masks of *leno*, *miles*, principal slave, and all female masks; in the second he eliminates the *senex* and the *adulescens*. New actor–actant relationships emerge as a consequence.

Scarcely has the prologue in *The Captives* proclaimed Plautus' high

moral intent in removing the lying *leno*, braggart *miles*, and evil *meretrix*
from the stage, when the parasite enters and proclaims that his nickname
is 'whore' (line 69). He later doubles as slave by performing the routine of
the 'running slave', gathering his cloak about his neck 'like slaves in
comedies do' (line 778). As the entertainer whose livelihood consists in
making people laugh, he becomes a metaphor for Plautus' comedy as a
whole. When he says that he has returned to the forum to find other
parasites ambling to no purpose (line 491), he refers to actors appearing
in the forum with their production. The triumph of the parasite in this
play is thus the triumph of the traditional comic formula. The plot deals
with the way one *adulescens*, supposed a slave, exchanges roles with his
master in order that the latter may escape from captivity. There can be no
question of the supposed slave Tyndarus wearing a slave mask, for the
audience knows from the beginning that he is a free-born Greek. The two
young men have been reared alongside each other, and share an identical
noble nature (lines 720, 419). To be sure, the two masks cannot be
identical, for certain distinguishing signs are mentioned in a description
of the *adulescens* who escapes: mouth (thin), nose (pointed), complexion
(pale), eyes (dark), hair colour (blond), hair texture (curled locks) (lines
647–8). In a comedy of Menander we should expect the other young man
to have reverse features, and for these features to be a key to character. In
Plautus these features are arbitrary, for the two yo'.ng men are not
differentiated psychologically.[34] The features cited are significant, rather,
for the way they establish a Greek-style face. While the parasite's mask is
grotesque, a sight that terrorizes the *puer* (lines 913–14), the masks of the
young men are in this instance good-looking. The visual interest lies in
the sight of an *adulescens* dressed in the stage costume of a slave. We know
of no precedent for this device in Greek comedy, and it is a characteristic
Plautine metamorphosis. One may guess that in the Greek source play
adapted by Plautus, 'Tyndarus' did wear a slave mask, did behave
creditably, and was not revealed to be of Greek birth. The figure of the
noble slave is incompatible with Roman ideology, and Plautus would
seem to have inverted the message of the Greek play by demonstrating the
triumph of birth over breeding. When Plautus' prologue describes the
two young men as each bearing the *imago* of the other (line 34), he
demonstrates how the Greek masking tradition has been assimilated by
the Roman.

In *The Persian*, the plot concerns the duping of the *leno*. This *leno*,
securely rooted in the genus of *leno*s (line 582), becomes a fixed point,
while every other mask mutates. The first slave becomes the *adulescens*,

obsessed with getting the girl he loves. The second slave dresses as a *miles*. The parasite is cast in the role of the *senex*, the cruel father, and his daughter, the *virgo*, is dressed as a *meretrix*. The real *meretrix* gains her liberty like a *mulier* or 'pseudo-virgin'. To complete the pattern, the *ancilla* acts the mature *meretrix* when she tries to seduce the *puer*. As in *The Captives*, the mutation of the Greek masks provides the means for a clear articulation of Roman values. It is again the parasite who is the vehicle for criticism or irony. While the parasite parodies the obsession of the Roman nobility with emulating the achievements of ancestors, it is his daughter the *virgo* who becomes the emotional centre of the play. In her borrowed prostitute's uniform, she articulates the dilemma of a woman torn between a duty of obedience and a concern for honour. The play deals with the plight of those who are poor in Roman society. The visual contradiction set up by the image of slave as rich youth, the *virgo* as prostitute illustrates a gap between illusion and reality. The man who is too poor to marry, the girl whose father can pay no dowry, succeed within a stage world that is not an escape from reality but an inversion of reality. The rules which the play flouts are at once the conventions of Hellenistic theatre and the conventions of Roman society.

PLAUTUS AND THE *COMMEDIA DELL'ARTE*

Comparisons with the *commedia dell'arte* can give us further insight into Plautus' system of masks. We see in the *commedia* how a restricted system of mask types is compatible with a diversity of mask names and specific mask designs. The Spanish Captain, for instance, may be incarnated by different actors under such names as Matamoros (Moor-slayer), Cocodrillo (crocodile), Spavento della Valle Inferno (scourge of the Valley of Death), and so on, but his role is always the same. Plautus in a similar way invents punning names for familiar masks each time they reappear.

The utopian Greek setting established in Roman comedy may remind us of the utopian Italian setting offered by Italian actors to foreign audiences. In the Paris of Molière, for instance, we know how the famous Arlecchino 'Dominique' would adopt his favourite role of 'Marquis de Sbroufadel', and would somersault into a frock-coat and out of a wig; how, dressed as a soldier, he would threaten to die for love in the way that Cleopatra died for Tarquin, and Aristotle died for Galen; or how, dressed as a doctor, he would feel the father's pulse as 'flesh and blood' of his sick daughter.[35] In all these instances, the Parisian audience saw the follies of

its own culture – its fashion, its poetic discourse, its pseudo-scientific
medicine – brought into relief. Beneath the contemporary disguise, it can
always see the familiar mask and costume of the Italian actor. A similar
double image is offered to the Roman spectator when a conventional
Roman moral discourse about *pietas* (reverence), *pectus* ('guts'), and *mos
maiorum* (ancestral values) emerges from an alien Greek mask. As Erich
Segal has demonstrated,[36] the Greek setting is associated in Roman
comedy with sexual and political licence. While many Romans deplored
Greek freèdom as decadent and destructive of all Roman values, the
intellectual and artistic achievements of Greece were much envied. The
Greek origins of the Plautine mask therefore affect the way the mask is
perceived. In a similar way, Italy was for seventeenth-century France the
mythical land of Machiavelli and Petrarch, pure evil and pure romantic
love. With its history of artistic triumph and political disaster, notorious
for its republican traditions and the libertinism of its courtesans, Italy
had connotations for Frenchmen not dissimilar to those which Greece
had for Romans.

Segal stresses the close relationship between the world of Plautus and
the Roman *ludi*. Plautus' comedy is inseparable from the Roman festival
in the same way that the *commedia dell'arte* is inseparable from the Italian
carnival. While *commedia dell'arte* actors borrowed their narrative
frameworks from classical Roman comedy, thcy turned to contemporary
carnivalesque practices in order to create specific masks, costumes, and
movements. In the same fashion, Plautus turned to Hellenistic comedy to
create a framework for his drama, but brought his plays to life by drawing
on an indigenous popular culture. Clearly he drew on this culture in order
to give Greek-style masks a visual interpretation meaningful to his
audience. The Plautine mask, like that of Arlecchino, seems to take on
animal and infernal attributes. It is not an imitation of observed human
features, but a symbol. Like all carnivalesque *commedia* masks, it liberates
the wearer from the hierarchical, sexual, gravitational, and ontological
constraints of normal existence.

The *commedia* mask is a half-mask, the Greek mask was a full mask.
The *commedia* actor develops a close relationship with his mask which he
wears for much of his career, while the Greek actor slips from one mask to
another. While the Greek mask effaces the actor's personality, the
commedia mask leaves part of the face visible, and establishes the sense
that a particular actor has a unique physical presence. It is difficult to
know where to place the Roman mask in this respect. Hellenistic comedy
is written for performance by three actors, actors whose personality

necessarily vanishes in the course of rapid doubling. Roman comedy does not observe this convention.[37] The interesting exception is the *Stichus*, which clearly is written to be played by three actors. Here, however, the same pair of actors play a pair of sisters, a pair of brothers, and then a pair of slaves who are brothers in love. It is the parallelism which integrates the play, and it is essential therefore that the audience be aware of the distinctive personalities of the three performers.

Plautus' comedy always assumes that the audience is aware of the actor's physical presence. I have pointed out already how the audience are reminded of the actor behind the stage masks of Nicobulus, of the *mulier* in *Casina*, of the *leno* in *The Rope*. In *The Persian*, when a disguise is needed, a visit to the costumier is recommended because he is under contract to supply all the costumes for the performance (lines 159–60). Examples of this kind of device are too numerous for me to cite more. It is reasonable to imagine that the masks used by Plautus would have offered the audience the same apprehension as the text of the player behind the role. Paulette Ghiron-Bistagne has brought to light a tradition of half-masks in the ancient world, and develops a rather unconvincing argument for the use of such masks by Atellan actors.[38] A more suggestive iconographic tradition is that which enlarges the mouth and eyes of the Hellenistic New Comedy mask, allowing the features of the actor to be discerned. The most striking example is a figurine from Asia Minor of the third century AD.[39] Here the trumpet mouth of the slave becomes a kind of picture frame, allowing the audience to discern or divine the movement of the actor's mouth. Such a mask would well suit the metatheatrical role of the slave as the 'poet' of a drama within a drama.[40]

The *commedia dell'arte* is famed as a tradition of improvisation. This does not necessarily mean that the actors invented their lines on stage; it means, rather, that the actor and not the dramatist was responsible for preparing the words to be spoken.[41] The job of the dramatist was to create a scenario, and the mask had such a strong identity that the wearer knew at once how to respond to the situation proposed by the dramatist. There is a close link between the masks of the *commedia* and the extemporal element, as Keith Johnstone explains in his description of mask workshops:

Scholars have advanced many reasons for the use of the Masks by the players of the Commedia dell'Arte, but they miss the obvious one – that Masks improvise for *hours*, in an effortless way... Masks don't fit so well into normal theatre, unless the director understands their problems... The biggest problem is that the Masks refuse to repeat scenes. Even when you tell them they are going to take part in a play, they insist on being spontaneous.[42]

Johnstone is influenced by eastern concepts of the mask, and describes how the actor becomes possessed by the spirit of the mask. He sees the masked actor as a person regaining the spontaneity of childhood, and a child's sense that everything is for the first time. He quotes the advice given by Vakhtangov to actors working on *commedia* characters:

I don't deny the importance of thinking, inventing and planning, but if you have to improvise on the spot (and that's exactly what we have to do), you must act and not think. It's action we must have – wise, foolish or naive, simple or complicated, but *action*.[43]

These observations are valuable for our understanding of Plautus' use of masks. It is clear that Plautus was deeply influenced by the extemporal techniques of the Atellan actors. His plays set up the illusion that the masks are improvising. In Menander's theatre, the neat crafting of the plot reassures the audience that the controlling hand of the poet is at work. The actions of the masks presuppose an element of prior thought. The action and dialogue articulate a set of moral choices, and these moral choices allow the audience to decode the *êthos* of the mask. In Plautus' theatre, the Aristotelian category of moral choice is absent. The masks express no *êthos*. Rather, the masks seem to behave in an unpremeditated, spontaneous manner as soon as they are confronted, before their Roman audience, with the situation proposed by a Greek playwright. The masked actors of Plautus break the conventions of *mimêsis*: they refer to the Roman context of performance, they move freely from speech to song, they experiment with novel impersonations. The masks have no past and no future: slaves, for instance, have no Asiatic homeland, no fears of punishment or hopes of freedom tomorrow, and they live only in and for the present;[44] young men likewise are interested in sex today, not marriage tomorrow, and a prostitute is as welcome as a bride.[45] Plautus, in short, is at pains to create an extemporal illusion for his masks, so that 'when you tell them they are going to take part in a play, they insist on being spontaneous'.

The *commedia dell'arte* has its sociological context in the rigid social structure of the French *ancien régime*, in Ducal and Spanish regimes in Italy, and in the Counter-Reformation. It has its roots in an aristocratic society where there was little social mobility and a strong sense of hierarchy.[46] Each mask is fixed in its particular theatrical category, just as each human being is fixed in his or her social category. The inversionary, utopian social structure of carnival and of *commedia* is made both possible and necessary by the hierarchical order of everyday life. In Victor Turner's terms, the stronger the sense of structure within a society, the stronger becomes the need for 'anti-structure' within the liminal time and space allotted to festival.[47] With the waning of aristocratic rule, and the emergence of the bourgeois idea that each individual creates his or her own economic, social, and moral destiny, the appeal of a system of fixed theatrical roles waned necessarily. There was no point in wearing a mask providing licence to subvert, when no clear order existed to be subverted.

The contrast between Rome and Greece can be seen in rather similar terms as a contrast between a hierarchical and a bourgeois society – although the term 'bourgeois' may create a false picture of the Hellenistic economy.[48] In Rome it was very difficult to move from one census grouping to another. A man's nature in the present was defined by the quality of his ancestors. Death masks rendered these ancestors a fixed and unchangeable element in the present. In Greek democratic society, on the other hand, there was no formal hierarchy within the citizen body – if one excludes vestiges of the pre-democratic past preserved in certain religious rites. In Athens, unlike Rome, political office was open to all citizens. In assemblies and lawcourts, a citizen had to keep judging the characters of his peers in order to decide how to vote. Theatrical structure correlates with social structure. Characters have to be judged. Explanations for their behaviour have to be sought in the way life has treated them, and the way they have responded. In a broader dimension, the Greek festival is structured as a celebration of mobility. Plays are written to provide opportunities for the virtuoso actor who can play any part. In the Roman world there was a corporate ethic of a very different kind. People were not judged by character alone, but by character in relation to family. Individuals were honoured or punished as members of a given group – the nobility, a particular regiment, prostitutes, the slaves of a particular household. The theatre reflected (and of course reinforced) this basic difference between an immobile society interested in group qualities and a mobile society interested in the qualities of each particular member. Both societies, of course, were equally committed to the system of slavery, and I shall examine in the next chapter the effect of slavery upon the world of the stage.

TERENCE

When we move ahead one generation to the comedy of Terence, much seems to have changed. The Greek comedy of Menander is no longer an alien form to be subverted but an aesthetic ideal to be imitated, though also modified to suit Roman tastes. Terence's prologues proclaim the

PLATES

1　Mosaic by Dioskourides from Pompeii, representing a scene from
The Girl Possessed

IA   Mask of a young man from Lipari, superimposed upon a sketch of
the central figure

2　Mosaic by Dioskourides from Pompeii, representing a scene from
The Ladies at Luncheon

3　Stone relief from Pompeii

4 Mosaic from Pompeii, representing Eros riding a tiger

5   Slave from Lipari

6   Mask of a youth from Lipari

7   Four young women from Lipari

supremacy of the writer. He invites the audience to be aware of the aesthetic control which he, the author, has over the performance. While Plautus seems to have learned his craft as an actor, Terence began as a writer, and he was accused of taking to drama too suddenly.[49] In this new theatre of the writer, the masks could no longer be allowed to 'improvise', for the writer had to protect himself from condemnation by literary critics for breaking the rules. The political context had changed by the time Terence wrote. The reactionary Roman traditionalism of Cato the Censor – which valued the ascetic element within the Greek tradition – now stood in sharp opposition to the philhellenism of the Scipios, which valued the aesthetic element. The biographical sources collected by Suetonius, agree unanimously in placing Terence amongst the Greek-speaking intellectuals gathered around Scipio the younger.[50] Dispute turns principally upon the homosexual basis of the relationship between Terence and this group. Suetonius' sources probably in the main built upon the fact that, as aediles, Scipio and his brother selected two of Terence's plays for performance at the funeral games of their father. The prologue to one of these plays, *The Brothers*, counters, or more probably manufactures, the rumour that Terence was helped in his writing by eminent men, implicitly Scipio and his associates. The respect with which Terence treats his Greek sources is an ideological phenomenon. While Plautus continually reminds his audience that he has Romanized and transformed his Greek sources, Terence allows nothing to distract from the idea that his stage is a street in Athens. Through his abolition of the sustained monologue and expository prologue, Terence shows himself more Greek than Menander, subjecting himself completely to the idea that a play is not a festive concelebration but a *mimêsis* of social reality.

The philosophy of the Greek Stoics is in evidence in Terence's writing. In accordance with Stoic materialism, Terence retains the principle that the *psychê* is knowable through its external manifestations. As in Menander, the actor is the hidden but material presence animating visible corporeal matter. The Stoics were much concerned with moral responsibility. While the masks of Plautus act rather than think, and their actions seem to have no consequences extending beyond the action of the play, Terence's masks cannot escape moral responsibility. In *The Brothers* we see, for instance, how two old men display contrasting philosophies of education, two young men contrasting attitudes to marriage. Present actions are seen as having consequences in future life. While Aristotle perceived most emotions as good or bad only in relation to the situation in which they are experienced, Stoicism tended to regard emotion in general as dangerous. Stoicism therefore did not encourage its adherents to make fine distinctions between different emotions, but gave credit to those who can conquer all emotions. As I observed in chapter 1, the binary structure of Terence's narratives sets up a clear opposition between those who surrender to pleasure, and those who reject emotion in preference for duty. Terence's plays are not Stoic tracts, but they are plainly shaped by an engagement with Stoicism.

We can make certain obvious deductions about Terence's use of the mask. His concern to imitate Greek practice would have necessitated a relatively close adherence to the Greek masking system. Unlike Plautus, he had no reason to subvert the visual language of Greek theatre. The polemical prologue to *The Self-Tormentor* expresses a rejection of Plautus' comedy of fixed types:

Be fair – give me permission to put across a quiet comedy in silence, so that we don't always have to have a Running Slave, an angry Senex, a greedy Parasite, an impudent Sycophant, a miserly Leno, all acted with the greatest noise and maximum effort.[51]

The argument interestingly reverses that offered two years earlier, when Terence justified his use of a rather similar body of stock types in *The Eunuch*: the Running Slave, a virtuous Matron, a wicked *meretrix*, a greedy Parasite, and a braggart *miles*. Terence's comedy of stock types, *The Eunuch*, brought instant success, while other plays seem to have gained a more mixed response. Terence was subject to conflicting pressures, and the masks which he used must have been in some sense an aesthetic compromise.

Terence's style is commonly distinguished from that of Menander by his tendency to generalize. This tendency has often been related to Terence's Stoic concern with 'humanity' rather than with one specific society.[52] I shall restrict myself to one representative example of this generalizing tendency. Chremes in *The Self-Tormentor* tells his son that parental severity follows a common pattern, for parents attempt to inculcate virtue in their sons, while sons 'enslave their minds to base desires' (lines 204–9); the son responds by claiming that fathers are unfair judges of *adulescentes* (line 213). The plays bear out the implications of this conversation, namely that all fathers have problems in common, and so do all sons. Terence's concern with the Stoic virtue of self-dominance in respect of all personal desires, his Stoic concept of man's common humanity, and the whole corporate ethic of Roman society allowed no space for the intricacies of Menander's masking system. Whether a person is reared in a hot or a cold climate, whether his metabolism inclines to melancholia, whether a youth is more or less than 25 years old – such questions are irrelevant, since they cannot excuse a man from moral responsibility. In *The Brothers*, for instance, we see how two young men are able to form their own moral choices in complete defiance of their respective backgrounds. Terence requires for such a play a system of masks which will establish a rather simple set of polarities – the angry country *senex*, the genial urban *senex* – and any more complex information would be redundant, impeding rather than assisting the audience's understanding of the poet's work.

Terence abandoned the finer points of Menander's naming conventions. In his adaptation of *The Eunuch*, Chairestratos is renamed Phaedria, Daos becomes Parmeno, Chrysis becomes Thais, and Simon becomes Laches.[53] Terence also incorporates two characters from Menander's *The Toady*: Gnatho the parasite retains his Menandrean name, but the soldier, Bias, is renamed Thraso. The name Chremes, given to an old man in three other plays of Terence, is here inexplicably given to a young man from the country. Since the names Chrysis, Daos, and Simon are used elsewhere in Terence, it is hard to see why Terence has for the most part rejected the names used by Menander. If part of Terence's originality lay in reconceiving the characters created by Menander, then the names may perhaps be a clue to the way he sought to reconceive the masks. It is possible that an important aesthetic choice lay behind, for example, the replacement of the dynamic mask of Daos with the more passive masks of Parmeno. On the evidence that we possess, it looks as if well-known mask names have been randomly chosen from within such categories as nurse, lover, soldier, or courtesan – but the reality may have been different.

It is safe to assume that Terence was not in a position to reproduce the nuances of Menander's system of masks. Terence's Roman audience did not possess the same cultural references as the Greek audience. Menander's masks require a familiarity with the principles of Aristotelian physiognomy, a science which rests in its turn upon broad cultural assumptions – upon Hippocratic physiology, upon a theory of education, upon a received ethical discourse which takes goodness as a mid-point, and so forth. Such cultural references were part of an everyday, commonsense attitude to life in the Greek world, but did not form part of a normal Roman understanding of how life was. It was not only the Roman audience for whom the Greek masking system was a closed book, however. Terence himself probably had a very restricted knowledge of the visual codes assumed by Menander.

We need to consider in this connexion how the Greek masking tradition was transmitted. There are many gaps in our knowledge. It is uncertain to what extent Menander inherited a coherent system of masks, and to what extent he created a system in the course of his career. We do know that Menander's death approximately coincided with the setting up of an organized guild of actors in Athens, a similar guild forming in the Peloponnese.[54]

Mask-making was traditionally the responsibility of a 'skeuopoios' ('maker of equipment'),[55] and Aristotle speaks of the great power of the skeuopoios in relation to the visual element of performance.[56] Pollux tells us that the skeuopoios came to have the alternative name of prosôpopoios (mask-maker) in the period of New Comedy.[57] We know that the Egyptian guild had a skeuopoios, but we do not know what relation his role bore to the himatiomisthês (literally 'hirer of cloaks') of the Greek guilds, who would contract to supply the costumes for a dramatic festival.[58] The question arises whether the himatiomisthês supplied the masks for a festival, or whether these were the personal property of actors. Webster suggested that masks must be designed to fit the head of a particular actor,[59] but this is implausible: four of Menander's plays as we have them, and thus perhaps most of his plays, require that a given mask be worn by more than one actor in the course of the performance.[60] It is more plausible that the prôtagônistês, the leading actor who competed for the acting prize, would like a Noh master have possessed a stock of masks for use by himself and his synagônistai or accomplices. A huge stock of masks would be needed, since the forty-four masks listed by Pollux are nowhere near adequate for performing the extant repertory of Menander, let alone the range of scripts that must have been available. The job of maintenance – repainting eyebrows, decorating a courtesan's hair with jewellery, making good all the damage that occurs on tour – must have been considerable. Given the close relationship between the mask and the performance, it seems to me most likely that a trio of actors carried their own set of masks on tour, while expecting costumes to be supplied upon arrival.

The institutionalizing of the guilds made for continuity. Yet in the century which separates Terence's youth from Menander's death and the formation of the guilds, change must have occurred. The multiplication of guilds must have meant that groups of actors diverged from the Athenian tradition. One must imagine conditions of rivalry rather than a pooling of information. One must imagine actors trying well-known roles in new masks, as in the Noh theatre, in order to create a fresh feel to the performance. One must imagine a progressive loosening of the link between mask and name, so that only well-known and boldly featured masks like Smikrines and Knemon would have allowed instant recognition. Bearing in mind this slow process of loosening, we must also differentiate the kind of knowledge available to the actor or mask-maker with access to the traditions of the guild from the kind of knowledge available to a lay spectator. There is no evidence that Terence had any professional involvement with the Greek theatre, and he would merely have gained a general sense of the kind of mask which belonged to a particular kind of role. Since he wrote for a cast of more than three actors, distinctions of character could to a greater extent be created through the distinctive vocal and physical traits of different actors. Terence's plays provide us with valuable information about Menander's texts, but we should not expect them to give us any useful information about the conventions of performance assumed by Menander. The plays provide evidence only of Roman practice.

CHAPTER 6

The four mask genera

We shall return now to the Hellenistic mask and examine how the four genera – old man, young man, slave, woman – came into being. We shall try to understand how this fourfold division came to be seen as the *natural* way in which a *mimêsis* of Greek society should be organized. Once we define the problem in these terms, we are of course committed to accepting that an art form is an ideological phenomenon. And we are forced to confront the question of how popular entertainment shaped or challenged the common-sense view of the world shared by most members of the Greek audience. The question which concerns us is a question about form, not about content. A dramatist in a particular play may have tried to communicate a message – about youthful morality, or attitudes to poverty, for instance. But any such message had to be transmitted via a channel – namely, the actor – and via a code – namely, the conventions of theatrical performance. It would have been comparatively easy for a Greek audience to grasp and reject the message – to emerge from the theatre feeling, say, that Menander portrayed slaves too sympathetically, women too sentimentally. It is always much harder for an audience to reject the code, the basic building-blocks of a performance – its stage, its narrative patterns, its masks, and so forth – for these constitute the language in which theatrical communication becomes possible. Much modern criticism of Menander is concerned with extrapolating the message. My objective in this book is to analyse the code, for it is only through the code, and the channel, that a message can be communicated. If the channel is not the actor but a printed page, and the reader tries to decode the message in the same way that he or she would decode a novel, the message extracted from the words Menander wrote will be of a particular and often inappropriate kind. My object is to lay bare the performance code which Menander and his audience shared, and to a significant extent we do not share. This performance code is what made communication in the theatre possible.

As I observed in my analysis of Pollux's catalogue, tetradic structures seem characteristic of Greek thought. A liking for fours, which can be traced back to the Pythagoreans, becomes almost a compulsion in the Hellenistic period. Some examples will illustrate the point. Theophrastos identified four sources of human action: sources that we might call personal, one's choice and one's nature, intersect with two impersonal sources, chance and necessity.[1] Democritus analysed colour in terms of two opposed pairs, black/white and red/green.[2] Just as Hellenistic dramatists worked with four mask types, so Hellenistic painters, we are told, worked with a palette of four colours.[3] Most important of all, in Hellenistic thought, is the fourfold division of hot/cold and wet/dry. This division is linked in complex ways to a perception of the natural world comprising earth, air, fire, and water, the year comprising four seasons, and the body containing four humours.[4] It is linked also to a system of physics based on the oppositions heavy/light and rare/dense.[5] Aristotle states that the four elements, hot and cold, wet and dry, are the basis of all physical distinctions, and that matter cannot be subdivided further.[6] In living organisms, these four are identified as the sole causes of 'life and death, sleep and waking, strength, age, illness, health'.[7]

From the pre-Socratics through to the Stoics, the same idea holds, that physiological health depends upon an equal balance of these four elements. In accordance with the democratic cast of Greek thought, a Pythagorean described the dominance of any one element as 'monarchical', while the proper balance was seen as 'equal rights'.[8] Mind and body were considered to be interlinked. Democritus carried materialism to its logical conclusion when he asserted that a person's physical composition, which varies according to his age and *pathos*, determines his *phantasia* – his 'imagination' or 'power of perception'.[9] Physiological theories of the hot and the cold, the wet and the dry, are thus fundamental to Hellenistic thinking about character. Bodily substances are all subject to imbalance, and an imbalance will affect both the appearance and the behaviour of a person. 'Of all our qualities, the hot and the cold are the most character-forming (*êthopoios*)', wrote one of Aristotle's followers in an essay on black bile.[10] The blood, which carries the breath of life to the heart, is naturally the most important fluid in Aristotelian thinking, and thick hot blood was seen as giving strength, thin cool blood intelligence and sensitivity, the ideal blood being hot and wet.[11] The quality of the blood was thought to be apparent through the quality of the skin and hair. Given these assumptions, the physiological features encoded in the mask necessarily gave the audience information about psychological states.

The four mask genera plainly correlate with the four elements as understood in Aristotelian thinking:

old man	cold and dry
young man	hot and wet
slave	hot and dry
woman	cold and wet

Age is understood as both a drying and a chilling process, while regenerative life is moist and warm.[12] Deficiency of heat causes greying of the hair – a kind of mould or disease of the hair.[13] The drying of the blood makes the complexion darker, whilst the chilling of the blood makes it livid.[14] The blood of the young man is lymphatic, wetter, and more abundant than that of the old man.[15] The male in general, however, is hot and dry in comparison with the female who is cold and wet.[16] His blood is hotter, and thus flows to the surface.[17] The young male thus embodies the hot/wet principle which in all forms of organic life is necessary for regeneration.[18] There remains, of course, much variation within the mask of the young man, for exercise in the open air dries the body; without exposure to the air, a wet warm surface becomes pale and putrified.[19] The tawny (*pyrrhos* – literally 'fiery' or 'burnt') hair of the slave can be explained by the erratic climate of the north: while the body is chilled, the external parts are dried by the sun.[20] Tawny hair is inferior, for hair only grows dark with moisture and nourishment.[21] The reddish complexion of the slave can be explained as nature's way of resisting a cold climate. The blood rises to the surface, but the fluids are not dried out. The cold thickens the skin in order to keep the heat in.[22]

The distinguishing features of the masks correlate with this system of thought. The woman (crones excepted) always has a whitish face. This pallor can be explained by the natural wetness and coldness of the female body. It is also assumed that the woman is pale because she lives indoors and 'shuns the light',[23] so her skin is not dried by the sun, her blood is not brought to the surface. We should take note too of a correlation with the social convention whereby fashionable women enhanced their pallor by painting their faces with white lead.[24] Bone structure is not of significance in relation to the four elements of hot/cold/wet/dry, and bone structure does not therefore differentiate male and female masks. Complexion, hair, mouth, and eyes are the critical features. It is not so much the natural colour and texture of the hair as the coiffure which distinguishes one woman from another. It is woman's social status rather than her character which tends to be the focus of the audience's attention. The woman has narrow eyes because she lives out of the light, and is naturally dazzled when she comes onto the street. Her role is not to look but to be looked at. Her mouth is less wide open than the young man's because her role is not to speak but to listen. The crones are an exception to all this, and constitute an anomaly in the neat tetradic system. By virtue of their age and loss of sexuality, they should in many respects be bracketed with old men.

Old men in our monuments are distinguished from young men principally by the fact that they have beards.[25] Shaving became customary in the age of Alexander, only a generation before Menander,[26] and the young are therefore beardless not so much because they are adolescent as because they are fashionable. Hair colour and skin texture distinguish old from young in obvious ways. The slave is distinguished from the free man by the distinctive stylized beard which forms a trumpet round the mouth. While the beard of the old man's mask is made of real hair, the beard of the slave is solid. By the time Plautus was writing, the beard had become vestigial, and could scarcely be recognized as such; the trumpet was simply a grotesque frame for a grinning mouth.[27]

When we compare the mask conventions of New Comedy with those of Old Comedy, we see that a new set of distinctions has emerged. In Old and Middle Comedy, the comic hero is characteristically neither old nor young, but in his prime. Beards did not distinguish the generations.[28] Equally, we find in masks and figurines related to earlier comedy no clear distinction between old men and slaves.[29] In Old and Middle Comedy, the padded stomach and leather phallus demonstrated the grotesqueness of the human animal. In the context of a religious festival, the audience were for ever reminded that they were watching human beings rather than gods. In New Comedy, this perception changes. The orchestral circle with its ritual associations has given way to a mirror-like stage. The play is presented as a *mimêsis* of social life, and the characters are fully clothed. The drama has absorbed Aristotle's view that man is by nature *politikos*, a social being. The masks and costumes represent man's social identity. The oppositions old/young and free/slave are now, in the theatre as in Aristotelian philosophy, seen as part of nature's plan.

My concern in this book is with New Comedy as a synchronic system, and an adequate diachronic exploration of each of the four mask genera would require much further research. It is not my intention to emulate the patient labours of T. B. L. Webster and J. R. Green who have confronted the question of origins in the course of cataloguing comic masks. I shall restrict myself to the observation that comedy, as a genre, provides the parameters for Webster's and Green's cataloguing. The evolution of the masks is sought within the confines of comedy. It seems to me, however, that since Menander's writing patently owes more to Euripides than to Aristophanes, one might reasonably expect that his masks too should owe more to the Euripidean tradition than to the Aristophanic. To a large extent, I believe, New Comedy borrowed and modified the relatively naturalistic mask conventions of late classical tragedy. This happened at the same time as Hellenistic tragedy on the high stage adopted a new idiom based upon the *onkos*, the raised head-dress connoting the marvellous or heroic status of tragic characters. The practice of reviving works of Old Comedy began in 339 BC and by 311 BC such revivals were a regular part of the Dionysia.[30] This must have given impetus to the creators of New Comedy to develop a new set of masks in a style wholly independent of Old Comedy.

It is amongst the young men's masks that a debt to tragedy is most obvious. Tragic heroes engaged on ephebic quests – like Perseus, Neoptolemus, or Orestes – must have had beardless, idealized features. Fourth-century terracotta miniatures of tragic masks found in Lipari confirm the evidence of vase-paintings that this was so.[31] We should likewise expect the admirable heroines of Menander to owe their features to figures like Iphigeneia and Aphrodite on the tragic stage rather than to the grotesque women of Aristophanes. The convention of the white face can be observed on some fifth-century vases which represent tragic performances.[32] Discussion of the evolution of the old man's mask is impeded by the fact that we have relatively few early examples from New Comedy. In the second and first centuries, the mask of the old man becomes increasingly grotesque, so that his lips, nose, and brow are scarcely distinguishable from those of a slave. The best-preserved mask of an old man in Lipari ('first grandfather', ex. 1, in Brea's MTGTL) has unquestionably handsome features and a mournful expression, and is valuable evidence for a Euripidean phase in the representation of old men. The mask of an old man found in Centuripe – his hair well groomed in an oriental style – confirms that old age is not necessarily grotesque in the early Hellenistic period.[33] Pollux, however, apparently names one old man's mask after the actor Hermon who played in Aristophanes,[34] a circumstance which suggests some continuity from Old Comedy to certain specific New Comedy types. We are looking at a system in flux in the late fourth century. The asymmetrical features of many old-man masks clearly represent a technique which evolved in response to the raised stage, and the new control which the actor had over the angle at which he presented his mask to the audience. It is in the slave that we can trace most clearly a direct line of evolution from Old Comedy. A comic slave mask found in Athens, for instance, with pointed trumpet and asymmetrical brows, is dated by Webster to before 325 BC.[35] In the case of the slave, there is room for speculation that perhaps the arched and projecting brows, and the prevalence of baldness, owe something also to the Euripidean satyr. The satyr, like the slave, represents mankind in his natural or uncivilized state. The independence of the three genres cannot be taken for granted.[36]

A diachronic analysis of Greek masks raises technical and methodological problems which are beyond the scope of this book. I shall pursue a synchronic methodology which involves seeking not for the history of a single given mask but for the relationship between one mask and another. Rather than seek to analyse that which constitutes a given mask type, I shall seek to analyse a system of differences. Let us clarify, first of all, the differences which distinguish one genus of mask from another.

Aristotle writes in the *Rhetoric* of three different ages: youth, prime, and old age. Youth is characterized by noble ideals, but a lack of self-control. Old age is characterized by utilitarian values and small-mindedness. The old are not hot-blooded but cowardly, for, of course, 'they are chill while the young are hot'. Men in their prime avoid the failings and enjoy the benefits of both conditions. Though men are placed in their physical prime at between 30 and 35, Aristotle accepts the Solonic tradition according to which the mind attains its prime at 49.[37] We see, therefore, that the young/old opposition developed in New Comedy is well suited to be a vehicle for defining an ideal intermediate state – a balanced condition defined by the opposite and imperfect conditions on either side.

Male is distinguished from female in Hellenistic comedy. This is a less obvious distinction than it seems, for many comic dramatists – Aristophanes frequently, Plautus in the *Casina*, Lucian in his *Dialogues of the Courtesans* – play at length upon sexual ambiguity, as women dress as men, men as women. Homosexuality is a taboo subject in Menander, as Plutarch noted with approval,[38] and we have no examples in the plays of transsexual disguise. Nothing enters the play to challenge the sense that the distinction between male and female is natural and absolute. There is no reason to believe that homosexuality was less prevalent in Athens in Menander's day than it had been a century earlier, and we have to seek ideological explanations for its omission. Where Plato the idealist celebrated homosexual love as the quest for an ideal of virtue and beauty ultimately unattainable in this world, Aristotle the materialist was interested in the biological task of propagation which nature seemed to ordain for human beings. He saw man as by nature a pairing animal, and celebrated the ideal of conjugal affection.[39] He deplored Plato's proposal to abolish the family, and portrayed the household as the primary component of the state.[40] We find no echo of Plato's argument that women should receive the same physical and intellectual education as men.[41]

Aristotle's biology confirmed his picture of the woman as the inferior partner in marriage. He states:

A boy resembles a woman in his shape, and a woman is as it were an infertile male. The female state derives from an incapacity – the incapacity by reason of natural coldness to concoct sperm from fully nourished fluid (i.e. blood, or the equivalent in bloodless animals).[42]

It is in line with this thinking that pallor rather than bone structure signifies the female within the system of masks. The woman lacks the heat to transform blood into semen; her blood is therefore discharged as menstrual fluid, in consequence of which the female is 'always pale with veins invisible, and has an obvious physical deficiency in comparison with males'.[43] Aristotle disagrees here with the Hippocratic view, according to which menstrual fluid is seminal.[44] In pregnancy he holds that the mother can shape the body of the foetus, but does not supply its *psychê*, and thus its powers of reason. It is her body, not her character, that transmits nourishment to the foetus.[45] Thus in the plays it is a woman's chastity and not the niceties of her character that is at issue.

One should note in this context that mothers and daughters belong to the same genus of masks. While fathers and sons are constituted as opposites, the 'talker' and the 'virgin' are not. We can explain this sociologically by observing that women married much younger than men, so that the mother of a marriageable girl need only be in her late thirties or early forties. We should take note also, however, of the underlying assumption that the woman is not expected to undergo a fundamental change of character as she grows older. Between youth and age there is no ideal condition or mental prime. Inferiority is not a state that the woman can escape.

While the woman is an infertile or deficient male in Aristotelian thinking, the slave is a 'living tool'.[46] The slave, like the woman, does not change his character with age, for he too can have no mean point of perfection. Aristotle's tortuous attempt in *The Politics* to justify slavery in principle has been described as 'perhaps the feeblest part of his whole

magnificent philosophical output'.[47] Aristotle was trying to answer the
egalitarian thesis that 'despotic relationships are not natural: slavery and
freedom exist by convention only, and nature makes no distinction –
hence we have not justice but force'.[48] In order to counter such views,
Aristotle attempted to demonstrate that slavery does indeed depend upon
differences in nature. Fundamental to his argument is the racial
distinction – part cultural, part climatological, part genetic – between
Greeks and barbarians. The monarchical system of government characteristic of barbarian lands is offered as proof that the inhabitants of these
lands are by nature suited to be ruled.[49] If certain men are by nature
suited to be ruled, and to undertake manual labour, then it follows that
these men should be differentiated physically as well as mentally.
Aristotle is obliged to concede that while it is 'nature's intention' to
differentiate the bodies of free men from those of slaves, in practice some
people have the physique but not the mind of free men, while others have
the mind but not the body.[50] This concession prepares the way for the
Stoic view of slavery, according to which true slavery is of the mind, while
the enslavement of the body is merely the result of chance.[51] It also
demolishes at a stroke the physiognomic axiom that the form of the body
changes the disposition of the *psychê*, and vice versa. Aristotle does not
explore these implications of his concession.

Aristotle's racialist theory of slavery made sense within the endoga-
mous citizen communities of the Greek world. The Stoic theory became a
necessary theory within the Roman world, where manumitted slaves
regularly became citizens. In Menander's theatre we should expect to see
some careful attempt being made at ethnological observation, but
evidence for such a project is lacking in our archaeological remains. We
perceive, rather, an ideological rupture within the mimetic project of
New Comedy. The theatrical mask depicts nature's intention, not
observed reality. The gaze of the foreign slave, it would seem, is
something that the citizen minority could not bring themselves to
contemplate. Observation was therefore abandoned in favour of a
symbolic representation of what was known to be. The slave was
constructed as a negative image, a systematic inversion of all the features
which characterized the ideal Greek male.

There is again a missing intermediate point in Menander's plays,
although the system creates the illusion of a spectrum. Men who are free
but not citizen-born have only a peripheral part, and seem generally to be
caricatured. Pollux's 'portrait' mask of a foreigner, as I have observed
already,[52] seems to fit the non-citizen bankers who appear in Plautus'

adaptations of Greek comedy; the pimp, who also appears regularly in Plautus, makes only a fleeting appearance in our textual remains of Menander; and we also come across the occasional foreign-born mercenary. At the other end of the spectrum, Pollux includes the mask of a 'freedman' within the genus of slaves. We should remember that when domestic slaves were manumitted in Greece, they were usually bound by a legal undertaking to serve their master until their master's death, and they continued to be regarded as slaves.[53] The conspicuous absentees are the urban poor, men disfranchised in large numbers under the regime of Demetrios of Phaleron, men who were citizen-born but earned their living like slaves through manual labour. We come nearest to such a figure in the parasite, who is on the margins of the leisured classes, or the boor, who works the land. In *Old Cantankerous*, Gorgias the Boor works the land alongside his slave, but at the end of the play we see him safely reabsorbed into the enfranchised, property-owning classes. Although, therefore, New Comedy creates the illusion that we see on its stage a cross-section of Athenian life, its system of oppositions conceals an ideological gap. This gap covers the blurred area within Athenian social life where a man who was a slave is free, a man who is free labours like a slave, a man who is Greek, rich, and educated is condemned to be of second-class metic status. This blurred area, within which the logical rationale for the Athenian political system breaks down, is obliterated from the world of the stage. Enough marginal figures people the boundaries for the gaps to be effectively camouflaged.

I should add, of course, that this last 'gap' which I have identified – between citizen and metic – is specifically a male gap. Courtesans and concubines are usually resident foreigners of intermediate status, and they are plentiful enough in Menander's plays. A 'citizen' woman is not actually part of the political community, but merely a person capable of bearing citizen males. All women are a priori of lower status. There is no ideological requirement, therefore, that the non-citizen woman should seem inferior to the citizen woman by nature, that is, physiognomically.

We have seen that the masking system of New Comedy is constructed around three absolute distinctions: young/old, male/female, free/slave. These three relationships – of father and child, man and wife, master and slave – are understood by Aristotle to be, analytically, the core components of the household.[54] Democracy and tyranny alike are characterized, for Aristotle, by a threefold failure of citizens – a failure to control children, to control women, and to control slaves.[55] The political system evolved in *The Politics* aims to restore orderly relationships whereby the male head of household maintains a 'despotic' control of his slave, a 'political' control of his wife, and a 'kingly' control of his child.[56] These three relationships are all referred to the paradigm of the *psychê* and the body.[57] Just as the rational *psychê* controls the irrational body, so must the male head of household control his irrational members.

Literary criticism in the 1980s has increasingly come to search for that which is unspoken in a literary text – the interpellated subject, the split between the enouncing and enounced self. Through exposing gaps in the system created by the text, the literary critic can uncover the ideological operations of the text. We can look at the theatrical system of New Comedy in a similar way, and see how sets of oppositions each rely upon an absent intermediate point. When we look at the genera of masks, we can say that one significant absence is the pivot of the whole masking system. This absentee is defined by what he is not: not a slave, not female, not old, not young – for these states all represent excesses or deficiencies. The absentee is the perfectly balanced person, neither too hot nor too cold, neither too wet nor too dry. He is poised between his physical and his mental primes. He is the complete citizen, the completely free man. He is in a sense the invisible *psychê* animating the visible body of New Comedy, just as the *mythos* is the *psychê* of the text, and the actor is the *psychê* animating the mask.[58] The stage wall in every performance is an insistent visual metaphor for this eternal absence. The central doorway, untenanted or tenanted by a god, stands as the vacant mid-point between the dwellings of two contrasted men. This doorway is the space of tragedy, the house inhabited by the better-than-life Hellenistic hero. In Hellenistic comedy, this space is a void. The audience are invited to fill this void with an ideal figure constructed in the imagination.

We can describe the ideological operation of this theatre as one of establishing a version of common sense, a sense of how life *naturally* is. The common-sense view of reality which New Comedy articulates is, I have argued, essentially an Aristotelian common sense. It is perhaps because he was educated in the Aristotelian school that Menander was able to articulate the problems of his age so clearly. Aristotle's ethical thinking was, broadly speaking, consensual. He took a set of widely held assumptions and codified them, organized them, provided them with a teleology, but he did not fundamentally change them. While Plato associated himself with a social and religious elite, and propounded radically heterodox views, Aristotle associated himself with the conventional thinking of the educated and prosperous sections of society. His theoretical ideas were bound up with a practical political programme.

Although Demetrios of Phaleron, who attempted to implement an Aristotelian system of government, was eventually driven from Athens as an enemy of democracy, Aristotle's understanding of the central problem in political life – how to find an acceptable mid-point between the excesses of the arrogant rich and the excesses of the anarchic poor[59] – continued to be seen as *the* political problem.

Aristotle was, as we have seen, the last of the major Greek philosophers to assert the primacy of the *polis* over the individual. The philosophers of Menander's generation, Zeno the Stoic and Epicurus, introduced a new perspective on man when they saw the individual as in the first instance a member of humanity, and the ensuing great debate between the Epicureans and the Stoics made sense in a world dominated by the mega-states of Macedon and Rome. The fact remains, nevertheless, that the *polis* was still the basic unit of organization in the Greek-speaking world during the Macedonian period, and, to a lesser extent, thereafter. The *polis* continued to require an ideology to justify its existence. The ethical and political thinking of Aristotle met that need.

In arguing that New Comedy fulfilled an ideological function, I do not wish to imply that it was a form of propaganda. I do not see much evidence for the theory that the poor abandoned the theatre following Demetrios' abolition of the theoric fund, and that the theatre subsequently limited itself to the concerns of the bourgeoisie.[60] New Comedy was a system for the working out of problems. The conventions of New Comedy set an agenda, but did not determine the outcome of the debate. Only to a limited extent did the performance allow its own parameters to be questioned. *The Arbitration* probably represents the maximum extent to which Menander allowed the verbal text to work against received conventions of presentation, depriving the audience of its secure premises.

We see a nascent questioning of sexual boundaries in *The Arbitration*, when the hero realizes that he is applying double standards, expecting one type of behaviour of his wife and another of himself. When the slave, citing Euripides, distinguishes nature's purpose for women from human convention (lines 1123–4), we glimpse the arbitrariness of the social order. When the hero describes himself as a 'barbarian' (lines 898, 924), and merely a 'human being' (line 912), the natural boundary between citizen and slave is in question. This questioning is reinforced when the good-hearted slave prostitute schemes for (and probably obtains in the lost part of the finale) her freedom. The male slave Onesimos laments that he, unlike her, will remain a 'snotty, dumbstruck' slave (line 561), contrasting the public image of the slave with the reality of a slave who is highly educated. The plot is on the brink of acquiring a new format, as a comedy of married life rather than a comedy about courtship. The play draws the audience's attention to its own artifice by pointing up the way it parodies tragedy (lines 327, 1125), and it concludes with a discussion of dramatic character. The slave tells Smikrines, whose miserly character is identifiable from the features of the mask, that a person's character is, as it were, installed by the gods as commandant, so must be placated, for gods have no time to deal individually with the inhabitants of one particular *polis*. The allusion is plainly to the Macedonian commandant whom Athens had to satisfy, and who ruled through Demetrios.[61] Implicitly, Menander's role as dramatist, which obliges him to allocate a particular mask to Smikrines, is likened to the role of a foreign general imposing a certain political order. Menander thus exposes in a subtle way the extent to which the conventions of his theatre are man-made rather than natural. The slave's remark about absentee gods has Epicurean overtones.[62] The assumptions of the new philosophy seem close at hand, and the play is beginning to seem self-referential rather than a mirror of the outside world. But Menander, in the end, never steps across the threshold of Aristotelianism.

The system of oppositions which I have outlined in this chapter is a Greek phenomenon, and makes no sense in relation to the assumptions of Roman culture. The free/slave opposition must be understood differently when the manumitted slave can become a citizen. In Rome, the manumitted slave became the *libertus* or *cliens* of his *patronus*. The wealthy Roman had a series of subservient dependants, of whom some were technically slaves and some free. The poor Roman may have been legally free, but he relied on his patron in order to exercise his legal rights. In Plautus, therefore, we see that the parasite serves as the representative of the poor citizen, and that his functions are to a large extent interchangeable with those of the slave. The relationship of clientage between a rich Roman and his poor dependants and political supporters has no Greek equivalent. The male/female opposition also has a different logic in Rome. Citizen women in Rome did not lead sequestered lives, and mingled freely with male guests. Courtesans, on the other hand, wore a recognizable uniform; they did not tend to visit the men's quarters of citizens' houses, but were visited in brothels. Free women had more economic independence in Rome, particularly when fatherless and widowed. The powerful dowered wife becomes a stock figure in Plautus, and there is much more interest in the strains of married life.[63] The relationship between old and young also changes its nature. Rome was a gerontocracy, since a man could not acquire property or function as an independent member of the citizen body until his father's death. Fathers in theory had power of life and death over their children as over their slaves.[64] There could be no sense that the rhythm of a man's life involved moving smoothly towards and away from his prime. The father in Plautus becomes the embodiment of power, usually compounding political power (he is a senator), financial power (dowries are fantastically large), and domestic power. While the young hero in Menander seems to be moving steadily towards maturity, the young hero in Plautus is concerned only with immediate gratification. Father and son have an absolute conflict of interests, and there can be no sense that between them lies a golden mean.

OLD MEN

We have seen the logic that lies behind the division of mankind into four parts. We must return now to Pollux's catalogue and examine the different species of mask within each genus. I shall attempt to identify the principal signifying elements which distinguish one mask from another within a genus.

Pollux first distinguishes two 'grandfathers'. Since all fathers in Menander have children who are either preparing to procreate or have just done so, the term 'grandfather' does not imply a different generation, but merely a feeling of greater age. An excellent example of an old man with cropped hair survives on Lipari (fig. 4).[65] This is no grotesque, but a man well preserved in his old age with a fine profile. When the mask is tilted back, the expression becomes increasingly tragic: the mouth drops, the eyes droop, and the hollowness of the cheeks is more apparent. The shaven head suggests a man in mourning. This would seem to be the type of father who has lost his children in their infancy, has acquired serenity in sorrow, and will recover his children in the course of the play. Brea places in the same 'first grandfather' category a very different old man.[66] Although the general shape of head is similar, the skin is not ochre but a more vigorous red-brown, the hair is fuller, the nose is not straight but slightly hooked. The eyebrows are indented in such a way that the eye narrows unevenly when the mask is lowered, making it possible for the actor to create a crafty expression. The forehead is angled back, and a line across it only becomes obvious when the mask is lowered. This line could also connote guile. Although Brea is struck by the benign, sad qualities of

fig. 4

the mask, this mood can easily be transformed. We have here a mask that cannot easily be reconciled with any of Pollux's mask types. It is a mask that could be used in a wide variety of plot situations.

Only one other old man exists in good condition in the Lipari collection. Brea identifies this mask as the pimp, even though the brows are only slightly 'clenched'.[67] A sneer is the most striking feature. One sees the mouth become much narrower to its right when the mask is lowered. The skin is pink, which, in conjunction with the fillet around the head and the baggy eyes, implies a drinker.[68] The pink complexion tallies with the baldness of the mask, for in Aristotelian theory the excretion of heat leads to baldness through a cooling of the brain. It is a common Greek idea that those given to sexual intercourse grow bald through excreting heat.[69] This face characterizes in a striking but never grotesque fashion a dissolute man. The emotional range is narrower than that of the other two old men, and the mask seems suited to a minor role. Brea's claim that this is a pimp seems as good a guess as any. The pimp was a proverbial hate figure in fourth-century Athens.[70] Menander gave him a minor role in *The Toady*, and doubtless in other plays that we know only from Roman adaptations.[71]

It is unfortunate that no asymmetrical old men have been found in Lipari. Pollux cites several instances, and the Pompeian material includes a good number. Menander's miser Smikrines probably wore such a mask. It is tempting to associate Smikrines with the mask of Lycomedes (etymologically 'wolfish cunning'), which Pollux tells us belongs to a busybody. Smikrines in *The Arbitration* knows that he is likely to be thought a 'busybody', and denies that he is one (line 656). In *The Sikyonian*, Smikrines has oligarchic sympathies, and hears oligarchs being attacked for 'holding their brows high' – 'snooty' rather than 'highbrow' in English parlance (lines 160–1). There would be comic possibilities in Smikrines' reaction if the mask does indeed hold only one brow high. Pollux tells us that the principal old man has his right brow raised, and Lycomedes 'the other'. In Aristotelian thinking, the right brow is normally raised in a higher arch than the left because the right is the dominant side.[72] The raising of the left brow thus denotes a higher degree of moral deviance.

The two old men who feature most prominently in Menander's texts are Laches and Demeas. The contrast between these two, so far as one can judge, seems to echo the contrast between the two old men with wreaths of hair in Pollux. The wreath or crown of hair adds height and thus dignity to the mask. The hooked nose and asymmetrical brow of Pollux's 'principal old man' suggest a less relaxed temperament than the level brows, lethargic gaze, and free-flowing beard of 'long streamy beard'. Menander's Laches, as MacCary noted, seems 'prone to violence'.[73] The surviving scene from *Title Unknown* is a build up towards an explosion of anger, and the surviving scene in *The Girl from Perinthos* stages an explosion of anger when Laches tries to have his slave burnt. In our text of *The Necklace*, Laches expresses frustration with the marriage which has rescued him from poverty, and we see this frustration vented in the Mytilenean mosaic.[74] In *The Harpist* we see a Laches proud precisely because he has managed not to lose his temper with his son. Demeas, by contrast, seems to have an equable temperament. I have suggested that the comedy of *The Girl from Samos* turns upon the way a sweet-tempered old man is finally forced into anger. In *The Man She Hated*, Demeas plays the fond father. He is described by a slave as looking 60 (i.e. no 'grandfather') and 'grizzled' (i.e. not bald or fully white) (lines 219–20). He may also be the man likened to a 'fat-faced pig' (lines 160–1). An anonymous papyrus represents Demeas calming and helping an agitated young man before the second old man of the play enters in an evil temper.[75] From the random, circumstantial evidence of the texts, we can at least formulate a conclusion expressed in the negative. Nothing in the surviving material contradicts the idea that Demeas is by nature placid and affectionate, in contrast to Laches who is uneven in both face and temperament.

There is a striking change when one turns from the masks of Lipari to the Pompeian material which records a rather later tradition. The mouths of old men have acquired a frozen grimace like that of slaves, and the brows and nose are also grotesque like a slave's. The idea that an old man can be handsome, or psychologically complex, seems to have vanished. The old man's mask from Centuripe confirms that the Lipari masks are not exceptional. The striking transition which the old man's mask undergoes in the late Hellenistic period may best be explained by the ideological problem thrown up by the slave. Under the influence of Stoic and Epicurean thinking, the slave could no longer be isolated as a grotesque. His nature becomes little different to that of the old man. Both are enslaved to immediate material wants.

SLAVES

Pollux pays close attention to the slave's hair, which in most of the masks is 'tawny'. The Greek term *pyrrhos* is usually translated as 'red', but one looks in vain at terracottas, frescoes, and mosaics for anything that in our system of colour terms we could describe as 'red'. *Pyrrhos* – from *pyr*, fire – implies burnt as much as flaming. Greek usage is not consistent. *Pyrrhos* for Aristotle is the colour of the lion, but in the *Physiognomics* the lion is *xanthos* while the fox is *pyrrhos*.[76] Plato describes *pyrrhos* as a mixture of *xanthos* and grey.[77] *Xanthos* is a blond colour, and characterizes the blond hair of Slavic peoples, whence the name Xanthias given to several slaves in Aristophanes.[78] *Pyrrhos* can describe the hair of a Scythian from north of the Black Sea.[79] A problem confronts us here because in Menander's day slaves were increasingly imported from Asia Minor,[80] a region in which we should expect the inhabitants to have dark hair. The tradition of tawny hair may well have been taken over from Old Comedy at a period when most slaves were from Europe. If we look at the hair colour of slaves in frescoes and mosaics, we see that their hair is either white or brown, the brown often having a reddish tinge. Although slaves ought for ethno-graphic reasons often to have black hair in New Comedy, for other

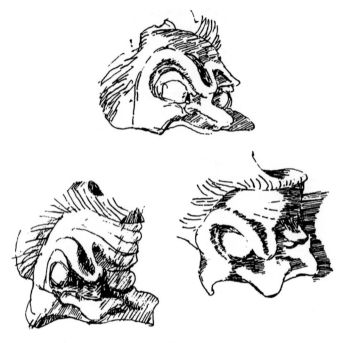

fig. 5

semiotic reasons they cannot. Aristotle saw tawny hair in humans as a
species of deficiency,[81] and dark hair is reserved in masks for certain free
men – apart from the *Cicada* whom we shall examine presently. For
ideological reasons, it proved impossible to model a slave's mask
according to the same rules as a free man's mask.

Pollux mentions only one asymmetrical slave mask, but the majority of
slave masks in the Lipari collection are asymmetrical. The asymmetrical
mask became popular for good reasons. The eyes of the slave are bulbous,
and he has a snub nose. The nose has no bridge, while the brow projects
forward to a point, creating a sharp overhang. The result of this facial
structure is that the mask becomes capable of looking sideways. When the
mask turns away from the spectator, the spectator nevertheless feels
watched. On some masks (see fig. 5), a zigzag formation of the eyebrows
also allows the actor to lower his head diagonally down left, yet still
appear to be looking forwards. The slave may thus easily seem to be
prying round corners, listening to other people's conversations. Conversely, when facing another character, his eyes seem to be evading

fig. 6

contact in a shifty manner. The trumpet beard acts as a frame for the lips. If one studies the Lipari masks, one can see how the top of the trumpet overhangs the lips, changing the expression according to the angle of vision. In a well-preserved example with white hair and zigzag brow (plate 5),[82] one can see how in the raised position the corners of the mouth curve up into a slight smile, a smile which becomes more pronounced when the mask turns away to the side. Lowered, the mask seems anguished (see fig. 6). The horizontal plane of the cheek above the trumpet becomes visible only when the mask is lowered, creating the sense of a jaw sagging in penitence. The brows, raised in a mischievous or mystified fashion, likewise become anguished when the mask is lowered. A narrow and projecting crown of hair loses its height as the mask is lowered, enhancing the impression of a contracting brow. On a bald mask, which Brea identifies as 'low-hair',[83] one can see how puffed-out eyebrows perform a similar function.

It is from Athenaeus and not Pollux that we learn that the masks of Maison and the Cicada belong to cooks.[84] There is no iconographic evidence to support the idea that cooks should be placed in a different category from slaves. In Menander's day, the practice was to hire cooks for banquets. These cooks might be freedmen or slaves granted some economic autonomy by their masters. A fragment from the authoritative study of masks by Aristophanes of Byzantium tells us that the mask of Maison was created by a Sicilian actor of that name.[85] The mask, we may guess, was borrowed from a Sicilian farce tradition.[86] In *Old Cantankerous*, the cook is appropriately named Sikon or 'Sicilian'. Another cook in New Comedy alleges that 'Sikon' was the originator of the cook's art,[87] and Athenaeus cites two other references to Sicilian cooks.[88] It is reasonable, therefore, to regard the Sicilian cook as a stock figure in New Comedy. The name Libys or 'Libyan' apparently belongs to a cook in Menander's *The Urn*.[89] The Mytilenean mosaic which depicts a scene from *The Girl from Samos* pictures a cook with dark, African features, and receding hair falling in long strands or twists that resemble modern dreadlocks.[90] Several problems are solved if we conclude that the *Cicada* mask belongs to an African cook. We can see why Pollux emphasized the dark complexion and dark curls of the mask, and how coils of hair about the mask could look like cicadas. We can see also how the tradition originated whereby the *Cicada* is a foreign cook, while *Maison* is of the city.[91] Although the *Maison* mask was usually used for a cook, it could also be used for other figures, such as a sailor.[92] Menander in *The Arbitration* casts a Carian as a cook. There seems no particular reason to associate Carians with good food, and in this instance Menander seems to have used an ordinary slave mask for a cook. The hirer of this particular cook is a man under stress, and has little concern for his stomach. The masking tradition was flexible enough to meet the demands of countless different dramatic situations. An extant Pompeian fresco gives us a good picture of a cook's mask that we may associate with *Maison*.[93] The white trumpet is particularly prominent against a red-brown face because there is so little hair. One can see why the alternative derivation from *masasthai* ('to chew') arose.[94] The 'chewer' mask is allocated in Hesychius' lexicon to a 'cook; alternatively, glutton'.[95]

It is clear from the mask names in Menander's texts that the ethnic origin of slaves was an important concern. Ethnic slave names are far more common in the theatre than they were in Greek life.[96] The racial stereotypes which feature in Aristotle's *Politics* are drawn from Hippocratic thinking about the effects of climate. According to Aristotle:

The races that live in cold regions and those of Europe are full of courage and passion but somewhat lacking in skill and brainpower; for this reason, while remaining generally independent, they lack political cohesion and the ability to rule over others. On the other hand the Asiatic races have both brains and skill but are lacking in courage and will-power; so they have remained enslaved and subject. The Hellenic race occupying a mid-position geographically, has a measure of both.[97]

A treatise attributed to Theophrastos advises that the best slaves are those which avoid the two extremes described by Aristotle.[98] Vitruvius develops a similar argument in favour of Roman racial superiority, placing the Romans midway between large, blond, straight-haired northerners and puny, dark, curly-haired southerners. The cold, damp climate of the north is alleged to produce much blood, hence a good temperament for battle, but to dull the intellect; the hot, dry climate of the south makes for clear thought and quick thinking, but little valour. Because Romans have a balanced temperament, they are clever enough to control northerners, strong enough to control southerners.[99] Another follower of Aristotle perceives a homology between the south/north opposition and the age/youth opposition, and speculates that the northern races may be newer.[100] All these ideas turn, in a manner that is now familiar to us, upon the theory of the golden mean. Racialist theory was no doubt linked to everyday practice. The evidence suggests that European slaves, because valued for manual labour, were particularly numerous in the mines.[101]

The representative northerner in Menander's texts is Getas, a Gete from the north side of the Danube. Herodotus regarded the Getes as the most manly of all the Thracian tribes, and Strabo regarded them as direct and honest.[102] One Gete in Menander celebrates the indomitable quality of his race by declaring:

All Thracians, and we Getes in particular – for that I boast to be my race – have little self-restraint.

He cites the polygamy of his countrymen to prove his point.[103] The aggressive character of a northerner is obvious in the way Getas in *Old Cantankerous*, with the help of the cook, manhandles a free old man onto the stage, insults him, and forces him to dance. The decadent household in which he serves fails to curb him. The lovelorn soldier in *The Man She Hated* has a more attractive Gete for his servant. Getas cannot understand his master's emotions, and the generosity which his master shows to a girl whom Getas dubs a barbarian, a lioness (line 311). The aggressive, impulsive mask of Getas is selected for this play as the ideal foil for the sensitive soldier who resists raping a girl who lies in his power. Getas plays a rather similar role in *The Hero*, where he cannot understand Daos' falling in love, and blames his diet. A fourth Getas in *The Girl from Perinthos* plays the leading part in the attempted burning of Daos. Daos is no European, but a Phrygian from Asia Minor. The name 'Daos' was a popular Phrygian name used to signify the universal Phrygian, just as 'Paddy' or 'Jock' might in Britain signify an Irishman or a Scotsman.[104] An interesting conversation takes place in *The Shield*, where a Gete, learning that Daos is a Phrygian, insults him as an effeminate. The Getes are manly, he claims, so the punishment mills 'groan with them' (lines 242–5). One reason why the Athenian audience was so interested in the ethnic background of slaves was because racial tension between slave groups made it impossible for slaves ever to unite in revolt.[105]

I analysed in chapter 3 the non-aggressive, imaginative character of Daos.[106] The popularity of the mask type is related to a particular Greek image of Phrygians. There is no lack of evidence to support Tertullian's statement that 'comedians represent Phrygians as cowards'.[107] The tradition goes back to Aristophanes,[108] and to the effeminate slave in Euripides' *Orestes*, and it survives in the mimes of Herondas.[109] From further south, Menander provides two examples of highly intelligent Syrian slaves. The Syrian burner of charcoal in *The Arbitration* produces much smooth rhetoric when laying claim to the valuables attached to a foundling. And a Syrian in *The Double Deceiver* perpetrates at least the first eloquent deception. In another work of New Comedy, a Syrian tries to deflate a braggart cook, showing himself familiar with the ample literature on the art of cooking.[110] Where the Phrygian was seen as effeminate, the Syrian was seen as the epitome of greed.[111] Syrians were associated with the ancient Babylonian civlization, and the manner in which they succumbed to the slave trade was ignominious.[112] They were also linked to the successful commercial culture of the Phoenicians.[113] The audience watching the duel of wits between education (Syrus) and native wit (Daos) would have had such racial stereotypes in mind. Neither Syrus nor Daos is the type to resort to violence, whence the comedy of their resorting to arbitration.

It is hard to judge the extent to which racial stereotyping was fixed by elements of the mask. It seems reasonable to guess that Daos wore an asymmetrical mask in accordance with his devious nature. While Getas' eyes should confront, those of Daos should evade. Our monuments, as we have seen, belie the information in Pollux that slaves had hair of uniform colour. We should expect Getas to have straight, blond hair and a more ruddy complexion. We should expect the Syrian to have darker, curlier hair, and darker eyes and skin.[114] It was probably a dark complexion which encouraged Menander to cast a Syrian as a charcoal-burner in *The Arbitration*. Given the pointers to ethnic origins in the texts, and the interest of Hellenistic science in the physical traits of different races, it seems to me that mask-makers would not have been able to avoid making complexion and hair correlate to some extent with race, however distorted the slave's facial features.

Pollux does distinguish the white hair of the freedman. The freedman should, on etymological grounds, be associated with Menander's Parmenon. A manumitted slave in Greece was normally freed under a deed of *paramonê*, which obliged him to continue *par(a)menôn* (staying with) his master, usually until the master's death.[115] In *The Girl from Samos*, Parmenon adopts a fatherly, moralistic tone towards his young master, before becoming the perpetual victim. The threat of a branding gains added poignancy if Parmenon is already technically manumitted. We have no other Greek texts against which to test Donatus' comparison between the unfaithful natures of Getas and Syrus and the loyalty of Parmeno.[116]

YOUNG MEN

Pollux's catalogue provides for four special categories – the boor, the soldier, the parasite, and the metic – and four normative types. Within the latter group, the main differentiating features are complexion, hair, and brows. The Lipari collection contains a large number of young men, ranging in a spectrum from the almost idealized to the grossly distorted. I shall begin with two of the most imposing and best-preserved masks surviving on the island, before passing on to a series of variants that may be termed 'parasitical'.

The mask listed by Brea as 'accomplished youth', ex. 4, has brick-red skin, red-brown hair, and grey eyes. This is a handsome face, and is seen to best advantage when one looks down upon it slightly so that the eyes and mouth flatten out. The mouth opens and the brow rises when the actor raises his head in response to something that he has seen or heard. The left eye and brow are pulled back slightly to create a face that is mobile rather than statuesque. It is clear from the tanned complexion that this youth has led an outdoor life. We may contrast the paler face of Brea's 'dark youth', ex. 24. The brows are here the prominent feature, constructed so as to signify intense thought when lowered (the horizontal wrinkle becoming prominent),[117] and anxiety when raised (the clenching becoming prominent). These anguished features are in striking contrast to the Dionysiac fillet which he wears about his head, and the mask might belong to an immature youth forced to marry a girl he does not love. This contrast between an admirable outdoor youth and a tense, introverted indoor youth may remind us of the contrast of temperaments which we examined in *The Sikyonian*.[118]

A mask with a similar tanned complexion to our outdoor youth is now in Glasgow (plate 6).[119] Though Brea claims this as another 'accomplished youth' (ex. 1), the eyebrows and forehead plainly bulge a little, and the profile of the nose is less good; the bulge in the centre of the forehead causes the eyes to slant when the mask is lowered; and the hair is not finely striated but curly, which suggests a soft or southern nature.[120] This is not therefore a handsome face, and one's first frontal view of it proves deceptive. This technique is echoed in other masks, where skin colour makes the negative character attributes more apparent. Thus in Brea's 'curly youth', ex. 27, we see a striking coffee-brown complexion, but a similar moulding of brow and eyes. The mouth and eyes slant down to the left slightly. The lips are thicker than normal, and when the mask is tilted down, the lower lip becomes prominent, creating a drooling effect. Brea's 'curly youth', ex. 22, has a fatter face, this time purplish-pink. The mouth is slightly more open on its right side. We find the same trick of the lower lip, which causes the weak chin to vanish. The bulge of the mid-forehead becomes noticeable when the mask is lowered, but the eyes remain visible and watching. Another variant – Brea's 'parasite', ex. 4 – has redder flesh, and wide, protruding eyes. These bulge with greed when the mask is raised, but become slanting and malignant when the jutting brow half-covers them in the lowered position. The nose is fleshy and slightly askew, and the ears are prominent. One may guess from Pollux that the nose and ears have been damaged through wrestling in the gymnasium. The complexion, like that of the previous mask, confirms that this man haunts the gymnasium and symposium in preference to the countryside. One might choose to attribute the mask to a parasite rather than a toady inasmuch as the focus is less upon the mouth – what the character says – than upon the eyes – what the character ogles. This whole group of masks can be linked to the type of the presentable young man who reveals his true *êthos* when he starts to cringe. One physiognomic treatise refers to the curved or broken body of a 'toady', another to his lowered brows and raised pupils.[121] The actor wearing this mask would tend to walk with a self-abasing stoop, but would watch all the time to see how his words are received.

We find in the Lipari collection, therefore, a wider range of parasitical types than Pollux's catalogue allows, and the divide between parasites and ordinary young men is far from clear. The same kind of spectrum is apparent in Menander's texts. Chaireas, the hero's cowardly friend in *Old Cantankerous*, is labelled 'the parasite' in our papyrus. His *métier* is to help friends to find a courtesan or bride, and he is used by the dramatist as an exemplar of an urban life style. Chaireas in *Title Unknown* seems to be spinning a yarn to help a friend. Chaireas in *The Shield* is an ineffectual youth, full of self-pity, and must offer a contrast to the soldierly hero. In these three instances, the 'Chaireas' mask is used for the hero's foil, a man with unsatisfactory psychological traits that point the audience towards a particular reading of the hero's face. A quite different style of parasite appears in *The Toady* and *The Sikyonian*, where characters bear the names or nicknames 'Jaw' and 'Beast'.[122] In both these instances, the young men are not Athenians but foreigners in the entourage of an itinerant mercenary. A highly distinctive toady mask must have been created for these roles.

The mosaic by Dioskourides which depicts a scene from Menander's *The Girl Possessed* (plate 1) confirms that the distinction between youth and parasite may be highly nuanced. Although Webster identifies both figures as ordinary youths, Brea sees the pair as toady and parasite.[123] Both masks are of a similar tanned complexion. The left-hand figure has normal, gently arched brows, and a good profile to his nose. He is clearly looking for a lead from the right-hand figure, who is beating a tambourine and dancing vigorously (as one sees from the movement of the hair). The artist has caught the head of the latter in a lowered position so that we can see the projecting lower lip, raised eyebrows, and eyes that stare forwards despite the angle of the mask and the angle of shadow. This mask, therefore, has parasitical attributes. The pair are playing corybantic music in order to test whether the heroine is really possessed, and the scheme is obviously at the instigation of the parasite–friend.[124] I shall explore the dramatic situation further in the next chapter. For the present it is enough to observe what the masks do to illuminate the relationship between the hero and his friend.

The popularity of the parasite type is striking, and may be explained by the place of the *kolax* (toady or flatterer) within a moral discourse about *philia* (friendship or love). Aristotle defines three types of *philia*: reciprocal (the pure type, love for the *êthos* of the other), hedonistic (characteristic of the young, and of sexual lovers), and utilitarian (characteristic of the old).[125] Pure friendship is, of course, a golden mean. It is seen in the *Eudemian Ethics* as a mid-point between the attitude of the foe and that of the toady, for *philia* is neither the frustrating (= foe) nor the fulfilling (= parasite) of every desire, but furthering right desires.[126] The distinction between 'friend' and 'toady' points up the fact that pleasure is not by definition good.[127] Theophrastos developed these ideas further in a treatise, *The Toady*.[128] This philosophical concern with the figure of the toady had a sociological basis in the rise of conspicuous private expenditure. Demetrios of Phaleron brought in legislation to control the scale and extravagance of private banquets.[129] When his relatively austere regime was ousted, and democracy was restored, the Macedonian 'liberator' of Athens surrounded himself with courtiers described as 'toadies'.[130] Greek traditionalists became particularly interested in the figure of the toady because he symbolized Persian-style subservience.

Plutarch, in his ethical tract *How to Tell a Toady from a Friend*, distinguishes the chameleon-like qualities of a real toady from the crab-like features of a stage parasite, whose 'body is nothing but belly, whose eyes look in all directions, a beast that crawls on its teeth'.[131] Plutarch's language implies that 'toady' is a conventional term in moral discourse, while 'parasite' is specifically a theatrical term. As a stage type, the toady can be traced back to 421 BC, when Eupolis staged a chorus of 'toadies'.[132] The term 'parasite' was coined by the playwright Alexis in around 350 BC. It was apparently introduced as the nickname given to a specific toady, a nickname derived from the title of a functionary who officiated at religious feasts.[133] The third parasite mask in Pollux, offered in a kind of footnote, the Sicilian parasite, can be related to the statement elsewhere in Pollux that the fifth-century Sicilian dramatist Epicharmus used the term 'parasite' for a toady.[134] It seems, therefore, that the three mask terms in Pollux relate to three phases in the evolution of the parasitical type. Outside Pollux's neat schema, parasite and toady are overlapping rather than strictly antithetical terms.

The parasite and the soldier are more truly antithetical. One holds himself too low, the other too high. While the parasite pretends to be inferior,[135] a braggart soldier, like Bias in Menander's *The Toady*, pretends to be better than he is. As in the case of the parasite, the distinction between the ordinary youth and the soldier is not sharply defined, and the evidence suggests a spectrum of types. In Pollux, the sign which signifies a soldier's mask is mobile hair, hair which wafts about when the actor shakes his head in rage. Thus we may imagine, for instance, that Polemon in *The Rape of the Locks* has waves of hair, in striking contrast to the shaven head of the girl he loves. Pollux distinguishes the straightforward braggart from a more sensitive variant, and Menander offers several examples of the latter. Two masks in Lipari characterize angry young men, and would be suitable for a soldier. One – listed by Brea as 'curly youth', ex. 21 – has blue eyes, red face, and a purplish tinge to his sweep of hair. The low, slightly asymmetrical brows connote anger when the mask is raised, grief when it is lowered – the basic emotional trajectory of Polemon. We see a similar sweep of hair and angry frown on another (listed by Brea as 'parasite', ex. 1). Here, however, the lowered brow and eyelid distort the form of the eye, and the snub nose has an aggressive pointed tip. This would be more suitable for Bias, whose character is predominantly negative.

The parasite or toady stands on one side of true friendship, the soldier on the other. From another point of view, we may say that the soldier serves to articulate a body of ideas about courage. Courage in Aristotle's thinking is again a mid-point, standing between recklessness and cowardice.[136] Thus in *The Rape of the Locks* Moschion is plainly a coward, while Polemon the soldier errs on the side of recklessness. To kill oneself for love, Aristotle states, is the act of a coward,[137] and this the soldier Thrasonides threatens to do in *The Man She Hated*. Roles like these require a mask which can be viewed in different ways at different points in the play.

The 'boor' is another Aristotelian category. The Greek term *agroikos* fuses the sociological concept of rusticity and the moral concept of insensitivity. The boor is contrasted by Aristotle with his opposite, the man who has no restraint in his passion for the pleasures of life. Amongst insensitive people, Aristotle writes, 'such most of all are those whom the comic poets portray as *boors*, people who avoid even moderate and necessary pleasures'.[138] Broad lips, a snub nose, and the dark colouring of one who works in the fields are cited by Pollux as signs of the boor. A mask of this kind makes a natural foil for a city youth with sensitive features and a taste for sexual pleasures. A contrast to this pattern is developed in *Old Cantankerous*, where, despite upbringing, the boor turns out to have a certain moral sensitivity, while the city youth proves able to respect the chastity of an unchaperoned virgin. According to the scheme of oppositions implicit in Pollux, while hostility and toadying stand on either side of true friendship, insensitivity and hypersensitivity stand on either side of a proper attitude to pleasure. While the boor is *anaisthêtos* (or insensitive), the 'portrait' mask belongs to an aesthete who dresses well, and tries, despite his years, to live the self-indulgent life of a youth. An alternative reading of Pollux's text, in lieu of 'with a scattering of grey hairs', gives 'with hollows in his cheeks'. If correct, this reading would establish a nice visual contrast between the fleshy features of the boor and the cadaverous features of the aesthete.[139]

When we turn to the mask names in Menander's texts, the name that we find again and again is 'Moschion'. We have already seen how Moschion is characterized by Choricius as one who rapes virgins.[140] His character embodies the Aristotelian category of *akrasia* – lack of self-control. Softness (*malakia*) and luxury (*tryphê*) are offered by Aristotle as synonyms.[141] Aristotle sets up an important distinction between the uncontrolled man and the dissolute (*akolastos*) man: the uncontrolled man is not unjust, but does unjust things. He pursues excessive and unprincipled bodily pleasures without any conviction that he is right, and is thus capable of being reformed. The roots of good behaviour have not been damaged.[142] It is because of this capacity for change that the uncontrolled man is such an interesting theatrical type. In all our texts, Moschion is weak but not vicious. In *The Girl from Samos* he has raped the heroine, and has had a wealthy, indulged upbringing. He has also had a privileged upbringing in *The Sikyonian*, for his father is an oligarch. He would seem to have raped a girl in *The Harpist*, and his father has made little effort to supervise his upbringing. He rapes a girl in *Title Unknown*, and his father seems anxious to spare him anxiety (line 44). He rapes a girl yet again in *The Changeling*, where he is evidently cast as the favourite, city-dwelling son, in contrast to the unloved, rustic elder brother. He tries to seduce a soldier's concubine in *The Rape of the Locks*, where he is good-looking (line 302), and has had no father to supervise him. The cognate 'Moschos' in *The Double Deceiver* is the youth who stays in Athens while the other youth has been hardened by foreign travel. His pedagogue condemns his *akrasia* when he falls in love with a courtesan (line 16). We can begin to visualize Moschion's mask. In terms of Pollux's distinction, he is reared in the shade, not in the sun. He must be well groomed, good-looking, and immature, his brow scarcely lined by experience. He correlates closely with Pollux's 'delicate youth', the youngest of the young men.

The mask of Moschion may be recognized on a silver cup found in

Boscoreale. The theme of the cup is the need to enjoy life's pleasures while one can, and the figures on it are all skeletons. In one group of figures, Epicurus helps himself to food while Zeno the Stoic wags his finger. In another group, Fate spins her thread while one figure crowns himself and another, too late, holds garland and skull apart. In the last group, 'Sophocles the Athenian' inspects a tragic mask, while 'Moschion the Athenian' inspects the comic mask of a young man. Another mask of an old man looks up at 'Moschion' and proclaims the moral that 'the world is but a stage' (*skênê ho bios*), while a musician proclaims, 'enjoy it while you can'.[143] This cup is one of a pair, and in the other Menander confronts Euripides. We know of no comic writer named Moschion.[144] The reason for naming Moschion in this context must be the fact that the mask stands for instant gratification, where the Sophoclean mask stands for the stoical endurance of suffering. Though tiny and damaged, we can see that Moschion's mask portrays a good-looking youth with an unlined face and a crown of finely striated hair.

WOMEN

The masks of the older women provide relatively few interpretive problems. The mask of the 'she-wolf' belongs to a bawd, like Philainis in *The Ladies at Luncheon*. The mask of the 'little housekeeper' belongs to a character like Simiche, the snub-nosed hag who keeps house in *Old Cantankerous*. The 'fat old woman' belongs to a more motherly type of servant, such as Sophrone, the nurse in *The Arbitration* and *The Hero*. The talker belongs to Myrrhine, the respectable wife in several plays.[145] The hair-style evidences her respectability. The open mouth of the theatrical mask necessarily sets up a contradiction with the image of respectability. Married citizen women lived sequestered lives and did not normally conduct conversations in public. Although the Greek *lektikê* is sometimes translated as 'chatterbox', I prefer the neutral 'talker', since it is force of circumstance which normally prompts Myrrhine to speak. Problems of interpretation increase when we try to identify Pollux's 'pseudo-virgin'. It has long been recognized that the mask belongs to heroines of the type who reveal their true status at the end of the play.[146] The term *pseudokorê* is sometimes translated too sentimentally as 'wronged maiden', for the '*pseudo-*' should be active as well as passive in its force. The cognate term *pseudo-parthenos* in Herodotus describes a girl who tries to conceal the loss of her virginity.[147] We confront a complex problem. Does the mask signify the fact of the rape, or does it represent the character changes that occur as a result of being raped?

We must re-examine Pollux's system of differentiation in respect of women. The virgin plainly resembles her mother, the talker: both have level brows and hair that has been smoothed at the sides (*parapsêsmenos*). The virgin's hair – though not her face – is identical to that of the young slave-girl. The mother's hair is not parted, for it goes 'all round'. The hair of the concubine also goes 'all round', and in this the respectable concubine differs from the unrespectable ex-courtesan. The hair of the practising courtesan, we gather, is neither smoothed down, nor does it go all round. It is not covered by a cloak in public and thus flattened, but is designed to be exhibited. While the 'nubile courtesan' simply binds up her hair, the 'mature courtesan' ('the ultimate in a courtesan' might be a more literal translation of Pollux's term) relies upon her arts rather than her body, and has curled her hair. The nubile courtesan has, literally, an 'unbeautified face' (*akallôpiston*), suggesting that the mature courtesan has reddened her face by applying rouge. We learn nothing about the faces of the three remaining courtesans, who are characterized by three exotic hair-styles. The fundamental distinction, then, lies between the respectable women who smooth their hair in order to cover it, and the courtesans who use their hair to display their sexual availability. We note also that when a respectable girl becomes an adult, and her hair grows too long, she no longer parts her hair but binds it round the head. All this helps us to understand the more complex case of the pseudo-virgin. The first pseudo-virgin looks like a newly wedded wife, not like a courtesan. Her hair retains its parting, but is partly bound round. A virgin would have worn her hair loose.[148] The virgin mask also has a darker skin colouring, a relic of her unsequestered childhood. The second pseudo-virgin has no parting, and is presumably a little older than the first.

We turn now from Pollux to Menander's naming conventions which we examined in chapter 3. We find a virgin mask required in *Old Cantankerous*. The *dramatis personae* in our papyrus lists the character simply as 'maiden – daughter of Knemon', and she receives no name in the dialogue, in accordance with the social convention which inhibited men from uttering the name of a respectable woman in public. This maiden lives on a farm, and has to fetch water from outside the house, so a slightly ochre complexion seems well justified. We find a nubile courtesan in Pythias in *The Ladies at Luncheon*. She is the daughter of a bawd, so a professional. Pythias has a similar role in Terence's version of *The Eunuch*, though we cannot be sure that she bore this name in Menander's original.[149] In Menander's *The Eunuch*, the attractive, mature courtesan is called Chrysis, and we also meet a Chrysis in *The Girl from Samos*. Terence and Lucian confirm that Chrysis is the mask name of an experienced courtesan.[150] The name means 'golden' and suggests that she should wear the mask of the 'golden courtesan'. Chrysis is living with a very rich man in *The Girl from Samos*, so golden ornaments would be appropriate. She appears to wear a bejewelled head-dress in the Mytilenean mosaic.[151] It is important theatrically that Chrysis, although living the life of a concubine, should wear the mask of a courtesan in this play. The mask reminds the audience of her origins, and of the life to which she may have to return; it lends plausibility to the idea that Moschion should be attracted to her, and it makes her altruism the more remarkable. For a low-status slave prostitute, we can look to Habrotonon in *The Arbitration*. While Chrysis is modelled upon the type of prostitute who was a free foreigner, and received negotiable 'gifts' rather than a fixed fee from her lovers, Habrotonon is modelled upon slaves who were hired out as 'music girls' at banquets at rates fixed by law.[152] Habrotonon appears in a similar role in *The Rape of the Locks*. She must have worn the mask which Pollux attributes to the 'slave-girl with smoothed hair' who serves a courtesan. She has no money with which to adorn herself. If her hair is parted and smoothed, then the uncertainty of the hero as to whether he raped her or the heroine is theatrically plausible.

The mask of Plangon is related to Pollux's pseudo-virgin. In *The Girl from Samos* she has been raped, and tries to conceal the fact. She appears on stage only at the end of the play for the wedding ceremony. In *The Hero*, Plangon is living as a servant; again she has been raped, and she marries when her true identity is revealed. In *The Ladies at Luncheon*, Plangon has been reared as a courtesan, and has lost her virginity to the man with whom she lives, and whom she will marry when her citizen birth is revealed. Plangon's fourth appearance, in *Old Cantankerous*, differs from these in that she is, so far as the audience knows, a virgin bride. What the mask in this instance needs to establish is a contrast between 'the maiden', who has grown up in the countryside, and Plangon, who has grown up in a decadent city environment, the daughter of a mother who enjoys orgiastic ceremonies. We can see a clear artistic purpose in Menander's decision to introduce the mask of a sexually experienced girl as Gorgias' bride. The meaning of the name Plangon – 'doll' – evokes the nature of the mask. This is a girl whose nature it is to be passive, the plaything of fate; a girl who has learned to make herself attractive to men, but does not do this with the sophistication of a courtesan. Because she has experienced sexual awakening, she looks like a 'newly-wed' rather than a bride-to-be. We can return to the ambiguous term 'pseudo-virgin' in Pollux with new confidence. The signifiers which Pollux identifies in the masks signify traits of character: they are not guides to the plot, and they rarely allow moral prejudgement.

Krateia (Conquest) in *The Man Who Was Hated* and Philoumene (Beloved) in *The Sikyonian* are also figures of marginal status. They are slaves in the possession of mercenaries, and turn out to be of citizen birth. They remain virgin until marriage, so do not seem to merit the title 'pseudo-virgin'. Philoumene could wear a virgin mask since she has only recently become nubile, but Krateia has not been reared from birth by her owner, and in the Mytilene mosaic she wears a high courtesan's headdress.[153] The range of masks offered by Pollux seems incapable of dealing with her particular status category. Another interesting mask is that of Glykera in *The Rape of the Locks*. Glykera (sweet) should be a pseudo-virgin, since she lives as a soldier's concubine, but turns out to have citizen birth. Glycerium in Terence's *The Girl from Andros* falls into this category. The interesting feature of *The Rape of the Locks* is that Glykera has had her hair cut off in the manner of Pollux's 'shorn poppet' to give her the humiliating appearance of a slave, and the audience must rely upon her facial features in order to read her character. Here again we find that Pollux provides a valuable guide to the structure of the masking system, but that his list does not cover all eventualities. We find also that a mask can be adapted to meet the particular requirements of a given play, while still remaining recognizably the same mask type.

When we turn to the archaeological evidence, we find that the younger female masks are the hardest to identify. The crones are a category apart, and present no particular problem. Pollux, in his description of the younger women, effectively only differentiates according to hair-style. His occasional reference to complexion does not help us greatly when we look at extant paintings and terracottas. When we look at the masks of Lipari and Centuripe, we find that changes of facial expression are subtle, and there are no strongly defined features, like wrinkles or raised brows, that can be quickly identified. It becomes understandable, when we look at the terracottas, why Pollux concentrated upon the hair. Unfortunately, female hair-style proves particularly susceptible to change over the years in accordance with changes of fashion. Brea relies upon masks from Centuripe to fill what he perceives as gaps in the range offered by the Lipari masks, but this is a hazardous procedure, since the Centuripe masks are of later date – probably a century later, half a century at best.

The only safe procedure is to analyse the Lipari masks as a set, and try to understand the principles of the system.

It seems easiest to start with a group of masks in which the hair is arranged in a series of vertical coiled tresses. In the two most handsome examples, the hair is wound into sixteen coils, and a long plait of hair is woven round the head above them to hold the coiffure in place.[154] In one, the profile of the nose is slightly less perfect, and the mouth is small, pursed as though calculating. These masks must belong to mature courtesans who have grown their hair over many years, and think nothing of spending hours preparing their coiffure. We see similar coils, more crudely prepared, in a group which Brea plausibly identifies as the ex-courtesan. These women are snub-nosed and ugly, though some sneer more than others.[155] Other courtesans display variants upon this style. One type, identified by Brea as the concubine, has only ten coils, but a tower of hair above. Another example with eight coils has her hair bound with a white head-band.[156] The profile of the nose is imperfect, and the face communicates duplicity when the head is lowered, for the lower lip gains prominence and the eye vanishes. A similar example, now in Glasgow, has a bulging forehead, slightly hooked nose, and asymmetrical eyebrows (plate 7A).[157] We can perceive in the Lipari masks, therefore, a normative courtesan style, with a range of facial expression running from the perfect features of the first woman with sixteen coils to the obviously flawed features of the Glasgow mask. To these normative courtesans, we must add some variants with distinctive hair-styles. The Stevenson collection in Glasgow contains several good examples from Lipari. Although Brea has found a good specimen of the 'little torch' hair-style, a better-preserved face with only the top-knot missing is in Glasgow. A pair of rosettes decorate the hair, and the thick lips suggest that this prostitute is not of Greek origins (plate 7B). A courtesan with her hair caught up in a bow cannot be identified in Pollux.[158] A heavily bejewelled, almond-eyed version is plausibly identified by both Brea and Webster as Pollux's golden courtesan: the thin, slightly twisted mouth and nose belie the elegance of the coiffure (plate 7C).[159]

The other young women found in Lipari all have a much simpler hair-style. The hair is held in place by a simple cord or tiara, and may seem more or less orderly beneath its restraint. There may be earrings. A mask in Glasgow obviously belongs to the virgin: the hair is parted and smoothed down, and there is no jewellery; the face is unsophisticated, and might belong to a peasant girl, such as Knemon's daughter in *Old Cantankerous* (plate 7D).[160] The most striking young woman's mask in

Lipari has pale skin (carefully toned by the artist), a perfect straight profile to the nose, well-shaped but not obviously erotic lips, and swathes of red-brown hair. The adornments are a simple tiara and earrings.[161] The hair is in an idealized classical style such as was used for Praxiteles' Aphrodite of Knidos. This mask cannot belong to a mature courtesan as Brea believes, for it suggests a more natural beauty. It belongs to a girl who has experienced the world, but has not been corrupted by it. The face represents the golden mean which the texts of New Comedy so artfully construct: the mean between the prostitute and the marriageable innocent. Several other good examples are also classified by Brea under the heading of mature courtesan. Brea's reasoning is based upon Pollux's note that this mask has 'curls round the ears', but Pollux refers, in my view, to hair that has been deliberately curled, and which does not merely go over the ears, but round about them (*peri ta ôta*). The basic distinction which Pollux's taxonomy sets up is between professional prostitutes who can never become brides and citizen-born women who will become brides. The prostitute whose hair is professionally organized may be beautiful and virtuous, or she may be ugly and vicious, but she is definitely not marriageable. The citizen-born woman whose hair falls naturally has not abandoned her natural innocence, and her character may yet be shaped by the rule of a husband. She is not corrupted, and therefore cannot be ugly.

The logic in Pollux's account is plain. The pseudo-virgin is someone capable of being transformed into a 'newly-wed'. The concubine has a hair-style which mixes elements of the wife and the ex-courtesan. The nubile courtesan is still almost an innocent, but her hair is now being disciplined. The pseudo-virgin masks of the type which we find in Lipari would be well suited to the type of the heroine who has been enslaved (*The Man She Hated*), or is thought to be a prostitute (*The Girl from Andros*, *The Eunuch*), or lives in a secret shrine (*The Phantom*), or pretends to be a religious fanatic (*The Girl Possessed*). The pseudo-virgin category, however, embraces many other possibilities also: most commonly the girl living at home and concealing her pregnancy or recent childbirth, but also the girl living with a man as his concubine (*The Ladies at Luncheon*), and the girl who has been through the marriage ceremony (*The Arbitration*). The Lipari masks do not on the whole seem suitable for these types of 'pseudo-virgin'. Pollux identifies the pseudo-virgin by hair wound round the top of her head, and for an example of this style we can look at the pair of frescoes in Pompeii and Herculaneum which derive from a common original.[162] A youth anxiously clutches a richly dressed girl, while a slave gives him some warning. This girl would seem to be a pseudo-virgin. The parting is clearly shown, the hair is held up in a bun secured with a band, and strands of red-brown hair emerge above the band. This hair-style, which fits Pollux's description, is in fact the orthodox style worn by girls before and after marriage.[163] It is the everyday normality of this style, I suspect, which prevents it from figuring amongst our terracotta miniatures. Without the accompanying costume and situation, the coiffure is not intrinsically theatrical. It is perhaps for the same reason that masks for the mother or talker are so hard to identify. The character is always of secondary interest in the texts, and her hair-style was probably too ordinary to seem worth reproducing.

The masks found in Centuripe in Sicily, now in the museum in Syracuse, include many women. These masks display a completely different range of hair-styles from those in Lipari, and create their own spectrum. At one end, we have a clear example of a virgin mask – a sober, square face, parted hair, and no hair-band or adornment.[164] At the other extreme we find rows of symmetrical curls or towering hair-arrangements that clearly belong to courtesans.[165] In between are a range of coiffures that might belong to pseudo-virgins of various kinds. The prevalence of closed mouths suggests that these masks are becoming works of art in their own right rather than theatrical replicas. If one knew the plays from which the characters came, one would be able to find the faces rich in psychological interest. These faces (so far as one can judge from photographs) recall Noh masks with their enigmatic expressions, and the sense that they have experienced many traumas. These female faces suggest a passive relationship to experience, where the male face is always dynamic.

It should not perhaps surprise us that the woman's coiffure assumes such importance within the system of masks. Menander's plays, broadly speaking, represent a moral choice on the part of the hero (the subject of the narrative), and a status transition on the part of the heroine (the object). The plot turns less upon the woman's character than upon her birth. The woman's face counts for something, of course – we can see that the profile of the nose is the critical signifier of beauty, the eyebrows the signifier of temperament – but what matters fundamentally is the way the woman arranges her hair, for this makes it clear to whom her body is available. If there is no clear-cut distinction between the face of a citizen-born woman and the face of a foreigner, this is because of the a priori assumption that the woman's *êthos* is inferior. The pseudo-virgin, strictly speaking, cannot ever become a citizen: she can only be recognized as someone fit to be guardian and nourisher of a citizen's seed.

Pollux's catalogue must be read as an intellectual construct. Like most scientific treatises of the period, it is not the product of a systematic scanning of the evidence. It is a theoretical model, modified by observation. As a construct, the coherence of Pollux's catalogue is impressive. It charts an ideal system, the underlying system that ought to exist, that exists in 'nature' rather than in observing reality. This does not prevent the catalogue from supplying us with invaluable evidence regarding the signifiers which the Hellenistic spectator learned to identify. The system of mask types implicit in Menander's naming conventions cannot be reconciled with the detail of the catalogue, but does prove entirely consistent with the archaeological evidence. In Menander's mask names and in the Lipari collection, we discern a system which follows the structure of the catalogue, but is much more flexible. Within the four genera as identified in Pollux, a set of interchangeable signifiers appear in numerous different combinations. Some combinations reappear to create a face that is known and recognizable by name, others may appear in one play only. As an assemblage of signifiers, the mask viewed in isolation may mean very little. It acquires meaning for an audience only when it is seen on stage in combination with other masks, and the signifiers are noticed because of the way they differentiate one mask from another. To repeat the axiom of Lévi-Strauss, 'a mask does not exist in isolation; it supposes other real or potential masks always by its side ... a mask is not primarily what it represents but what it transforms'.[166] The soldier is a transformation of Moschion, the miser a transformation of the gentle old man, the bride a transformation of the courtesan, and so on. To sum up our findings, let us review the cast list of *Old Cantankerous*, and see how the masks of that play set up a system of oppositions.

The two old men have mask names that seem to be unique, for they do not appear in other plays. Knemon, the first old man, is a case study in 'cantankerousness', and the focus of the play is this new and precisely defined character type. The 'cantankerous' man is a type which Aristotle opposes to the 'complaisant' man, two extremes which serve to define an intermediate *êthos* which has no name but is akin to *philia*.[167] The second old man, Kallipides, is a relaxed *bon viveur*, and epitomizes the 'complaisant' type. Aristotle criticizes the 'complaisant' man for treating everyone alike, where the ideal type will make distinctions in the way he treats men of high and low rank. Today we may admire Kallipides' willingness to bestow his daughter on a peasant, but Aristotle would have had reservations. Kallipides complies with his son's request too quickly, and tolerates his wife's excesses too easily. Having established the character of Knemon in the first four acts of the play, we see that Menander introduces at the end of the play a mask which inverts the features of Knemon's mask. This forces the audience to define or sense the presence of an ideal mode of conduct somewhere in the mid-point between these two extremes. The audience are not allowed to leave the theatre thinking that a simple negation of cantankerous misanthropy is enough. The moral issues are more complex. The sting in the tail of the play, when Kallipides' ill-disciplined slaves maltreat Knemon, reinforces this questioning.

The masks used for the other characters are or became stock masks in Menander's theatre. Knemon's estranged wife bears the mask of Myrrhine, Pollux's talker. This is contrasted with the mask of Kallipides' wife, the unrestrained lady who marches her household up to the mountain to hold an orgiastic feast. The alternative version of the talker mask, according to Pollux, has curly hair, and the negative, southern associations of curly hair would seem to fit well enough. If we continued to follow Pollux, we might infer that Sostratos, the son of this lady, likewise has curly hair. Pollux's curly youth is young and has an outdoor complexion. In *Old Cantankerous*, Sostratos goes hunting, and is later seen to be sunburnt (line 754). The Sostratos of *The Double Deceiver* is the foil to Moschos, the city youth, and is the one who travels abroad. If the curly youth mask is indeed akin to that of Sostratos, then we can imagine how the audience might notice similarities between Sostratos' *êthos* and that of his mother. The second youth is Chaireas, 'the parasite'. The juxtaposition of Sostratos and a youth with parasitical features sets up questions about *philia*, and the extent to which Sostratos is self-interested. Having encouraged his audience to sympathize in the first act with Sostratos' rejection of his parasitical friend, and of the urban values which that friend represents, Menander in the second act sets up a juxtaposition of Sostratos and the rustic boor. The ugliness of the boor mask makes it hard for the audience to idealize the antithesis of urban living, the life of a peasant. Gorgias toils alongside a slave. His boorishness – his negative attitude to pleasure – comes to the fore when he refuses to join the celebrations at the shrine. The meaning of the mask comes into question again when the city slave at the end of the play taunts

Knemon with being a 'boor' (line 956). I have commented already on the contrast between the virgin mask worn by Knemon's daughter and the pseudo-virgin mask worn by Kallipides' daughter. While the union of Sostratos and the virgin implies that a reconciliation of town and country is possible, the incongruous union of boor and pseudo-virgin undermines the sentiment, and calls the possibility of reconciliation into question.

We pass on to the slaves. Simiche, the menial with, according to Pollux, four molars, stands as a fitting emblem for Knemon's life style. The ugliness of her mask suggests the ugliness of his life. There is a purposeful irony in the way Daos, the intelligent Phrygian slave, labours on the land while Getas the virile Thracian arrives carrying a huge pile of cushions. Normal expectations are reversed, and the audience can sense that the world is not organized for the best. Daos, having used his asymmetrical mask to eavesdrop, tries in his usual tricky way to ensnare Sostratos. Getas is more direct. His blunt insolence to Sostratos is rewarded with a promise of food (line 573). He uses brute force in true Thracian style to make the injured Knemon submit to his wishes. His companion is a Sicilian cook, and the mask is chosen to show that Kallipides' family can afford the best.[168] We should infer from Pollux that Sikon is bald. The lechery which baldness implies comes into play when Sikon evokes the dancing of drunken girls. He is more verbal and less violent than Getas.[169] The other slave with a speaking part is Pyrrhias ('fiery'), who appears in the first act as Sostratos' 'fellow hunter' (line 71). The 'running slave' routine which he performs may be characteristic of the role, since Pyrrhias makes a similar entry in *The Sikyonian*. The running slave is contrasted with the young man who, after a fashion, stands his ground. The pairing of Sostratos and Pyrrhias is also significant because it points up Sostratos' 'complaisant' tendency to fraternize with social inferiors.

The slaves are not adjuncts to the action but are integral to the play's possible meanings. The test which Sostratos undergoes in order to win the girl involves taking a slave's mattock and doing a slave's work. It is an ironic test for a man who persists in treating slaves as equals. Knemon, on the other hand, is consistently treated as a slave by Sikon and Getas.[170] The action of the play, therefore, blurs the free/slave boundary whilst the system of masks presents the slave/free distinction as natural and absolute. Attempts to read the text in some kind of isolation from the performance are necessarily flawed. It is all too easy to read Menander's text as a broadly naturalistic comedy of manners, and to assume that this is somehow an innocent or unprejudiced reading. To read the play as a naturalistic text is to impose modern ideas about personality. It is to impose the idea that human personality has some kind of existence independent of race and class, that human beings are individuals first, and members of a social unit second. These assumptions are post-Aristotelian. The intellectual project behind Menander's plays is the search to define the good citizen, not merely the good human being. Goodness is a function of free moral choice, in its dialectical relationship with moral disposition. The free citizen, the citizen who is truly free to choose, can only be defined in relation to that which he is not, the slave. Once we look at the text in terms of an Aristotelian psychology, based upon the study of types, rather than a modern psychology, premised upon a doctrine of the uniqueness of the individual, we find that the relationship of text and performance changes. The masks are not a barrier to understanding. We have to shake off Arnott's sense of 'the limitations put on Menander's character drawing by his genre' and his admiration for the way Menander manages to 'refine the grossness out of the conventional traits'.[171] Menander's organization of 'conventional' mask types created in the theatre works of art of remarkable complexity.

CHAPTER 7

Costume and movement

Two ancient texts describe the costume of New Comedy. First Pollux . . .
(The glosses in brackets are mine.)

The costume of comedy is the *exômis* [lit. 'off the shoulder'], an unmarked white
chiton; not stitched up on the left side; not fulled.
Old men have a cloak and hooked stick.
Young men have a Phoenician or a dark purple cloak.
Wallet, stick, and leather garb for *boors*.
While young men wear a purple costume, *parasites* wear black or grey – excepting
white in *The Sikyonian*, where the parasite is about to marry.
Belonging to *slaves*, in addition to the *exômis*, is a small white cloak called an
enkolombôma or . . . [text corrupt].
The costume of the *cook* is double, and is not fulled.
As for the costume of women in comedy, that of *old women* is quince or sky-
coloured, excepting priestesses, who wear white. *Bawds* or mothers of
courtesans have a purple band round the head.
Young women wear white or linen [i.e. a yellowish colour, unlike the white of
natural wool], except heiresses who wear white with a fringe.
Pimps are dressed in a dyed chiton, with a floral wraparound, and carry a straight
stick; the stick is called an 'if-you-please'.
Also to *parasites* belong a strigil and an oil flask, while *boors* have a crook.
For some women also, a 'by-the-elbow' and 'same-on-both-sides', which is a full-
length chiton, with a ring of sea-purple [i.e. as a border].[1]

The second is from Donatus:

Old men in comedy are dressed in white, which is reputed the most traditional
colour, while young men are given opposite colours.
Slaves wear a scanty costume, by virtue of their traditional poverty, or so that they
can move more freely.
Parasites enter with their cloaks twisted up.
Bright clothes are given to those who are happy, worn-out clothes to those in
hardship; purple is given to the rich, . . . [text corrupt] to the poor.
A purple chlamys [a cloak fastened at the shoulder] is put on a soldier, foreign
dress on a girl.

The pimp wears a multi-coloured cloak, courtesans are given yellow [i.e. a dye obtained from weld] on account of their avarice.

Syrmata [trained robes] are so called from the way they are trailed, which is a fashion derived from Ionian luxury. The same wear on persons in grief signifies heedless self-neglect.[2]

These two texts complement each other, and contain few contradictions. Pollux mentions a play by Menander, but does not say that his description applies exclusively to New Comedy. While Pollux is more concerned with isolating a technical vocabulary, Donatus is concerned with what the costumes mean.

The system of differences established by the masks correlates with the system of costumes. The costume shows the spectator, without any possibility of confusion, which category of mask he is looking at. The old man is distinguished by his substantial white cloak, and his hooked stick. The young man is distinguished by his boldly coloured cloak, which contrasts in colour with the chiton. The slave has a tiny cloak, which does not cover the *exômis*. Women have full-length chitons. Old women wear cloaks on top of these chitons dyed in a plain, feminine colour, while the fabric used for the cloaks of young women (courtesans apart) has not been dyed.

Within the separate mask genera, some basic variables are noted. While most old men dress in a plain, traditional style, the foreign pimp dresses in a flamboyant, decadent outfit. We should recall also that the portrait mask of the foreigner is associated by Pollux in his mask catalogue with a decorative hem. Thucydides describes the wearing of plain clothes as a Greek cultural innovation first initiated by the Spartans[3] and the sense that decorative clothing belongs to foreigners remains through the period of New Comedy.

Young men wear 'purple'. Sea-purple, the dye of the murex, was a basic status symbol in antiquity: the purple stripe or laticlave worn by the Roman nobility is the most famous instance of this correlation between purple and rank. 'Purple' could come in many tints. A Greek treatise on colour tells us that 'when purple is being dyed, and the blood-red substances are added, initially grey-browns and blacks and sky colours appear: only when the dye-stuff has been adequately boiled does the bright, clear sea-purple emerge'.[4] The Phoenicians were thought to have discovered 'purple', and Phoenician or Tyrian purple was the most valued.[5] The dark purple to which Pollux refers must be a mixed dye.[6] The parasite is less wealthy than the man with 'dark purple', and can only afford black or grey. The quality of the true purple could easily be discerned in the theatre because the colour changed in relation to the angle of light.[7] The soldier is distinguished from the young man not by the colour of his cloak but by its style, a style allowing more freedom of movement. The boor's garment is made from an animal hide, and has cost him nothing.

The slave wears a scanty costume which signifies his low social status and allows him a freedom of movement denied to other characters. His cloak is a token rag of a garment appended to the chiton. The cook, who is a slave of higher status, wears a cloak that is 'double', that is, twice the length of the regular slave's *enkolombôma*, and wound round the body twice. The slave's basic garment, the *exômis*, is described elsewhere in Pollux as being worn over one shoulder, and thus being at once a chiton and a cloak.[8] A lexicon adds that it is 'belted like a chiton, but thrown over one shoulder like a cloak; comedians use the term both when the garment is worn and when it is draped'.[9] A scholiast tells us that the single-shouldered chiton worn by workers is not sewn up on one shoulder and that the double-shouldered chiton 'is sometimes said to be the servile chiton'.[10] The term *exômis* cited by Pollux refers in the first instance, therefore, to the single-shouldered chiton which was worn by Aristophanic slaves, and can be seen in numerous illustrations of slaves in *phlyax* comedies.[11] In all the *phlyax* illustrations the slave wears his *exômis* over the left shoulder in the conventional Greek manner, so when Pollux says that the *exômis* is not stitched up on the left side, he must mean that the fabric is thrown over the shoulder and not stitched into place under it. In all representations of New Comedy, the slave wears a symmetrical chiton covering both shoulders. We must assume, therefore, that the traditional term '*exômis*' was retained when the slave's costume was reconceived in the period of New Comedy and gave way to the double-shouldered 'servile chiton'.

Courtesans and the old are the only women to wear dyed fabrics. The choice for a young woman is between a traditional Doric-style *peplos* of plain wool, and a fashionable Ionian chiton and cloak made of linen. Ionian luxury was proverbial in Menander's day.[12] We should expect virgins with no experience of the world to wear traditional wool, with perhaps a fringe as a sign of wealth; we should expect the more fashionable type – soldiers' concubines and so forth – to wear an Ionian costume, usually bordered with purple. The Ionian costume hung in a more interesting manner, and was harder to maintain. A remark of Lucian's is illuminating in relation to female costume. He describes how the beautiful woman wears earrings but not lots of gold, a simple headband to keep the luxuriant hair in check, and some purple: only the courtesan wears an outfit entirely of purple.[13] Beauty is understood as a mid-point between the natural and the artificial.

The system described by Pollux and Donatus is rigorously codified, but not inflexible. The rules can be changed in special circumstances, as for example in Menander's *The Sikyonian*, where Theron the parasite seeks to marry his master's former mistress. Similarly, we can see in *Old Cantankerous*, where our text is intact, how Menander plays with the costume code. The hero arrives wearing a fashionable chlamys, which should be the wear of a soldier. The garment is regarded by the peasants as a symbol of urban decadence, and he removes it to win favour with Knemon (lines 364ff). We may guess from his mother's prophetic dream that he not only takes a peasant's mattock in order to dig, but also puts on a peasant's leather coat (line 415). Conversely, in *The Man She Hated*, we should expect the soldier hero Thrasonides to wear a chlamys, yet the Mytilene mosaic and a related clay mould show him wearing an ample civilian cloak.[14] He has renounced violence for love. He is also not involved in front-line warfare, and resents the fact (A33–36). His mental constraint seems inseparable from the physical constraint which a full cloak imposes upon his body.

The system of costumes is based upon conventions of dress outside the theatre, but is far more rigorously ordered. We must remind ourselves once more that Menander's theatre was not naturalistic in the modern sense – particularly in visual terms. The actors played against a neutral stage wall. Under their chitons, they wore body-stockings. Masks changed the proportion of head and body. Because all plays were performed by a cast of three, male and female characters had to be of the same height. Costumes had to be simple so that they could be thrown on and off in an instant. Visual detail had to be isolated and simplified if it was to be seen at a distance. Reality, in short, had to be signified, not reproduced, as is clear when we look at the world outside the theatre.

The white costume of the old men in comedy signified traditionalism. It is difficult to imagine that all young men in Athens actually wore dyed cloaks while old men did not, and many young men must have worn pale colours, and old men bold colours. There is no evidence that slaves in Athens wore any kind of uniform. Slaves mingled freely and worked alongside free men. The system of slavery, whereby slaves outnumbered citizens by a ratio of nearly twenty to one,[15] flourished in practice because slaves did not perceive themselves as a homogeneous body. A fifth-century oligarch complained that he could not strike a slave in Athens for fear of mistaking his identity, 'for so far as clothing and general appearance are concerned, members of the *dêmos* look just the same as slaves and metics'.[16] Equally, it is clear that courtesans in Athens, unlike Rome, had no recognizable uniform. Suidas refers to the Athenian custom whereby courtesans wore floral or flower-coloured costume. Sumptuary legislation in Syracuse barred all women save courtesans from wearing flower-coloured costume or garments with purple borders. In fifth-century Sicily, flower-coloured clothes were taken to be a sign of the courtesan's profession, while Lucian, as we have seen, refers to purple as the wear of courtesans.[17] In Greek social life, it seems, courtesans merely dressed luxuriously, yet the stage tradition, Donatus tells us, called for yellow. Aristophanes often refers to a *krokôtos*, a long chiton dyed yellow, in an erotic context.[18] The saffron cloak was an innovation which came from Ionia, and was, we are told, first worn in Greece by a Theban musician early in the fourth century.[19] Yellow dye comes from the flower of the saffron, or, in a cheaper variant, from the weld, so the yellow cloak of the courtesan falls into the category 'flower-coloured'. This yellow cloak, although Donatus' moralistic interpretation of the meaning of yellow probably has Roman roots, provides a clear instance of the general principle that governs Hellenistic costume. The complexity of normal social life is simplified, so that its essential nature can be made clear.

To each role type is attached not only a particular mask and costume but also a particular system of movement. This is obvious, for example, through the way every old man carries a hooked stick. These sticks are said to have been introduced into the theatre by Sophocles,[20] and appear in all iconographic representations of old men. They are a focus around which the actor can construct a walk perceived to be an old man's walk. Outside the theatre, most old men do not need sticks to support themselves, but inside the theatre the stick is a convenient sign of age and authority.

The same physiognomic logic which governs the mask must also govern movement. This principle, as we saw in chapter 3, declared that the movements of the *psychê* change the morphology of the body, and vice versa. The physiognomist who followed up Aristotle's work on the relationship between human and animal traits, for example, worked his way systematically through toes, feet, ankles, legs, thighs, hips, belly, back, chest, shoulders, and neck before analysing the face. Let us look at the shoulders as an example of his method:

Those in whom the shoulders and blades are well jointed have strong *psychês* – this applies to the male. Those in whom the shoulders are weak and lack jointing

fig. 7

have soft *psychês* – this applies to the female. I repeat what I said about the feet and thighs. Those whose shoulders move freely are free in their *psychê* – the evidence is clear, for there is a correlation with the visible form of freedom. By the same correlation, those whose shoulders are immobile and hunched together have no freedom.[21]

As in the system of masks, we see male distinguished from female, free from slave. The Aristotelian 'natural' slave, the person whose nature is to be a slave, must logically have a body that lacks freedom of mobility and self-determination. If we look at the representation of slaves in frescoes, we can see a clear code of movement. The legs are apart, the knees are turned outwards, the buttocks are projected backwards and the stomach forwards. The head is sunk into the shoulders and the shoulders raised, so that the neck vanishes and the actor seems smaller. The example (fig. 7) is from a fresco which I shall discuss at the end of this chapter.

Quintilian, in his advice to an orator, comments on the shoulders in a similar vein:

Raising or contracting the shoulders is rarely acceptable, for this shortens the neck and creates a gesture that is low and servile, and almost deceitful in the way men feign fawning, admiration, fear.[22]

Comedy preserves an absolute distinction between the servile body and the free body, just as it preserves a distinction between the male body and the female, the young and the old.

The parasite was another type with a distinctive set of movements. We saw in the last chapter how his mask lends itself to a lowered position, and correlates with the 'curved or broken body' which a physiognomist attributes to the toady. I also cited Plutarch's description of the parasite's movements, a description which Plutarch apparently borrowed from a play by Diphilus.[23] Pollux refers to the parasite's oil flask and strigil which show that his natural home is the gymnasium, where he scrapes off his patron's sweat. Although the parasite in Plautus' *Stichus* auctions off these conventional attributes along with his jokes,[24] it seems unlikely that the parasite always carried these items. The striking feature of the parasite was his movement. Donatus refers to the writhing manner in which the parasite gathers up his cloak as he enters. In his commentary on Terence's *The Eunuch*, Donatus associates the exclamation of Gnatho the parasite – 'Gods immortal!' – with a parasite's gesture, and later in the same scene, 'How I am galling him!' calls for a 'parasitical gesture and face', while the slave responds with a similar 'servile gesture'.[25]

Quintilian's description of two Greek actors gives us some sense of the link between movement and character types. Demetrius is said to be at his best playing gods, young men, virtuous old men and slaves, mothers, and respectable old women. Stratocles is at his best with sharp-tempered old men, rascal slaves, parasites, pimps, and the more frenetic roles.

Demetrius' voice was more cheery, Stratocles' more cutting. More remarkable qualities, and not shared by the other, were a throwing away of the hands, presenting sweet exclamations for the benefit of the auditorium, catching the air in his costume as he walked, and sometimes making a movement with his right side, which would not have suited anyone else but Demetrius: for in all these he was helped by his size and wonderful appearance. What suited Stratocles were his way of running, his agility, a laugh which might not be very appropriate to the mask, but which he consciously produced for the sake of the populace, and also a contraction of the neck. If either actor had tried the other technique, it would have looked repulsive.[26]

Stratocles plays agile characters with distorted bodies like parasites and slaves, and we note the trick of contracting the neck and raising the shoulders to suggest servility. Demetrius plays the virtuous characters for preference, particularly the amorous hero. His art lies in the way he

uses his hands, and deploys his cloak. The Greek cloak left the right
shoulder bare, and it is thus with the ribs on his right that Demetrius
makes an expressive sigh, while keeping the fabric of his cloak immobile
with the left arm.

It was not for nothing that the Romans called their adaptations of
Greek comedy the *palliata*, the 'cloaked comedy'. The Greek cloak
(*himation*) was a simple rectangle of cloth, and no pins or belts held it in
place. One might imagine that this placed a restriction upon the physical
freedom of the actor, since one hand had always to be holding the cloak in
place. The movement of the fabric, when skilfully controlled by an actor
like Demetrius, evidently created a far bolder and more visible theatrical
effect than a movement of the hand alone could have done. Donatus cites
the way cloaks were often allowed to trail, either as a sign of decadence, or
as a sign of self-neglect. The decadent Ionian style of trailing the robe was
made famous by Alcibiades.[27] The technique of gradually allowing an
orderly toga to fall into progressive disarray is recommended by
Quintilian to the Roman orator as a way of signifying the orator's passion,
and is borrowed from the orators of fourth-century Greece.[28] In the first
scene of Plautus' adaptation of *The Ladies at Luncheon*, the despairing
virgin refuses to cease trailing her cloak, since she feels that the way she
treats her cloak is a metaphor for the way she is herself treated.[29]

It is tempting to make comparisons with the *commedia dell'arte*, where
we again find that a particular system of movement is associated with
particular mask types. There are, however, important differences. The
commedia actor had to play only one role, while the Hellenistic actor had
to play many. The *commedia* actor could exploit his own bodily
idiosyncrasies to a far greater extent. When Stratocles cultivated his
idiosyncratic laugh, he failed to be true to the role that he was playing; but
in the *commedia dell'arte*, the actor and his role were closely identified,
and no such problem could arise. While the costume of the *commedia*
actor moulded the body of the actor, and left the body free to perform
virtuoso acrobatic feats, the cloak of the Hellenistic actor did not so much
mould the body as conceal it. The art of the actor lay in suggesting,
through the movements of the cloak, the body beneath, which might
belong to an adolescent girl, a virile soldier, or a decrepit crone. In the
commedia the characters have no inner life. Their complete being is
expressed through their physical responses, and everything is externalized. In the Hellenistic theatre, the assumption is always that there
exists a hidden *psychê*. There is the sense always of a two-way traffic
between body and *psychê*. Costume is an integral part of this system of

representation, according to which the art of the actor lies in suggesting the hidden reality. The *psyche* cannot be externalized, its existence can merely be inferred. The one body that is rendered more or less visible in Hellenistic theatre is the body of the slave. The visibly grotesque body of the slave reinforces the illusion that, conversely, an ideal body is hidden beneath the hero's cloak. It is implicit that the slave's servile *psyche* is also capable of being externalized. His image on the stage, exposed and knowable, corresponds with his social reality as a chattel, a reified human being, a body at someone else's disposal.

While the *commedia dell'arte* is a carnivalesque form, and by definition indecorous, we find in Hellenistic comedy an aesthetic code based on ideas of decorum. A key text on the aesthetics of comedy is found in Aristotle's *Ethics*, where Aristotle defines the golden mean between vulgar buffoonery on the one hand, and morose boorishness on the other. Propriety is an aspect of this intermediate disposition.

Propriety means saying and listening to things which are congruent with being decent and free. There are appropriate jests for a man of this kind to utter and listen to. The jesting of a free man differs from that of a slave, the jesting of an educated man from that of an uneducated man. You can see this in comedy, Old and New. In the former, laughter was caused by saying the shameful, in the latter it is caused by suggestion. And this marks a considerable gain in elegance.[30]

Many of the terms in this passage are difficult to translate. The word which I have translated in the traditional way as 'jest' means, more broadly, 'sport', the play of a child. The word used for 'propriety' means literally 'towards the right-hand side', and relates in an obvious way to body-language and the convention that the left hand should be passive. The word used for 'elegance', *euschêmosynê*, literally 'being well formed', has an obvious bearing upon the well-made structure of Menander's texts, but the concept has a bearing also upon the *schêma* of the actor, his 'gesture' according to the vocabulary which we examined in chapter 1. We see in this passage Aristotle developing an ideal of comedy in which (a) the comedy is seen to be suitable for an educated, free man, (b) the purpose of the comedy is to reveal *êthos*, and (c) the comedy does not turn upon explicit slanders and obscenities, but works through suggestion. On all these counts, the carnivalesque comedy of Aristophanes was unacceptable.

In Quintilian, we begin to see how these ideas of decorum apply to gesture and movement, although we must read his text with some caution. Quintilian traces his theories about the physical performance of the orator back to the practice of Demosthenes, who, as we saw in chapter

1, drew freely upon the teaching of actors. Longinus in the third century AD was still advising orators to study the best tragedians and comedians.[31] Other Greek teachers of oratory were less happy about the relationship of stage and lawcourt. Philodemos, noting that many rhetoricians relate the art of performance in oratory to tragedy, comedy, mimes, and so forth, cannot bring himself to reject the principle, but suggests that since actors reject the possibility of learning from teachers of rhetoric, it is better to accept that there are two different spheres of *hypokrisis*.[32] In the Roman world, where actors were of lower status, a more studied attempt was made to analyse fundamental differences between the actor and the orator. The arts of both actor and orator became rigorously codified in accordance with a general cultural concern for order and hierarchy.

Cicero made clear his dislike for the theatrically manipulative oratory of the age of Menander, and set out his views about the difference between oratory and acting. While gesture in the theatre aims to express the words, he wrote, gesture in oratory expresses *universam rem* (the whole affair). In the theatre, gesture 'demonstrates' meaning, in oratory it 'signifies' a meaning. For the actor, in other words, physical expression relates to the immediate experience of the character in the here and now, while for the orator there is always a referent elsewhere. The orator's audience should perceive a gap between the signifier (the movement of the body, or inflexion of the voice) and the signified (an emotive situation located in another time and place). The orator's posture, Cicero argues, should be drawn from a military context rather than from the theatre. Hand movements should be less detailed, and should follow the words rather than elicit (*exprimere*) the words. The face and eyes, denied to the masked actor, should be central to the orator's performance. The face is the *imago* of the soul, the eyes its *indices*.[33] The logic of the argument is clear. The spectator reads the face of both actor and orator, but needs to sense that behind the orator's face lie true feelings. In the theatre there is no reference to a reality outside the world of the play. Gestures must seem to elicit the words, so that the words seem rooted in impulse rather than considered.

Quintilian shares Cicero's broad perspective, and follows up his discussion of the acting of Demetrios and Stratocles by observing that he wishes to train orators, not actors. To support Cicero's argument about detail, he cites the opening lines of Terence's *The Eunuch*, where the hero, having been rejected once by the courtesan, expresses his dilemma whether or not to continue to pursue her. Quintilian describes the actor's characteristic pauses for indecision, modulations of the voice, and inclinations of the head in different directions. The description is evidence of the meticulous care paid by actors to voice and movement, and of the audience's appreciation of this care. Oratory, concludes Quintilian, 'has a different flavour, and should not be overly spiced. It consists in acting, not imitation.'[34] This last formulation was adapted from Cicero's adage that the good orator is the 'actor of truth, while the stage performer is the imitator of truth'.[35]

Quintilian offers the general comment that posture is more expressive even than the hands. He analyses the way the orator should stand:

To stand with the right foot extended, and extend the same foot and hand [sc. since gestures are normally made with the right hand] is wrong. To put the weight on the right is, however, allowable, provided the chest is not projected – although the gesture belongs more to comedy than to oratory. It is bad, too, when resting on the left foot, to lift the right, or balance it on the toes. To straddle the feet beyond the norm is wrong if one is standing, and if one is carrying out a movement it is virtually obscene.[36]

We see here a very precise analysis of decorous movement. The theatrical slave, who walks with legs apart, embodies the antithesis of decorum. The ideal is one of balance without symmetry. To project the right hand and foot creates a symmetry of hand and leg, and an imbalance in the body as a whole. To put the weight entirely on the left foot, so that the right appears redundant, also creates an imbalance. If the weight is transferred to the right, as the theatre freely permits, then the chest should counterbalance. Similar thinking underlies Quintilian's teaching about the hands. The hands should not be raised above the shoulder or below the stomach, since this destroys the proportion of the whole. The movement of the right hand should be from left to right, so that it ends on a point of balance. A movement of the hand from right to left must be accompanied by a sympathetic movement of the left shoulder towards the hand. The left hand must not move in isolation.[37] We must remember all the time the asymmetrical nature of Greek costume, which required that the movement of the right arm balance the weight of fabric on the left. A whole aesthetics of gesture can be perceived in Quintilian's remarks, related to the idea that the free man is one who (a) keeps his body and *psychê* in equilibrium, and (b) is not subject to any organizing principle exterior to himself. This is the code of bodily decorum of which comedy must take account. If slaves and parasites are the negation of decorum, young men must be the embodiment, otherwise the dramatic tension is lost. Although individual characters and movements may shatter decorum – and the play would have no interest if they did not – the stage picture, like the five-act structure of the text, must embody an overall harmony in order to be aesthetically pleasing.

One may turn for comparison to codes of movement governing other theatrical forms. The theory of *contrapposto*, or counter-position, became fundamental to neo-classical performance. Jelgerhuis directed his actors to study classical sculptures in the museums in order to learn how to stand and move. His actors were taught to ensure that no part of their bodies should be on the same body plane. The head should be off-set against the neck, and legs, arms, and hands against their opposites. The body should be flexed and turned. The weight should be on one foot.[38] We may imagine that Hellenistic actors learned in a similar way to create a balanced stage image. The similarities are important, but so too are the differences. Pictures of neo-classical actors differ enormously from pictures of Hellenistic actors. In the neo-classical theatre, actors are always portrayed with the body in maximum tension, but in representations of Hellenistic actors the body is relaxed and in movement. The neo-classical actor was concerned to represent a *pathos*, or passion, and at climactic moments presented the audience with a tableau which encapsulated such a passion in a pure and extreme state. The Hellenistic actor also was concerned to represent emotion, but he represented emotion in the context of an *êthos*, which has necessarily a continuous rather than a momentary existence. This helps to explain why the pose, or tableau, was not developed as a technique. The mask too was not conducive to a tableau, but came to life when seen in movement. Theophrastos in his treatise on *Hypokrisis* discussed a related phenomenon. He records that the actor who fixed his gaze on something while performing was said to be turning away from the audience.[39] The mask had to be kept in motion in order to hold the audience's attention. In Japanese theatre likewise we can see how the technique of the *mie*, or pose, belongs to the bourgeois Kabuki style, where the mask has been abandoned.

The system of movement in the pre-baroque *commedia dell'arte* can also be contrasted with the Hellenistic system. Let us look, for example, at two representations of an old man eavesdropping. In a painting from Herculaneum, an old man spies upon a slave, who is cavorting with the stage piper while a significant bundle lies at his feet (see sketch: fig. 8).[40] The old man's left foot points to the slave, while his right almost points to the audience – not quite, because a right angle would be unacceptable. The body is thus twisted round. The neck is lowered, the head raised. The weight is on the left foot, and the arms rest on a stick. The line of the

fig. 8

stick echoes the line of the back and right leg, creating a sense of equipoise. The whole figure creates an equilateral triangle which balances another triangle created by the slave and girl.

If we look at how *commedia dell'arte* actors eavesdrop in this situation, we find a different kind of stage picture. The actor's art consists in defying gravity. In the *Recueil Fossard*, Pantalone in this precise situation projects a disembodied head through the curtain, and the beard takes on an aggressive dynamic of its own.[41] While the training of the *commedia* actor is based upon the principle of isolation, the training of the Hellenistic actor must have emphasized the *Gestalt*.

Pantalone's costume was designed so that the body, in its bright red, skin-tight suit, might emerge from and retreat into the folds of a black cloak. The white cloak of the Hellenistic old man, by concealing the body, leaves the audience to imagine the contours of the torso beneath. The actor is not free to isolate torso, arms, or legs because of the cloak, which the left arm always supports. The figure of Pantalone is visually arresting in itself, but the figure of the Hellenistic old man is only interesting in relation to the composition as a whole, which is to say to the dramatic situation. The slave balances the old man. The slave's knees are wide apart and face the old man, while the upper torso is twisted towards the girl. He is in movement while the old man is still. His tiny green cloak, in servile fashion, is draped across his right shoulder, and the right arm is moving towards the girl in a line that draws us from the bundle towards her face. We see a movement, not a tableau. There are no curves as in the *commedia* picture, only angles, and every angle carries a relationship. Visual relationships bring the scene to life.

In the *commedia dell'arte* the actor draws the audience's attention to his own physicality. In the seduction scene portrayed in *Fossard*, we see the real knees of the man playing the serving-maid, and become aware of the actor's own physical presence. The unnaturally straight line of Pantalone's beard contrasts with the unnatural curve of Arlecchino's spine. That which is physically impossible becomes possible. Arlecchino's leg becomes a snake-like phallic symbol, acquiring an existence separate from the body. In the Hellenistic theatre, by contrast, no part of the composition is isolated. We see how the slave's *êthos* allows him to become distracted from his bundle. We can reconstruct a coherent *êthos* within the slave because there is no sign of the actor beneath the role, and everything in the stage picture confirms that coherence is possible. The slave's legs are a sign of his *êthos* rather than his carnal passion. While Pantalone shows us his thoughts through the eccentric movement of his head, the Hellenistic old man compels us to deduce his thoughts through our understanding of the logic of the situation.

Let us examine now some of the other better-preserved illustrations of New Comedy. The two mosaics of Dioskourides are the two best-preserved monuments, and plainly derive from third-century originals. The one which depicts the opening scene of *The Ladies at Luncheon* (plate 2)[42] is particularly informative about costume. Fragments of Menander's original text confirm that Plautus' adaptation gives us a broadly faithful rendering of the dramatic situation. Plangon, the pseudo-virgin, is being visited by the bawd Philainis and by the bawd's daughter Pythias. Philainis, having acquired Plangon as a changeling, gave her to the hero to be his concubine after he had raped her at the Dionysia (frag. 382). The hero now intends to marry, and Plangon must therefore leave his house and take up the life of a regular courtesan. In the course of the play, her citizen birth will of course be revealed, and she will marry the hero. The mosaic represents the bawd on the right drinking wine, a young woman in the centre apparently speaking, and a young woman on the left apparently listening anxiously. On the extreme right, half hidden behind the stage wall, is an unmasked boy dressed to represent the slave-girl who will shortly remove the bawd's wine, and the table (frag. 385). On the table are a sprig, a censer, and a little dish. Pliny tells us that the seed of the cultivated myrtle improves the smell of the mouth, even if eaten a day previously, and that this was eaten in Menander's *The Ladies at Luncheon* (frag. 391). This identifies for us the objects on the table. Plangon is being taught how to make herself seductive – either to win back her partner, or to make a success of her future life as a courtesan.

Webster, Lilly Kahil, and Erika Simon identify the central figure as Plangon, following the Mytilene mosaic which depicts the same scene.[43] The Mytilene mosaic gives us the characters' names, and places Plangon in the centre, the bawd on the left, and Pythias on the right. The artist has not simply reversed his original, for in his mosaic the bawd sits on a chair while the two young women share a couch; in Dioskourides, the left-hand woman sits on sumptuous cushions on a stool, while the bawd and central figure are seated close together. We know from the Mytilene represent-ation of *The Girl Possessed* that the Mytilenean series derives from a different original. We also know that the artist was capable of mislabelling his characters, and that the costumes in the Mytilene series reflect the conventions of a much later period. There are no prima-facie grounds, therefore, for assuming that Plangon is the central figure in Dioskourides' mosaic. The costume code makes it plain that she is not. Donatus tells us that courtesans wear yellow, and a bawd in a Pompeian mosaic is also dressed strikingly in yellow.[44] The two women dressed in yellow are thus the two professional courtesans; mother is distinguished from daughter by the purple stripes in her chiton. The left-hand figure is dressed in the expensive attire of a woman living as the concubine of a wealthy citizen: her undyed cloak is bordered with purple. Her place, on the cushions, makes it clear that she is the hostess, while her two visitors seem to perch. She is not fingering a prostitute's worry-beads, as Erika Simon suggests, but the fringe of her cloak. She is represented as the anxious listener, while the professionals give her instruction. Pythias, young enough to rely upon her youth in order to attract, wears the mask of the nubile courtesan: her hair is bound tight with a thin white ribbon. Plangon has her hair bound up in a respectable headband, and some wild strands signify her emotional condition. It is not possible to comment on the nuances of facial expression because the cheek and mouth of Pythias, and the eye of Plangon, are damaged. We notice, however, that by presenting the mask in profile, the actor of Plangon shows the fine straight profile of the nose to the audience, which is a sign of the woman's good free-born character.

The mosaic is less informative about movement, since the characters are all seated. All the actors support their cloaks with the left hand, while the right hand is mobile. The gesticulation of the central figure shows the audience who is speaking, since, of course, there can be no movement of the lips. The straddled legs of Plangon show her resistance to the idea of playing the seductress. The folds of the cloak are very obvious, and we can see how each character carries her cloak in a different way. Pythias has her cloak neatly organized. The bawd had covered her head as a respectable woman should when going in public, but the covering is coming off as the wine takes effect, and she grips the fabric rather than allowing it to hang. Plangon's cloak is not worn gracefully, and the play of the tassels picks out the anxious movement of her hands.

One other feature worth comment is the sleeves. Plangon has brown sleeves, while the two courtesans have yellow sleeves. It seems almost inevitable that such sleeves must have been retained by the actors for the duration of the performance. If so, then the actor playing Plangon could be recognized throughout the performance as the *prôtagonistês*, the lead actor who alone competed for the prize.[45] In Dioskourides' other mosaic,[46] the two young men wear identical sleeves while the third actor – almost certainly a mute rather than the *prôtagonistês* – wears white sleeves.

In this mosaic, depicting the title scene from *The Girl Possessed* (plate I), we see two young men performing a corybantic dance. A Mytilenean mosaic and a fragment of text help us to interpret the situation. The Mytilene mosaic apparently shows an earlier moment in the same scene. The slave Parmenon is gesturing towards the house, and looking at Kleinias. Kleinias wears a wreath and red-brown cloak, and is presumably Parmenon's master. In his right hand he holds an object that might be a tambourine. On the left of the picture, Lysias, also wreathed, is playing the castanets and dancing. He is clearly a parasite, for he has a prominent stomach like a slave's, and a scanty slave-style cloak passing over the left shoulder and tied under the right arm, in conjunction with the mask of a free young man. The extant fragment of text begins with a passage of reported speech, which most editors assign to Parmenon. In this reported speech, the possessed girl, the heroine of the play, is addressed by someone who should be a pimp, since he inhabits an inn. The pimp refers to the young man, to the girl receiving gifts, to her wearing a wreath, and to her madness. Kleinias concludes that the girl's madness is real, but Lysias proposes putting the matter to the test, and instructs the piper to play. Kleinias expresses admiration – at the music, obviously, and also probably at a demonstration dance performed by Lysias.

In Dioskourides' mosaic, the slave has gone, probably to fetch the girl, and his exit will have allowed the actor to change roles. The differentiation of the two young men is more subtle than in the Mytilene mosaic. The friend on the right, as we saw in the last chapter, has a mask in the parasitical style, which he presents in the lowered position. The hero in the centre presents his face in half profile, so we can see that the line of the nose is true. The friend, having suggested the test, is the leader and demonstrates a vigorous dance. Kleinias watches, and beats with castanets that look very insubstantial in relation to the tambourine. Both men have tied their cloaks around their waists in order to have their hands free. While the parasite has a purple cloak, Kleinias has a white cloak. This marks out the cautious hero of the play as a man who does not follow fashion, but dresses like an old man. The parasitical mask of Kleinias signifies the quality of his character, and not abject poverty. He resembles the parasite in *Old Cantankerous*, rather than the parasite in *The Toady*. The mosaic also includes an unmasked slave-boy and the piper. The latter is not the stage musician, since the actor is masked and the costume is not a Dionysiac gown. The imperfect profile of the nose informs us of her character. Her greenish cloak has a brown rim, suggesting an attempt at elegance.

The Naples relief (plate 3)[47] yields no information about colour, but is useful evidence for gesture and movement. In this stone relief a young man enters drunk, supported by his slave, while a flute girl accompanies the revel. An angry old man, doubtless the young man's father, is restrained by an old man of more benevolent features. The slave must be played by a mute actor, and the musician seems to be played by a maskless boy who has puffed out his cheeks to simulate playing.

The masks of the two old men are distinguished by the form of the mouth, which creates the difference of temperament. Both old men have asymmetrical eyebrows. The brows of the central old man are twisted, so that head and eyes seem to move in opposite directions. While the left hand, stick, and left foot point to the drunken youth, the right foot and right arm point away. The mask is thus presented almost frontally to the audience, so that the effect of rolling eyes, moving between friend and son, is maximized. The angry old man's beard appears in photographs to be pointed: on the monument itself, however, it appears to be broken, so that the original would have fallen in five tresses rather like that of the benevolent old man. This would be logical if the two old men were brothers, as in Menander's *The Brothers* adapted by Terence. As in *The Brothers*, so in the relief it is the angry old man who is the rich brother, or, more accurately, the one with an affluent life style. The braid or fringe bordering his cloak marks a clear difference of status. The angry old man also has a more elaborate coiffure, and his stick suggests authority. His posture is an excellent example of *contrapposto*; no two parts of the body, finger included, are on the same plane. The two old men are carefully contrasted: one rests on his left leg, the other on his right. The benevolent old man has his left brow raised in humour, but at this intense moment of the play it is the right brow which is presented to the audience. The youth is performing a dancing step. The legs are pointing in one direction, the head and upper torso in another, so that the audience again gets a good view of the mask, and particularly of the eyes. He waves a party-goer's garland in the air. The slave walks with bent knees, so that he appears to be a small man, although played by a full-size actor. The slave's mask is asymmetrical, so that he appears to be simultaneously squinting up at his young master and across at the stick of his old master. His nose has no bridge, a feature shared by the old men but not by the young man. The young man, with his fine profile, is thus literally someone who can only look forwards, and is incapable of being devious.

Let us turn finally to two frescoes in the house of Casca Longus in Pompeii. Scenes from comedy alternate with scenes from tragedy on the walls of the atrium. It is interesting, as we pass across these examples, to observe how theatrical pictures in Pompeii are placed in the public part of the house near the street, the part used for a symposium. Pictures of sexual activity are located in secret, private areas. Pictures of gods, hunting, water creatures, and the wilderness are situated at the furthest remove from the street, around the shrine devoted to the household gods. Hellenistic theatre deals with the social dimension of man, not with the private or religious dimensions.

The better-known picture represents a slave giving a warning to two lovers. A picture found in Herculaneum derives from the same original, as we saw in chapter 5.[48] This slave has a symmetrical mask, so he would seem to be trusty rather than devious. He illustrates the conventional slave stance: legs straddled, shoulders raised, buttocks and stomach extended. He has wrapped his cloak round the stomach, and supports the stomach with his right hand. The usual technique is used to make the body dynamic: the legs face forward, the upper torso is turned towards the lovers, and the head is turned away in the direction of the threat. The slave's left index finger is the focus of the picture, clearly visible against the neutral stage wall. The right hand would have been used for admonition, and the gesture of the left, projecting from the cloak, suggests secrecy. The pigeon-toed stance of the young man echoes that of the woman, and shows his lack of courage. In his anxiety he has allowed his brown cloak to slip so that it hangs to the ankle. His feet point to the danger, but the shoulders turn away. The woman is sumptuously dressed in blue chiton and a cloak of plain fabric bordered with purple. (The cloak is plainer in the Herculaneum version, but there she wears jewellery to create the same effect.) The mask, as we saw in the last chapter, implies that she is the pseudo-virgin of the plot, the young man's mistress whom he has perhaps liberated from slavery, and certainly will marry at the end of the play. The woman may be played by the lead actor, since the other two actors wear tights of identical colour.

The second fresco in the house of Casca Longus is something of an enigma in respect of the central figure.[49] It forces us to consider how rigorously the costume code was applied. On the left is a cook sitting next to a cooking-pot, on the right is a boy actor, who has gathered up his cloak anxiously. The cook wears the bald mask of *Maison*, and he has wound his hands in his double-length white cloak to restrain himself from an act of physical violence against the central figure. His body is bent forwards away from the central figure, while his face turns to glare at him. The problematic central figure gestures with the right arm towards the

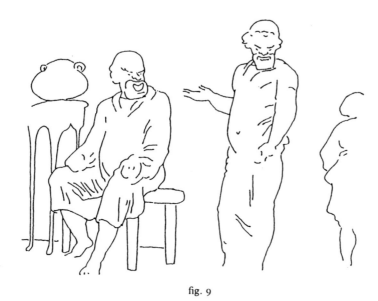

fig. 9

cooking-pot, while the left arm is clasping the cloak towards a distended stomach. The cloak has slipped off the shoulder and hangs to the calf. This costume ought to belong to a slave or to an old man, and the posture suggests a slave. The problem is that the central figure appears to have the face of a young man, with strange bunches of hair round the ears. This figure is generally taken, despite what Pollux states about costume, to be a parasite. My own inspection of the fresco leads me to believe that this is an optical illusion caused by damage to the fresco. The black mark, which appears in photographs to be a mouth, is no such thing. The white neck conceals the vestiges of a trumpet mouth, and we see in fact the bowed head of the household slave.

In this sketch of the painting (fig. 9), the face of the central figure has been reconstructed, following the surviving silhouette, in order to give an idea of how the painting might originally have looked. The hair seems to be in the style of the low-hair slave mask, and is probably crowned with a garland. Perhaps the slave has been carousing, the meal is ruined or uncooked, and his head now hangs in penitence; or perhaps he is bringing news that the wedding-feast has been cancelled, and is shrugging off the cook's fury. The boy is probably, as in *The Shield*, the cook's assistant. A small technical point, illustrated by these two pictures, confirms that we must take the evidence of Pollux seriously. The slave in the first picture wears a cloak the cloth of which has been fulled. It is therefore of a richer, yellower colour than the chiton. The cook's cloak has not been fulled, and it is therefore of the same colour as the chiton.

Many other frescoes from Pompeii could be analysed in a similar fashion in order to demonstrate how consistent the conventions of costume are. It is unfortunate that so many were excavated at an early date and have been allowed to vanish, so that we have to rely upon descriptions and poor photographs. Sometimes we have only sketches – a particular disappointment in the case of the fresco which seems to represent a soldier and the distinctive walk of his parasite.[50] A number of frescoes in Delos have been excavated much more recently. Although badly damaged, these are of early date, and confirm that the evidence which comes to us from southern Italy represents standard Hellenistic practice. Of particular interest is the Delian fresco which depicts a figure in the costume and mask of a slave half hidden behind a huge shield. This must illustrate Menander's play *The Shield*, in which Daos returns from the war with the shield of his supposedly dead master.[51]

CHAPTER 8

Language and voice

The French mime Etienne Decroux, explaining the value of his art to speaking actors, sets out some simple but fundamental principles about dramatic writing:

Unlike the novelist, the playwright forces himself not to put his whole thought into words. Sometimes he removes an adjective which completed the sense of the idea that he had, and still has, for the noun; sometimes he removes an adverb which completed the sense of the idea that he had for the verb ... because it is to the actor that he entrusts part of the responsibility of expression.

The actor, called interpreter in the sense of intermediary or 'middleman', is an author of dramatic music: which he composes, though without writing down a note, to accompany the words of the man who is called the author ...

If 'I will kill you' is written, and if the writer was thinking, 'I will kill with pleasure,' the actor, of course, says only 'I will kill you,' but does so in such a way that the audience infers that the man thinks of committing this murder with pleasure. The two ideas, one of action and the other of manner, reach us at the same time, by the same voice and by the same route. Is that not marvelous? The text on its own is not capable of such a feat since it proceeds sequentially ...

How can I find a non-pejorative name for writing which, partially empty – on purpose, let it be stressed – leaves room for the speaker?

– Already this word 'empty' seems a denigration.

Shall I call the text hollow, or poor, or thin, or incomplete, or insufficient? All of these imply contempt, instead of praise, since a sentence which says enough for the reader says too much for the stage.

Let us make a decision, nevertheless: to qualify a text, I shall alternate between these two adjectives: rich and poor, while letting it be understood that I prefer the poor one. And here is the law: the richer the text, the poorer the actor's music must be ...

Baudelaire is richer than Molière, whose works in turn are richer than those attributed to the *commedia dell'arte* ...

In the course of an evening with friends, you can read Baudelaire sitting down; but in order to do justice to Corneille you must take off your jacket; and in order to play a text in *commedia dell'arte* style, you must strip down to your shorts.[1]

This perspective could not have been formulated by an English actor, for
two reasons that are closely related: there is no comparable mime and
physical theatre tradition, and there persists the tradition of the 'rich'
Shakespearian text. In the twentieth century as in the seventeenth, the
English theatre has tended to project the author's music at the expense of
the actor's. If we look at Greek comedy in relation to Decroux's law, we
may say that Aristophanes created a 'rich' text, Menander a 'poor' text.
Aristophanes wrote in an age which valued the author above all other
theatrical artists, and Menander wrote in an age which valued the actor. I
quoted in my first chapter Aristotle's lament that 'actors now count for
more than poets'. Aristotle comments elsewhere that spectators eat
sweets in the theatre when they are bored with the actors: he does not
speak of them being bored with the play.[2] The positive theatrical value of
Menander's texts needs to be assessed in relation to their emptiness, to
the space which they leave for the music of the actor. This is not a task
which conventional literary criticism finds easy.

The problem was one with which Aristotle at least grappled. As we saw
in chapter 1, he distinguished the different styles proper to written and
performed texts:

When compared, the works of 'writers' appear thin in public debates, while those
of orators, when held in the hand and read carefully, appear amateurish – the
reason being that they suit debate. So, when performance is removed, speeches
made to be performed do not fulfil their proper function but appear banal – for
instance asyndeton and frequent repetition, properly disallowed in writings, are
part of the debating style of orators: for they are performable.[3]

Aristotle illustrates his argument about repetition by citing the way the
actor Philemon varied his delivery of repeated expressions. He states that
asyndeton (the absence of conjunctions) likewise calls for variety of tone
and *êthos* in delivery, since conjunctions have the reverse effect of
imposing unity. Asyndeton and repetition, Aristotle goes on, also create
an illusion of something extra. Three verbs unlinked by conjunctions
create the impression of many actions, a name repeated three times
creates the impression that much is known about the person who bears
this name. Aristotle concludes his argument by distinguishing the
impressionistic style of political oratory (his metaphor is from *skia-
graphia*, chiaroscuro) from the more precise style of oratory in the
lawcourt, where the audience is smaller and grasps ideas more quickly.[4] A
student of Aristotle some four hundred years later illustrated the
argument about asyndeton by quoting Menander's line:

edexamên, etikton, ektrephô, phile.
(I took, I gave birth, I nurture, dearest.)

The lack of conjunctions is said to force even an unwilling speaker to
'perform' the line. Link the verbs with 'and', and all emotion vanishes.
Because of Menander's predominantly discontinuous style, the critic
claims, people 'perform' Menander, while they only 'read' the plays of
the playwright Philemon.[5]

This Aristotelian reasoning is in harmony with that of Decroux. In
Decroux's terms, Menander's line leaves the actor space to supply the
missing adverbs, the adverbs which express the manner of the woman's
taking a man, giving birth, and nurturing her child. The discontinuous
syntax encourages the actor to articulate separately the emotion behind
each event. In Aristotle's terms, the gaps allow the audience to reconstruct other events – pregnancy, early infancy, the current predicament.
The emotion seems the greater because of the illusion of something
extra – an illusion that is created in the theatre better than in the study.
Menander's skill as a playwright lay in his ability to create a 'poor' text.
Plautus' language is more obviously 'rich' in the sense that it is full of
metaphor, assonance, word-play, and so on. It is more Shakespearian,
and thus more accessible to English taste. If we compare the language of
Menander with that of Plautus, we can see that the two writers create very
different kinds of space in which the actor must create his music.

Barthes's analysis of the difference between the language of French
classicism and the language of modern poetry provides a useful starting-
point for the exercise of comparison. Barthes writes that:

In [classical language] no word has a density by itself, it is hardly the sign of a
thing, but rather the means of conveying a connection... In classical speech,
connections lead the word on, and at once carry it toward a meaning which is an
ever-deferred project. In modern poetry, connections are only an extension of the
word, it is the Word which is 'the dwelling place'... Thus under each Word in
modern poetry there lies a sort of existential geology, in which is gathered the total
content of the Name, instead of a chosen content as in classical prose and poetry.[6]

Menander's ideals are not dissimilar to those of French classicism. He
does not defamiliarize words and offer them as free-standing signs, but
allows words to become transparent in order that the audience may
concentrate upon the thought that lies behind them.

An obvious speech to analyse in order to illustrate this principle is
Sostratos' monologue late in the second act of *The Double Deceiver*, and

the short exchange leading up to it (lines 13–30). We can see how Plautus
has translated this passage into his own theatrical idiom in *The Two
Bacchises* (lines 495–520). The young man's monologue follows a
conversation with his friend's father and friend's pedagogue. Having
learned that his friend is consorting with his courtesan, the young man
resolves to return the money of which his father has been defrauded in
order that the courtesan will have no power over him. The speech thus
represents a turning-point in the plot.

I shall refrain from quoting the passage in English because of the
intractable problem of translation.[7] Norma Miller in her Penguin
translation of the monologue introduces a sequence of nouns where
Menander has used verbs and adjectives: claws, fighter, hosts of heaven,
act, wiles, pockets. Geoffrey Arnott in his Loeb translation introduces
different nouns: grief, catch, oaths, bitch, lock, stock and barrel, blarney.[8]
English, particularly in the context of stage dialogue, seems to require
this concretization. Menander's preference for constructions using verbs
places the emphasis upon what Barthes calls 'connections'. He rarely
allows a single vivid word to be 'the dwelling place' of meaning – for
meaning is not within the word but somewhere beyond it. So for example
when the pedagogue has the exit line:

elaun' ekeinon				*ton akratê*	
assail him				the uncontrolled	
hapantas	*aischynei*	*gar*	*hêmas*	*tous*	*philous.*
all	he shames	because	us	the	dear.

Arnott translates:

assail / That libertine! He shames us all, his friends.

Miller translates:

keep at him. He's lost all control, he's a disgrace to all who love him.

And Plautus renders:

concastiga		*hominem*	*probe,*		
really-chastise		the man	decently		
qui	*dedecorat*	*te,*	*me amicosque*	*alios flagitiis*	*suis.*
who	dishonours	you,	me and friends	other by flagrancies	his.

Arnott places the focus on the concrete 'libertine' and 'friends', where
Menander uses an adjectival construction connecting back to the
pronoun. Miller introduces the nouns 'control' and 'disgrace' – these
things which the youth has lost and become acquire an independent
existence. Plautus brings the speech to a climax on the noun *flagitiis*, the

flagrant deeds that the youth has done. Plautus' choice of vocabulary is striking. The word *concastiga* is a word that draws attention to itself as a variant on the normal *castiga*, and *probe* is not the qualifying adverb that one would anticipate.

In Barthes's terms, there is an 'existential geology' beneath the words emphasized in Plautus. Internal alliteration in the two verbs *concastiga* and *dedecorat* helps the actor to milk the words for what Barthes calls their 'total content'. The audience can relish the fact that the word is a sign rather than a meaning. There is a dissociation between signifier and signified, the word and the thought behind the word. The three-part rhetorical flourish *te, me, amicosque alios* becomes comic because it has taken leave of thought: the pedagogue has forgotten to include his master, the boy's outraged father standing next to him. The text encourages the actor to make his performance as big as possible, in order that the chastisement, the dishonour, the flagrancies may seem to be on a larger-than-life scale. Plautus demands what Dupont calls 'an aesthetics of redundance, a fullness to excess'.[9] The lines of Plautus' pedagogue are in trochaic rather than iambic metre, and thus to be chanted rather than spoken. The actor does not have to replicate everyday manners, but can develop an amplified vocal and physical style.

In Menander's text, none of the pedagogue's words are individually remarkable. The audience are aware not of the words but of the 'chosen content', the thought behind the words. We should recall the ancient definitions of *hypokrisis* which call upon the actor to relate his performance not to the actual words but to 'what is said'.[10] There is no sense of a dissociation between word and thought, signifier and signified. The language is structured in order to emphasize situation – the tension between the *akratê* off stage and the *philous* on stage. The final word in the Greek prompts a question: does the speaker really deserve, socially and morally, to be numbered amongst the 'dear ones' of the youth off stage? While the climactic *flagitiis suis* in Plautus needs to be played for redundance, for the 'fullness to excess' of flagrancy, the final but linguistically trite *tous philous* of Menander draws the audience's attention to the mingled emotions of all three figures on stage. Much is buried beneath an unremarkable word, and all would be destroyed if the actor played for the essence or totality of *philia*, 'dearness'.

In the monologue which follows, Menander's text maps out a thought process. The audience follows the twists and turns of the young man's reasoning as anger turns to a desire for vengeance, and he reaches his decision to return the money. The speech allows for movement, as the actor moves towards and away from the courtesan's house. The effect of thought is created by discontinuous syntax: asyndeton, the particle *men* ('on the one hand') not followed by its expected *de*, and by the speaker referring to himself successively in the third, first, and second persons.[11] In Plautus' version we find quite different devices. The first part of the speech is adapted to become the vehicle for a three-part gag, as an expression of hatred is converted to an expression of love. Although Plautus uses iambics for the monologue to create a more confidential tone, the lines are end-stopped in order to create the rhythm of the punch-line, and the audience are always aware that they are listening to verse, to a linguistic construct. The second part of the speech uses similes and alliteration to create the sense of emotion to excess. There is no attempt to map out a sequence of thoughts leading to an irreversible decision. The structured gags, alliteration, and rhetorical similes do not create halts and gaps but continuity and momentum. A very different kind of energy is generated. The climax of Menander's speech is a proverb, 'telling a tale to a corpse', which evokes the feeling of death beneath the speaker's anger. When translated by Plautus into a flurry of words, the emotion is nothing but anger, total anger. All is on the surface, nothing is hidden.

One could develop a similar comparison between the old man's speech in Menander's *The Necklace* and the adaptation of the speech by Caecilius, a Roman playwright who died sixteen years after Plautus.[12] The old man is angry with his wife, who has dismissed a slave-girl. In Menander, sarcasm finally emerges in a burst of anger, followed by a decision to do nothing. There is more momentum in this speech, more concrete language, but nothing distracts the focus from the speaker's state of mind, from his impotent resentment. In the Latin text we find, as in Plautus, virtuoso similes, alliteration, and internal rhyme, all of which encourage the audience to notice the brilliance of the expression. The old man in Menander is obsessed by the size of his wife's nose. The mosaic which represents a scene from Menander's play does not portray a grossly distorted face,[13] and the evocation of the nose tells us much about the speaker's state of mind. In Caecilius, the climax is a little vignette in which the old man creates a picture of the wife and her younger female friends. The vignette is a a piece of musical virtuosity, designed to be sung rather than spoken, creating through music the ambiance of gossiping women, and the emotions of the speaker (or rather, the singer) are for a brief moment forgotten. Caecilius favours variety rather than continuity. Menander shows himself in his text to be master of the unspoken. When his old man states that he will keep silent about 'the night, the foundation of many ills', the audience are encouraged to imagine those events of the night. In Caecilius' version, the old man states baldly that his wife accused him of secretly having intercourse with the servant-girl. Nothing is left unsaid. The audience's attention is fixed not upon an implicit mental condition but upon the external expression.

The contrast between Menander and his Roman imitators might be explained by a different attitude to stage time. In Menander, stage time equates with real time. Lapses of time take place only during choral interludes. The audience thus have the sense that they are living and thinking at the same speed as the characters on stage. They have to follow and make sense of the rapid mental jumps which characters make in the play, trying to make their own thought processes work as quickly. There is always a sense that time is short, that a decision has to be made at the end of the speech. The iambics provide a steady, almost imperceptible beat that prevails for most of the play. In the Roman writers, the rhythm is largely provided by the piper. There are regular switches from speech to chant or song. Time can be accelerated. Having no act break after the monologue in *The Two Bacchises*, Plautus is content for the young man to hand over the money and explain everything to his father off stage in the space of three lines. And time can be slowed down, so that there is space for gags, similes, and vignettes before the plot proceeds on its way. While Menander's plays take place in real time, real time in Plautus is suspended. Plautus' use of time makes sense in the context of the Roman festival, where the constraints of everyday time are suspended for the audience.

In Menander, syntactical discontinuities are set within a narrative that is rigorously organized. In Plautus we find narrative discontinuity but greater syntactical continuity. The different methods of the two writers correlate with different techniques of acting. In the iconography which I examined in the last chapter, we saw how players of Greek New Comedy created a unified stage picture in order to throw the emphasis upon 'connexions', upon the relationships between the three speaking actors on stage. The interest lies in the situation rather that in the individual characterizations. We lack iconographic evidence for Plautus, but the implications of the texts are clear enough. I showed in my analysis of the *Curculio* in chapter 5 that each successive characterization is presented as distinctive and physically grotesque. Plautus presents words and masks alike as free-standing signs. There is no transparency, no attempt to make the audience focus on the signified at the expense of the signifier, upon thought and feeling at the expense of the language, upon an *êthos* at the expense of the mask, upon the character type at the expense of the actor.

The Hellenistic definitions of *hypokrisis* which I quoted in chapter 1 have a much sharper meaning once one analyses Menander's style in these terms. The concern is always with the *pragmata* – what is done, the situation – and with the *legomena* – what is said. The actor is not concerned with the *lexis* – the saying, the style – but with what lies behind the *lexis*. He is concerned not with physical routines, but with the underlying situation. He is concerned not with the mannerisms of a character type or mask, but with its hidden *êthos*, an *êthos* which can only be made clear through decision-making. In Plautus the emphasis is upon 'how', not 'what' – how things are done, how things are said. The interest is not in the thought, feeling, and decision behind an action, but in the action itself.

Plutarch, in an essay which compares Menander with Aristophanes, condemns Aristophanes for failing to give appropriate language to different types of character, so that one cannot tell 'if it's a son talking or a father, a farmer or a god, an old woman or a hero'. Paradoxically, he then praises Menander's language for its homogeneity:

> Speech in Menander lives and breathes as one through the way it is intermixed, such that, when making its way through many *pathê* and *êthê*, and fitting every type of mask, it seems uniform, and preserves its consistency in a diction that is common, banal and needy. However, if the action requires something high-faluting or noisy, it is as if he opens all the holes on his pipe, then quickly and convincingly stops them, restoring the voice to normality. There have been many respected craftsmen, but no workman has made a sandal, no property-man a mask, and no one a cloak that is identically suited to a male, a female, a youth, an old man, and a domestic slave. Yet Menander has so mixed his style that it has the measure of every nature and condition and age.[14]

The striking contrasts occur not between certain types of character but between certain portions of the action.

When Plutarch refers to Menander opening the holes on his *aulos*, he alludes to the trochaic passages which seem to occur once or twice in every play, when the piper accompanied the actors.[15] The piper was a highly paid performer,[16] and these musical scenes obviously had an important role in integrating the action of the play with the Dionysiac context of the festival and the choral interludes. The use of trochaics was borrowed from tragedy, and could be used to draw the audience's attention to links between the two genres (an aspect of New Comedy which I discussed in chapter 1). Aristotle distinguished iambics, as the speech of the many, from the trochaic rhythm which has the feel of a comic dance,[17] and he described the music of the pipes as being orgiastic rather than concerned with *êthos*.[18] In *Old Cantankerous*, there is a 'high-faluting' (*terateias*) passage in Act IV, when Knemon on the *ekkyklêma* makes his mock-tragic recantation; and there is a 'noisy' passage of tetrameters (in this case, iambic) accompanied by the piper in the final act, when, as the feast proceeds off stage, two slaves torment Knemon with a vision of the dance, and force him to participate. *The Girl from Samos* follows a similar pattern, with trochaics used for the whole of the energetic fourth act with its climactic chase sequence, and for the latter part of the fifth act when the wedding feast is being made ready. In *The Rape of the Locks*, the convention is manipulated. The impetuous soldier is in such a hurry in the final act that there is no time for an off-stage feast to be prepared. The trochaics are placed at the start of Act II, to create an ironic context. Moschion's mother has received the supposed courtesan into her house, the courtesan has bathed, a meal is prepared, and Moschion anxiously considers how to seduce her. The music creates the ambiance of a wedding, pointing up the hollow nature of Moschion's adolescent fantasies.

Plutarch's description of a 'needy' (*hypo tên khreian*) style can be likened to the 'poor' style of Decroux. Other theatrical accoutrements – the shoes, the mask, the cloak – need to be changed when the actor switches from one role type to another, but the type of speech does not need to alter. Plutarch's emphasis is very different from that of modern criticism, which has tended to stress Menander's ability to individuate characters through patterns of syntax and distinctive oaths. Sandbach sees Menander's procedure as essentially one of selection. This procedure 'selects from life and modifies what it selects, but with a tact that leaves a result that seems lifelike'.[19] This formulation ties Sandbach to the idea that the artist imitates rather than constructs reality. I find it more helpful to follow Plutarch's assumption that one constructs a theatrical language just as one constructs a pair of shoes, a mask, or a garment.

It is the slave whose speech is most obviously constructed. Slaves imported from Syria, Asia Minor, and the Danube must have spoken a variety of broken forms of Greek, but none of this emerges in the language, even though the geographical origins of slaves may be brought to the attention of the audience. There is no hint either, amongst the free-born, of a Sikyonian, or a Rhodian, or a Corinthian accent. All speech is reduced to a single Attic idiom. The unique exception which proves the rule is the stage Doric given in *The Shield* to a free man who disguises himself as a doctor. Dialect is taken by the audience as a sign of disguise, not as a sign of a certain upbringing. Menander's Atticism has an ideological basis. Cicero describes how Aeschines attacked Demosthenes because his vocabulary was not pure enough, in order to impugn his patriotism.[20] The unsullied Attic of Menander's dialogue cannot be dissociated from the Athenian values which the plays express. It is tied to the same code of decorum which governed movement and gesture. If Menander had given Daos a Phrygian accent, to take a simple example, this would not have been seen by the audience as a higher degree of realism. The accent would probably have been interpreted as a sign that Daos was by nature an imbecile. Sustained systematically, a Phrygian voice could, arguably, have been seen as a statement that Asian values were on a par with those of Athens – but only if parallel changes had taken place in the systems of mask, movement, and costume.

The actor no less than the writer was concerned to conceal his artifice. Aristotle's *Rhetoric* is, as usual, illuminating:

So those who do it [i.e. use fine or exotic language] must conceal the fact, and appear to speak not artificially but naturally. The latter convinces, the former does not. Like a blended wine, a person with designs is mistrusted. So, for example, the voice of Theodoros convinced, in comparison with the voices of other actors, for his voice seemed to be that of the speaker, while other voices [seemed to] belong to a different speaker. The concealment works when one draws from everyday diction in order to compose one's speech. Euripides did this, and was first to point the way.[21]

The everyday dialogue of a Euripides or a Menander requires a particular skill in the actor. There must be no awareness of the presence of the actor, or of human artifice. The voice must 'convince' (or 'persuade') the audience that it is the voice of the character represented. The ideal seems an obvious one, but in practice it was not. Quintilian gives an interesting example of how the deception can break down, citing two scenes from plays by Menander:

Comic actors likewise seem to me very much at fault when, suppose they are playing the role of a youth, but it turns out that in the course of some exposition they quote the words of an old man (as in the prologue of *The Urn*) or of a woman (as in *The Farmer*), they then speak with a tremulous or an effeminate voice. Thus some forms of imitation can be wrong, even in those whose whole art consists in imitation.[22]

The double illusion of the imitated imitating exposes the actor's artifice. The audience are reminded that they are watching a display of skill, and

that the actor imitating the young man may, a few minutes later, reappear
in the mask of the old man or the woman. In Plautus, such a problem
would simply not occur. Doubling was not central to the actor's art. The
quotation in direct speech could become an excuse for parody, for excess.

Clearly the Greek actor did change his voice when he changed his
mask. When Philodemos writes of the proper voice needed for political
oratory, he draws an analogy with the absurdity that would be felt if a
boy's voice emerged from a large hirsute mask.[23] Lucian complains of
how actors might win prizes through glaring and gaping, yet have small,
thin, feminine voices, more abject than Hekabe or Polixenes, when
wearing the mask of Agamemnon, Kreon, or Herakles.[24] The voice
should not, therefore, be out of keeping with the mask. However, within
the broad categories of voices recognized as young, old, or feminine, there
is no evidence that the voice was used to create distinctive characterizations. In a theatre which relied so heavily upon doubling, there were
limits to the flexibility of any one voice. As we saw in chapter 1, the
emphasis was upon the ability of the voice to register the shifting
emotions of the play. The key text is again in *The Rhetoric*, where
Aristotle describes the nature of *hypokrisis*:

It is [located] within the voice, in the way the voice is used for each emotion –
when it should be loud or small or between, and in its pitch, whether it should be
high or deep or between, and in what rhythms are used for each [emotion] (for
there are three aspects to be examined, namely volume, harmony, and rhythm).
The prizes are almost always taken by such men in dramatic contests, and just as
actors there now count for more than poets, so it is in political contests, because of
the corrupt state of politics.[25]

Aristotle adds a few lines later that the actor's art is, historically, rooted in
the voice, which is 'the most imitative of all our parts'.[26] A somewhat
different approach to the voice was suggested by Theophrastos. Theophrastos traced the origins of singing in the emotional states of pain,
pleasure, and inspiration, and, working with a theory of catharsis,
analysed how such emotions changed the speaking voice to give it a
musical quality.[27] This research was in line with his view that, of all the
senses, hearing most easily stirred the emotions.[28]

If we return to the young man's monologue in *The Double Deceiver*, we
can see that the speech ranges through a gamut of emotions: fatalism
turning to reflection, to anxiety, to fury, to resolve, to despair. In the old
man's speech in *The Necklace* we see sarcasm with flickerings of self-pity
turning to anger turning to fatalism. The task of the actor's voice is to
clarify these emotions. There is no need for a characterful voice – a voice

particularly suited to an impulsive 25-year-old who has been out in the world, or to a bad-tempered impoverished old man of good family. This would be superfluous detail. The audience can read with its eyes the characteristics of the mask. It can infer from the words what thought processes prompt the different emotions, and it can evaluate the actions that stem from these thoughts and emotions. It can form a view of the speaker's *êthos* through relating the mask to the actions. The job of vocal inflexion is primarily to represent the emotions – not, of course, that *êthos* and *pathos* can ever finally be disentangled.

Hellenistic actors took very seriously the task of training the voice. Their training was based upon certain assumptions about how the voice functioned. Aristotle's definition of 'voice' is as follows: 'The striking of the air exhaled by [the agency of] the *psychê* in those parts [namely throat, lung, and heart] through the so-called windpipe [*artêria*] constitutes voice.'[29] The voice is thus directly linked to the *psychê*. This understanding lies behind Theophrastos' statement that mastery of *hypokrisis* involved harmonizing the movement of the body with the *tonos* (tone) of the *psychê*, and by the tendency of Hellenistic acting theory to differentiate body from voice.[30] Although Aristotle does not give a clear account of how the *psychê* operates upon the voice, we can discern two underlying assumptions. First, breathing is taken to be a cooling process. The life-principle depends upon heat, and food is concocted to produce heat; thus, for example, the old die when they have lost their ability to produce heat.[31] Secondly, air is the medium through which the *psychê* transmits life, for a kind of breath (*pneuma*) runs through the bloodstream.[32] For these reasons, the actor's voice would seem to give a more direct access to the *psychê* than any other element in his performance.

The eleventh chapter of *Problems*, written by a scientist of the Aristotelian school, is a study of the voice in its many aspects, and the writer has learned from the experience of actors. He notes, for example, the difficulties that actors have when they first come on stage: because of nervousness, he says, actors will start by using a small voice which they know they can control, and they only risk increasing the volume when they have gained full control.[33] He relates all vocal effects back to the four fundamental physical qualities of hot and cold, wet and dry. The voice, therefore, becomes the sign of a physiological condition. This underlying but insistent assumption allows us to understand the interface between the voice of the Hellenistic actor and his mask.

The author of *Problems* relates volume to the amount of air expelled, and pitch to the speed with which the air is expelled through the windpipe. He ponders why men in their prime have deep voices, but women, boys, eunuchs, and old men have high voices. Because of weakness, there is less air to be expelled, he argues, thus the air can move faster. Also the windpipe (like the duct from the testicles) is narrower, again causing the air to be expelled faster. The tremulous quality of an old man's voice is explained by a lack of control, which is in turn connected to a lack of heat.[34] Another scientist of the Aristotelian school, in an essay entitled *On Things Heard*, distinguishes the pure or 'white' voice of the young from the rough or 'grey' voice of the old. He compares the workings of the voice to those of a reed pipe, and argues that the sclerotic voice of an old man may be clearer than the soft voice of a young man, although it is less controllable and less flexible.[35]

Two emotions which the author of *Problems* analyses with particular care are nervousness and fear. Nervousness (*agônia*) seems to be a species of fear. The heart loses heat, causing the tongue to tremble. Some internal paralysis, caused by chilling, results in a stutter. Yet in nervousness the voice is low, in fear it is high. In fear, the heart has little strength to expel much air, but in nervousness (a kind of embarrassment) the blood rushes to the head, which causes the air to thicken and emerge more slowly.[36] Habitual stuttering is related to melancholia, for the melancholic is in the power of his imagination and tries to speak before he has formulated the words.[37] Stuttering is also a feature of anger, for the angry breathe quickly and expel much breath – though it is uncertain whether such stuttering is best explained by the emission of heated breath, or by the chilling of the windpipe.[38] It is not hard to imagine how the actor playing the young man's monologue in *The Double Deceiver* could profit from this kind of analysis. The situation calls for anger, but also for an element of anxiety (the embarrassed, nervous, hot-headed kind of fear), for the youth knows that the courtesan has a hold over him. The final image of the corpse suggests a chilling as the decision is made. The power of imagination, as the youth pictures the lovers off stage, may also make him inarticulate. Menander's asyndeton and erratic syntax plainly call for a halting delivery. The actor's task is therefore to integrate halting breath with halting verse in order to create his performance. The heating and cooling process correlates with changes in the rhythm of the verse.

Diet is another topic discussed in *Problems*. We learn that actors trained before they breakfasted in order not to damage their voices. Food makes the windpipe moist, so making the voice rougher, and there is risk of damage to the windpipe. Certain foods, like leeks and garlic, clear the larynx and are beneficial to the voice.[39] Another writer on theatre mocked a tragedian who ruined his voice by eating too many artichokes – so it seems that actors could be obsessed by the effects of diet upon their voices. One is reminded of the famous actor known to Stanislavski who placed a thermometer in his soup and wine.[40] The author of *Problems* is also interested in acoustics. He discusses the direction in which the voice travels, and the clarity of an echo. He notes that the singing of a chorus is less distinct when the floor of the *orchêstra* is covered with chaff. When he discusses the way empty earthenware vessels in a building increase the echo, and bronze vessels do so even more, it is hard to doubt that he again has theatrical practice partly in mind. Vitruvius describes at length the practice in Greek theatres of setting up inverted urns, preferably of bronze, to improve resonance. The urns described by Vitruvius are tuned according to musical theories set down by a pupil of Aristotle.[41] Voice is understood as part of the human organism, working according to the laws of physics and biology.

It may be helpful to compare the Hellenistic actor's understanding of voice with that of the Stanislavskian actor. Stanislavski starts with the same basic idea that the written text is incomplete:

The whole point of any such creation is the underlying subtext. Without it the words have no excuse for being presented on the stage. When they are spoken the words come from the author, the subtext from the actor. If this were not so the public would not make the effort of coming to the theatre, they would sit at home and read the printed play.[42]

With such a premise Menander could have agreed – until he began to question Stanislavski's definition of the 'subtext' as 'the manifest, the inwardly felt expression of a human being in a part, which flows uninterruptedly beneath the words of the text, giving them life and a basis for existing'.[43] One does not sense in Menander's writing these two levels of 'the manifest' and 'the inwardly felt'. When a woman in *The Cherry Orchard* is in total despair, she seems to speak of trivia: 'our thermometer is broken'.[44] Characters in Menander would never express feeling as indirectly as this. 'If I were called "darling", simply, I should sacrifice to all the gods!' says the despairing soldier in *The Man She Hated*.[45] These words do not set up a gap between the manifest semantic content of the words and the feeling expressed, for Menander's soldier has no subconscious. The excellent Hellenistic actor, we recall, conforms his acting to 'what is said', not to 'what is inferred'.[46] Because there is no sense that Menander's soldier has a subconscious, the actor can aspire to obliterate the disparity between the signifier (the words) and the signified (the thought, feeling).

In Stanislavski we regularly find two levels. When the talented student actor in *Building a Character* impersonates a critic, the harsh voice which helps to create this character is discovered intuitively and unexpectedly. The actor is subsequently dismayed when he has to learn the techniques of intonation, phonetics, pauses, and so forth. There is a tension between the actor's reliance upon feeling and his reliance on technique. I quoted in chapter 4 Stanislavski's remark that 'a characterization is the mask which hides the actor-individual. Protected by it, he can lay bare his soul down to the last intimate detail.'[47] In Menander we find a less mystical concept of 'soul', for the *psychê*, though immaterial, is linked in a material way to the body. The pathology of the emotions (*pathê*) and the pathology of the body are indisseverable. Without a physical manifestation, an emotion has no existence. There is thus a much closer association between what is said and done on stage and the feeling presumed to lie behind the action. The actor's voice does not need to oscillate between two opposed levels of text and subtext. The mask in Menander is a characterization which, though it hides the actor's face, cannot hide his *psychê*, for the *psychê* is more readily accessible via the voice. There is no private area of inner being which the actor needs to conceal or expose. His task is to find a single psychosomatic level of coherence, where the *êthos*, the emotions, the blood and the breath of the 'mask' coalesce. The actor's understanding of another human being's 'character' and his technical control over his own body are aspects of a single process.

The different visual and acoustical sign systems which comprise Menander's theatre are linked by virtue of a coherent materialist philosophy. Aristotelian philosophy has, I think, no parallels before or since in the scope of its ambitions. It offered an integrated understanding of humanity in all its political, ethical, metaphysical, biological, and artistic aspects. In the New Comedy of Menander, this philosophy was the basis for an integrated understanding of theatre. The achievement of this 'New' form was quite different from that of classical tragedy. The great tragic theatre of the fifth century stemmed from the historical collision of democracy and heroic feudalism, of science and Olympian religion. We do not find the same sense of irreconcilable opposites in the Hellenistic theatre that has come down to us. What we see instead is a desire for synthesis, a bringing together of opposites. This reconciling of opposites can be seen, on the level of theatre production, as embracing the reconciliation of actor and writer.

The historical logic behind the equipoise of actor and writer was

glimpsed by Aristotle when he related the rise of the actor to the
increasing importance of performance within the democratic political
system. ('. . . just as actors there now count for more than poets, so it is in
political contests, because of the corrupt state of politics'.) The Athenians
required their politicians to be performers, but they also accepted that
they should be philosophers. In the theatre, the Athenians respected the
art of the performer, but they also respected the role of the dramatist-as-
teacher. The historian of western theatre so often finds that great writers
and great actors belong to different eras. In the twentieth century,
theorists of the actor's art, from Artaud to Barba, have often found the
author something of an intrusion. Moments of convergence – Chekhov
and Stanislavski, for example – are rare. One plainly does find this kind of
convergence in the time of Menander, when both parties shared a
common level of sophistication in pursuit of their single art. Plautus
seems less of a historical rarity – the actor turned playwright, working
more from instinct than from theory. To the pragmatic English, he tends
perhaps to be a more appealing figure.

The most-often quoted critical comment on Menander is doubtless
that of Aristophanes of Byzantium: 'O Menander and Life, which of you
imitated the other?'[48] The paradox of Menander's theatre is that it
appears to be the most imitative of life, the most naturalistic of all ancient
forms of theatre; and yet upon examination it turns out to be the most
rigorously coded. In order to imitate life, it manipulates theatrical signs.
At every point we find a strategy of concealment. Meaning is, in
Barthes's phrase, 'an ever-deferred project'. The actual words efface
themselves, throwing the attention on the *legomena*, the 'what-is-said'.
Every trace of the actor's body is effaced, beneath mask, cloak, and tights.
Body-language is never remarkable in itself, but draws attention to the
situation represented. Concealed behind the figures physically represented on stage is deemed to be an *êthos*. The *êthos* is an aspect of the *psychê*,
the invisible presence which animates the visible organism. Pursuit of
this hidden *psychê* leads us towards the most mystificatory area of
Aristotelian thinking, the gap between appetite and the reasoning mind.
Êthos is an aspect of the *psychê* capable of following reason,[49] but the
nature of this 'reason' remains mysterious.

A close examination of the system of masks exposes one particularly
striking area of concealment. What appears to be a cross-section of
Athenian life is in fact a construct based upon ideological assumptions.
The problems which Aristotelian rationalism could not deal with –
slavery, female intelligence, the arbitrariness of citizenship laws – become

the basis for constructing an ideal framework, an image of the *polis* as it ought to be. Within these non-rational or ideological parameters, rational debate can take place, and we should not of course underestimate the importance of these debates. Behind these debates lies an unspoken emptiness. The untenanted central doorway representing the home of the gods remains through every performance as a visual symbol of the irrational and unknowable: an empty space at the heart of the play.

The sign systems of Menander's theatre are designed to appear coherent and complete, in order to create the ultimate illusion that reason can apprehend reality. In Plautus' theatre, it is made plain that reason has no such ambitions. The coherence of Menander's stage world is demolished. Theatrical signs boldly proclaim themselves for what they are: actors earning their fee, Grecian cloaks supplied by a costumier, formulaic narrative patterns, verses composed by a poet. The audience perceives, always, that there is a gap between the *énoncé* and the *énonciation*, and it takes its pleasure from witnessing the construction and demolition of signs. In Menander's theatre, this gap between the *énoncé* and the *énonciation* was as far as possible effaced.

Does this mean, therefore, that Menander's theatre was a dishonest theatre? Such a question broaches a vexed and paradoxical area of artistic ethics. Athens was, with all due allowance for the restricted nature of the franchise, a democracy. In the lawcourts and in the public assembly, the art of persuasion was something that every citizen had to master. It is no coincidence that this society spawned a theatre which aimed to persuade that its stage replicated life. The more the realism of Menander's theatre 'convinced' the spectator, the more the spectator admired and examined the techniques of persuasion used. This is the central paradox of Menander's theatre. The Athenian spectator learned, in the theatre, adaptive skills of character analysis and presentation that served him well when speaking and voting in the courts and public assemblies.

In Rome, the level of democracy was minimal, and the sources of power were everywhere visible. The nobility made themselves prominent with signs of their power: the purple laticlave, the death masks of their ancestors, the clients in attendance. As in Roman political culture, so in Roman theatre, everything was visible. There were no hidden strategies for manipulating public opinion. The Roman theatre audience was accustomed to a different political sign-language. While in Athens – to take a simple example – the gesticulating arm of Cleon was a *sêmeion*, a probable sign connoting the felt emotion of the speaker, rejection of tradition, and a certain concept of freedom, in Rome the senator's laticlave was a *tekmêrion*, a certain sign denoting nobility.[50] The question of inference did not arise. Plautus' aim within this political culture was not to expose and refine a system of signs, but to subvert signs. Social and aesthetic rules are systematically broken in his plays. The ethos of Plautus' Rome was the military ethos of command-and-obey, not the democratic ethos of persuade-and-be-persuaded, and the principal theme of his plays is authority and disobedience. There is no interest in the democratic art of persuasion. Plays, therefore, do not need to be 'convincing' or to 'resemble life'.

One should end, perhaps, by considering the relevance of this study to contemporary performance practice. Having traced a subtle and long-lived tradition of masking, I find myself at once sympathetic towards and deeply opposed to Peter Brook's distinction between 'mysterious' and 'extraordinary' mask traditions of the east and the 'sordid' use of the mask 'common to the Western art theatre'. In the west, Brook argues, in almost Platonist terms, the subconscious fantasies of designers are superimposed upon the subjectivity of actors to create a kind of double lie.[51] Brook found a particular inspiration in Balinese actors, and his description of how a Balinese actor holds a mask and gazes at it may remind us of Greek practice:

He looks at it for a long while, until he and the mask begin to become like a reflection of each other; he begins to feel it partly as his own face – but not totally, because in another way he goes towards *its* independent life. And gradually he begins to move his hand so that the mask takes on a life, and he is watching it . . . It's obvious, in a way, that each mask represents a certain type of person, with a certain body and a certain tempo and inner rhythm, and so a certain breathing. As he begins to feel this, and as his hand begins to take on a corresponding tension, the breath changes till a certain *weight* of breathing begins to penetrate the actor's whole body; and when that is ready, he puts on the mask. And the whole shape is there.

Our actors can't do it that way – and shouldn't, because that belongs to a whole tradition and training.[52]

Brook perceives the profound difficulties which confront contemporary western actors when trying to work within a masking tradition that comes from outside their culture. He is right to stress these difficulties. There are, however, mystificatory overtones in this description of the eastern actor which we should beware of.

Brook is not one to be defeated by cultural difference, and he argues that there are ways in which western actors can come to terms with some eastern masks, using western methods. He distinguishes the 'strictly coded' masks of certain cultures, for which one needs to know 'the language of the signs', from 'so-called realistic, naturalistic masks', such as those of Bali, which express 'certain specific *but universal* human characteristics'. When one contemplates these Balinese masks, he claims, 'you see, first and foremost, Old Man – Beautiful Girl – Sad Man – Astonished Man – and then only secondarily, you see: Oh yes, they are Oriental'.[53] I find myself out of sympathy with Brook's thinking when it takes this turn, when he suppresses cultural difference in favour of a universal human condition. The closer I examine a given masking tradition, the more striking I find is its specificity. We can read any given mask, as we can read any text, by translating it, and imposing our own conceptual systems upon it, but we do not thereby share the same understanding of the mask as its creators and intended wearers. The masks of Menander's theatre could also, no doubt, be classed among Brook's 'so-called realistic, naturalistic masks', and Brook's actors would no doubt be able to discern '*universal* human characteristics' within them. I have tried to show in this book the extent to which Brook's dichotomy between the 'strictly coded' and the 'realistic' is false. One cannot represent reality without a language of signs. To accept and explore *different* theatrical languages seems to me more valuable than to search for the universal.

Notes

PREFACE

1 On the relationship between structuralism and stagecraft, see Oliver Taplin, *Greek Tragedy in Action* (London, 1978); Simon Goldhill, *Reading Greek Tragedy* (Cambridge, 1986); David Wiles 'Reading Greek Performance', *Greece and Rome* 34 (1987), 136–51; Simon Goldhill, 'Reading Performance Criticism', *Greece and Rome* 36 (1989), 172–82.

2 The work is not, of course, complete, nor ever will be. I regret that I was not able to benefit, while writing this book, from the second and third volumes of Geoffrey Arnott's Loeb edition of Menander's plays, nor from the third and greatly expanded edition of *Monuments Illustrating New Comedy*, revised by A. Seeberg and J. R. Green, and due to be published as *Bulletin of the Institute of Classical Studies*, Supplement no. 50.

INTRODUCTION: TWO TRADITIONS OF WRITING

1 All references to Menander's life are collected in the Körte–Thierfelder edition of Menander's plays (Leipzig, 1959). See the convenient summary in W. G. Arnott, *Menander*, vol. 1 (Cambridge, Mass. and London, 1979), pp. xiii–xix.

2 Plutarch, *Demetrius* 26.

3 *Poetics* V. 1–2.1449a.

4 *Poetics* XXV. 11.1460b.

5 *Poetics* XXIV. 6.1459b; *Rhetoric* III. vi. 1.1407b, III. vii. 2.1408a.

6 *Republic* X. 606.

7 *Eudemian Ethics* II. x. 30.1227b; *Rhetoric* I. ix. 32.1367b; *Poetics* VI. 24.1450b.

8 *Nicomachean Ethics* II. i. 1.1103a, II. vi. 15.1107a, etc.

9 As in *The Arbitration, The Changeling, The Harpist, The Necklace, The Peplos-Bearer, The Girl from Perinthos, The Phantom, The Girl from Samos, The Wet-Nurse, Ladies at Luncheon.*

10 As in *Old Cantankerous* 964, *The Man She Hated* 459–60, *The Sikyonian* 418–19, *The Girl from Samos* 731. On garlands for actors, see RAGA, p. 186. On garlands for authors, see Plutarch, *Moralia* 785B, Athenaeus VI. 241F.

11 *Moralia* 712A.

12 See, for example, T. B. L. Webster, *An Introduction to Menander* (Manchester, 1974), p. 1.

228

13 See Webster's chapter on 'The Tragic Code' in *An Introduction to Menander*. Cf. also A. G. Katsouris, *Linguistic and Stylistic Characterization: Tragedy and Menander* (Ioannina, 1975).
14 See MC, pp. 382, 302.
15 The seminal study is Erich Segal, *Roman Laughter* (Harvard, 1968). See more recently Florence Dupont, *L'Acteur-roi* (Paris, 1985).
16 The seminal study is Marino Barchiesi, 'Plauto e il metateatro antico', *Il Verri* 31 (1970), 113–30.
17 *Curculio* 591.
18 *Pseudolus* 407. Barchiesi's interest in this passage is echoed in Niall W. Slater, *Plautus in Performance: the Theatre of the Mind* (Princeton, 1985).

1 TEXT AND PERFORMANCE

1 *Poetics* XVI. 8.1462a (tr. M. E. Hubbard).
2 DFA, pp. 126–7.
3 *Rhetoric* III. i. 4.1403b.
4 DFA, p. 100.
5 Diogenes Laertius V. 36.
6 For a sustained exploration of this debt see A. Barigazzi, *La formazione spirituale di Menandro* (Turin, 1965).
7 *Cambridge History of Classical Literature*, vol. I, ed. P. E. Easterling and A. M. W. Knox (Cambridge, 1985), p. 425.
8 'Ménandre et la société athénienne', *Chronique d'Egypte* 32 (1957), 84–100, esp. pp. 88, 95.
9 Aelian, *Historical Miscellanies* XIV. 40.
10 *Rhetoric* II. viii. 12–13.1386a; *Poetics* XIII. 2.1453a.
11 *Poetics* XIII. 3.1453a.
12 *Ion* 535 c–e.
13 *Ion* 536a.
14 *Rhetoric* III. vii. 4–6.1408a.
15 cf. S. C. Humphreys, *The Family, Women and Death* (London, 1983), p. 65.
16 *L'Ecole du spectateur* (Paris, 1981), p. 332.
17 Aulus Gellius, *Attic Nights* VI. 5.
18 cf. F. H. Sandbach, *The Comic Theatre of Greece and Rome* (London, 1977), p. 71.
19 According to the census of Demetrios of Phaleron cited in Athenaeus VI. 272c.
20 *On the Orator* III. lix. 222.
21 Roland Barthes, *Essais critiques* (Paris, 1964), pp. 258–9. I have borrowed some phrases from the English translation by Peter W. Mathers, *Theatre Quarterly* 33 (1979), 29–30.
22 See, for example, T. Kowzan, *Littérature et spectacle* (The Hague and Paris, 1975).
23 G. Capone, *L'arte scenica degli attori tragici greci* (Padua, 1935).
24 RAGA.

25 *Greek Drama in its Theatrical and Social Context* (Cardiff, 1976).
26 Plutarch, *Pericles* 5.
27 Walcot, *Greek Drama*, p. 74.
28 *The Rape of the Locks*, 171; *The Two Bacchises*, 1072, etc.
29 *Politics* VIII. vii. 1342a.
30 *Rhetoric* III. 1.7.1404a.
31 *Rhetoric* III. ii. 10.1405a.
32 *Rhetoric* III. i. 5.1403b.
33 *Rhetoric* III. xii. 2.1413b.
34 Philodemos, *Rhetorica* I. 196 (ed. Sudhaus); Cicero, *On the Orator* III. lvi. 213; Longinus, *Art of Rhetoric* in *Rhetores Graeci*, ed. Spengel (Leipzig, 1894), I. 311–568 1–2.
35 See Bruno Zucchelli, ʹΥποχριτης – *origine e storia del termine* (Genoa, 1962), p. 71 n. 60.
36 Dionysius of Halicarnassus, *Demosthenes* 53.
37 Demosthenes, *On the Crown* 287.
38 Athenaeus, XIV. 620b.
39 The term *'theatrokratia'* is coined by Plato in *Laws* III. 701a.
40 W. S. Ferguson, *Hellenistic Athens* (London, 1911).
41 Cited in Philodemos, *Rhetorica* I. 197 (ed. Sudhaus).
42 Cited by Athanasius in his preface to Hermogenes, *Peri Staseon*, in *Rhetores Graeci*, ed. H. Rabe (Tübingen, 1931), p. 177.
43 *On the Orator* III. 216.
44 Dionysius of Halicarnassus, *Demosthenes* 53.
45 The texts are printed in Bruno Zucchelli, ʹΥποχριτης – *origine e storia del termine*, and are from (i) scholiast on Dionysius of Thrace; (ii) scholiast on Theon of Alexandria; (iii) Longinus, *Art of Rhetoric*; (iv) Plutarch, *Table Talk*; (v) Athanasius of Alexandria, sophist – preface to Hermogenes, *Peri Staseon*.
46 Philodemos, *Rhetorica* I. 193 (ed. Sudhaus).
47 *On Sense and Sensible Objects* VI. 437a.
48 Eugenio Barba, *Beyond the Floating Islands*, tr. J. Barba, R. Fowler, J. C. Rodesch, S. Shapiro (New York, 1986), p. 53.
49 *On Sense and Sensible Objects* VI. 445b.
50 *On the Soul* I.i.403a; I.iv.408b.
51 See John Onians, *Art and Thought in the Hellenistic Age* (London, 1979), pp. 54–8.
52 F. H. Sandbach, 'Menander and the Three-Actor Rule', in *Le Monde grec: hommages à Claire Préaux*, ed. J. Bingen (Brussels, 1975), pp. 197–204; cf. DFA, pp. 279ff and see G. M. Sifakis, *Studies in the History of Hellenistic Drama* (London, 1967), pp. 74ff and table 3.
53 *L'Ecole du spectateur* (Paris, 1981), p. 333.
54 Plutarch, *Moralia* 347F.
55 *Poetics* IX.9.1451b; XVII.5–8.1455b.
56 *Poetics* VI.13, 19.1450a.

57 A. J. Greimas, *Structural Semantics: an Attempt at a Method*, tr. D. McDowell, R. Schleifer and A. Velie (Lincoln, Nebraska & London, 1983), pp. 202–7; cf. V. Propp, *Morphology of the Folk Tale*, tr. L. Scott (Austin, 1968).
58 See MC, p. 470. Sandbach infers from Plautus that *Ladies at Luncheon* is set in Sikyon. See also p. 15 above.
59 For references, see MC, p. 531.
60 *Politics* I.i.11.1253a.
61 See DFA, pp. 60, 61, 269.
62 This form is used in *The Arbitration* 887, *The Fishermen* frag. 24, *Old Cantankerous* 194, 659, 666, *The Girl from Samos* 269, 329, 447, 683, 734, and in Fragment 656. An alternative form of address to '*theatai*' – 'spectators' – appears in Menander's Corinthian play *The Rape of the Locks* 171. Possibly there was a more significant female presence in the Corinthian audience.
63 On this subject, see David Wiles, 'Marriage and Prostitution in Classical New Comedy' in *Themes in Drama. 11: Women in Theatre*, ed. J. Redmond (Cambridge, 1989), pp. 31–48.
64 'Verso un antropologia dell' intreccio. Le strutture semplici della trama nelle commedie di Plauto', *Materiali e discussioni per l'analisi dei testi classici* 7 (1982), 39–101.
65 Bettini, *ibid.*, 52.
66 Diogenes Laertius v.79.

2 SPACE

1 Vitruvius v.vi.2; vii.2.
2 Plautus, *The Little Carthaginian* 17–18, clearly implies that some spectators sat *in proscaenio*.
3 Cited in Aristotle, *Rhetoric* III.iv.1.1406b.
4 Plato, *Republic* VII.514–19.
5 HGRT, fig. 300a. Bieber, in her discussion in HGRT, interprets this as an actor. The figure is, however, not looking at the mask shown in the painting, and does not have the tousled hair of an actor. See RAGA, p. 106.
6 G. M. Sifakis, *Studies in the History of Hellenistic Drama* (London, 1967), p. 48.
7 For an account of tapered *paraskênia* in Southern Italy, see most recently Karina Mitens, *Teatri greci ispirati all'architettura greca in Sicilia e nell'Italia meridionale c. 350–50 a.C.* (Rome, 1988), esp. p. 26.
8 See, for example, Fiechter's reconstructions of Oropus, New Pleuron, Ephesus, Athens: HGRT, figs. 427, 438, 447, 467.
9 Livy VII.ii.3–4.
10 A. W. Pickard-Cambridge, *The Theatre of Dionysus in Athens* (Oxford, 1946), p. 197.
11 HGRT, p. 123.
12 F. E. Winter, 'The Stage of New Comedy', *Phoenix* 37 (1983), 38–47.

13 Vitruvius v.iii.8.
14 Vitruvius v.viii.1–2; on the reflective quality of the orchestral floor, see Pliny, *Natural History* xi.cxii.270; A. N. Modona, *Gli edifici teatrali greci e romani* (Florence, 1961), p. 61.
15 Vitruvius v.v.7.
16 See the Pseudo-Aristotelian *Problems* xix.48.922b.
17 MINC nm 1, nm 2. For the dating, see T. B. L. Webster, *Greek Theatre Production*, revised edition (London, 1970), p. 26. The best colour reproductions are to be found in B. T. Maiuri, *Museo nazionale: Napoli* (Novara, 1971).
18 See p. 107 below.
19 See Modona, *Gli edifici teatrali greci e romani*, p. 27.
20 François Canac, *L'Acoustique des théâtres antiques: ses enseignements* (Paris, 1967), pp. 80–1, 122–7.
21 The wall supporting the stage is taken to be the *proskênion* in Delos in Sifakis, *History of Hellenistic Drama*, p. 44. There is an Athenian reference to a removable *proskênion* in Athenaeus 587B – see Pickard-Cambridge, *Theatre of Dionysus in Athens*, p. 157. We cannot be certain whether this refers to the upper or lower level.
22 Pollux iv.123.
23 Sifakis, *History of Hellenistic Drama*, pp. 44–5.
24 Douris cited in Athenaeus xii.536a.
25 Pollux iv.126; Vitruvius v.vi.8.
26 Sifakis, *History of Hellenistic Drama*, pp. 51–2.
27 For the distinction between *skênai* at stage level and small panels called *pinakes* at ground level, see *ibid.*, p. 50 n. 3.
28 Vitruvius v.vi.8; for the relationship between the *periaktoi* and the *parodoi*, see W. Beare, *The Roman Stage*, revised edition (London, 1968), appendix B.
29 Pollux iv.126–7.
30 In a *Life of Aristophanes* cited in Pickard-Cambridge, *Theatre of Dionysus in Athens*, p. 236 n. 3. An example of blind adherence to this theory is to be found in the Penguin translation of Terence.
31 Plautus, *The Two Bacchises* line 170 must be an entry from the harbour. Lines 235ff imply the possibility of an exit to the Peiraeus, though the speaker changes his mind and goes to the forum instead. Forum and harbour are on opposite sides in Plautus' *The Captives*, as is shown in Beare, *Roman Stage*, p. 248.
32 HGRT, figs. 473–4.
33 Pollux iv.131.
34 Scholiast on Aristotle, cited in Beare, *Roman Stage*, p. 295.
35 MINC ns 25.
36 Pollux iv.124.
37 Vitruvius v.vi.3.
38 Pollux iv.124. Pollux refers to a play by the 'Middle Comedy' playwright Antiphanes in this context.
39 G. E. R. Lloyd, *Polarity and Analogy* (Cambridge, 1966), pp. 51ff.

40 T. B. L. Webster, *An Introduction to Menander* (Manchester, 1974), p. 82.
41 At *Old Cantankerous* 5, Pan says that the farm is on the right. He is speaking to the audience, so presumably their viewpoint is assumed. At line 909, one actor instructs another to go right from the old man's house towards the shrine. Here 'right' must mean stage right, since the speaker is not speaking in the first instance for the audience's benefit. W. G. Arnott, in the new Loeb edition of Menander, vol. 1 (Cambridge, Mass., and London, 1979), p. 185 n. 1 and p. 338 n. 1, makes the reverse assumption, for no stated reason.
42 See below p. 205.
43 Pollux IV.123; Pickard-Cambridge, *Theatre of Dionysus in Athens*, pp. 47, 53.
44 See Webster, *An Introduction to Menander*, pp. 119–20; other possible shrines are noted on p. 81.
45 MINC NP 28. Reproduced in H. G. Beyen, *Die Pompejanische Wanddekorationen* (The Hague, 1938), vol. 1, plate 132.
46 On movable statues, see P. D. Arnott, *Greek Scenic Conventions* (Oxford, 1962), p. 68.
47 MINC NP 21 = HGRT, fig. 771.
48 MINC NP 27.
49 *Délos*, 27 (Ecole française d'Athènes, Paris, 1970), pl. 24, no. 1–2.
50 *The Girl from Samos* 309, 444, 448, 455, 474, 567, 570. For the distinction between the *agyias* and the *agyieus bômos*, see P. D. Arnott, *Greek Scenic Conventions*, p. 45; the central altar is also regarded as the *agyieus* in Webster, *Introduction to Menander*, p. 81.
51 Frag. 592, probably from *The Priestess*.
52 MINC YM 2 and IT 80. The mould is reproduced in HGRT, fig. 793. In *Introduction to Menander*, p. 166, Webster argues that the young man at the centre of the mosaic is the heroine's brother. This is implausible, since the artist in every case aims to render the title scene of the play. My interpretation follows Kahil's view, and Webster's earlier view in MINC p. 301, in identifying the central figure as the soldier. For the relationship between the mould and the mosaic, see S. Charitonidis, L. Kahil and R. Ginouvès, *Les Mosaïques de la maison du Ménandre à Mytilène* (Bern, 1970), p. 60. I follow Kahil's view, accepted by Karl Schefold, and not by Webster, when I identify the central figure in the mould as again being the soldier. If my interpretation of the iconography is sound, then the Greek title would be more correctly translated as '*He Who Was Hated*', since in the final act the hero has come to hate himself.
53 Cf. Froma Zeitlin's psychosexual analysis of space in 'The Power of Aphrodite: Eros and the Boundaries of the Self in the *Hippolytus*', in *Directions in Euripidean Criticism*, ed. Peter Burian (Durham, N.C., 1985), pp. 74ff.
54 The instruction *eiskukleit' eisô me* – 'wheel me in' – at line 758 seems conclusive evidence for the device: see MC, pp. 239–41.
55 Pollux IV.128; Sifakis, *History of Hellenistic Drama*, p. 51.
56 *Greek Theatre Production*, p. 26. Unfortunately the mosaic cannot accurately

record the effect of morning light in the Theatre of Dionysus as Webster believes, for in Athens the east end of the stage is slightly north of east, and the sun in January or March could not enter at this angle.

57 MINC YM 2. This is another of the Mytilenean series reproduced in Charitonidis, Kahil and Ginouvès, *Les Mosaïques de la maison du Ménandre à Mytilène*.

58 MINC NM 1, NM 2 (= my plates 2 and 1), IM 3, NP 6, NP 8, NP 13, NP 22, NP 26, NP 38. Bieber reproduces several: HGRT, figs. 371, 383, 401, 770. On the use of boys, see G. M. Sifakis, 'Boy Actors in New Comedy', *Arktouros: Hellenic Studies Presented to B. M. W. Knox*, ed. G. W. Bowerstock, W. Burkert, and M. J. C. Putnam (Berlin and New York, 1979), pp. 199–208.

59 MINC NP 22 = HGRT, fig. 770; *Délos*, 27: 180–1: note on fig. xix.

60 Cicero, *Pro Murena* XII.26.

61 For classical practice, see HGRT, fig. 9; DFA, figs. 35 and 36. For Hellenistic practice, see the Naples mosaic representing a satyr chorus in their dressing-room: HGRT, fig. 36. For non-theatrical practice, see, for example, the Pompeian painting of musicians: Naples Museum Inv. no. 9021.

62 MINC NP 45 = HGRT, fig. 328. The piper is not masked, and wears a gown similar to that of the piper in the satyr chorus mosaic (see note 61 above).

63 On this convention, see G. E. Duckworth, *The Nature of Roman Comedy* (Princeton, 1952), pp. 106–7.

64 For documentation of this convention, see John Blundell, *Menander and the Monologue* (Göttingen, 1980), pp. 11–16.

65 See David Bain, *Actors and Audience: A Study of Asides and Related Conventions in Greek Drama* (Oxford, 1977), chapter 7.

66 HGRT, fig. 630.

67 See John Blundell, *Menander and the Monologue*, pp. 20–1.

68 At the time of writing this section, I had not consulted N. J. Lowe's valuable study of spatial parameters in 'Tragic Space and Comic Timing in Menander's *Dyskolos*', *Bulletin of the Institute of Classical Studies* 34 (1987), 126–38.

69 See John Onians, *Art and Thought in the Hellenistic Age* (London, 1979), pp. 120–1.

70 Aristotle, *Rhetoric* III.xii.5.1414a.

71 The standard discussion of doorways is Beare, *Roman Stage*, appendix G. In Terence's *Phormio*, for instance, although Betty Radice in the Penguin translation envisages three houses, there is no evidence that the pimp's house is shown on stage: the pimp's entry in mid-conversation at line 485 is far more easily played as an entry from the *parodos*.

72 MINC NP 28. Reproduced in Beyen, *Die Pompejanische Wanddekorationen*, vol. I, pl. 132. Cf. p. 46 above. For a recent discussion of the relationship between Pompeian paintings and stage design, see Alix Barbet, *La Peinture murale romaine* (Paris, 1985), pp. 44ff.

73 Donatus' Commentary on *The Brothers* line 578; *The Eunuch* line 845.

74 Beare, *Roman Stage*, appendix C.

75 *The Eunuch* 290, 534 (the harbour); 230ff, cf. 763 (the forum); 629, 971 (the country).

76 The most recent editor of the play states that the scene is set in the *vestibulum* or enclosed entranceway, but this hardly resolves the problem of staging: Hubert Petersmann, *Stichus* (Heidelberg, 1973), pp. 40–1.

77 The goddess seems to stand in a special relationship to the Roman theatre. The first permanent Roman theatre incorporated a sanctuary of Venus. HGRT, p. 182.

78 Plautus, *The Little Carthaginian* 32; Vitruvius v.iii.1; etc. For the comparative social position of women in Greece and Rome, see David Wiles, 'Marriage and Prostitution in Greek New Comedy', *Themes in Drama 11: Women in Theatre*, ed. J. Redmond (Cambridge, 1989), pp. 31–48.

79 For a sustained analysis of framing techniques in Plautus, see Niall W. Slater, *Plautus in Performance: the Theatre of the Mind* (Princeton, 1985).

80 *The Little Carthaginian* 17.

81 The actor is sighted 'at the end of the *platea*' (line 278). Since this phrase cues rather similar entries in Terence's *Phormio* (line 215) and Plautus' *Three Dollar Day* (lines 839, 1006), it is possible that such a technique was used in source plays by Apollodoros and Philemon.

82 See HGRT, figs. 485, 488, 489 for the central position; figs. 483, 491 for actors using the steps.

83 Sifakis, *History of Hellenistic Drama*, pp. 131–2. Sifakis also quotes a reference from Athenaeus Mechanicus to steps placed against the proscenium for the use of actors.

83 Entry lines from *Thersytes* and *The Play of the Wether*, cited in William Tydeman, *The Theatre in the Middle Ages* (Cambridge, 1978), pp. 82–3.

85 The classic treatment is Erich Segal, *Roman Laughter* (Cambridge, Mass., 1968). An important study of the sociological tensions underlying medieval and Renaissance carnival is E. Le Roy Ladurie, *Carnival at Romans*, tr. M. Feeney (Harmondsworth, 1981).

86 See Claude Nicolet, *The World of the Citizen in Republican Rome* (London, 1980), pp. 364–73.

87 Cicero, *Pro Flacco* VII.16 – discussed in E. Frézouls, 'La Construction du *theatrum lapideum* et son contexte politique', in *Théâtre et spectacles dans l'antiquité: actes du colloque de Strasbourg, 5–7 Nov. 1981* (Strasbourg, 1983), pp. 193–214.

88 Livy XXXIV.54.4–8; for seating in the later Roman theatre, see Elizabeth Rawson, 'Discrimina Ordinum: the lex Julia theatralis', *Papers of the British School at Rome* 55 (1987), 83–114.

89 Plutarch, *Cicero* 13.

90 I cannot accept the theory of Richard C. Beacham that the buildings which loom above the stage façade in frescoes such as the one in 'The Room of the Masks' in the House of Augustus in Rome are part of a second-stage façade placed behind the main façade. See his educational video package 'Staging Roman Comedy' (University of Warwick Audio Visual Centre, 1987). His book *The Roman Theatre and its Audience* is forthcoming (London, 1991).

91 Florence Dupont, *L'Acteur-roi* (Paris, 1985), p. 252.
92 Anne Ubersfeld, *L'Ecole du spectateur* (Paris, 1981), p. 332.
93 Aristotle, *Nicomachean Ethics* II.i.3.1103a.
94 Pollux IV.129. Terence may use such a window in *The Eunuch* 788ff, but the staging is not certain.
95 HGRT, figs. 484, 501, 535.
96 Anne Ubersfeld, *L'Ecole du spectateur*, p. 69.
97 Plato, *Phaedrus* 246–7, 253–4.
98 Aristotle, *Rhetoric* I.x.7.1369a; *Nicomachean Ethics* I.xiii.9.1102a; *On the Soul* III.x.433b.
99 Aristotle, *Nicomachean Ethics* II.ii.6.1104a.

3 THE SYSTEM OF MASKS

1 *Poetics* V.2.1449a.
2 The fullest classical discussion of Menander's debt to Euripides is Quintilian XI.69.
3 *On Aristotle and Greek Tragedy* (London, 1962), p. 45.
4 J. Lecoq (ed.), *Le Théâtre du geste* (Paris, 1987), p. 115; for earlier work with the neutral mask, see, for instance, John Rudlin, *Jacques Copeau* (Cambridge, 1986), pp. 46–8.
5 *Aristotle and Greek Tragedy*, p. 260.
6 'The Closet of Masks – Role-Playing and Myth-Making in *The Orestes* of Euripides', *Ramus* 9 (1980), 69.
7 Carl Robert, *Die Masken der neueren attischen Komödie* (Halle, 1911); T. B. L. Webster, *Greek Theatre Production*, revised edition (London, 1970), and *Monuments Illustrating New Comedy*, revised edition, BICS Supplement no. 24 (London, 1969); A. W. Pickard-Cambridge, *Dramatic Festivals of Athens*, revised by J. Gould and D. M. Lewis (DFA) (Oxford, 1968); L. Bernabò-Brea *Menandro e il teatro greco nelle terracotte liparesi* (MTGTL) (Genoa, 1981).
8 *Menander*, vol. I (Cambridge, Mass. and London, 1979), pp. xxxii–xxxiii.
9 *ibid.*, p. xxxii.
10 MINC AS 6, IS 10 = HGRT, figs. 316–17.
11 Gould and Lewis see 'no reason to doubt' that a lottery was employed: DFA, p. 94.
12 *Aristotle and Greek Tragedy*, p. 45.
13 Umberto Eco, 'How Culture Conditions the Colours We See', in *On Signs*, ed. M. Blonsky (Oxford, 1985), pp. 157–75.
14 *The Way of the Masks*, tr. S. Modelski (Washington, 1982), p. 144.
15 *Metaphysics*, IV.ii.21.1004b.
16 *Metaphysics*, V.x.4.1018b.
17 *Metaphysics* X.vi.1057a–b.
18 *Metaphysics* X.ix.1058b.
19 Theophrastos, *Metaphysics* VII.18–VIII.19.

20 MINC NM 6.
21 Pollux, *Onomastikon* IV.143–154.
22 Athenaeus XIV.659a; cf. Hesychius' *Lexicon* s.v. Tettix.
23 RAGA, p. 103.
24 MTGTL, p. 19; cf. the masks in the Bristol University Theatre Collection, illustrated in Glynne Wickham, *A History of the Theatre* (Cambridge, 1983).
25 MTGTL, pp. 21–2.
26 MTGTL, p. 15.
27 Robert, *Die Masken der neueren attischen Komödie*, pp. 34–5, 48–9, etc.
28 *Peri diaphoras komoidon* (ed. Kaibel), p. 5.
29 Quintilian XI.iii.74.
30 MINC NM 5, NM 4; for a colour reproduction of the second, see B. T. Maiuri, *Museo nazionale: Napoli* (Novara, 1971), plate 97.
31 MTGTL, p. 13.
32 DFA, p. 230.
33 *History of Animals* I.i.488b.
34 *History of Animals* I.viii.491b.
35 *De physionomica liber* 12; cf. Aristotle, *Parts of Animals* II.ii, II.iv.
36 *Physiognomics* VI.814b.
37 cf. *History of Animals* I.ix.491b; and Loxus in *De physionomica liber* 25.
38 *Physiognomics* IV.806b.
39 MTGTL, p. 13.
40 *Prior Analytics* II.xxvii.70b.
41 *Rhetoric* I.ii.18.1357b.
42 See the pseudo-Aristotelian *Problems* XXX.i.953–5.
43 Aristotle cited in *De physionomica liber* 81. I have translated *inflexa* as 'arched'.
44 *History of Animals* I.ix.491b; cf. Pliny XI.cxiv.273–4.
45 *Physiognomics* VI.812b 25–8.
46 Pollux II.49; raised brows were often associated with superciliousness: cf. Aristophanes, *Acharnians* 1069; Demosthenes, *On the False Legation* 314, etc.
47 MINC NS 25 = HGRT, fig. 324. Having inspected this relief, I think it likely that the beard which appears pointed in photographs is in fact broken. See below p. 205.
48 I am grateful to Oliver Taplin for showing me his unpublished paper 'Menander the Dramatist' which deals with the centrality of anger in *The Girl from Samos*.
49 W. T. MacCary, 'Menander's Characters: their Names, Roles and Masks', *TAPA* 101 (1970), 277–90; 'Menander's Slaves: their Names, Roles and Masks', *TAPA* 100 (1969), 277–94; 'Menander's Old Men', *TAPA* 102 (1971), 303–25; 'Menander's Soldiers: their Names, Roles and Masks', *American Journal of Philology* 93 (1972), 279–98.
50 P. G. McC. Brown, 'Masks, Names and Characters in New Comedy', *Hermes* 115 (1987), pt 2, 181–201. I am grateful to Peter Brown for showing me a copy of his article prior to publication.
51 *Comicorum Graecorum Fragmenta in Papyris Reperta*, ed. C. Austin (Berlin

and New York, 1973), text no. 257; for a translation, see *Select Papyri*, vol. III, ed. D. L. Page (Cambridge, Mass. & London, 1941), text no. 65, or the Penguin edition of Menander, pp. 252–4. In my reading of this papyrus, the scene turns upon the idea that Nikeratos is friend to both old man and youth. While Nikeratos embraces the old man and calls him 'friend' (*hetaire*) at line 26, the young man watches aside and meditates upon the singleness of *hetaireia* (line 32), before confronting Nikeratos with questions about the nature of his friendship. Nikeratos' apparent intimacy with the old man motivates the youth's belief that Nikeratos is himself scheming to marry the old man's daughter.

52 The original names are recorded by a scholiast on Persius, *Satires* V.161.

53 *For Roscius Amerinus* 46. In Caecilius' adaptation, the name of the younger brother has apparently been changed from Moschion to Eutychus, so we have no certainty that Menander used this mask in this particular play: see frag. 428 K–T.

54 Claude Vatin attributes the prevalence of male celibacy to the exposure of girls at birth: *Recherches sur le mariage et la femme mariée à l'époque hellénistique* (Paris, 1970), pp. 228–37.

55 T. B. L. Webster, *An Introduction to Menander* (Manchester, 1974), p. 98, develops a similar line of argument, and concludes that Chairestratos in *The Shield* is in his early thirties.

56 Gorgias in *The Farmer, Old Cantankerous, The Hero*; Smikrines in *The Shield, The Arbitration*, and in Choricius XXXII.73 (ed. Förster–Richstieg), which seems to be a quotation from *Faithless* – see Webster, *Introduction to Menander*, p. 120.

57 *The Farmer, Old Cantankerous, The Hero, The Rape of the Locks*. Although in the last instance there is no evidence that Myrrhine appeared on stage, the evidence of audience expectations is clear.

58 *The Eunuch, The Girl from Samos*.

59 *The Arbitration, The Rape of the Locks*.

60 *The Arbitration, The Hero*; cf. Terence, *The Eunuch, Phormio*.

61 *The Rape of the Locks, Papyrus Hamburgensis* 656 (for a translation, see p. 255 of the Penguin edition of Menander, ed. N. Miller). Doris is also apparently the recipient of orders in Pap. Oxy. 2658 (Austin no. 245). We do not know the nature of Doris's roles in *The Dagger* and *The Toady*.

62 *On the Dance* 29.

63 Epigrams by Asclepiades and Callimachus: *Anthologie grecque*, ed. P. Waltz (Paris, 1931), VI.311, VI.308 cited in RAGA, pp. 103 and 108.

64 'Speech on behalf of those who live by acting plays of Dionysus', *Choricius Gazaeus: Opera*, ed. R. Förster and E. Richstieg (Stuttgart, 1929), XXXII.73 – discussed by MacCary in 'Menander's Characters', 277–90.

65 See note 56 above.

66 MC, p. 648.

67 *Misopogon* 349c, 342a.

68 Commentary on *The Brothers* I.1.

69 Menander, *The Girl from Andros* frag. 40; cf. also Aristophanes, *Birds* 160–1. M. Collignon, in the *Dictionnaire des antiquités* s.v. *matrimonium*, discerns myrtle in vase paintings of brides. M. Détienne, in *The Gardens of Adonis*, tr. J. Lloyd (Brighton, 1977), overstates his case when he argues for the erotic associations of myrtle. Myrtle was also used at funerals – cf. Euripides, *Alcestis* 172.

70 *The Double Deceiver, The Man She Hated, The Girl from Samos, The Imbrians*, and probably *The Misogynist*; Austin texts no. 244 (perhaps Menander's *The Urn*) and no. 252.

71 *The Hero, The Harpist, The Rape of the Locks, The Necklace, Title Unknown*; also in Austin texts no. 250, 255, 266.

72 Alexis, *The Furnace*, Krobylos, *The False Changeling: Poetarum Comicorum Graecorum Fragmenta*, ed. A. Meineke (Paris, 1894), pp. 562, 710.

73 For Arnott's view, see p. 70 above; while Arnott's concern is with character, Webster's emphasis is upon the way masks allow the audience to predict plot: *Introduction to Menander*, pp. 89–94.

74 'Menander's Slaves', 277–94, especially 285–8.

75 Pap. Oxy 11 (Austin text no. 254): for a translation, see *Select Papyri*, vol. III, ed. D. L. Page (Cambridge, Mass. and London, 1941), text no. 62.

76 Pap. Hibeh 5 = Austin text no. 244: for a translation, see *Select Papyri*, vol. III, ed. D. L. Page, text no. 64; Pap. Lund 4 = Austin text no. 263.

77 *Menander: Plays and Fragments*, tr. Norma Miller (Harmondsworth, 1987), p. 229.

78 *Nicomachean Ethics* I.xiii.9.1102a; I.xiii.19.1103a.

79 *Nicomachean Ethics* VI.ii.4.1139a.

80 *Nicomachean Ethics* II.v.1–6.1105b.

81 *Nicomachean Ethics* II.i.1.1103a.

82 *Nicomachean Ethics* VI.xiii.5.1144b.

83 *Nicomachean Ethics* I.ii.8.1094b.

84 *Nicomachean Ethics* I.xiii.1.1102a.

85 'Intimations of the Will in Greek Tragedy', in J.-P. Vernant and P. Vidal-Naquet, *Tragedy and Myth in Ancient Greece*, tr. J. Lloyd (Brighton, 1981), p. 28; cf. A. Dihle, *The Theory of the Will in Classical Antiquity* (Berkeley, 1982), esp. pp. 55–6.

86 *Poetics* IX.4–5.1451b. S. H. Butcher, in *Aristotle's Theory of Poetry and Fine Art* (New York, 1951), pp. 36–7, 376–9, conjectures that the text is at fault, and that *tychônta* should be preceded by a negative.

4 MASKS EAST AND WEST: CONTRASTS AND COMPARISONS

1 Athenaeus XIV.659a – see DFA, p. 178 n. 6.

2 For a correlation of mask types with play types, see P. G. O'Neill, 'Masks in Japanese No Drama', *aarp: Art and Archaeology Research Papers* (June, 1975), 36–47.

3 *On the Art of the Nô Drama: the Major Treatises of Zeami*, tr. J. Thomas Rimer and Yamazaki Masakazu (Princeton, 1984), pp. 10–17.

4 *ibid.*, pp. 151–6.

5 I have consulted Yoshinobu Inoura and Toshio Kawatake, *The Traditional Theatre of Japan* (Tokyo 1981), p. 115, and the lists of Morita Toshirô (modified by R. Teele), Mark J. Nearman, and Nakamura Yasuo, collected in *Nô/Kyogen Masks and Performance: Essays and Interviews Compiled by Rebecca Teele*, ed. Mime Journal (Claremont, 1984), pp. 8–11, 59–64, 114–20. Kunio Komparu, *The Noh Theatre*, tr. J. Corddry (New York and Tokyo, 1983), uses this tetrad on pp. 232–3, but offers a more complex taxonomy on the pages which follow.

6 *Nô/Kyogen Masks and Performance*, p. 61.

7 P. G. O'Neill, 'Masks in Japanese No Drama', 45.

8 Athenaeus xiv.659a.

9 *Etymologicum Magnum* 376.48: see, however, DFA, p. 224.

10 Suidas s.v. Thespis; scholiast on *Frogs* 406.

11 RAGA, p. 103, cites ID 1421 as an example.

12 *Nô/Kyogen Masks and Performance*, p. 173.

13 *On the Art of the Nô Drama: the Major Treatises of Zeami*, p. 238.

14 'Recollections and Thoughts on Nô: an Interview with Kongô Iwao, Head of the Kongô School of Nô', in *Nô/Kyogen Masks and Performance*, pp. 74–92.

15 Jacques Lecoq (ed.), *Le Théâtre du geste* (Paris, 1987), p. 115.

16 Donald Richie, 'Nô Masks', in *Nô/Kyogen Masks and Performance*, pp. 17–19.

17 Nakamura Yasuo, 'Nô Masks: Their History and Development', in *Nô/Kyogen Masks and Performance*, p. 123.

18 *Nô/Kyogen Masks and Performance*, p. 61.

19 *ibid.*, p. 58.

20 Komparu, *The Noh Theatre*, p. 229.

21 *ibid.*, pp. 78, 84–5.

22 Kanze Hisao, 'Life with the Nô Mask', in *Nô/Kyogen Masks and Performance*, pp. 72–3.

23 See J. J. Pollitt, *Art and Experience in Classical Greece* (Cambridge, 1972), pp. 174ff.

24 *Nô/Kyogen Masks and Performance*, p. 123.

25 Aristotle, *Problems* xxxi.7.958a.

26 Accomplished youth, ex. 4: MTGTL, fig. 247 and plate xxiv.

27 *ibid.*, p. 128.

28 Observations by Gerhäuser on reflected light from the seats are quoted in the course of a useful discussion of lighting in Siegfried Melchinger, *Das Theater der Tragödie* (Munich, 1974), p. 131.

29 MINC NM 1 = HGRT, fig. 347: see p. 48 above and p. 202 below.

30 Keith Johnstone, *Impro* (London, 1981), p. 185.

31 'Okina: an Interview with Takabayashi Kôji, Actor of the Kita School', in *Nô/Kyogen Masks and Performance*, p. 99.

32 *ibid.*, pp. 99–100.

33 See Mario Prosperi, 'The Masks of Lipari', *The Drama Review* 26 (1982), 25–36.
34 François Jouan, reviewing a revival of the production in 1989 in Pisa: *Cahiers du GITA* 5 (1989), 224–6.
35 One Japanese mask, the *Okina*, is donned not in the mirror room but before the audience. This exceptional mask functions as a symbol, not as a personality. See *Nô/Kyogen Masks and Performance*, pp. 51–5.
36 Fronto, *On Eloquence* v.i.37.
37 HGRT, fig. 36.
38 HGRT, fig. 109. For authors gazing at masks, cf. the Lateran/Princeton reliefs of Menander: HGRT, figs. 316, 317; the Alexandrian theatre ticket representing Menander: HGRT, fig. 320; the Lyme Park relief: HGRT, fig. 201; the relief in Vienna: HGRT, fig. 300b; and Naples Museo Nazionale no. 6700.
39 *Nô/Kyogen Masks and Performance*, pp. 72, 70.
40 Quoted by Mark J. Nearman in *Nô/Kyogen Masks and Performance*, p. 43.
41 Monica Bethe, 'Nô Costume as Interpretation', in *Nô/Kyogen Masks and Performance*, p. 148; on the combination of specific wigs and masks, see Komparu, *The Noh Theatre*, pp. 300–2.
42 Nicola Savarese (ed.), *Anatomia del teatro* (Florence, 1983), p. 134.
43 *Nô/Kyogen Masks and Performance*, p. 146.
44 A. S. F. Gow and D. L. Page, *The Greek Anthology: Hellenistic Epigrams* (Cambridge, 1965), ii.185. However, Paulette Ghiron-Bistagne, *Recherches sur les acteurs dans la Grèce antique* (Paris, 1976), follows Wilamowitz in taking the epigram to refer to a damaged terracotta model: RAGA, p. 103.
45 See, for this broad understanding of Dionysus, Charles Segal, *Dionysiac Poetics and Euripides' Bacchae* (Princeton, 1982), pp. 10–17.
46 Paulette Ghiron-Bistagne, in RAGA, p. 107, derives this conclusion from Lucian, *Menippus* 16. Unfortunately the text does not specify that it was on stage that the mask was removed. We should note, however, that unmasked actors certainly appeared with the dramatist at the Proagon at the start of the festival: DFA, p. 68.
47 *No/Kyogen Masks and Performance*, p. 19.
48 Zenchiku, quoted by Nearman in *Nô/Kyogen Masks and Performance*, p. 45.
49 Plato, *Laws* 645–6, 671.
50 Cited by Jean Duvignaud in *L'Acteur – esquisse d'une sociologie du comédien* (Paris, 1965), p. 24.
51 *Tutte le opere di Carlo Goldoni*, ed. G. Ortolani, third edition (Milan, 1954), vol. I, p. 349.
52 *Building a Character*, tr. E. R. Hapgood (London, 1979), pp. 29–30.
53 *Man and Superman* (Harmondsworth, 1946), p. 45, originally published in 1903.
54 Tom Davies, cited in George Taylor, '"The Just Delineation of the Passions": Theories of Acting in the Age of Garrick', in *The Eighteenth-Century English Stage*, ed. K. Richards and P. Thompson (London, 1974), p. 61.

55 Charles LeBrun, *A Method to Learn to Design the Passions*, tr. J. Williams (London, 1734), p. 13. The original French text was written *c*. 1670 and published in 1698.

56 *ibid.*, pp. 20–1.

57 'An Essay on the Art of Acting', in *Works* (London, 1753), p. 356. Joseph R. Roach cites and discusses an earlier version of Hill's text in *The Player's Passion* (Cranford, N.J., 1985), p. 80.

58 Hill, *ibid.*, p. 409.

59 See, for example, James Parsons, *Human Physiognomy Explained* (London, 1747). George Taylor, in *Players and Performances in the Victorian Theatre* (Manchester, 1990), also cites Lavater's *Physiognomical Bible* of 1772, translated by the playwright Thomas Holcroft in 1789, and Franz Joseph Gall's theory of phrenology, popularized in George Combe's *Constitution of Man* (London, 1828). I am grateful to George Taylor for allowing me to consult a draft chapter prior to publication.

60 Johannes Jelgerhuis, *Theoretische lessen over de gesticulatie en mimiek* (Amsterdam, 1827), tr. A. S. Golding in *Classicistic Acting: Two Centuries of a Performance Tradition at the Amsterdam Schouwburg* (Lanham, 1984), p. 339.

61 *ibid.*, p. 365.

62 *ibid.*, pp. 340–1.

63 *ibid.*, p. 361.

64 See, for example, F. Taviani and M. Schino, *Il segreto della commedia dell'arte* (Florence, 1982), p. 435.

65 See *ibid.*, pp. 309–21.

66 Flaminio Scala, *Il teatro delle favole rappresentative* (Venice, 1611), tr. by H. Salerno as *Scenarios of the Commedia dell'Arte* (New York and London, 1967).

67 See Cesare Molinari, *La commedia dell'arte* (Milan, 1985), pp. 23–6 on the normative structure, and pp. 142–3 on Cecchini.

68 *Il segreto della commedia dell'arte*, pp. 375–6, 449.

69 Preface to *A Duke and No Duke* (1693), reprinted in *Themes in Drama. 10:Farce*, ed. James Redmond (Cambridge, 1988), pp. 101–10.

70 See, for example, G. Casanova, *History of My Life*, tr. W. Trask (New York and London, 1967–71), vol. IV, pp. 81–2, vol. VII, p. 254, vol. VIII, pp. 203–9.

71 Limojon de St-Didier, *La Ville et la république de Vénise* (Paris, 1680), p. 369.

72 E.g. in Mantua in 1608: see K. M. Lea, *Italian Popular Comedy* (Oxford, 1934), p. 315.

73 *La Ville et la république de Vénise*, pp. 380–1.

74 *ibid.*, p. 368.

75 E.g. in *Il festino* (1754), III.iv; *Le massere* (1755), III.iii.

76 *The Book of the Courtier*, tr. J. Bull (Harmondsworth, 1967), pp. 118–19.

77 Marino Berengo, *La società veneta alla fine dell' '700* (Florence, 1956), p. 72; Casanova, *History Of My Life*, IV, p. 75.

78 *La Ville et la république de Vénise*, p. 353.

79 *ibid.*, p. 380.

80 See, for example, the diagram by F. Le Rousseau reproduced in J. R. A. Nicoll, *The World of Harlequin* (Cambridge, 1963), p. 71.

81 Comments made during a seminar at the Centre for Performance Research, Cardiff, on 4 February 1989. For the diabolic origins of the Arlecchino mask, see Ludovico Zorzi's comments in *Arte della maschera nella Commedia dell'arte*, ed. D. Sartori and B. Lanata (Florence, 1983), pp. 74ff.

82 *Il segreto della Commedia dell'Arte*, p. 12.

83 *ibid.*, p. 449.

84 Enzo Petraccone, *La commedia dell'arte* (Naples, 1927), p. 138, Originally published in 1699 under the title *Dall'arte rappresentativa*.

85 DFA, pp. 30–3.

86 Demosthenes, *On the False Legation* 287; Plutarch, *Moralia* 527d.

87 Semos, quoted in Athenaeus 622.

5 THE ROMAN MASK

1 *On the Dance* 79.

2 Polybius VI.56.

3 Juvenal III.175; Martial XIV.176; Seneca, *Epistles* XXIV.13, *On Anger* II.xi.4.

4 Suidas s.v. Thespis; scholiast on *Frogs* 406; Virgil, *Georgics* II.385. Wooden masks worn in the worship of Artemis were said to be worn 'after the Italian fashion': Hesychius s.v. *kyrittoi*.

5 The fundamental account is Polybius VI.53; cf. Diodorus XXXI.xxv.2; Ovid, *Fasti* I.591; Juvenal VIII.19ff, Martial II.90, Vitruvius VI.iv.6, Pliny, *Natural History* XXXV.6. Suetonius, *Vespasian* 19 refers to an *archimimus* playing the part of the dead emperor in this ritual.

6 DFA, p. 218.

7 Suetonius, *Caligula* 27, *Nero* 39.

8 Livy VII.2.12.

9 Festus s.v. *personata*.

10 See above p. 113.

11 *Epistles* II.i.173.

12 *The Comedy of Asses* 11, *The Merchant* 10; for the biographical implications, see, for example, Florence Dupont, *L'Acteur-roi* (Paris, 1985), p. 348. A. S. Gratwick notes that 'Titus' and 'Plautus' also have theatrical associations and appear to be stage names: 'TITVS MACCIVS PLAVTVS', *Classical Quarterly* 23 (1973), 78–84.

13 Ovid, *Fasti* VI.651ff; Livy IX.30.5–10; Valerius Maximus II.v.4; Plutarch, *Roman Questions* 55.

14 See J. G. Frazer, *The Fasti of Ovid* (London, 1929), vol. IV, p. 306.

15 Livy VII.ii.3–5.

16 See Yves Bomati, 'Phersu et le monde dionysiaque', *Latomus* 45 (1986), 21–32. I am grateful to Birgitte Ginge for this reference. On the Etruscan origins of Roman theatre, see HGRT, pp. 147–8, Florence Dupont, *L'Acteur-roi*, pp. 136–40.

17 E.g. Pierre Grimal, 'Le Théâtre à Rome', in *Actes du IXe congrès à Rome, 1973*, ed. Assoc. Guillaume Budé (Paris, 1975), pp. 288–9; Florence Dupont, *L'Acteur-roi*, p. 80; F. Della Corte, 'Maschere e personaggi in Plauto', *Dioniso*

46 (1975), 163–93; Chiarini in G. Chiarini and R. Tessari, *Teatro del corpo, teatro della parola: due saggi sul "comico"* (Pisa, 1983), pp. 113–14.

18 *The Roman Stage*, revised edition (London, 1968), appendix 1.

19 *Cambridge History of Classical Literature*, vol. 2: *Latin Literature*, ed. E. J. Kenney (Cambridge, 1982), p. 83.

20 *Grammatici Latini*, ed. Keil, vol. 1, p. 489.

21 Donatus on *The Eunuch* I.6, *The Brothers* I.6.

22 See Florence Dupont, *L'Acteur-roi*, pp. 147–55.

23 Festus 446 (Lindsay); cf. Livy XXVI.37.13.

24 *Natural History* XXXVI.114.

25 See HGRT, figs. 542–3.

26 See HGRT, figs. 551–3.

27 Livy XXXIX.22.2, 22.10.

28 See Eric S. Gruen, *The Hellenistic World and the Coming of Rome* (Berkeley, 1984), vol. 1, p. 252.

29 MINC NP 6 (=HGRT, fig. 395), NP 46.

30 Cesare Questa, 'Maschere e funzioni nelle commedie di Plauto', *Materiali e discussioni per l'analisi dei testi classici* 8 (1982), 9–64.

31 I am in complete agreement here with A. S. Gratwick. See *Cambridge History of Classical Literature*, vol. 2: *Latin Literature*, p. 104; on the parallel between Plautus' stock characters and the *commedia dell'arte*, see John Wright, *Dancing in Chains: the Stylistic Unity of the comœdia palliata* (Rome, 1974), p. 104.

32 cf. Plutarch, *Roman Questions* 10.

33 See M. F. Della Corte, 'La tipologia del personaggio della Palliata', *Actes du IXᵉ congrès à Rome, 1973*, ed. Assoc. Guillaume Budé (Paris, 1975), 354–93, p. 365.

34 On the separation of psychological and physical traits in Plautus, see Silvia Magistrini, 'Le descrizioni fisiche dei personaggi in Menandro, Plauto e Terenzio', *Dioniso* 44 (1970), 79–114.

35 My examples are taken from the '*Receuil de Dominique*', the notebook of Domenico Biancolelli printed in S. Spada, *Domenico Biancolelli – ou l'art d'improviser* (Naples, 1969).

36 *Roman Laughter*, second edition (New York, 1987), pp. 31–4; on the Greek setting, cf. also Pierre Grimal, 'Le "Truculentus" de Plaute et l'esthétique de la palliata', *Dioniso* 45 (1971–4), pp. 532–43.

37 See Chiarini's comparison of doubling principles in Menander and Plautus: G. Chiarini and R. Tessari, *Teatro del corpo, teatro della parola*, pp. 109–14.

38 'Les Demi-masques', *Revue archéologique* (1970), 332–82. I prefer the explanation that these masks were designed for flute players, and that the mouths are uncovered for this reason.

39 MINC ZS 7 (=HGRT, fig. 420); cf. FS 5.

40 cf. chapter 1 above, pp. 32–3.

41 See Taviani's reassessment of the evidence in Ferdinando Taviani and Mirella Schino, *Il segreto della commedia dell'arte* (Florence, 1982), pp. 309ff.

42 *Impro* (London, 1981), p. 181.

43 *ibid.*, pp. 147–8, citing N. Gorchakov, *The Vakhtangov School of Stage Art.*

44 See Erich Segal, *Roman Laughter*, pp. 141ff.

45 See my 'Marriage and Prostitution in Classical New Comedy', in *Themes in Drama: 11, Women and Theatre*, ed. James Redmond (Cambridge, 1989), pp. 31–48.

46 On the correlation between dramatic and social structures, see my unpublished doctoral thesis, 'The Servant as Master: a Study of Role Definition in Classical and Renaissance Popular Comedy', Bristol University, 1979.

47 See *The Ritual Process: Structure and Anti-Structure* (London, 1969).

48 For an attempt to understand Menander as a man who wrote for a 'bourgeois' society, see M. I. Rostovtzeff, *The Social and Economic History of the Hellenistic World* (Oxford, 1941), especially pp. 1, 118.

49 *The Self-Tormentor*, 23.

50 Suetonius' biography is preserved by Donatus. His sources go back to the second century BC. For a cautious view of the notion of a 'Scipionic circle', see Sander Goldberg, *Understanding Terence* (Princeton, 1986), pp. 13–14.

51 *The Self-Tormentor* 35ff. My translation is adapted from that by M. Winterbottom.

52 For a sceptical view, see again Sander Goldberg, *Understanding Terence*, pp. 10–12.

53 We owe this information to a scholiast on Persius, *Satires* V.161, and to Donatus' note on *The Eunuch* 971.

54 DFA, pp. 281–2.

55 Aristophanes, *Knights* 232.

56 *Poetics*, VI.28.1450b.

57 Pollux II.47.

58 DFA, p. 311; for a discussion of the *himatiomisthês*, see G. M. Sifakis, *Studies in the History of Hellenistic Drama* (London, 1967), pp. 81–2.

59 Quoted in G. M. Sifakis, *ibid.*, p. 55.

60 See F. H. Sandbach, 'Menander and the Three-Actor Rule', in *Le Monde grec: hommages à Claire Préaux*, ed. J. Bingen (Brussels, 1975), pp. 197–204.

6 THE FOUR MASK GENERA

1 See W. W. Fortenbaugh, 'Theophrastus on Fate and Character', in *Arktouros: Hellenic Studies presented to B. M. W. Knox*, ed. G. W. Bowerstock, W. Burkert and M. J. C. Putnam (Berlin and New York, 1979). For the relation to Menander, see also Fortenbaugh's article, 'Theophrast über den komischen Charakter', *Rheinisches Museum* 174 (1981), 245–60.

2 Theophrastos, *On the Senses* 73–82.

3 Pliny, *Natural History* XXXV.50.

4 See G. E. R. Lloyd, *Polarity and Analogy* (Cambridge, 1966), pp. 44, 74.

5 Theophrastos, *On the Senses* 59.

6 *On Generation and Corruption* II.ii.330a 24.

7 *Parts of Animals* I.ii.648b.
8 See Lloyd, *Polarity and Analogy*, pp. 20–1. E. C. Evans 'Physiognomics in the Ancient World', *Transactions of the American Philosophical Association* NS 59, pt 5 (1969), has a full discussion on pp. 17–27.
9 Theophrastos, *On the Senses* 64.
10 Aristotle, *Problems* XXXI.1.955a.
11 *Parts of Animals* II.ii.648a.
12 Aristotle, *On Length of Life* V.466a; cf. *Problems* XXXI.1.955a.
13 Aristotle, *Generation of Animals* V.iv.784b.
14 Aristotle, *Problems* XXXVIII.9.967b; also VIII.1.887b.
15 Aristotle, *History of Animals* III.xix.521a.
16 Aristotle, *Problems* IV.25.879a.
17 Aristotle, *Generation of Animals* VI.i.765b.
18 See G. E. R. Lloyd, 'Hot and Cold, Wet and Dry in Greek Philosophy', *Journal of the Hellenic Society* 84 (1964), 92–106, esp. 101–2.
19 Aristotle, *Problems* XXXI.14.958b; XXXVIII.3–4.967a.
20 *Problems* XXXVIII.2.966b; cf. Hippocrates, *Airs, Waters, Places* XXIV.34.
21 Aristotle, *On Colours* VI.797b.
22 Aristotle, *Problems* XIV.16.910b; cf. *Airs, Waters, Places* XX.
23 See Plato, *Laws* VI.781c; cf. *Phaedrus* 239c.
24 Xenophon, *Economist* X.2; cf. Aristophanes, *Assembly-Women* 878, *Wealth* 1,064.
25 A bearded youth does, however, appear on the Aixone monument of 313 BC – dated by Webster, however, to 340 BC. See DFA, fig. 25 and discussions on pp. 49 and 216.
26 Athenaeus 564f–565d.
27 For the process of evolution, see MINC 14–15.
28 See *ibid.*
29 See, most obviously, the New York series of terracotta figurines: DFA, figs. 92–5; cf. MTGTL, nos. C2, C3, C4. There is still room for confusion in the Amphipolis plaque of *c.* 300 BC: MINC XT 1.
30 DFA, p. 83.
31 MTGTL, nos. A6–A15.
32 The white-faced female mask is represented in HGRT, figs. 74 and 34; it is also clearly represented in a vase painting of a *phlyax* comedy: HGRT, fig. 535 = MTGTL colour plate X.
33 Not catalogued in MINC. A photo was displayed in the Museo Eoliano, Lipari, in 1988.
34 *Etymologicum Magnum* 346, 48; cf. scholiast on Aristophanes, *Clouds* 542, and hypothesis to Aristophanes, *Peace*.
35 T. B. L. Webster, *Monuments Illustrating Old and Middle Comedy*, second edition, Institute of Classical Studies (London, 1969) at p. 96 (pl. VII).
36 See p. 102 above.
37 Aristotle, *Rhetoric* II.xiv.1390a–b; Solon frag. 27. Cf. *Politics* VII.xiv.6 and II.1335a–b.

38 *Moralia* 712c.
39 *Nicomachean Ethics* VIII.xii.7.1162a.
40 *Politics* II.i.1260bff.
41 Plato, *Laws* VI.781, VII.804–6, *Republic* V.451–7.
42 *Generation of Animals* I.xx.728a.
43 *Generation of Animals* I.xix.727a.
44 See R. Joly (ed.), *Hippocrate*, vol. XI (Paris, 1970), p. 17.
45 *Generation of Animals* II.iii.737a, *Politics* VII.xiv.9.1335a.
46 *Politics* I.ii.4.1253b.
47 G. de Ste Croix, in *Slavery and Other Forms of Unfree Labour*, ed. L. Archer
    (London, 1988), p. 28.
48 *Politics* I.ii.3.1253b.
49 *Politics* I.ii.18.1255a, III.ix.3.1285a.
50 *Politics* I.ii.14–15.1254b.
51 See, for example, G. de Ste Croix, *The Class Struggle in the Ancient Greek
    World* (London, 1983), pp. 418–19; Yvon Garlan, *Les Esclaves en Grèce
    ancienne* (Paris, 1982), p. 142.
52 See p. 135 above.
53 See, for example, Yvon Garlan, *Les Esclaves en Grèce ancienne*, pp. 91–2.
54 *Politics* I.ii.1.1253b.
55 *Politics* VI.ii.12.1319b.
56 *Politics* I.v.1–2.1259a–b.
57 *Politics* I.ii.10.1254–b.
58 See p. 27 above.
59 See, in particular, *Politics* IV.ix.1295aff.
60 The theory of the 'bourgeois' audience owes much to V. I. Rostovtzeff, *The
    Social and Economic History of the Hellenistic World* (Oxford, 1941),
    pp. 1, 115. On the relevance of disfranchisement, see W. S. Ferguson,
    Hellenistic Athens (London, 1911), p. 73; for a challenge to this view, see A.
    Blanchard, *Essai sur la composition des pièces de Ménandre* (Paris, 1983),
    pp. 387–8.
61 For the existence of the garrison, see, for example, Plutarch, *Demetrius* 8.
62 MC, p. 378.
63 See my article 'Marriage and Prostitution in Classical New Comedy' in
    Themes in Drama 11: Women and Theatre, ed. J. Redmond (Cambridge,
    1989), pp. 31–48.
64 See Erich Segal, *Roman Laughter* (Cambridge, Mass., 1968), pp. 18–19: cf. J.
    Crook, 'Patria Potestas', *Classical Quarterly* NS 17 (1967), 113–22.
65 MTGTL, first grandfather, ex. 1 – fig. 227, plate XXIIc.
66 *ibid.*, ex. 2 – plate XXII a–b.
67 *ibid.*, plate XXIII.
68 Cf. Aristotle, *Physiognomics* VI.811b 15, 812a 34.
69 Aristotle, *Generation of Animals* V.vii.783b; *Problems* IV.18.878b; Plato,
    Republic V.454c; Hippocrates, *On the Nature of the Child* 20.
70 See, for example, Aeschines, *Against Timarchos* 188.

71 E.g. *Thrasyleon*, adapted by Turpilius; *The Brothers 'B'*, adapted by Terence.

72 Aristotle, *Parts of Animals* III.ix.671b; Pollux II.49 describes raised brows as a sign of arrogance.

73 T. W. MacCary, 'Menander's Old Men', *TAPA* 102 (1971), 303–25. The scene which MacCary quotes from *The Hero* cannot stand as evidence.

74 MINC YM 2 (A2).

75 Pap. Hibeh 4: *Select Papyri III*, ed. D. L. Page (London, 1941), text no. 63.

76 Aristotle, *Generation of Animals* V.vi.785b 18; *Physiognomics* VI.812a 15–17.

77 *Timaeus* 68c.

78 *Acharnians* 242, *Birds* 656, *Wasps* 2, *Frogs* 1.

79 Hippocrates, *Airs, Waters, Places* 20; Aristotle, *Problems* XXXVIII.2.966b.

80 See Yvon Garlan, *Les Esclaves en Grèce ancienne*, pp. 60–1.

81 Aristotle describes *pyrrhotês* (tawniness) as a deficiency of the hair in *Generation of Animals* at V.v.785a 19.

82 MTGTL, principal slave, ex. 2: fig. 329.

83 MTGTL, fig. 338.

84 Athenaeus XIV.659a; Festus s.v. *Moeson*; Athenaeus also cites Polemon on the Sicilian origins of Maison.

85 Athenaeus XIV.659a.

86 A. Giannini, 'La figura del cuoco nella commedia greca' *Acme* 13 (1960), 137ff.

87 Sosipatros, quoted in Athenaeus IX.378a.

88 Athenaeus XIV.661e–f.

89 See Colin Austin (ed.), *Comicorum Graecorum Fragmenta in Papyris Reperta* (Berlin and New York, 1973), text no. 244, note to line 188; K. Gaiser, *Menanders 'Hydria'* (Heidelberg, 1977).

90 MINC YM 2 (A5), conveniently reproduced on the cover of *Menander: Plays and Fragments*, tr. N. Miller (Harmondsworth, 1987). The term 'cicada' (*tettix*) was used of the ringlets into which an athlete's hair was bound: see M. M. Evans, *Chapters on Greek Dress* (London, 1893), p. 64.

91 Athenaeus XIV.659a; cf. Hesychius s.v. *tettix*. There can be no question that *Maison* represented a citizen cook, as Athenaeus states. Citizen cooks performed ceremonial duties only: see Guy Berthiaume, *Les Rôles du mageiros* (Leiden, 1982). Athenaeus confuses the issue by stating that only one dramatist, Poseidippus, portrayed slave cooks. Athenaeus is obviously referring to a situation in which a man owns and keeps a slave cook for his personal use rather than hire a slave cook in the customary manner.

92 Festus s.v. *Moeson*; Philodemos cites '*Maison*' as a type who is not only uneducated but lacks all common sense: Philodemos I.189.17 (ed. Sudhaus).

93 MINC NP 8; for a reproduction, see *Analecta Romana Instituti Danici* 12 (1983), 77.

94 Athenaeus cites Chrysippus the Stoic: XIV.659.

95 Hesychius s.v. *Maison*.

96 M. I. Finley, *Economy and Society in Ancient Greece* (London, 1981), p. 171.

97 Aristotle, *Politics* VII.vi.1.1327b. I have used the Penguin translation by T. A. Sinclair (Harmondsworth, 1962).

98 Aristotle, *Œconomica* I.v.5.1344b.

99 Vitruvius VI.i.3–11.

100 Aristotle, *Problems* XIV.15.910a.

101 M. I. Finley, *Economy and Society*, p. 104.

102 Herodotus IV.93; Strabo VII.iii.7–8; on the bloodthirsty nature of Thracians in general, see Thucydides VII.29.4.

103 Menander frag. 794–5; on the Polygamy of Getes, cf. Herodotus V.v.

104 N. Lascu, 'Intorno ai nomi degli schiavi nel teatro antico', *Dioniso* 43 (1969), 97–106.

105 Aristotle, *Politics* VII.ix.9.1330a; Plato, *Laws* VI.777c; Aristotle *Œconomica* I.iii.1344b 18.

106 See above pp. 95–8.

107 Tertullian, *On the Soul* XX.3.

108 *Birds* 1244–5.

109 Herondas II.100.

110 Hegesippus, *Brothers*, in Athenaeus VII.290b.

111 Polemo, cited in *De physiognomica liber* 14; Firmicus Mathematicus I.i, I.iv.

112 Strabo XIV.v.2.

113 On the greed of Phoenicians, see Plato, *Republic* IV.xi.436; Plato, *Laws* V.747c.

114 Strabo I.ii.34 records that Syrians resembled Arabs and Armenians in their build. He mentions the dark skin of Syrians at XII.iii.9. *De Physionomia Liber* 14 refers to frizzy hair in connexion with the greed of Syrians.

115 In manumission inscriptions, Paramonos is a more common form than Parmenon: see Kurt Treu, 'Zu den Sklavennamen bei Menander', *Eirene* 20 (1983), 39–42; cf. above p. 158.

116 See chapter 3, p. 93 above.

117 For the wrinkle as a signifier of thought, see Pollux II.49.

118 See above, pp. 88–9.

119 MINC ST 89. Webster has published a photograph in *Scottish Art Review* 12, no. 1 (1969), 7, fig. 12.

120 For curly hair as a species of deficiency, see Aristotle, *Problems* XXXIII.18.963b; for curly hair as a signifier of cowardice, see Aristotle, *Physiognomics* VI.812b 30–3. Cf. *History of Animals* VIII.x.5.596b on curly hair as a sign of weakness in sheep, and IX.xliv.7.629b on curly hair as a sign of weakness in lions.

121 *De physionomica liber* 76, and 83.

122 In *The Toady*, Gnatho ('Jaw') seems to be a nickname for Strouthias. On the common use of nicknames for parasites, see W. G. Arnott, 'Alexis and the Parasite's Name', *Greek, Roman & Byzantine Studies* 9 (1968), 161–8.

123 MINC NM 2; MTGTL, p. 189.

124 See p. 204 below.

125 *Nicomachean Ethics* VIII.iii.1156a.

126 For Aristotelian definitions of the *kolax* or toady, see *Eudemian Ethics* VII.4.7.1239a; *Nicomachean Ethics* IV.vi.9.1127a and VIII.viii.1.1159a.

127 *Nicomachean Ethics* X.iii.11.1173b.

128 Athenaeus VI.254d.

129 Demetrios restricted the number of guests to twenty: Athenaeus VI.245. For the scope of his legislation, see W. S. Ferguson, *Hellenistic Athens*, chapter 2.

130 Athenaeus VI.253a, 261b.

131 *Moralia* 54b; see below, p.oo.

132 Athenaeus VI.236e.

133 I entirely accept the arguments of W. G. Arnott in 'Alexis and the Parasite's Name'.

134 Pollux VI.35; cf. scholiast on *Iliad* XVII.577. Arnott, *ibid.*, assumes that Epicharmus created the character but not actually the name of the 'parasite'.

135 Aristotle, *Nicomachean Ethics* VIII.viii.1.1159a.

136 *Nicomachean Ethics* III.vii.12.1116a.

137 *Nicomachean Ethics* III.vii.13.1116a.

138 *Eudemian Ethics* III.ii.5.1230b.

139 For this reading, see MTGTL, p. 157. On the fleshy features of the boor, see Aristotle, *Physiognomics* III.807b.

140 See p.92 above.

141 *Nicomachean Ethics* VII.i.4.1145a.

142 *Nicomachean Ethics* VII.viii.3–5.1151a.

143 F. Baratte, *Le Trésor d'orfèvrerie romane à Boscoreale* (Paris, 1986), pp. 65–6. The drawing, unfortunately, is of poor quality, and makes the masks appear grotesque, which they are not. The second cup is catalogued in MINC as NJ 2.

144 Clement of Alexandria, *Stromata* VI.ii.14.4, mentions a Moschion the Comedian, but this is generally taken as an error for Moschion the tragedian, a minor third-century writer of unknown origin. The mask on the cup is a comic mask, so this tragedian cannot be intended.

145 *The Rape of the Locks, The Hero, The Farmer, Old Cantankerous.*

146 DFA, p.228. This interpretation was first offered in A. K. H. Simon, *Comicae Tabellae* (Emsdetten, 1938), p. 101.

147 Herodotus IV.180.

148 cf. M. M. Evans, *Chapters on Greek Dress*, p.65.

149 In Terence, Pythias refers to Thais as *era* (mistress) at lines 654 and 883, but she behaves more like Thais' daughter. This may point to a difference in Greek and Roman social conditions. Pythias is a courtesan in Lucian's *Dialogues of the Courtesans*.

150 See Terence, *The Girl from Andros*; Lucian, *Dialogues of the Courtesans*.

151 MINC YM 2(5), conveniently reproduced in the cover of *Menander: Plays and Fragments*, tr. N. Miller (Harmondsworth, 1987).

152 Aristotle, *Constitution of Athens* 50.2.

153 MINC YM 2 (B3).

154 MTGTL, pseudo-virgin, exx. 1 and 2. Ex. 2 has the more perfect features.

155 MTGTL, 'talker with grey strands', exx. 10, 11, 12, 18. Ex. 10 has a particularly marked sneer.

156 MTGTL, 'mitred courtesan', ex. 1.

157 Probably to be identified as MINC ST 92.

158 MTGTL, 'curly' ex. 2 = MINC ST 99.

159 MTGTL, 'golden courtesan', ex. 1 = MINC ST 97.

160 MINC ST 100 = MTGTL, virgin, ex. 4.

161 MTGTL, mature courtesan, ex. 12, plate xxxix.

162 MINC NP 6, NP 46.

163 See C. Daremberg and E. Saglio (eds.), *Dictionnaire des antiquités* (Paris, 1875–1912) s.v. *coma*, citing Winckelmann. See esp. fig. 1,822.

164 MINC ST 43.

165 MINC ST 42, ST 53.

166 See above, p. 72.

167 *Nicomachean Ethics* IV.vi.1126b. The Greek terms are *dyskolos* and *areskos*.

168 Athenaeus XIV. 661 e–f.

169 At line 945, Getas states that 'the man is soft' (*malakos hânêr*). Sandbach in MC, p. 282, assumes that this means that Knemon is softening. Arnott, in his Loeb translation, takes the comment as an aside, referring to the cook's effeminate gestures. My analysis of the masks supports Arnott's rendering. The un-soft Getas remains silent during the cook's evocation of the orgy, then takes the lead in manhandling Knemon into the feast.

170 See Sikon's use of *beltiste*, his mode of address for a slave: lines 497, 503, 911, 921.

171 See above, p. 70.

7 COSTUME AND MOVEMENT

1 Pollux IV.118–20.

2 Donatus, *On Comedy* VIII.6–7.

3 Thucydides I.vi.2.

4 Aristotle, *On Colours* V.797a 5ff.

5 See Meyer Reinhold, *History of Purple as a Status Symbol in Antiquity* (Brussels, 1970), p. 6, p. 11 n. 2; cf. Xenophon, *Cyropaedia* VIII.iii.3.

6 cf. Pollux VII.48; Léon Heuzey, *Histoire du costume antique* (Paris, 1922), p. 110.

7 See C. Daremberg and E. Saglio, *Dictionnaire des antiquités* (Paris, 1875–1912) s.v. *purpura*; see also Léon Heuzey, *Histoire du costume antique* (Paris, 1922), p. 109.

8 Pollux VII.47.

9 Hesychios s.v. *exômis*.

10 Scholiast on Aristophanes, *Knights* 878.

11 Aristophanes, *Wasps* 444; HGRT, pp. 481, 504, 509, 511, 414, 515, 526, 528, 533, 535.

12 Theophrastos, *On Pleasure*, cited in Athenaeus XII.526d.

13 Lucian, *On the Hall* 7.
14 MINC YM 2 (B3); IT 80 = HGRT, fig. 793; both are reproduced and their relationship discussed in S. Charitonides, L. Kahil and R. Ginouvès, *Les Mosaïques de Ménandre à Mytilène* (Bern, 1970).
15 See Yvon Garlan, *Les Esclaves en Grèce ancienne* (Paris, 1982). Garlan shows why the figures which Athenaeus cites from the census of Demetrios of Phaleron should be accepted.
16 Pseudo-Xenophon, *Constitution of Athens* I.10–12.
17 Suidas, cited in C. Daremberg and E. Saglio, *Dictionnaire des antiquités*, s.v. *meretrix*; Phylarchus cited in Athenaeus XII.521b; Diodoros XII.2.
18 For a description of the garment, see the scholiast on *Women at the Thesmophoria* 261, and on *Frogs* 46; cf. *Assembly-Women* 332, 879; *Lysistrata* 44, 220; Plutarch, *Moralia* 785e; Athenaeus 155c, 440c.
19 Suidas 2657 s.v. Antigenides; Democritus of Ephesus, cited in Athenaeus XII.525c.
20 RAGA, p. 142, citing the anonymous *Life of Sophocles*. Casual allusions in Menander confirm that he wrote with the convention of the stick in mind: *The Arbitration* 248, *The Shield* 378.
21 Aristotle, *Physiognomics* VI.810b–811a.
22 Quintilian XII.iii.83; cf. Pollux II.135: Pollux cites a statement attributed to Aristotle that the short-necked man who draws up his shoulders is crafty.
23 *De Physionomia Liber* 76; see above, p. 174. The quotation from Plutarch is listed by Kock as Diphilus fragment 133.
24 *Stichus* 226–31.
25 Commentary on *Eunuch* II.ii.1, II.ii.43.
26 Quintilian XI.iii.179–80.
27 Plutarch, *Alcibiades* 1; Plato, *Alcibiades* I.122; Demosthenes, *On the False Legation* 314.
28 Quintilian XI.iii.144–9; cf. Lycurgus, *Against Leocrates* 41; Aeschines, *Against Timarchus* 26.
29 *The Casket Comedy* 115.
30 Aristotle, *Nicomachean Ethics* IV.viii.3–6.1128a.
31 Longinus, *Art of Rhetoric*: Spengel, *Rhetores Graeci* (Leipzig, 1894), I.196.
32 Philodemos, *Rhetorica* I.194 (ed. Sudhaus).
33 Cicero, *On the Orator* III.lix.220–1.
34 Quintilian XI.iii.181–2.
35 Cicero, *On the Orator* III.lvi.214.
36 Quintilian XI.iii.125.
37 Quintilian XI.iii.109–19.
38 *Classicistic Acting*, ed. A. S. Golding (Lanham and London, 1984), pp. 291ff.
39 Theophrastos, cited in Cicero, *On the Orator* III.lix.221.
40 MINC NP 45 = HGRT, p. 328.
41 P. L. Duchartre, *The Italian Comedy*, tr. R.T. Weaver, revised edition (New York, 1966).
42 MINC NM 1. See my earlier discussions on pp. 48–9, 107–8.

43 MINC YM 2 (A6); MINC p. 299; Lilly Kahil, 'Remarques sur l'iconographie des pièces de Ménandre', in *Ménandre* (Fondation Hardt, Geneva, 1970), pp. 231–51; Erika Simon, *The Ancient Theatre*, tr. C. E. Vafopoulou-Richardson (London, 1982), pp. 32–3.

44 MINC NP 25.

45 RAGA, pp. 116–18.

46 MINC NM 2.

47 MINC NS 25 = HGRT, p. 225; cf. my discussion in chapter 2, pp. 42–3.

48 MINC NP 6 = HGRT, p. 395; MINC NP 46; cf. my discussion in chapter 5, p. 133.

49 MINC NP 8. Webster interprets the central figure as a parasite. The first photograph was published in *Notizie degli scavi di antichità: Accademia Nazionale dei Lincei* 7 (1929), plate 22. The fresco is no. 3 in A. K. H. Simon, *Comicae Tabellae* (Emsdetten, 1938). Simon interprets the figure as a youth in a long chiton, addressing the audience.

50 HGRT, fig. 371. For variations offered by three different copyists, see Carl Robert, *Die Masken der neueren attischen Komödie* (Halle, 1911), figs. 7–9, 48–50.

51 *Délos*, 27 (Ecole française d'Athènes, Paris, 1970), pl. 24.3. Although the frescoes are dated to the late second century BC, U. Bezerra de Meneses, the excavator of the frescoes, notes that a fresco illustrating tragedy depicts no *onkos*, so this example at least must relate to fourth-century practice.

8 LANGUAGE AND VOICE

1 Etienne Decroux, *Words on Mime*, tr. M. Piper (Claremont, 1985), pp. 33–6.

2 Aristotle, *Rhetoric* III.i.4.1403b; *Nicomachean Ethics* X.v.4.1175b.

3 Aristotle, *Rhetoric* III.xii.2.1413b.

4 Aristotle, *Rhetoric* III.xii.5.1414a.

5 Demetrius, *On Style* IV.194.

6 From *Writing Degree Zero*, in Roland Barthes, *Selected Writings* (London, 1983), pp. 54–8.

7 The Oxford text reads:

Λυ.   αὐτῶι, Σώστρατε,
χρῆσαι πικρῶς, ἔλαυν' ἐκεῖνον τὸν ἀκρα[τῆ.
⟨ἅ⟩παντας αἰσχύνει γὰρ ἡμᾶς τοὺς φίλουσ.
(ΣΩΣΤΡΑΤΟΣ)
ἤδη 'στιν οὗτος φροῦδος. ενπλη[
τούτου καθέξει. Σώστρατον προήρπασας.
ἀρνήσεται μέν, οὐκ ἄδηλόν ἐστί μοι—
ἰταμὴ γάρ—εἰς μέσον τε πάντες οἱ θεοὶ
ἥξουσι. μὴ τοίνυν [.]ον[
κακὴ κακῶς τοίνυν—ἐ[π]άγ[αγε, Σ]ώστρατε·
ἴσως σε πείσει· δοῦλο[

ἐγὼ μάλισθ', ἡ δ' ὡ[σ κενὸν συ]μπεισάτω
ἔχοντα μηδ[έν·   τ]ῶι πατρὶ
τὸ χ]ρυσίον· πιθαν[ευομέν]η γὰρ παύσεται
ὅταν] ποτ' αἴσθητα[ι, τὸ τῆς πα]ροιμίας,
νεκρῶι] λέγουσα [μῦθον. ἀλλ'] ἤδη [με] δεῖ
ἐλθεῖν ἐπ' ἐ]κεῖνον.

8 Menander, *Plays and Fragments* tr. Norma Miller (Harmondsworth, 1987), p. 176; *Menander*, vol. I, ed. and tr. W. G. Arnott (Cambridge, Mass. and London, 1979), pp. 153–5.

9 Florence Dupont, *L'Acteur-roi* (Paris, 1985), p.252; cf. above, p. 63.

10 See above, chapter 1, p. 22.

11 The point about changes of person is noted by Sandbach, in MC, p. 121.

12 The two passages are compared by Aulus Gellius in *Attic Nights* II.23. I have followed the text in the Budé edition, ed. R. Marache (Paris, 1967). I have made some use of the commentary in John Wright, *Dancing in Chains: the Stylistic Unity of the comœdia palliata* (Rome, 1974), pp. 120–6.

13 MINC ΥΜ 2 (Α2).

14 'Epitome of a comparison between Aristophanes and Menander': Plutarch, *Moralia* 853.

15 See MC, p. 36, and above, p. 50.

16 See the laws of Euboea cited in RAGA, pp. 181, 185.

17 Aristotle, *Rhetoric* III.viii.4.1408b.

18 Aristotle, *Politics* VIII.vi.5.1341a.

19 F. H. Sandbach, 'Menander's Manipulation of Language for Dramatic Purposes', in *Ménandre*, Foundation Hardt, vol. XVI, ed. E. G. Turner (Geneva, 1970), p. 114.

20 Cicero, *Orator* VIII.26–7.

21 Aristotle, *Rhetoric* III.ii.4–5.1404b.

22 Quintilian XI.iii.91.

23 Philodemos, *Rhetorica* I.199 (ed. Sudhaus).

24 Lucian, *Nigrinus* XI.

25 Aristotle, *Rhetoric* III.i.4.1403b.

26 *Rhetoric* III.i.8.1404a.

27 Theophrastos fragments XC, LXXXIX.14 (ed. Wimmer). Theophrastos no doubt builds upon the discussion in Aristotle, *Politics* VIII.vii.1341b.

28 Fragment XCI (ed. Wimmer).

29 Aristotle, *On the Soul* II.viii.420b.

30 See above, pp. 21, 23.

31 Aristotle, *On Respiration* VIII.474a–b, XVII–XVIII.479a–b.

32 Aristotle, *Generation of Animals* III.xi.762a.

33 Aristotle, *Problems* XI.62.906a.

34 *Problems* XI.34.903a, 62.906a.

35 Aristotle, *On Things Heard* 801b.802a.

36 *Problems* XI.31, 36, 32, 53.902b–903b, 905a.

37 *Problems* XI.38.903b.

38 *Problems* XI.60.905b.
39 *Problems* XI.22.901b, 11, 12.900a, 39.903b.
40 Juba, cited in Athenaeus VIII.343f; Constantin Stanislavski, *Building a Character*, tr. E. R. Hapgood (London, 1950), p. 107.
41 *Problems* XI.23, 25.901b; Vitruvius V.iv–v.
42 *Building a Character*, p. 115.
43 *ibid.*, p. 113.
44 Anton Chekhov, *Plays*, tr. E. Fen (Harmondsworth, 1959), p. 395.
45 *The Man She Hated* A 90.
46 See above, p. 22.
47 *Building a Character*, p. 30; see p. 114 above.
48 Cited in MC, p. 21, from Syrianus' commentary on Hermogenes.
49 Aristotle, *Eudemian Ethics* II.ii.1.1220b; cf. *Rhetoric* I.x.9.1369a, *On The Soul* III.x.433a.
50 See p. 18, above.
51 Peter Brook, *The Shifting Point* (New York, 1987), p. 217.
52 *ibid.*, pp. 220–1.
53 *ibid.*, p. 225.

Select bibliography of secondary sources

Aloni, Antonio, 'Il ruolo dello schiavo come personaggio nella commedia di Menandro', *Centro ricerche e documentazione sull' antichità classica* 8 (1976/7), 25–41

Anderson, M. J., 'Knemon's Hamartia', *Greece and Rome* 17 (1970), 119–217

Arnott, P. D. *Greek Scenic Conventions*, Oxford, 1962

  An Introduction to the Roman World, London, 1970: chapter 3, 'The Rome of Plautus'

Arnott, W. G., 'Alexis and the Parasite's Name', *Greek, Roman & Byzantine Studies* 9 (1968), 161–8

  Menander, Plautus, Terence, Oxford, 1975

  Menander, vol. I, Cambridge, Mass. and London, 1979

  'Time, Plot and Character in Menander', *Papers of the Liverpool Latin Seminar. Vol. 2*, ed. F. Cairns, Liverpool, 1979, pp. 343–60

  'Moral Values in Menander', *Philologus* 125 (1981), 215–27.

Bain, David, *Actors and Audience: A Study of Asides and Related Conventions in Greek Drama*, Oxford, 1977

  '"Plautus vortit barbare"', in *Creative Imitation and Latin Literature*, ed. D. West and T. Woodman, Cambridge, 1979, pp. 17–34

Barbet, Alix, *La Peinture murale romaine*, Paris, 1985

Barchiesi, Marino, 'Plauto e il metateatro antico', *Il Verri* 31 (1970), 113–30

Barigazzi, A., *La formazione spirituale di Menandro*, Turin, 1965

Barthes, Roland, *Essais critiques*, Paris, 1964

  Selected Writings, ed. S. Sontag, London, 1983

Beare, W., *The Roman Stage*, revised edition, London, 1968

Bernabò-Brea, L., *Menandro e il teatro greco nelle terracotte liparesi*, Genoa, 1981

Berthiaume, Guy, *Les Rôles du mageiros*, Leiden, 1982

Bettini, Maurizio, 'Verso un antropologia dell' intreccio. Le strutture semplici della trama nelle commedie di Plauto', *Materiali e discussioni per l'analisi dei testi classici* 7 (1982), 39–101

Beyen, H. G., *Die Pompejanische Wanddekorationen*, The Hague, 1938

Bieber, Margaret, 'Maske', in Pauly-Wissowa, *Real-Encyclopädie*, vol. XIV (1930), 2070–105

  The History of the Greek and Roman Theater, revised edition, Princeton, 1961

  Ancient Copies: Contributions to the History of Greek and Roman Art, New York, 1977

Blanchard, A., *Essai sur la composition des pièces de Ménandre*, Paris, 1983

Blundell, John, *Menander and the Monologue*, Göttingen, 1980

Bomati, Yves, 'Phersu et la monde dionysiaque', *Latomus* 45 (1986), 21–32

Brook, Peter, *The Shifting Point*, New York, 1987

Brown, P. G. McC., 'Review: *Menandro e il teatro greco nelle terracotte liparesi*', *Liverpool Classical Monthly* 9.7 (1984), 108–12

'Masks, Names and Characters in New Comedy', *Hermes* 115 (1987), pt 2, 181–201

Cambridge Ancient History: Vol. VII. Part 1. The Hellenistic World, ed. F. W. Walbank, A. E. Astin, M. W. Frederiksen and R. M. Ogilvie, Cambridge, 1984

The Cambridge History of Classical Literature, Vol. 2: Latin Literature, ed. E. J. Kenney, Cambridge, 1982

Vol. 1: Greek Literature, ed. P. E. Easterling and A. M. W. Knox, Cambridge, 1985

Canac, François, *L'Acoustique des théâtres antiques: ses enseignements*, Paris, 1967

Capone, G., *L'arte scenica degli attori tragici greci*, Padua, 1935

Caputi, Anthony, *Buffo: the Genius of Vulgar Comedy*, Detroit, 1978: chapter 6, 'The Plautine Play'

Charitonidis, S., L. Kahil and R. Ginouvès, *Les Mosaïques de la maison du Ménandre à Mytilène*, Bern, 1970

Chiarini, G. and R. Tessari, *Teatro del corpo, teatro della parola: due saggi sul 'comico'*, Pisa, 1983

Crook, J. A., 'Patria Potestas', *Classical Quarterly* NS 17 (1967), 113–22

Daremberg, C. and E. Saglio (eds.), *Dictionnaire des antiquités*, Paris, 1875–1912

Davies, J. K., 'Athenian Citizenship: the Descent Group and the Alternatives', *Classical Journal* 73 (1977/8), 105–21

Decroux, Etienne, *Words on Mime*, tr. M. Piper, Claremont, 1985

Della Corte, F., 'Maschere e personaggi in Plauto', *Dioniso* 46 (1975), 163–93

'La tipologia del personaggio della Palliata', *Actes du IXe congrès à Rome, 1973*, ed. Assoc. Guillaume Budé, Paris, 1975, 354–93.

Délos, vol. 27, *L'îlot de la Maison des Comédiens*, ed. P. Bruneau and others, Ecole française d'Athènes, Paris, 1970

vol. 29, *Les Mosaïques*, ed. P. Bruneau, Ecole française d'Athènes, Paris, 1972

De Ste Croix, G., *The Class Struggle in the Ancient Greek World*, London, 1983

Détienne, M., *The Gardens of Adonis*, tr. J. Lloyd, Brighton, 1977

Dihle, A., *The Theory of the Will in Classical Antiquity*, Berkeley, 1982

Duckworth, G. E., *The Nature of Roman Comedy*, Princeton, 1952

Dumont, J.-C., *Servus: Rome et l'esclavage sous la république*, Rome, 1987

Dupont, Florence, *L'Acteur-roi*, Paris, 1985

Duvignaud, Jean, *L'Acteur – esquisse d'une sociologie du comédien*, Paris, 1965

Eco, Umberto, 'How Culture Conditions the Colours We See', in *On Signs*, ed. M. Blonsky, Oxford, 1985, pp. 157–75

Evans, E. C., 'Physiognomics in the Ancient World', *Transactions of the American Philosophical Association* NS 59, pt 5 (1969)

Evans, M. M., *Chapters on Greek Dress*, London, 1893

Ferguson, W. S., *Hellenistic Athens*, London, 1911

Finley, M. I. (ed.), *Slavery in Classical Antiquity*, Cambridge, 1960

Flacelière, R., *Love in Ancient Greece*, tr. J. Cleugh, London, 1962

Fortenbaugh, W. W., 'Theophrastus on Fate and Character', in *Arktouros: Hellenic Studies Presented to B. M. W. Knox*, ed. G. W. Bowerstock, W. Burkert and M. J. C. Putnam, Berlin and New York, 1979, pp. 372–5

'Aristotle's *Rhetoric* on Emotions', in *Articles on Aristotle. Vol. 4. Psychology and Ethics*, ed. J. Barnes, M. Schofield and R. Sorabji, London, 1979, pp. 133–53

'Theophrast über den komischen Charakter', *Rheinisches Museum* 174 (1981), 245–60

Foucault, Michel, *The Uses of Pleasure*, tr. R. Hurley, Harmondsworth, 1986

Fraenkel, Eduard, *Elementi Plautini in Plauto*, tr. F. Munari, Florence, 1960

Frézouls, E., 'La Construction du *theatrum lapideum* et son contexte politique', in *Théâtre et spectacles dans l'antiquité: Actes du colloque de Strasbourg, 5–7 Nov. 1981*, Strasbourg, 1983, pp. 193–214.

Gaiser, K., *Menanders 'Hydria'*, Heidelberg, 1977

Garlan, Yvon, *Les Esclaves en Grèce ancienne*, Paris, 1982

Gentili, Bruno, *Theatrical Performances in the Ancient World*, Amsterdam, 1979

Ghiron-Bistagne, Paulette, 'Les Demi-masques', *Revue archéologique* (1970) 232–82

Recherches sur les acteurs dans la Grèce antique, Paris, 1976

Giannini, A., 'La figura del cuoco nella commedia greca', *Acme* 13 (1960), 135–216

Giglioni, Gabriella Bodei, *Menandro o la politica della convivenza*, Como, 1984

Gill, Christopher J., 'The Question of Character and Personality in Greek Tragedy', *Poetics Today* 7 (1986), 251–73

Goldberg, Sander, *The Making of Menander's Comedy*, London, 1980

Understanding Terence, Princeton, 1986

Goldhill, Simon, 'The Great Dionysia and Civic Ideology', *Journal of Hellenic Studies* 107 (1987), 58–76

Gomme, A. W. and F. H. Sandbach, *Menander – a Commentary*, Oxford, 1973

Gratwick, A. S. 'TITVS MACCIVS PLAVTVS', *Classical Quarterly* 23 (1973), 78–84

Green, J. R., 'Additions to *Monuments Illustrating Old and Middle Comedy*', *Bulletin of the Institute of Classical Studies* 27 (1980), 123–31

Grimal, Pierre, 'Le "Truculentus" de Plaute et l'esthétique de la palliata' *Dioniso* 45 (1971–4), 532–43

'Le Théâtre à Rome', in *Actes du IXe congrès à Rome, 1973*, ed. Assoc. Guillaume Budé, Paris, 1975, 249–305

'Existe-t-il une morale de Plaute?', *Bulletin de l'Association G. Budé* 34 (1975), 485–98

'Jeu et vérité dans les comédies de Plaute', *Dioniso* 46 (1975), 137–52

Gruen, Eric S., *The Hellenistic World and the Coming of Rome*, Berkeley, 1984
Handley, Eric, (ed.), *The Dyskolos of Menander*, London, 1965
  Menander and Plautus: a Study in Comparison, London, 1968
Heuzey, Léon, *Histoire du costume antique*, Paris, 1922
Hopkins, Keith, *Conquerors and Slaves*, Cambridge, 1978
Humphreys, S. C., 'Public and Private Interests in Classical Athens', *Classical Journal* 73 (1977/8), 97–104
  The Family, Women and Death, London, 1983
Hunter, R. L., *The New Comedy of Greece and Rome*, Cambridge, 1985
Inoura, Yoshinobu, and Toshio Kawatake, *The Traditional Theatre of Japan*, Tokyo, 1981
Jelgerhuis, Johannes, *Theoretische lessen over de gesticulatie en mimiek*, Amsterdam, 1827, tr. A. S. Golding in *Classicistic Acting: Two Centuries of a Performance Tradition at the Amsterdam Schouwburg*, Lanham, 1984
Johnstone, Keith, *Impro*, London, 1981
Jones, John, *On Aristotle and Greek Tragedy*, London, 1962
Jones, W. and C. R. Morey, *The Miniatures of the Manuscripts of Terence Prior to the Thirteenth Century*, Princeton, 1931
Katsouris, A. G., *Linguistic and Stylistic Characterization: Tragedy and Menander*, Ioannina, 1975
Komparu, Kunio, *The Noh Theatre: Principles and Perspectives*, tr. J. Corddry, New York and Tokyo, 1983
Konstan, David, *Roman Comedy*, Ithaca, 1985
Kowzan, T., *Littérature et spectacle*, The Hague and Paris, 1975
Lascu, N., 'Intorno ai nomi degli schiavi nel teatro antico', *Dioniso* 43 (1969), 97–106
LeBrun, Charles, *A Method to Learn to Design the Passions*, tr. J. Williams, London, 1734
Lecoq, Jacques (ed.), *Le Théâtre du geste*, Paris, 1987
Lévi-Strauss, Claude, *The Way of the Masks*, tr. S. Modelski, Washington, 1982
Lloyd, G. E. R., 'Hot and Cold, Wet and Dry in Greek Philosophy', *Journal of the Hellenic Society* 84 (1964), 92–106
  Polarity and Analogy, Cambridge, 1966
Long, Timothy, *Barbarians in Greek Comedy*, Carbondale and Edwardsville, 1986
Lowe, N. J., 'Tragic Space and Comic Timing in Menander's *Dyskolos*', *Bulletin of the Institute of Classical Studies* 34 (1987), 126–38
MacCary, W. T., 'Menander's Slaves: their Names, Roles and Masks', *TAPA* 100 (1969), 277–94
  'Menander's Characters: their Names, Roles and Masks', *TAPA* 101 (1970), 277–90
  'Menander's Old Men', *TAPA* 102 (1971), 303–25
  'Menander's Soldiers: their Names, Roles and Masks', *American Journal of Philology* 93 (1972), 279–98

MacCary, W. T. and M. M. Willcock (eds.), *Plautus: Casina*, Cambridge, 1976
Magistrini, Silvia, 'Le descrizioni fisiche dei personaggi in Menandro, Plauto e
    Terenzio' *Dioniso* 44 (1970), 79–114
Maiuri, B. T., *Museo nazionale: Napoli*, Novara, 1971
Méautis, Georges, *Le Crépuscule d'Athènes et Ménandre*, Paris, 1954
Melchinger, Siegfried, *Das Theater der Tragödie*, Munich, 1974
Ménandre, ed. E. G. Turner, Fondation Hardt, Geneva, 1970
Meyerhold on Theatre, tr. and ed. E. Braun, London, 1969
Miller, Norma (ed.), *Menander: Plays and Fragments*, Harmondsworth, 1987
Mitens, Karina, *Teatri greci ispirati all'architettura greca in Sicilia e nell'Italia
    meridionale c. 350–50 a.C.*, Rome, 1988
Modona, A. N. *Gli edifici teatrali greci e romani*, Florence, 1961
Mossé, Claude, *Athens in Decline*, tr. J. Stewart, London, 1973
Nicoll, J. R. A., *The World of Harlequin*, Cambridge, 1963
Neiiendam, Klaus, 'Theatrical Murals at the House of Publius Casca Longus',
    Analecta Romana Instituti Danici 12 (1983), 72–9
*Nô/Kyogen Masks and Performance: Essays and Interviews Compiled by Rebecca
    Teele*, ed. Mime Journal, Claremont, 1984
Onians, John, *Art and Thought in the Hellenistic Age*, London, 1979
Otto, Walter F., *Dionysus: Myth and Cult*, tr. R. B. Palmer, Bloomington, 1965:
    chapter 6, 'The Symbol of the Mask'
Paratore, E. (ed.), *Plautus: tutte le commedie*, Rome, 1976
Pavis, Patrice, *Languages of the Stage: Essays in the Semiology of Theatre*, New
    York, 1982
Petrone, Gianna, *Morale e antimorale nelle commedie di Plauto*, Palermo, 1977
    Teatro antico e inganno: finzioni Plautine, Palermo, 1983
Pickard-Cambridge, A. W., *The Theatre of Dionysus in Athens*, Oxford, 1946
    Dramatic Festivals of Athens, revised by J. Gould and D. M. Lewis, Oxford,
    1968
Pollitt, J. J., *Art and Experience in Classical Greece*, Cambridge, 1972
Préaux, Claire, 'Ménandre et la société athénienne', *Chronique d'Egypte* 32
    (1957), 84–100
Prosperi, Mario, 'The Masks of Lipari', *The Drama Review* 26 (1982), 25–36
Questa, Cesare, *Il ratto dal serraglio: Euripide, Plauto, Mozart, Rossini*, Bologna,
    1979
    'Maschere e funzioni nelle commedie di Plauto', *Materiali e discussioni per
    l'analisi dei testi classici* 8 (1982), 9–64
Rawson, Elizabeth, 'Discrimina Ordinum: the lex Julia theatralis', *Papers of the
    British School at Rome* 55 (1987), 83–114
Reinhold, Meyer, *History of Purple as a Status Symbol in Antiquity*, Brussels,
    1970
Roach, Joseph R., *The Player's Passion*, Cranford, N.J., 1985
Robert, Carl, *Die Masken der neueren attischen Komödie*, Halle, 1911
Rostovtzeff, M. I., *The Social and Economic History of the Hellenistic World*,
    Oxford, 1941

Rousselle, Aline, *Porneia*, Paris, 1983

Russell, D. A. and M. Winterbottom (eds.), *Ancient Literary Criticism*, Oxford, 1972

Sandbach, F. H., 'Menander and the Three-Actor Rule' in *Le Monde grec: hommages à Claire Préaux*, ed. J. Bingen, Brussels, 1975, pp. 197–204
   The Comic Theatre of Greece and Rome, London, 1977

Sartori, Donato and Bruno Lanata (eds.) *Arte della maschera nella Commedia dell'arte*, Florence, 1983

Savarese, Nicola (ed.), *Anatomia del teatro*, Florence, 1983

Scala, Flamino, *Il teatro delle favole rappresentative*, Venice, 1611, tr. H. Salerno as *Scenarios of the Commedia dell'Arte*, New York and London, 1967

Segal, Charles, *Dionysiac Poetics and Euripides' Bacchae*, Princeton, 1982

Segal, Erich, *Roman Laughter: the Comedy of Plautus*, 2nd edn, New York, 1987

Serbat, M. G., 'Théâtre et société au second siècle avant J.-C.', *Actes du IXe congrès à Rome, 1973*, ed. Assoc. Guillaume Budé (Paris, 1975), 394–403

Sifakis, G. M., *Studies in the History of Hellenistic Drama*, London, 1967
   'Boy Actors in New Comedy', *Arktouros: Hellenic Studies Presented to B. M. W. Knox*, ed. G. W. Bowerstock, W. Burkert and M. J. C. Putnam, Berlin and New York, 1979, pp. 199–208

Simon, A. K. H., *Comicae Tabellae*, Emsdetten, 1938

Simon, Erika, *The Ancient Theatre*, tr. C. E. Vafopoulou-Richardson, London, 1982

Slater, Niall W., *Plautus in Performance: the Theatre of the Mind*, Princeton, 1985

Sonkowsky, Robert P., 'Delivery in Rhetorical Theory', *TAPA* 110 (1959), 256–74

Spada, S., *Domenico Biancolelli – ou l'art d'improviser*, Naples, 1969

Stanislavski, Constantin, *Building a Character*, tr. E. R. Hapgood, London, 1979

Tandoi, Vincenzo, 'Noctuini oculi', *Studi italiani di filologia classica* 33 (1961), 219–41

Taplin, Oliver, *Greek Tragedy in Action*, London, 1978
   'Menander the Dramatist', unpublished lecture

Taviani, Ferdinando and Mirella Schino, *Il segreto della commedia dell'arte*, Florence, 1982

Taylor, George, '"The Just Delineation of the Passions": Theories of Acting in the Age of Garrick', in *The Eighteenth-Century English Stage*, ed. K. Richards and P. Thompson, London, 1974, pp. 51–72
   Players and Performances in the Victorian Theatre, Manchester, 1990

Treu, Kurt, 'Zu den Sklavennamen bei Menander', *Eirene* 20 (1983), 39–42

Turner, E. G., 'Menander and the New Society of his Time', *Chronique d'Egypte* 54 (1979), 106–26

Ubersfeld, Anne, *L'Ecole du spectateur*, Paris, 1981

Vatin, Claude, *Recherches sur le mariage et la femme mariée à l'époque hellénistique*, Paris, 1970

Vernant, J.-P. and P. Vidal-Naquet, *Tragedy and Myth in Ancient Greece*, tr. J. Lloyd, Brighton, 1981

Walcot, Peter, *Greek Drama in its Theatrical and Social Context*, Cardiff, 1976

Walton, J. Michael, *The Greek Sense of Theatre: Tragedy Reviewed*, London, 1984

Webster, T. B. L., *Monuments Illustrating New Comedy*, revised edition, BICS Supplement no. 24, London, 1969; a revised and expanded edition by A. Seeberg and J. R. Green is forthcoming as BICS Supplement no. 50

Studies in Later Greek Comedy, revised edition, London, 1970

Greek Theatre Production, revised edition, London, 1970

An Introduction to Menander, Manchester, 1974

Monuments Illustrating Old and Middle Comedy, 3rd edn, revised by J. R. Green, BICS Supplement no. 39, London, 1978

Wiles, David, 'The Servant as Master: a Study of Role Definition in Classical and Renaissance Popular Comedy', unpublished Ph.D. thesis, Bristol University, 1979

'Menander's *Dyskolos* and Demetrios of Phaleron's Dilemma', *Greece and Rome* 31 (1984), 170–80

'Reading Greek Performance', *Greece and Rome* 34 (1987), 136–51

'Greek Theatre and the Legitimation of Slavery', in *Slavery and Other Forms of Unfree Labour*, ed. Léonie Archer, London, 1988, pp. 53–67

'Taking Farce Seriously: Recent Critical Approaches to Plautus', in *Themes in Drama. 10: Farce*, ed. J. Redmond, Cambridge, 1988, pp. 261–71

'Marriage and Prostitution in Classical New Comedy', in *Themes in Drama. 11: Women in Theatre*, ed. J. Redmond, Cambridge, 1989, pp. 31–48

Williams, Gordon, *Tradition and Originality in Roman Poetry*, Oxford, 1968

Winter, F. E., 'The Stage of New Comedy', *Phoenix* 37 (1983), 38–47

Wright, John, *Dancing in Chains: the Stylistic Unity of the comoedia palliata*, Rome, 1974

Zeami, *On the Art of the Nô Drama*, tr. J. Thomas Rimer and Yamazaki Masakazu, Princeton, 1984

Zeitlin, Froma, 'The Closet of Masks – Role-Playing and Myth-Making in *The Orestes* of Euripides', *Ramus* 9 (1980), 62–73

Zorzi, Ludovico, *Arte della maschera nella commedia dell'arte*, ed. D. Sartori and B. Lanata, Florence, 1983

Zucchelli, Bruno, Ὑποκριτής – origine e storia del termine, Genoa, 1962

Index

Character and mask names are here italicized

actants   27–9, 32, 135, 138
act-breaks   7, 56
acting (Lat. *actio*)   see *hypokrisis*; mask, techniques of masked acting
action (*praxis*)   27–8, 143
actor (*hypokritês*)
   boy actors 48, 50, 65, 202, 205, 207; casting 71, 194; dominance of 9–10, 103; double awareness of 12; geographical mobility of 29, 103, 133; guilds of 38, 104, 148; mutes 50, 203; principal actor (*protagonistês*) 43, 148, 203; relationship to role 32, 109–11, 120, 122, 126–7, 141–2, 195, 218–19; three-actor rule 4, 26, *see also* doubling; training of 220–2
acoustics   38–9, 40, 52, 55, 222
adulescens (youth in Roman comedy)   134, 135, 139, 146, 162
aedile (magistrate in charge of *ludi*)   8, 60–2, 145
Aesopus   110, 111
African cook   168
agora (market-place)   42–3
Alexis   174
alleyways   *see* entries
altar   36, 46–7, 51, 66, 96
anagnôrisis (recognition)   3, 28–9, 46
anger   90, 175
animals
   on stage 51; related to Roman masks 137–8; studied by physiognomists 86–7
Apollo Agyieus   47
Aristophanes   2, 5–6, 17, 65, 68, 154, 170, 210, 216

Aristophanes of Byzantium   168, 224
Aristotelian school, treatises from   20, 86, 88, 151, 169, 210, 220–1
Aristotle
   influence on Menander 2, 10, 159, 223; methodology 44, 66, 73, 97, 120; *Poetics* 2–4, 9, 68, 73, 97, 98; *Rhetoric* 12, 19–20, 86, 87, 116, 120, 155, 210, 218, 219; views: on actors 20, 210, 218, 224; on age 152, 155, 174; on character (*êthos*) 2–3, 6, 12, 64–5, 68, 70, 97, 174–6, 184–5, 187; on comedy and laughter 2, 68, 99, 196; on emotions 12, 20, 25, 86, 87, 119, 120, 143–4; on human physiology 69, 151, 156; on *mimêsis* 2–4; on narrative structure 3–4, 27; on oratory 13, 210, 219; on performance 9–10, 19, 210, 219; on physics 151; on physiognomics 86–7; on Plato 2, 9, 12, 66, 156; on politics 20, 66, 158–60, 219; on the primcy of the *polis* 30, 32, 47, 98, 153, 187; on respiration 116, 220; on signs 87–8; on slavery 152, 156–7, 169, 193; on the soul 20, 25, 66, 111, 159, 220; on virtue 97–8, 119, 174–6, 185, 187; on visual perception 23–4, 55; on women 152–3, 156
Arlecchino   125–6, 201
Arnott, W.G.   70–1, 87, 94, 187, 212
asides   52–3, 59
Atellan comedy   130–1, 134, 138, 142
Athenaeus   78
Athens   *see* Atticism; audience; *polis*; Theatre of Dionysus

Lightning Source UK Ltd.
Milton Keynes UK
UKOW050337270312

189638UK00001B/115/A